SOVIET-AMERICAN DIALOGUE ON THE NEW DEAL

SOVIET-AMERICAN DIALOGUES ON UNITED STATES HISTORY
VOLUME 1

General editors: Eugene F. Yazkov
Richard D. McKinzie

SOVIET-AMERICAN DIALOGUE
ON THE
NEW DEAL

EDITED BY OTIS L. GRAHAM, JR.

University of Missouri Press
Columbia, 1989

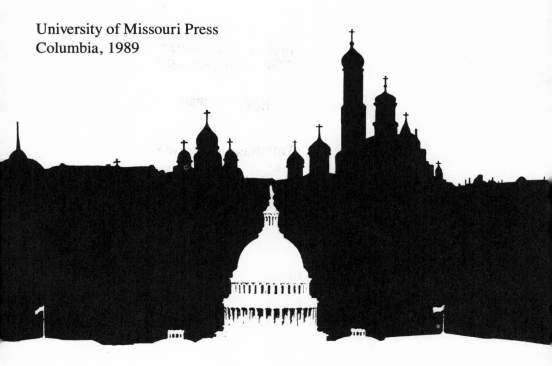

Copyright © 1989 by
The Curators of the University of Missouri
University of Missouri Press, Columbia, Missouri 65211
Printed and bound in the United States of America

Library of Congress Cataloging-in-Publication Data

Soviet-American dialogue on the New Deal / edited by Otis L. Graham, Jr.
    p.   cm.—(Soviet-American dialogues on U.S. history series)
    Includes index.
    ISBN 0-8262-0612-3 (alk. paper)
    1. New Deal, 1933-1939. 2. United States—Politics and
government—1933-1945. I. Graham, Otis L., Jr. II. Series.
E806.S782   1989
973.917—dc19   88-27559
                                                       CIP

∞™ This paper meets the minimum requirements of
the American National Standard for Permanence of Paper
for Printed Library Materials, Z39.48, 1984.

IN MEMORY OF NIKOLAI SIVACHEV, 1934–1983

CONTENTS

SOVIET PREFACE

In introducing American readers to this first volume of a series of books designed to establish a scholarly dialogue between scholars of American history in both our countries, we would like to explain the development of American Studies in the Soviet Union and how the idea of this book evolved. The road to publication was not easy. Not a few political disagreements have weighed on relations between our countries, and there are deep ideological differences between Soviet and American historians. In these few paragraphs, the [Soviet] members of the editorial board would like to direct the reader's attention not to those difficulties, but to developments that made this project possible.

In the Soviet Union there is genuine interest in American society and its past, in the history of its material and spiritual culture. Despite the ideological differences that have characterized relations between our governments, there have been opportunities to cooperate. In 1933 the USSR and the United States found a common ground and, in the national interests of our peoples, established diplomatic relations. The most striking example of Soviet-American cooperation has been the fight against our common enemies, German fascism and Japanese militarism, during World War II. The shared danger encouraged our people to resolve quite complicated military and political problems, and the unity of the coalition against Hitler was the decisive factor in victory. However, many years thereafter the Cold War complicated relations between our governments and infused the whole field of international relations with serious problems. By the 1950s confrontational policies had led to an impasse, and considerable political courage was required to lead the world out of it. Yet, even under those difficult circumstances, political dialogue did continue. Political dialogue was most memorable, of course, during detente, when favorable conditions existed for developing better relations between our governments.

The problems of normalizing Soviet-American relations are obvious, but we believe they are surmountable. Experience tells us that with good will, readiness to compromise, meaningful dialogue, and collaboration, we can cooperate in the establishment of peace, while we compete in the area of improving the lives of our peoples. We understand full well that political dialogue is positively reinforced by the expansion of contacts in other spheres, particularly in science and culture. It was in that context that we came to the idea of publishing a series of Soviet-American volumes.

The books planned for publication are intended, in part, to acquaint Americans with the nature of American Studies in the USSR. We offer, therefore, a few words about the establishment and development of American Studies in the Soviet Union. In comparison to the study of other national histories—those of France, England, Germany—American Studies in the Soviet Union is young. Its establishment is connected with the names of A. V. Efimov, L. I. Zubok, and V. I. Lan, Soviet scholars who published their first serious works in the 1930s.

Research on American history broadened rapidly in the Soviet Union after World War II with the training of a cadre of professional American historians. Moscow State University played a large role in that expansion. The efforts of I. S. Galkin, A. V. Efimov, G. N. Sevastianov, and V. M. Khvostov brought forward a new generation of Americanists who began to form American Studies literature and programs. During the 1960s and 1970s there emerged a whole army of talented scholars. Today the work of these individuals shapes the character of American Studies in the Soviet Union: I. A. Beliavskaya, N. N. Bolkhovitinov, G. A. Vorontsov, R. S. Ganelin, I. A. Geyevsky, I. P. Dementiev, V. V. Zhurkin, V. P. Zolotukhin, R. F. Ivanov, G. P. Kuropiatnik, V. L. Malkov, U. M. Melnikov, R. S. Ovinikov, P. F. Petrovsky, E. I. Popova, N. V. Sivachev, G. A. Trofimenko, A. A. Fursensko, V. G. Furayev, G. N. Tsvetkov, A. N. Yakovlev, N. N. Yakovlev, E. F. Yazkov, and others.

Centers for American Studies have formed: the Institute of U.S. and Canadian Studies of the Academy of Sciences of the U.S.S.R. (director, G. A. Arbatov); the Institute of World Economic and International Relations of the Academy of Sciences of the U.S.S.R. (formerly headed by N. N. Inozemtsev, and later by E. M. Primakov); the section on the history of the United States and Canada of the Institute of General History of the Academy of Sciences of the USSR (headed by G. N. Sevostyanov); the Department of Modern and Contemporary History of the School of History at Moscow State University (originally headed by I. S. Galkin, and now by E. F. Yazkov); Leningrad State University; and the Institute of the International Workers' Movement of the Academy of Sciences of the U.S.S.R. (director, T. T. Timofeev). A certain division of labor has evolved among these centers for American Studies.

Topics and periods of American history which have aroused the strongest interest among Soviet researchers have been socioeconomic history, workers' and democratic movements, social policies of the United States government, international policies and military political doctrine, and the history of social thought. The periods of greatest interest to Soviet historians are the Revolutionary War, the Civil War, the Progressive Era, the New Deal, and the sociopolitical history of the postwar period. The intensive development of American Studies in the Soviet Union has led to regular publication of a number of periodicals that examine a wide variety of issues. *The U.S.A.: Economics, Politics, and Ideology*, managing editor V. M. Berezhkov, has been published since 1970, and the *American Annual*, managing editor G. N. Sevastyanov, since 1971. Publication of the interdisciplinary annual *Problems of American Studies*, managing editor E. F. Yazkov, began somewhat later. In addition, American history topics are examined from time to time in the pages of our leading historical journals, *Questions of History* and *Modern and Contemporary History*.

At the same time our leading specialists in American Studies were researching the basic issues of American history, they were preparing new cadres of scientific workers. These new scholars entered the field of American history in the late 1970s and early 1980s. Among them are A. G. Arbatov, A. U. Borisov, V. I. Borisiuk, V. A. Valtsov, K. S. Gadzhiev, N. A. Kosolapov, M. I. Lapitsky, A. S. Manykin, V. A. Nikonov, V. O. Pechatnov, S. M. Plekhanov, P. T. Podlesny, A. A. Popov, U. N. Rogulev, N. A. Sakharov, V. A. Savelev, I. M. Saveleva, V. V. Sogrin, D. N. Stashevsky, V. I. Terekhov, V. A. Ushakov, A. I. Utkin, and B. M. Shpotov. They have significantly broadened study of the multifaceted history of the American people. The history of political parties and political institutions, sociopolitical activities of business, ideopolitical alignments at the extreme poles of the American political spectrum, movements among the rank and file in American unions, regional aspects of American international policies—this is only a short list of subjects which, in addition to traditional topics, are beginning to be developed by American historians in the Soviet Union.

Today the next generation of young scholars is emerging. We hope they make their own contributions to our science and find their own place in the field.

A leading role belongs to the School of History at Moscow State University, the Institute of General History, and the Institute of U.S. and Canadian Studies in training these Americanists. Because the project presented here for the reader's consideration has resulted from the efforts of Moscow State University and the University of Missouri, we offer a brief description of the collective of American historians at Moscow State University.

The study of American history is conducted in the Department of Modern and Contemporary History, which for many years was headed by Professor I. S. Galkin. In 1977 the department created a special laboratory in which to study American history. Its first leader was the well-known academician Professor N. V. Sivachev.

Scholars who worked in this laboratory concentrated their efforts on the evolution of one of the most important elements of politics in the United States—the two-party system. One co-worker in the laboratory, A. S. Manykin, has published a book, *The History of the Two-Party System of the United States.* The laboratory collective has published a series of articles on the same topic, as well as two volumes of essays on the two-party system in modern times. A number of doctoral dissertations covering critical events in the history of the two-party system were defended between 1979 and 1985. These dissertations expanded our understanding of the functions of this institution and its role in the political history of the United States. In subsequent volumes in this series, we intend to acquaint American readers with portions of these works and, the editorial board hopes, stimulate a useful debate.

The establishment of scientific contacts and reciprocal exchanges came about slowly. A milestone on this road was the agreement in 1958 that established exchanges between the USSR and the United States in the areas of science and culture. N. V. Sivachev did much to expand contacts between Soviet and American historians. A number of direct agreements between Moscow State University and American universities were signed as a result of his initiative. And in 1974 a continuous contact was established through the Fulbright Program.

Many American scholars have come to Moscow State University through this program: Leon Litwack, Robert Kelley, David Brody, Edward Pessen, David Cronon, Richard Jensen, E. B. Smith, Peter Walker, George Fredrickson, Winton Solberg, John Milton Cooper, and Darrett Rutman. Two representatives of the University of Missouri, Richard McKinzie and Eugene Trani, have also participated as Fulbright scholars and have played key roles in the evolution of this volume.

Since the program began, Soviet students specializing in American history have taken a special course during the second semester taught by an American professor. Each course concludes with an oral examination. The ideological differences between Soviet students and American instructors stimulate lively scholarly discussions. Such scientific debates are a necessary component in the development of young specialists, and they are also of interest to the American scholars. During their stay in Moscow, visiting American scholars have the opportunity to better acquaint themselves with daily life in the Soviet Union, understand how the Soviet people live, and compare the reality of Soviet life with certain stereotypes widespread in the West. They also have the opportunity to acquaint themselves with the state of American Studies in Soviet historiography. They can observe that their Soviet colleagues study American history scientifically, and that in interpreting the course and character of American society they rely on methodological practices characterized by a thorough analysis of multiple sources.

Extended discussions led scholars at Moscow State University and the University of Missouri to the conclusion that dialogue between historians in our countries is quite possible and is useful to the wider scholarly community. Thus was born the idea of publishing this series.

Each volume in this series will address a major topic in American history and will consist of ten to fifteen articles previously published in scholarly journals in the Soviet Union. These articles, in the opinion of the Soviet members of the editorial board, best illustrate current Soviet historiography on each topic. Each article will be followed by a comment prepared by an American scholar who works in the same field. The Soviet authors retain the right to respond to these comments.

The members of the editorial board selected the New Deal as the topic of the first volume. A number of factors explain this choice. First, there is the significance of this period in American history. The works of such American historians as Arthur Schlesinger, Jr., Richard Hofstadter, Frank Freidel, Henry S. Commager, William Leuchtenburg, Otis Graham, Jr., James Sundquist, James Patterson, Richard Polenberg, and others very clearly illustrate the role the Roosevelt administration played in forming the socioeconomic and political infrastructure of American society. Although Soviet historians interpret the causes and consequences of the New Deal differently, they agree that it was a very great determinant of subsequent developments in American capitalism.

The second factor influencing the selection of this topic is its popularity in Soviet historiography. Soviet ideas about the New Deal and its place in American history are detailed in the works of N. V. Sivachev, V. L. Malkov, and a number of other historians. And, inasmuch as this volume is dedicated to the memory of N. V.

Sivachev, a man who did so much to develop Soviet-American scholarly connections, and whose enthusiasm, in the final analysis, made possible this project of our two universities, the editorial board found it appropriate to select as the topic of the first volume the subject he most favored. Selecting this topic is an expression of the gratitude that all of us, both Soviet and American participants of the project, feel toward N. V. Sivachev and his memory.

Soviet contributors to this volume are prepared to discuss any points that seem debatable to their American colleagues. We hope this exchange of views will be an impetus to further study of the important, complicated, and interesting question: what was the New Deal?

The editorial board would like to use this occasion to share its immediate plans with readers. In the next volume we plan to address the American Revolution, the very important historical significance of which is acknowledged in the USSR. As a result of that momentous event, a new, independent nation appeared on the political map of the world, and its people made a great contribution to civilization. It is our thought that American readers would be interested to learn how this event is treated by Soviet historians. The third volume of the series will address Russian-American relations. It seems to us that this topic is also timely, as knowledge of past diplomatic relations between our countries offers lessons pertinent to the present and the future. Finally, the fourth of the currently planned volumes will address the history of the American two-party system. This topic is most important to the American historians at Moscow State University. We would like to acquaint American readers with their work.

In conclusion, allow us to express the hope that the first volume of this Soviet-American cooperative effort will be an important step on the road to establishing scholarly dialogue between specialists with common interests. In looking to the future, publication of this series may, in our opinion, create new opportunities for cooperation between the scholars of our two countries; and such cooperation may facilitate a new kind of political thinking that is so necessary for both scholars and politicians and, more generally, for all people in these complicated and crucial times.

SOVIET MEMBERS OF THE EDITORIAL BOARD

Eugene F. Yazkov, Moscow State University
Igor P. Dementiev, Moscow State University
Alexander S. Manykin, Moscow State University
August Mishin, Moscow State University
Yuri N. Rogulev, Moscow State University
Grigori N. Sevastyanov, Institute of General History, Academy of Sciences of the U.S.S.R.
G. A. Trofimenko, Institute of U.S. and Canadian Studies, Academy of Sciences of the U.S.S.R.

AMERICAN PREFACE

Historians trained in the United States are constantly reassessing the "meaning" of the American past. On occasion they feel compelled to explain how and why interpretations have changed over the years. Although their approaches are multiple and their first premises diverse, most are persuaded that succeeding generations, each confronted with different problems, view the past with an eye toward understanding the antecedents of their own preoccupations. Home-trained Americanists also note the procession of discovery—the ever-increasing quantity and variety of cultural documentation (manuscripts, oral testimonies, folklore, music, film, photographs, art) that expand and illuminate the base on which historians build. They give credit to individuals for brilliant insights. They allude to new methodologies, often inspired by work in other disciplines and, recently, by technology, that enable scholars to extract new answers from old materials.

Seldom in these discussions about the "meaning" of the past does one find reference to, or even acknowledgment of, the work of foreign scholars who study American history. And yet, it is safe to say that most American history read throughout the world is written by foreigners. The lamentable failure of Americans to learn foreign languages is probably the main reason the writing of outsiders has been neglected or ignored. Doubtless, also, there is a view that no one can understand America better than Americans.

Honest people can and do argue whether the proper purpose of studying history or any intellectual discipline is to aid in the quest of some political condition. Without denying the validity of the question, it seems clear that life in a world shrunken by satellite communications, no-win weaponry, interdependent commerce, and unprecedented people-to-people contact has created a climate in which the assessments of outsiders are no longer mere curiosities. These assessments must figure into the ongoing efforts of Americans to achieve accommodation and stability.

Although little of it has circulated in the United States, a large body of work on American history has been produced in the Union of Soviet Socialist Republics since World War II. Beyond a very few U.S. Americanists fluent in Russian, a handful of scholars who have taught American history courses in the Department of Modern and Contemporary History at Moscow State University under the auspices of the government's Fulbright exchange program have come to know something about Soviet views on the American past. Each spring semester since 1974, an American historian has been in residence to teach (in English) and to discuss history with faculty and students.

Much credit for this extraordinary and unbroken procession of American historians to Moscow, and for the training and receptivity of Moscow State's students and faculty, goes to the late Nikolai Sivachev. As chair of the Department of Modern and

Contemporary History and the American Studies program, Sivachev emphasized the need for a sophisticated familiarity with recent American scholarship, research in American archives, and development of the critical, technical, and literary skills that mark professionals. Sivachev also championed frank exchanges of views with U.S. colleagues. This, during years in which serious Soviet-American dialogues often had broken down in other areas. Sivachev set an example in his own research and publications and by delivering, in 1982, the first paper by a Soviet Americanist at the annual meeting of the American Historical Association. Eugene Yazkov, Sivachev's colleague and successor, has sustained the example and delivered the first paper by a Soviet Americanist at the annual meeting of the Organization of American Historians in 1987. Not the least of the contributions of the U.S. Fulbright exchange program, whose officers worked with Sivachev and Yazkov to facilitate the Moscow exchange, has been a substantial addition of important books on American history to Moscow State's library. The result of all these efforts is a graduate program in American Studies in which the students' Soviet (Marxist-Leninist) perspective is augmented by an understanding of U.S. approaches and methods that has impressed most of the visiting Fulbright professors.

Enlightening as frequent small-group discussion and one-on-one conversations with students and faculty proved, most of the American visitors have nonetheless felt a need to grasp a larger body of Soviet scholarship and to examine more thoroughly the foundations and structure of Soviet arguments. More, to historians accustomed to taking their information and fashioning their own contributions through the written word, most oral exchanges seem somehow less than precise and definitive.

Fulbright scholars at Moscow State and their Soviet hosts readily agreed that facilitating an ongoing dialogue among professional historians and familiarizing more Americans with Soviet accounts of U.S. history would be mutually beneficial to scholars and the people of both nations. As discussions progressed, Americanists and officials at Moscow State and those at the University of Missouri–Kansas City agreed to collaborate in the preparation of a series of books, Soviet-American Dialogues on United States History. The agreement signed in 1986 by Rector A. A. Logunov (for Moscow State) and Chancellor George A. Russell (for the University of Missouri) makes possible the dissemination, in English, of Soviet-authored articles on selected topics in American history. The planners sought to promote a true scholarly dialogue by adopting the medium and format historians know best—written presentation (the Soviet articles), written comment by a second party, and written response by the presenter.

The structure and general subject matter of the series are the responsibilities of a fourteen-member editorial board (seven Soviets, seven Americans). The Soviet members, representing not only Moscow State but also the larger community of Soviet Americanists, choose the topic for each volume and the articles that best reflect current Soviet scholarship. The articles are selected from Russian-language journals circulated in the USSR. The American members of the board, all of them former Fulbright professors at Moscow State, choose an American editor for each volume. The editor, a ranking scholar on the specific topic, in turn selects distinguished U.S. specialists to write commentaries on the Soviet-authored articles and himself writes an overview of the subject and the exchange of views. Finally, the Soviet authors may, if they wish, respond to the commentators.

It is worth repeating that the spirit of the endeavor is that of dialogue, not summary judgment. The American members of the editorial board hope that issues raised in this and future volumes of Soviet-American Dialogues on United States History will prompt continued exchanges of ideas and commentary among historians of the two countries. They also dare to hope the exchange will be interesting and enlightening to the community at large, that future explanations of trends and changing interpretations in American history will include the contributions of foreign scholars, and that better understanding in the field of history will be symbolic of better understanding between the Soviet and American peoples.

AMERICAN MEMBERS OF THE EDITORIAL BOARD

Otis L. Graham, Jr.

INTRODUCTION

There can be no more gratifying occasion for scholars than the mutual enlarge-ment of knowledge through international scholarly discourse. Surely the Ricardian theory is correct here, even if nowhere else, when it encourages us to expect trade in the form of intellectual interchange to be advantageous in both directions. Foreign visitors Alexis de Tocqueville and Lord Bryce, among others, have taught Americans to expect benefits from outsiders' views of our society. Such views are a valuable import that puts no American out of work.

It would be difficult to name two nations more in need of deeper knowledge of each other's history than the United States and the Soviet Union. Historical under-standing requires interchange and collaboration among professional historical com-munities, and after years of too little of this, there has recently been a favorable turn. The Joint U.S.-Soviet Commission on the Humanities and Social Sciences has been at work negotiating protocols to regulate scholarly exchanges between the two coun-tries, and the seventh of such protocols was signed early in 1988. The protocol endorses twelve history and archaeology programs, among them the biennial collo-quium of Soviet and American historians, and other programs leading to conferences on historical subject matter. The biennial colloquium of historians now approaches its seventh occasion, to be held in 1989 in the USSR.[1]

Thus this volume in a projected series of Soviet-American historical dialogues among "Americanists" comes into being within the context of a broad augmentation of scholarly interchange between these two societies. It builds upon the burgeoning research commitment to U.S. studies that is described by the Soviet members of the Editorial Board in the Soviet Preface to this book. The germinal idea for the volume grew out of the professional contacts made between American Fulbright lecturers and their colleagues at Moscow State University. The immediate beneficiaries of such

1. I am grateful to Samuel R. Gammon, executive director of the American Historical Associa-tion, for a summary of the exchanges in the humanities and social sciences with the Soviet Union, which, in his words, "have been continuous since the first cultural exchange agreement between the governments of the USA and the USSR in 1958" (Gammon to the author, 22 February 1988). Thanks are also due to Professor Lewis Hanke, an irresistible force on behalf of improved interna-tional understanding, for correspondence acquainting me with earlier work on U.S.-Soviet scholarly exchanges, which includes a pioneering volume on the other Americas, Russell H. Bartley's *Soviet Historians on Latin America* (Madison, 1978). Hanke would surely urge the early abandonment of the term *Americanists* as denoting those who study the United States, though the terms *North Ameri-canists* and *Latin Americanists* are not fully satisfactory, for, among other things, requiring that Canada and the U.S. be thought of together. For this essay, the term *Americanist* designates a scholar whose professional interest is the history of the United States. I am especially grateful for the dedica-tion and resourcefulness of Richard McKinzie, who supervised translation and gave wise counsel at every point. Samuel H. Baron and Donald J. Raleigh offered valuable insights, and Pamela Fesmire provided able administrative assistance.

collaborative inquiries will be the scholarly communities in both nations. The larger audience includes the American people, who may read these exchanges in English, the Russian people, and all others who draw upon this and subsequent collaborations.

The focus of this book is the "New Deal," a burst of internal reform in the United States as the nation passed in the 1930s through an era of intense national difficulty. There was a time when those interested in New Deal scholarship found themselves reading American authors almost exclusively. British authors contributed to the literature from time to time, and scholars with the requisite language skills could consult writings by historians from West Germany, Scandinavia, Italy, occasionally India or Japan. But Russian "Americanists" were not much read in the United States in earlier decades. Had I been asked a year ago to name those Soviet writings on the New Deal upon which I had drawn in my own work (necessarily, given my inadequacies, in English), the answer would probably have consisted mainly of citations to the work of that admirable scholar and colleague who shared with me an apprenticeship with Richard Hofstadter—Professor Nikolai Sivachev. Certainly I had read the book by Sivachev and Nikolai Yakovlev, *Russia and the United States* (1979), and Sivachev's articles on the New Deal published in *Soviet Studies in History* and in *Labor History.* Yet the Soviet and American historical communities were widely separated, and Samuel H. Baron probably stated the prevailing Western view (in this case, of Soviet writing on Russian history) when he wrote in the *American Historical Review* in 1972 that "Soviet historiography represents an alien 'continent' whose exploration hardly repays the effort, and dialogue between Soviet and Western students of Russian history is well-nigh impossible."[2]

Certainly in U.S. studies one could not claim that there was a flourishing international scholarly exchange, with the Soviets or otherwise. U.S. Americanists would have said that there was not much scholarship being published abroad, and at some point in the past this was undeniably true. But scholars outside the U.S. who were interested in American history and life were justified in observing that U.S. historians had developed a certain insularity that would not serve them well as the overseas community of Americanists augmented its size and improved the quality of its professional work. When Louis Hanke compiled his invaluable *Guide to the Study of United States History Outside the U.S., 1945–1980*, the essay on U.S. history in

2. See Nikolai V. Sivachev and Nikolai N. Yakovlev, *Russia and the United States* (Chicago, 1979); Sivachev, "The Realignment of the Two-Party System of the United States During the New Deal," *Soviet Studies in History* 22 (Spring 1984); and Sivachev, "The Rise of Statism in 1930s America: A Soviet View of the Social and Political Effects of the New Deal," *Labor History* 24 (Fall 1983). The useful journal *Soviet Studies in History* produces English translations of Soviet historical writing. Most of this is on Russian history, but occasionally there are writings on the American past, as for example the Sivachev article cited above, which appeared with articles on Lyndon Johnson's "Great Society" and on the Democratic Party in 1861–1862 in a special issue in memory of Sivachev; see also Nikolai N. Bolkhovitinov, "The Results and Tasks of the Study of the History of Russian-American Relations," *Soviet Studies in History* special issue (Fall 1986). For the quotation from Baron, see his "The Transition from Feudalism to Capitalism in Russia: A Major Soviet Historical Controversy," *American Historical Review* 77 (June 1972): 716.

Canada informed readers that American historians were apparently not paying much attention to the work of their Canadian colleagues—work written mostly in English, and growing in both volume and quality. Whatever the merits of this observation, one learns from Hanke's *Guide* that the writing of American history is not a national, but an international industry. There has in recent years been a remarkable expansion of published research on American history conducted by foreigners and published abroad. The present volume represents an effort to enlarge the exchange between U.S. Americanists and their colleagues in the country said by Professor Norman Saul to be the world's second producer of works on U.S. history—the Soviet Union.[3]

***

Not surprisingly, the New Deal is seen differently, since the craft of history itself is pursued in a different mode, by Soviets and Americans.

Let us begin with American scholarship. It is characterized by a wide-ranging variety of methods and points of view, but one may speak of central preoccupations and themes which give the American, or Western, scholarly enterprise a certain common ground of argument. Most American historians of the New Deal, in the 1940s and 1950s when seminal histories began to appear, tended to emphasize the vast changes which State policy had brought to their nation's economy and polity, and to cast these in a favorable light as remedies for the basic flaws of a capitalist economy. The New Deal, perceived as "liberal"—that is, incremental and nonsocialist— reform which left an altered and consequently healthier capitalism in place as the nation's economic system, had adequately, even admirably, met the needs of the occasion. As for causation, U.S. historians tended then (and now) to be eclectic, citing the economic pressures of the Depression, political influences exerted by an electorate newly mobilized by class and ethnic sensibilities, and the leadership of Franklin Roosevelt and his shifting collection of reformers.

3. Saul, *Soviet Historians on Domestic American History* (International Communication Agency of the U.S., 24 September 1980). See also Robert Kelley, "Teaching U.S. History at Moscow State University, 1979," in *Guide to the Study of United States History Outside the U.S., 1945–1980*, ed. Lewis Hanke (White Plains, N.Y., 1985), and the symposium "The View From Abroad," *Reviews in American History* 14 (December 1986), a report from the Bellagio Conference on American History, with accounts of historical work in Britain, France, Italy, West Germany, Poland, and Japan. See also Kelley, "The Study of American History Abroad," *Reviews in American History* 15 (March 1987), an assessment of recent Japanese and Italian writing. On Soviet perceptions of the American past, see, in addition to the essay in Hanke's *Guide*, Leo Okinshevich, ed., *United States History and Historiography in Soviet Writings, 1945–1970* (Santa Barbara, Calif., 1975), Hans Rogger, "America in the Russian Mind—Or Russian Discoveries of America," *Pacific Historical Review* 47 (February 1978), and N. N. Bolkhovitinov, "The Status and Tasks of Studying the History of the United States in the Soviet Union," *Soviet Studies in History* 16 (Spring 1978). In Sigmund Skard's *American Studies in Europe* (2 vols.; Philadelphia, 1958), the Soviet Union's output (combined with that of Tsarist Russia) received 27 pages, while Germany received 148, France 78; but this was many years ago.

One would hardly expect Soviet historians to see matters in this way, but they were not at that time active participants in the historiographical discussion. The 1960s brought change to American views of the New Deal, as a relatively small number of historians exerted a large influence in a more critical direction. The "New Left" interpretation presented the New Deal's changes as modest in scope and marginal in impact, at a time when American society was not only in need of, but also politically ready for, more sweeping economic measures in a socialist direction.

Mainstream New Deal scholarship was influenced by such arguments, but not fully persuaded. Here I compress a great deal of historical discussion to observe that in the 1970s and 1980s the dominant view among U.S. historians might be designated as a more complex, mature version of the earlier interpretation that the New Deal represented, on the whole, substantial and necessary liberal reforms. We have no reliable methods and no strong professional interest within American scholarship to determine the views of the dominant majority, but it is my impression that most historians engaged in writing about the New Deal still hold generally to what may be called a Liberal interpretation. Yet the influence of "New Left" writing, along with the accumulation of monographs, has tended to foster a more mixed appraisal of the impact and benefits of governmental policy during the 1930s, along with a deeper appreciation of the intractability of social problems.

Certainly the scholarly discussion of the New Deal, in books, journals, meetings, and elsewhere, spreads across a wider range of views than a generation ago. Unlike the 1950s, a number of historians find that the New Deal did not represent sufficiently vigorous or effective intervention to assist the victims of capitalism's rough habits. Unlike the 1960s, a small number of scholars—surprisingly few, given the resurgence of neoclassical economic thought in American intellectual life generally within recent years—write from a free-market commitment, arguing that the State attempted far too much and reduced the general welfare by impairing the vital dynamics of capitalism. In general, American historians of the New Deal display much less agreement over just what should have been done (and not done) by the State in the 1930s than one found a generation ago, when the vast majority conveyed the belief that the New Deal was headed in all the right directions and sadly had not been able to reach all of its goals.

More strikingly, there is a growing awareness of the complexity of social change in those days, of the limits upon the meliorist impulse which the New Deal so confidently represented, of the frailties of human knowledge then and now. American scholarship on the 1930s now conveys a strong sense, undoubtedly nourished by the discouraging performance and prospects of American liberal governments from the middle 1960s forward, that the 1930s were not the plastic juncture for social reform they were usually thought to be. There is, among contemporary historians, a perception of narrowing horizons, a widespread conviction that historians had earlier underestimated the limits that confined and blunted the reformist and dissenting impulses of the 1930s. To some extent the impediments of which we are increasingly aware derived from hesitations and disputes within the Roosevelt administration and coalition. More importantly, they inhered in the surrounding political, economic, and social environment. This is nowhere more evident than in the area of labor or working-class history, where a current of "laborite realism," in Nelson Lichtenstein's phrase, no longer sees the 1930s as full of radical possibilities. U.S. scholarship on political economy in the 1930s may be said now to be most concerned with a more intense examination of the concrete economic and social consequences of State reforms and interventions and of the barriers and obstacles to reform encountered in American political institutions and culture, limiting the New Deal and accounting for the outcomes which historians find more ambiguous in effect and implication than a generation ago.[4]

Still, the New Deal must continue to seem, to U.S. historians taken as a whole, as the best deal that might have been arranged, for polls of historians on the "greatness" of American presidents have in the 1980s recorded a change, with Franklin D. Roosevelt passing George Washington to be ranked as the second "greatest" president of the United States.[5]

***

It will readily be seen from the Soviet historians' essays in this volume that they view the matter differently. At the root of this appears to be the ideological commitment of the Soviet historians to Marxist-Leninist social theory and the sociopolitical system within which Soviet scholarship is generated. From this Marxist-Leninist perspective and the historic experience of Soviet society, these historians derive their interpretive structure—"the working class," or "the masses," are primal forces who deserve to and will win, the "monopolists" or "bourgeoisie" are the adversaries of progress. American history for them must have an underlying dynamic of class struggle and thus an evolutionary direction—the same general direction, though naturally a different timetable and configuration of events, as other industrialized capitalist societies. Thus the American past may only be understood as the struggle of class forces along a track punctuated by economic and social crisis characteristic of all capitalist systems. The era of the 1930s in America was an especially severe

4. See Lichtenstein's review-essay (based upon Robert H. Zieger's *American Workers, American Unions, 1920–1985* [Baltimore, 1986]) "Labor History in the Realist Vein," *Reviews in American History* 15 (June 1987); see also Ronald Radosh, "The Corporate Ideology of American Labor Leaders from Gompers to Hillman," *Studies on the Left* 6 (November–December 1966), and Melvyn Dubofsky, "Not So 'Turbulent Years': Another Look at the American 1930s," *Amerikastudien/American Studies* 24 (1979). A recent appraisal of the New Deal from a neoclassical, free-market viewpoint is Robert Higgs, *Crisis and Leviathan* (New York, 1987). There are a number of recent appraisals of the state of New Deal scholarship; one might begin with Harvard Sitkoff, ed., *Fifty Years Later: The New Deal Evaluated* (New York, 1985), to be supplemented with Otis L. Graham, Jr., and Meghan R. Wander, eds., *FDR, His Life and Times: An Encyclopedic View* (Boston, 1985).

5. This ranking of FDR in polls of American historians was reported in Robert K. Murray and Tim Blessing, "The Presidential Performance Study: A Progress Report," *Journal of American History* 70 (December 1983).

crisis, and Soviet historians agree that the political events of that time brought "a categoric shift in the social development of the country," in the words of Nikolai Sivachev. Roosevelt presided over a "process by which American monopoly capitalism developed into State-monopolism" or, as he and other Russian authors preferred, "State-monopoly capitalism."

And what of this process and its results, this New Deal? Here the Soviet essays present unresolved interpretive points of view. At times it seems that they present the New Deal as a Good Thing. Since the American working class in the 1930s appears by several measures to have been decisively supportive of the New Deal, Soviet historians give many indications that they, too, look with favor on the New Deal's efforts to extend the regulatory and welfare State. Presumably these were all steps in the right direction, i.e., toward socialism, rather than strengthening capitalism for its long struggle with the inevitable. But in other places the Soviet historians' outlook appears to be that the New Deal was a Bad Thing, what American radical historians would call a "corporate-liberal" alliance to co-opt mass demands into harmless concessions and to shore up capitalism with various State supports. Indeed, the Soviets appear to see the New Deal as a mixture of both, and Sivachev offers a model in which a structure of economic subsidies and regulation ushered in "State-monopoly capitalism" to save the existing order, but welfare measures and the Wagner Act inaugurated a more humane welfare state or "State socialism" which the working class was correct to have demanded and won. Grounds for Soviet approval of even this compromised result appear in Sivachev's observation that the New Deal was a "left-center variant" of the new State-monopoly political economy. Apparently, though none of the Soviet authors state it in exactly this way, this left-center variant was preferable both to the old order of the 1920s and to the "right-center" variant to which the Republican Party was slowly being converted by its most enlightened capitalist leadership.

***

In such an exchange of views between historical materialists and mostly pluralists, one might have expected wide-ranging *Methodenstreit*, a war of methodological principles. But this largely fails to appear. To be sure, the Soviets claim to practice "scientific" history, a problematical idea which the American historians question but which is not squarely joined (see Pechatnov's comment in his Response below: "scientific analysis . . . in our academic discourse has quite a different connotation and in this particular case should have been more accurately translated as 'scholarly analysis' "). The American historian Lawrence Stone has written that "all Marxist historians are, and always have been, social historians," but from the evidence in this volume that statement would have to be carefully defined or abandoned altogether. The Soviet historians of the New Deal are methodologically conventional. While convinced that class forces drive events, their eyes are on the story told in the political superstructure.[6]

By this observation I mean nothing invidious. The same may be said for many American historians. Yet I mean to convey something more than simply that the Soviets approach a series of political events with the tools of political historians, as do their American counterparts. They do so, it seems from these essays, along a narrower (they might well say, a more carefully focussed) and more traditional range than is currently the practice in the West. A generation ago, American historians of the New Deal and political historians generally conducted their research and writing in the belief that elections and lawmaking, parties and politicians, were centrally important. The Soviets operate chiefly from this base in the essays published here, but many American historians have moved their research efforts from elections and lawmaking to formerly neglected arenas of struggle—administrative rulemaking, bureaucratic implementation, judicial interpretation. And some have moved their research out from the Capital to the provinces, and in labor history especially have turned attention away from formal institutions such as unions and political parties to the workplace and community where they find and analyze those elements of ethnic, racial, gender, and religious background which cut across and complicate class identification. The Soviets, possibly because they have fewer scholars to deploy, or because they are certain that they know where the commanding heights thrust above the details and wish to concentrate there, remain focussed upon political parties, labor unions, and legislative battles in Washington, D.C., areas where American scholarship concentrates less single-mindedly now than a generation ago.

The nature of the subject decrees that this will be State-centered history on both sides, even though American scholarship has turned considerable attention to state and local levels and to the social structures and processes beneath governments. U.S. historians of the New Deal, with few exceptions, practice political history without an explicit theory of the State. They have made some use of the descriptive label and model of "the Broker State" or "interest-group liberalism" as developed by political scientist Theodore Lowi and others.[7] But large arguments have not centered upon such concepts, nor upon related theoretical formulations of "Who Rules America," in the phrase so important to the work of sociologists such as C. Wright Mills, G. William Domhoff, and others. Yet there are signs of change, indications that the discussion of New Deal history is becoming more closely meshed with the growing debate in (primarily) political science and sociology over the nature of the American State in the twentieth century.

This debate has centered principally over the degree to which the State may and

6. Stone, "Resisting the New," *New York Review of Books*, 17 December 1987, 62.

7. See Lowi, *The End of Liberalism* (New York, 1969), and for some applications to the 1930s, Otis L. Graham, Jr., *Toward a Planned Society: From Roosevelt to Nixon* (New York, 1976), chap. 1, and Graham, "The Broker State," *Wilson Quarterly* 8 (Winter 1984).

does act autonomously, defying the considerable power of the economic and social groupings in our industrial-capitalist, white male Anglo-Saxon Protestant–dominated society. Here the 1930s are a seminal time. If there was ever an era when the American elites of industry and finance were frequently defied, and power in private society rearranged by State action, it was the 1930s. Was this the autonomous State?

Sifting the Western social science literature, there may be said to be three main positions on this matter. There is the venerable Marxist view that the State in capitalist societies is in all times and places simply the "executive committee of the bourgeois class" and does what it is told (i.e., is not autonomous). Then there is the perception that the State serves the interests of the capitalists faithfully, but those interests must be broadly conceived. For in reality the capitalists are often—or even usually—divided, indecisive, confused, or objectively wrong about where their real interests lie. In the twentieth century, it has often been in the real interest of the ruling class to yield a bit in dangerous circumstances and purchase a modicum of social harmony, co-opting the masses. "Capitalists" may not always see this, but the State is potentially capable of, and occasionally does take the lead in, certain concessions to workers and other noncapitalist groups. In other words, the State is quasi-autonomous, capable of actions not dictated by, and perhaps even disliked by, leading capitalists, but always confined to a role as the "system maintainer" and thus tied to the capitalist interest.

Then there is the third broad view, capacious enough to encompass certain Marxists along with all pluralists, that there are many interests in society including the State's interest itself, but there are no monolithic classes or invariable winners. In this view the State is often the instrument of some class or social interest, is potentially available for anticapitalistic as well as capitalistic purposes, yet frequently escapes such manipulation in order to pursue some interest of the State itself, such as social stability or military adventurism. Its potential for social action at any given time and the key to unravelling its history thus resides not in some rigid class theory of social causation but in the actual contours of contemporary power. These, as Skocpol's comment in this volume argues, are composed not merely of the political expressions of class power but also the institutions—electoral, legislative, bureaucratic—which define the capacities of the State and both limit and channel its activities.[8]

8. Not cited or discussed by the Soviets in the New Deal articles here is the work of American social theorists on the State, authors such as Ralph Miliband, James O'Connor, G. William Domhoff, Fred Block, Theda Skocpol, and others who have made important contributions to the literature on the State. For an introduction to that literature, see Martin Carnoy, *The State and Political Theory* (Princeton, 1984); Peter B. Evans, Dietrich Rueschemeyer, and Theda Skocpol, eds., *Bringing the State Back In* (Cambridge, 1985); Stephen Krasner, "Approaches to the State: Alternative Conceptions and Historical Dynamics," *Comparative Politics* 16 (January 1984); R. Benjamin and S. Elkin, eds., *The Democratic State* (Lawrence, Kans., 1985); Skocpol, "Political Response to Capitalist Crisis: Neo-Marxist Theories of the State and the Case of the New Deal," *Politics and Society* 10 (1980); William E. Leuchtenburg, "The Pertinence of Political History: Reflections on the Significance of the State in America," *Journal of American History* 73 (December 1986); and G. William

There are many variations on these positions, and there is an argument winding down through them as to whether a general theory of how the State will act may be derived from the historical materials of the 1930s or from the modern experience of capitalist societies generally. U.S. historians are increasingly joining the political scientists, sociologists, and others in this discussion, much of it rooted in empirical examination of the 1930s.

And what do the Soviets have to say on these matters, as expressed in these essays? My purpose in raising this question is not to interpose my answer between the reader and his or her own discovery, but to urge that the effort be made. The Soviets do not at first blush appear to engage directly the Western arguments about the nature of the American State. Yet they are deeply interested in the matter, and their mixed views on what might be called American State theory seem to me the unstated central theme of this book. To fully perceive their positions, and to appraise them in the light of the American historians' reactions to them, readers must do some translating for themselves.

In the process there will be other discoveries. American historiography—indeed, I should say "First World" historiography in the large, including Western and non-Western societies where U.S. history is seriously pursued—is characterized by continual and visible internal argument. A set of essays by multiple authors on virtually any subject is a diet spiced by much disagreement. Scholarship is more than the piling up of facts; it requires the probing of points of contention where interpretations are in conflict. Any line of argument will bring one authority into collision with another, into either gentle or stern claims that some deceased or even quite animated contemporary has written in error and got the story wrong. What moves our collective efforts of historical reconstruction is disputation, disagreement, challenge. Agreement exists within "schools," perhaps, but certainly not within the circles of nationality. Nationality merely confers a common language as a vehicle for a continual discussion which will contain much agreement and indeed aims at complete accord upon The Truth, but which is energized by disagreement.

At first appraisal, reading these essays, the Soviets are remarkably otherwise. They carry on explicit disputes with "bourgeois" scholars from other societies, but do not take issue with each other or with Soviet predecessors, and appear, for this reason and because of a common basic interpretive position, to be in agreement. Only a close reading reveals an occasional divergence in Soviet historians' views on a given issue.

But this contrast with Western scholarship can be drawn too sharply, and the mode of Soviet scholarship in this respect may be misunderstood. Professor Norman Saul, in a report on Soviet historiography prepared for the U.S. government in 1980, wrote:

Domhoff, "Corporate-Liberal Theory and the Social Security Act: A Chapter in the Sociology of Knowledge," *Politics and Society* 15 (1986–1987).

It would appear that life for Soviet Americanists is rather dull, with each monopolizing a reserved topic and all following the same basic line of interpretation. Private conversations, however, lead me to believe that this is not necessarily the case. There exist opportunities for verbal debate and broader discussion of varying interpretations, at least of those found in American sources.[9]

Undoubtedly the Soviets have a different view of this, and it should be noted that conditions are surely much changed since Saul wrote his report in 1980. Whatever may be the intellectual climate in which Soviet Americanists work, there have certainly been episodes of sharp internal disagreement among Soviet historians of Russia itself, as for example at the revisionist conference on the origins of Russian capitalism that was held in 1965 at the height of the Khrushchevian ferment.[10] The eleven essays in this volume are now in evidence for English-language readers and may be assessed against Saul's observation. It should be noted that they were written at various times between 1970 and 1984—BG, "before Gorbachev." Much is changing in the Soviet Union as this volume goes to press, as General Secretary Mikhail Gorbachev pursues *glasnost* in the realm of ideas and *perestroika*, restructuring, within the economy. The editor of *Soviet Studies in History* reported "unprecedented excitement" in the ranks of "those of us who monitor developments in Soviet historiography" at the publication, in a 3 May 1988 issue of *Izvestia*, of an article in which the Soviet historian S. V. Tiutiukin had been quoted as saying, "The time has come to rid history of various extraneous features and deformations, to return her civic spirit, honesty, and fortitude. Moreover, we must put an end to the irresponsibility, the negligence, the feckless repetition of stock phrases, and to the superficiality of which there is more than enough in historical science."[11]

Westerners reading these words do not know the validity of such observations, but that they were published in *Izvestia* represents a sea change, it would seem, in Soviet intellectual life, which includes history. Even as this book goes to press, observers of Soviet intellectual life report that the sort of changes Tiutiukin called for within the world of Soviet historiography are indeed much in evidence. If that sea change continues and alters Soviet historical practice, this will presumably be evident in the work they publish in the later 1980s and 1990s, against which these eleven essays may serve as one baseline of comparison.

In any event, from these essays themselves we may see that "life for Soviet Americanists," in Saul's phrase, does not include unanimity, the Soviets always speaking with a single voice. As David Brody points out in his commentary here on the essays by Popov and Borisiuk, one Soviet historian writing on labor history appears to see the American State in the 1930s as co-opting the organized workers as corporate

9. *Soviet Historians*, 13.
10. See the review of V. I. Shunkov et al., eds., *The Transition from Feudalism to Capitalism in Russia: Materials from the All-Union Discussion* (Moscow, 1969), in Baron, "The Transition from Feudalism."
11. Donald J. Raleigh, "Editor's Note," *Soviet Studies in History* 26 (Summer 1987): 3.

liberal theory might predict, while the other—and the Galkova essay on late New Deal politics cuts in a similar direction—depicts the Roosevelt regime as forcing the capitalists to concede gains the working class desired.

This unresolved interpretive position on the role of the U.S. State, in Soviet essays written prior to 1985, represents a not insignificant tolerance of diversity which runs against some Western stereotypes of Soviet intellectual life. The contrast in scholarly procedures in this regard are sharp enough, between historians of the West and the Soviet Union, but it is important to discover that differences are not absolute. The Soviets indeed present a more united view when it is time to publish, whatever their modus operandi in the prepublication labors that are not visible through these essays. But it is not an absolutely united view.

***

Other contrasts could be drawn between Soviet and U.S. approaches to history in general and to the New Deal in particular, but it is time for the editor to give way to the historians' discussions to follow, where these contrasts will be abundantly evident. I should note, however, one last feature of professional exchanges such as this. It is the familiar impediment of language difference. This project reminded all those involved that language, at once the primary medium of human communication, acts also as the eternal confounder of human understanding. The Russian essays were translated into English by a Russian-language specialist, ably overseen by Professor Richard McKinzie of the University of Missouri–Kansas City. The U.S. historians had to assume that they were indeed reading what the Russians intended to say, as must the American readers of this volume. Every care has been taken in this regard, but the editor and participants in this enterprise were reminded at every turn that the misunderstandings and unclarities lurking in discourse carried on in one language are more than doubled when there are two.

***

Nikolai Sivachev and Nikolai Yakovlev, in their book *Russia and the United States*, noted that the effort to overcome the divisive heritage of the long Cold War would be "no easier than the docking of *Soyuz* and *Apollo* in space." Despite the difficulties, they wrote, "we have a great deal to learn from each other."[12] This project is conceived in that spirit. If we learn from each other, we may yet find that sharp differences of basic interpretation remain, the Soviet conception of American reality continuing to diverge from the range of views found in the American (and Western) scholarly community. The learning would then be reflected not in notable consensus, but in ever more factually rich, methodologically and conceptually sophisticated accounts written in both nations. Or there might be a different evidence of learning—some movement, some shifts in perspective and technique, even in

12. Sivachev and Yakovlev, *Russia and the United States*, xiii, 268.

places some convergence upon what the story really was and what it means. This series of four volumes of Soviet-American dialogues should give concrete experience in the benefits—for how could it be otherwise?—of broadened intellectual interchange.

At first, when parties of equivalent abilities and commitment begin an exchange of views, there is the hope of conversion of the other. That hope persists to the end, and is not always unrewarded. But life teaches us to expect and in time to find some gratification in a different result, the evolution of all views toward understandings that are more complex and more closely adequate to the task of describing and comprehending historic reality.

Convergence is a word often used when Soviet-American relationships are discussed, and there is generally less dispute over whether there is any of it than over how far it will proceed toward similarities. Two historians have recently called attention to the logic of convergence as it works upon these two polarized societies. Historian Robert Kelley, after a year on a Fulbright Lectureship at Moscow State University, wrote an essay in which the differences between the two societies were seen as less impressive than the many ways in which they shared common features and were seen to be converging toward closer identities. Acknowledging the well-known differences, Kelley noted that both these great powers with nuclear status and large military establishments have recently fought humbling wars in Asia; both are physically large; both have people characterized by a certain warmth of spirit who are said to be lacking in European sophistication; and both are ruled by a dominant "white" culture at the center of an ethnically and racially diverse population within which separatist impulses seem to be on the increase. A popular recent book, Yale historian Paul Kennedy's *The Rise and Decline of the Great Powers*, casts both the U.S. and the Soviet Union as declining imperial powers, moved down the slope of world power due to common factors of age, rigidity, and the "imperial over-stretch" of excessive and sustained military expenditure.[13]

These American observations of parallel developments within the two societies, nations accustomed to think of themselves as presenting irreconcilably opposed models of the world's future, found resonance in Mikhail Gorbachev's injunctions to his countrymen (published in English in 1987 as *Perestroika: New Thinking for Our Country and the World*) to energize their sluggish economy by borrowing from capitalist principles which assert the importance of individual incentives, decentralization, efficiency as measured in market verdicts, and an increase in proprietorship.

Yet these are only harbingers, perhaps, of a different future. Historical scholarship on the American past, as that scholarship is pursued within the two nations, cannot

13. Kelley, "Comparing the Incomparable: Politics and Ideas in the United States and the Soviet Union," *Comparative Studies in Society and History* 26 (October 1984); Kennedy, *The Rise and Decline of the Great Powers* (New York, 1987). On the theme of convergence, a headline writer for a local newspaper seemed to close the circle of time when General Secretary Gorbachev's visit to Washington in late 1987 was given front-page coverage under the heading "Gorbachev Opens Drive for New Deal" (*Raleigh News and Observer*, 8 December 1987).

yet be characterized as converging. It is strikingly divergent. But the Soviets are committing greater resources to the study of U.S. history and seek more frequent and substantial scholarly interchange with the West. No one knows, and we would not want anyone to instruct us, as to where this should or will lead. We take the early steps with optimism that subsequent exchanges in this series of volumes, and elsewhere, will enlarge historical understanding.

***

The parts of this volume are arranged in the following general pattern: a translated article by a Soviet historian; a Comment by an American historian; and finally a Response from the Soviet author. This general pattern has not been followed rigidly for a number of reasons. The death of Nikolai Sivachev precluded responses to the two American discussions of his articles, and V. L. Malkov responded to only one of the two American commentators on his articles. Similarly, Theda Skocpol, David Brody, and James T. Patterson have each commented on two Soviet articles because of the closely related content of those articles. It is hoped, though, that this general pattern of scholarly dialogue will help the reader comprehend both the similarities and the dissimilarities in Soviet and American views of U.S. history.

Chapel Hill, North Carolina
October 1988

N. V. Sivachev

1 THE NEW DEAL OF F. ROOSEVELT

The socioeconomic reforms and ideopolitical changes in the middle and late 1930s known as the New Deal (from the beginning of Roosevelt's administration on 4 March 1933 until the problems connected with World War II at the end of the decade) constitute one of the most important periods in American history. During the past decade the historiography of the New Deal has been shaped by differing views on the relationship of reform to sharp class and political conflict. The meaning of what occurred from 1933 to 1939 has become an integral part of American political and intellectual life. History and contemporaneity merged.

During the 1930s attitudes toward the New Deal were formed strictly along political lines. Several conceptions of those years were short-lived; however, others had a more solid scientific-historical base and have become a part of contemporary historiography. The view that Roosevelt's reforms were fascist did not last long.[1] The idea that the New Deal was "socialism" or "socialism" and "fascism" at the same time was taken more seriously.[2] As the "fascist" aspect of this accusation faded, the New Deal became more closely identified with "socialism."

The early historiography of the New Deal included a liberal apology based on the Rooseveltian belief that government regulation was a positive force in modern life. The major historian H[enry S.] Commager was among the founders of this interpretation.[3] The formation of a conservative and sharply critical (although not extremist) interpretation of the New Deal resulted from the labors of the Republican president of the University of Wisconsin, G[lenn] Frank,[4] and of R[aymond] Moley, a Democrat and member of Roosevelt's "brain trust." Moley left the New Dealers to join the critical Right during the second half of the 1930s.[5]

The first thorough historical investigation of the New Deal was an apologetic book by B[asil] Rauch.[6] The most visible leaders of liberal historiography—Commager, R[ichard] Hofstadter, A[rthur M.] Schlesinger, Jr., L[ouis M.] Hacker, W[illiam E.] Leuchtenburg, F[rank] Freidel, J[ohn D.] Hicks, C[arl N.] Degler among them—

1. E. Francis Brown, "The American Road to Fascism," *Current History* (July 1933). This essay by N. V. Sivachev was first published in the Soviet journal *Questions of History,* 1981, no. 9, 45–63. This English translation is by Brenda Kay Weddle.

2. H[erbert C.] Hoover, *The Challenge to Liberty* (New York, 1934).

3. Commager, "Farewell to Laissez-Faire," *Current History* (August 1933); "Regimentation: A New Bogy," *Current History* (July 1934). In the creation of the apologetic concept of the New Deal, a large role was played by a book by journalist E[rnest K.] Lindley, *The Roosevelt Revolution: First Phase* (New York, 1933).

4. Frank, *America's Hour of Decisions: Crisis Points in National Policy* (New York, 1934).

5. Moley, *After Seven Years* (New York, 1939).

6. *A History of the New Deal, 1933–1938* (New York, 1944).

later virtually sanctified the New Deal, although they were moderately critical of some of Roosevelt's policies.[7]

Conservative historians were less impressive. The names of J[ohn T.] Flynn and E[dgar E.] Robinson[8] are prominent in anti-Roosevelt publications and political rhetoric.[9] Conservative critics placed in doubt, if not the basic need for Roosevelt's reforms, then the way they were carried out. These conservatives questioned the extent of government's incursion into the prerogatives of private enterprise and its many concessions to the lower classes. Despite all these differences between liberal and conservative historians, they were united by the fact that they completely separated [Herbert] Hoover's policies from those of the New Deal. Liberal historians believed that when New Dealers disassociated themselves from Hooverism they had taken a progressive step; conservatives thought the decision was rash, and often found in it malicious intent.

By the beginning of the 1960s, the argument about whether or not the New Deal had been necessary was itself history. Consensus historiography, which discredited the idea of sharp conflict in American history, held that Roosevelt's reforms generally had been positive. They were seen as consequences of the maturing of the democratic idea. This interpretation underestimated the role of the workers' struggle for social progress and exaggerated the effect of New Deal changes in the socioeconomic fabric of American life.

A radical element that subjected the New Deal to sharp criticism from the Left appeared in American historiography on the crest of the democratic wave that existed during the 1960s and 1970s. There were at least two important features in the work of W[illiam] A. Williams, B[arton J.] Bernstein, P[aul K.] Conkin, H[oward] Zinn, and other radical historians (most of whom identified themselves with the "New Left," although a few—Conkin, for example—preferred not to be associated with this sociopolitical movement). The first feature was an emphasis on the fact that Roosevelt's reforms sought to weaken the labor movement and to strengthen the unstable position of major capital. The second feature was stress on the ineffectiveness of economic reform of the period; that is to say, the economy of the United States stood on its own legs not as a result of the New Deal, but as a result of World War II.[10] However, radical historians weakened their work by including a great deal

7. Hacker, *Shaping of the American Tradition* (New York, 1947); Commager, *The American Mind* (New Haven, 1950); Hofstadter, *The Age of Reform: From Bryan to FDR* (New York, 1956); Schlesinger, *The Age of Roosevelt* (Cambridge, 1957–1960); Hicks, *Republican Ascendancy, 1921–1933* (New York, 1960); Leuchtenburg, *Franklin D. Roosevelt and the New Deal, 1932–1940* (New York, 1963); Degler, ed., *The New Deal* (Chicago, 1970); Freidel, *Franklin D. Roosevelt: Launching of the New Deal* (Boston, 1973).

8. Flynn, *The Roosevelt Myth* (New York, 1948); Robinson, *The Roosevelt Leadership, 1933–1945* (Philadelphia, 1955).

9. See the anti-Roosevelt anthology edited by J[oseph J.] Boskin, *Opposition Politics: The Anti-New Deal Tradition* (Beverly Hills, 1968).

10. Bernstein, "The New Deal: The Conservative Achievement of Liberal Reforms," in his

of speculation, and they lacked a sense of historical methodology. This prevented a proper evaluation of both the reforms of the 1930s and the differences between Hooverism and the New Deal. Nevertheless, these radical ideas had no small effect on American historiography of the New Deal. New Leftists did insist on a comparative analysis of American socioeconomic developments before and during the "Great Depression."

From 1962 to 1966, more than one hundred new books and articles in the United States addressed the assumption that there was continuity between the 1920s and 1930s, or conversely, that there was a rupture between the Hoover regime and Roosevelt's New Deal.[11] A view that the foundations of the New Deal lay in the 1920s and early 1930s gradually developed, but nothing was settled in regard to Roosevelt's innovations.[12] Liberal historians deliberately set for themselves an easy task: they asked whether the New Deal was a revolution, and then easily justified a negative answer. This, however, hardly dealt with the heart of the problem. The conclusion among "New Leftists" that there was a continuity of conservatism was based on the fact that both Hooverites and New Dealers served the monopolists—i.e., both presidents had fought socialism. In other words, these authors did not regard the anticapitalistic appearance of far-reaching social reforms as important, nor did they consider that Roosevelt's service to the monopolists included the possibility of significant changes in the structure of capitalism.

The works of bourgeois historians ignored the process of governmentalization that

Towards a New Past: Dissenting Essays in American History (New York, 1968); Williams, *The Contours of American History* (Chicago, 1966); *New Deal Thought,* ed. Howard Zinn (Indianapolis, 1966); Conkin, *FDR and the Origins of the Welfare State* (New York, 1967); for the "new leftists" in American historiography see V. L. Malkov, "On the Question of the Modern Composition of American Bourgeois Historiography: The Crisis of Methodological Bases and the Practice of Concrete Investigation," in *Criticism of Modern Bourgeois and Reformist Historiography* (Moscow, 1974); *American Historiography of Interpolitical Problems in the Post-War Period* (Moscow, 1974); I. P. Dementiev, "Basic Directions and Schools in American Historiography of Post-War Times," *Questions of History,* 1976, no. 11; K. S. Gadzhiev, "Several Problems of Contemporary American 'New Left' Historiography," *Questions of Methodology and History of Historical Science* (Moscow, 1977).

11. [Richard S.] Kirkendall, "The New Deal as Watershed: The Recent Literature, *Journal of American History* 54 (March 1968). This is related to the historiographical section of A[lbert U.] Romasco, "Hoover—Roosevelt and the Great Depression: A Historiographic Inquiry into a Perennial Comparison," in *The New Deal,* ed. John Braeman et al. (Columbus, Ohio, 1975), 1:3–26.

12. Of the latest works we note two monographs. E[lliot F.] Rosen criticizes the concept of continuity and offers the thought that the New Deal broke sharply with the Hoover tradition (*Hoover, Roosevelt, and the Brain Trust: From Watershed to New Deal* [New York, 1977], 40). E[llis W.] Hawley is more cautious in his judgment. He concludes that America continued to search "for a liberal, but orderly mechanism of change of power in 1933" (*The Great War and the Search for a Modern Order: A History of the American People and Their Institutions, 1917–1933* [New York, 1979], 213).

underlay Roosevelt's reforms, overestimated the roles of Hoover and Roosevelt, and underestimated the role of the working class in bringing about progressive social reform. The critical potential of radical historians, who came close to an understanding of the class character of the New Deal, was weakened by the absence of a dialectical approach to the historical process. Their vision of the history of the 1930s was inadequate to the extent that they did not understand the complexity of American capitalism's state-monopolistic development.

In Soviet historiography the New Deal is studied as a "categoric shift in the social development of the country."[13] It is the result of the process by which American monopolistic capitalism developed into state-monopolism. [Editorial note: For more information about terms used by Soviet historians in describing American history, see N. V. Sivachev and E. F. Yazkov, *History of the USA Since World War I* (Moscow, 1976), and E. F. Yazkov, ed., *The U.S. Two-Party System: Past and Present* (Moscow, 1988).] The Leninist theory and analysis of state-monopolistic capitalism explains the nature of governmentalization that ran its full course in the United States in the beginning of the twentieth century, the catalytic role of the crisis of 1929–1933, the significance of political activity among certain bourgeois groups adept at social maneuvering to prompt and accelerate action, and the bourgeois character of governmentalization. Leninist analysis shows both the speculation of raising questions about a "Roosevelt revolution" and the dogmatism of radical historians who found nothing new in the New Deal because its supporters defended and strengthened capitalism.

New Deal economic policy took two directions. One involved deep institutional reforms that brought an increased government role in production; the other involved deficit financing. Both these directions intertwined; both prompted the private monopolies that formed the economic base to show sympathy for the idea of state-monopoly.

The new administration and Congress first had to take up bank-financing problems. At the beginning of March 1933, the previous banking system of the United States had practically ceased to function. By that time, 5,504 banks with deposits of $3.4 billion were closed and, by presidential decree, were under government control.[14] Only "healthy" banks would resume functioning. The cleanup of banks conducted by the government led to the liquidation of weak banks and strengthened the concentration of banking capital. In 1932 there were 6,145 national banks with combined deposits of $22.3 billion in the United States. Within a year there were significantly fewer—4,897, with deposits of $20.8 billion. According to data for 1939, 5,203 national banks with capital of $33.1 billion operated in the United States.[15] With a 15 percent reduction in the number of banks from 1933 to 1939,

13. Malkov, *The New Deal in the United States: Social Movements and Social Policy* (Moscow, 1973), 362.

14. *Public Papers and Addresses of Franklin D. Roosevelt* (New York, 1938–1950), 2:27 (hereafter *FDR Public Papers*).

15. *Historical Statistics of the United States: Colonial Times to 1957* (Washington, 1961), 626.

assets rose by 37 percent. The Reconstruction Finance Corporation (RFC), an agency established by Hoover, played a large role in reorganizing the banks. The RFC lent $7.3 billion from 4 March 1933 to 23 October 1937, most of it to fortify banking institutions.[16] A special law separated deposit banks from investment banks. From 1933 to 1935 reform legislation affecting the Federal Reserve System (operational since 1913) increased the role of government and reduced the prerogatives of bankers.

In 1933–1934 the government gathered up all gold and forthwith devalued the dollar by 41 percent.[17] The fears of Hoover and of all supporters of his monetary policy were realized. New Dealers justified devaluation in the name of helping the masses of debtors and of improving access to credit for both the government and private enterprise. The belief that American business might improve its position in foreign markets also was of some importance. All this was aimed at enlivening business activity in order to restore some of the losses suffered by capitalists who had gained great fortunes on the "hard dollar." Devaluation of the currency and government pressures to ease access to credit created an inflationary mechanism in the American economy, the effects of which were not fully apparent until after World War II.

Regulation of the stock exchange was linked closely to the banking and monetary measures. Wall Street bosses wanted to preserve the "private club status"[18] of the exchange with its freedom from restrictive rules. But the consequences of the exchange's orgy were too dramatic. Two laws to regulate and impose some order on the exchange of securities were passed in 1933–1934. The Securities and Exchange Commission (SEC), created in 1934 and still operative today, began to prescribe rules for issuing and trading shares. By 1937, 3,500 companies had applied with the commission to register shares in the amount of $13 billion.[19] As a result of another law in 1935, significantly better regulation of holding companies was achieved. This measure, like banking reform, was not antimonopolistic, but state-monopolistic. In 1938 the Investment Bankers Association reported to the SEC that there were 730 bank investors in the country, but the investment business was dominated by thirty-eight banks. Comprising only 5 percent of all investment banks, they issued 91 percent of the shares. Six major banks (1 percent) controlled 57 percent of the investment business. The House of Morgan alone managed 23 percent of all shares—as much as 692 other banks.[20]

Attempts to bring recovery to the debilitated industrial system turned in the direction of state-monopoly. The major efforts were contained in the National Industrial Recovery Act (NIRA), passed on 16 June 1933.[21] Even during the Hoover admin-

16. *FDR Public Papers*, 2:403–4.
17. Ibid., 3:64–76.
18. R[alph F.] De Bedts, *The New Deal's SEC: The Formative Years* (New York, 1964), 198.
19. *FDR Public Papers*, 2:213–15, 3:90–92.
20. D[avid D.] Lynch, *The Concentration of Economic Power* (New York, 1947), 127–28.
21. *Documents of American History* (New York, 1949), 2:452–56.

istration a number of major businesses had suggested measures to regulate competition, but Republicans lacked spirit for breaking with "rugged individualism." Business itself insisted on greater daring from the Democrats. The organ of business circles, *Business Week*, published an editorial on 10 May 1933 that put the issue point-blank: "The American businessman at this moment is utterly weary of the ruthless competitive struggle. It has been too much for him; he has survived so far, but he is spent. He is willing, he feels just now, to surrender some part of his freedom of action to achieve some degree of stability." *Business Week* noted a "general agreement among the leading businessmen" that regulatory measures were needed in the areas of production, sales, and labor. "Let industry formulate its own codes of practice," the magazine urged, and proposed that government "supervise these self-formulated codes." "Limit this, if you like, to the period of the emergency,"[22] concluded the mouthpiece of monopoly.

This was precisely what was done. The NIRA allowed associations of employers to formulate "codes of fair competition" and allowed the president to sanctify them. Violation of code provisions could result in suppression by the Federal Trade Commission, active since 1914. The codes prescribed the volume of production, prices, rules of sale, and even the conditions of labor.[23] For the duration of the law, which was limited to two years, antitrust laws were suspended for fields that adopted codes. Although antitrust legislation had never been a real barrier against monopolization, this official disarmament of the antitrust mechanism stressed the government's interest in a stronger concentration of production and capital. This government action forced the development of industrial cartels. The codes were written and adopted by industrial trade associations. Some five hundred new employers' associations wrote codes for fields that involved 95 percent of all industrial workers. The Temporary National Economic Commission, established in 1938 for the purpose of investigating concentration and monopolization, showed that "economic" and "political" centralization significantly increased during the New Deal.[24] While the two hundred largest industrial corporations controlled 49.4 percent of the nation's industrial production in 1929, it had risen to 57 percent in 1939. Nearly 29 percent of America's wealth belonged to them in 1939.[25]

The agricultural policy of the New Deal passed through several stages, the basic landmarks of which were laws enacted in 1933, 1936, and 1938.[26] The essence of the policy was simultaneous encouragement of lower production and higher prices.

22. *Annals of America* (Chicago, 1968), 15:208–9.

23. *FDR Public Papers,* 2:276–77.

24. *Investigation of the Concentration of Economic Power: Final Report and Recommendations of the Temporary National Economic Committee* (Washington, 1941), 5.

25. *Investigation of the Concentration of Economic Power,* Temporary National Economic Committee, monograph no. 21 (Washington, 1940), 299–300.

26. For a circumstantial analysis of this problem, see E. F. Yazkov, "Agricultural Policy of the Roosevelt Administration and the Farmers' Movement in the United States in 1933–1935," *Modern and Contemporary History,* 1957, no. 3; V. P. Zolotukhin, *Farmers and Washington* (Moscow, 1968).

Large farmers agreed to withdraw a significant part of their land from cultivation and to reduce other forms of agribusiness in return for a large government stipend. This money bought a great deal, having been squeezed from the already shrunken economy. On the whole, the agricultural measures of the New Deal were dictated by the interests of major capitalistic farmers. But the government did grant some benefits to small farmers that eased their tax burden, and price supports and tax relief did slow the rate at which farms were destroyed. Compared to 1932, the number of bankruptcies in 1939 was down by 71 percent; mortgage liabilities had decreased by 23 percent (down $2 billion). Farmers' cash incomes, including government premium payments, rose from $4.7 billion in 1932 to $8.5 billion in 1939.[27] But parity prices (the relationship between prices of goods that farmers sold and those they bought) remained far below the base level of 1909–1914. In 1936–1937, the parity price level rose to 92–93 percent, and in 1938–1939 fell to 78–77 percent.[28] Thus the agricultural crisis was not overcome before the war. New Deal measures helped to stabilize the situation somewhat, but more than anything they strengthened the position of large and powerful agrarians, enabled major capital to penetrate deeply into the agricultural economy, and facilitated formation of state-monopolistic principles by which this important branch of the economy would operate.

Once they had been handed the reigns of government, Democrats were convinced it was impossible to fulfill their election promises of cutting government spending and balancing the budget. Practical needs of the day forced New Dealers to turn to deficit financing. Increased government spending was dictated by two important conditions: first, the already difficult economic situation was made worse by the failure of private business to undertake industrial capital investment; and second, and more evident and urgent, an unemployed army of many millions expected material aid from government. Investments in industrial and social life were linked inseparably. Both demanded repudiation of traditional wisdom about the budget—which mostly rested on reducing the limit on what could be spent during a fiscal year.

The argument over when, whether, and to what degree Roosevelt became a Keynesian economist persists in American literature to this day. The state-monopolistic theory of J[ohn Maynard] Keynes featured an active role for government in the economy and sanctioned expansion of government spending without regard to possible budget deficit. Both were features of the New Deal, not as a result of reading Keynes (although his works were studied attentively by many American economists, including some of Roosevelt's advisors and aides), but due to the pressure of circumstances. In 1933 the government revealed plans for a grandiose hydroelectric station in the basin of the Tennessee River and created a special Tennessee Valley Authority (TVA). By means of government investment, numerous aspects of life in the region would be reconstructed. But the political right wing bitterly attacked the TVA as the embodiment of "socialism"—even though it was the very image of state-monopoly.

---

27. *FDR Public Papers*, 1938, 94.
28. *Historical Statistics of the United States*, 283.

While New Dealers caused government to intervene in the economy quite apart from any influence of Keynes, in the area of budgeting they departed from orthodoxy because of real needs and the inculcation of Keynesian thought in the United States.

The specific character of New Deal economic policy was determined by tension between deficit financing (the policy of "priming the pump") and the belief of most New Dealers in balancing the budget. Very few supporters of deficit financing came forward in 1933–1934 during the early stage of the New Deal, but those crisis years proved to be a great teacher. During the second stage of the New Deal, which became evident in 1935, advocates of deficit spending had much greater influence in Roosevelt's circle. Then, the economic crisis of 1937–1938 further opened the science of economics and economic policy to Keynesian thinking. From 1936 to 1937 the budget deficit had decreased sharply—from $3.5 billion to $0.2 billion.[29] But in an address to Congress on 14 April 1938, Roosevelt recommended a major increase in government spending. In his subsequent "fireside chat" he admitted that a precipitate drop in state spending during 1936–1937 had been one of the basic causes of the recession of 1937–1938.[30] The budget deficit rose significantly; it amounted to $2 billion in 1938 and $2.2 billion in 1939.[31] The war greatly heightened this trend.

Although New Dealers did not acknowledge Keynesian ideas about deficits as consistent and positive weapons in economic policy, they nevertheless implemented this primary aspect of Keynesian theory more than did the English. In 1929 general private investment amounted to $35 billion (in 1954 prices), and the value of goods and services purchased by government agencies came to $18.5 billion (of which $2.9 billion was spent by the federal government). In 1938 the relation between the two categories had changed. Private investment had fallen to $15.5 billion, and government purchases had increased to $28.8 billion (of which $11.4 billion was attributable to the federal government). This change encouraged the growth of the government debt. In 1929 government debt amounted to $29.7 billion, with $16.5 billion of that amount incurred by the federal government. By 1939, government debt was $58.9 billion, with $42.6 billion owed by the federal government.[32] The increase of the federal portion was particularly important. In 1929 it was 58.9 percent of all government debt, and in 1939 it was 72.3 percent.[33] Government circles gradually had to change their thinking about Keynesianism in order to rationalize the deficit and the debt. At the end of the decade the president himself was among those who, though not yet Keynesian, had ceased to feel their former trepidation about deficits.

New Deal financial and economic measures, which were seen by their initiators as devices for rescuing the economy from depression and as barriers against a new recession, fell far short of the intent. The beginning of a new, unexpected economic crisis in 1937 was the best proof. Compared to 1936, the index of industrial produc-

29. R[obert] Lekachman, *The Age of Keynes* (New York, 1966), 115.
30. *FDR Public Papers*, 1938, 221–48.
31. Lekachman, *The Age of Keynes*, 115.
32. *Historical Statistics of the United States*, 143, 664.
33. Ibid.

tion had fallen by 16.4 percent by 1938.[34] The dubious means of applying anticrisis therapy, through the "built-in stabilizers"[35] created by New Dealers' economic policies, undoubtedly strengthened the development of state-monopoly. The index of industrial production in 1938 was 53.3 percent higher than in 1932, and 120 percent higher by 1940. The pattern of federal spending also had changed: from 1932 to 1938 expenditures rose by almost 100 percent, from $4.266 billion to $8.449 billion, and from 1932 to 1940 by 136 percent—to $10.061 billion.[36] Admittedly, using 1932 (the lowest point in the Depression) as the date for comparison weakens proof of the thesis that federal expenditures outstripped other economic growth; but the figures are nevertheless convincing. The great change in the movement of these indicators would be particularly striking if the latter years of the 1920s were used as the point of comparison: production from 1927 to 1940 increased by 32 percent, and federal expenditures by 185 percent.[37] Government expenditures are one of the most important components in state-monopolistic capitalism. The sharp and steady growth of government expenditures over a relatively short time is a persuasive quantitative measurement of proof of the transformation of monopolistic capitalism in America into state-monopolism.

While the New Deal economy was evolving into state-monopolism, the approach to resolving social problems was becoming that of state socialism. In the United States state socialism was particularly liberal; it was reflective of the broad and deep maneuvering of the masses in behalf of a number of urgent demands. For the first time in American history social policy was consistent with needs. Such factors as the deepening socioeconomic crisis and the rise of democratic movements among the masses had a decisive influence on its formation. According to official data, 13 million people did not have work in 1933. In 1937 the number of the unemployed had decreased to 7.7 million, but in 1938 it jumped again to 10.4 million. And in 1939, the figure was 9.5 million, that is, 17.2 percent of the work force.[38] Indeed, the number of unemployed for all these years was actually significantly higher. Secretary of Labor F[rances] Perkins stated that in 1933 it reached 18 million.[39] According to trade union statistics, nearly 12 million were unemployed in January 1940, and 8.2 million in April 1941[40] (at a time official data showed only 5.6 million unemployed).[41] The most important trait of international political development was the rise of the workers' and democratic movement. During the Depression and particularly during the New Deal, the United States entered this movement and the country seethed.[42]

34. Ibid., 409.
35. E. Hansen, *Post-War Economy of the United States* (Moscow, 1966), 52.
36. *Historical Statistics of the United States,* 409, 724.
37. Ibid.
38. Ibid., 73.
39. Perkins, *The Roosevelt I Knew* (New York, 1946), 182.
40. *CIO News,* 8 March 1940, 21 July 1941.
41. *Historical Statistics of the United States,* 73.
42. See also Yazkov, *The Strike Movement of the Agricultural Proletariat in the United States in*

The workers' and democratic movement of the period under review was a militant offensive in support of broad sociopolitical goals. Foremost were demands for effective aid to the unemployed. These included legislation to create social insurance, legislation to set a minimum wage and a maximum work day, recognition of trade unions and collective bargaining, help for debt-ridden farmers and other workers, and guarantees of civil rights for even the most discriminated-against minority. The masses demanded a stop to the spread of fascism and a stop to events that threatened the unleashing of a new world war. The country experienced the most dramatic shift to the left since the second American revolution [i.e., the Civil War and Reconstruction]. A powerful new alliance of industrial unions arose—the Congress of Industrial Organizations (CIO)—in which the Communists exercised great influence. In 1932, there were 2,857,000 members of trade unions in the United States. By 1939 the two federations of unions (AFL and CIO) had enrolled 8,980,000 workers.[43] During the middle and second half of the 1930s, the Communist Party of the United States occupied a stable position in unions and other organizations of the masses for the first time. In 1938 the ranks of the Communist party contained 75,000 members.[44] Socialist thinking was having considerable influence among American intellectuals. American Socialist leader N[orman] Thomas had every reason to call the 1930s the "red decade."[45] In the midst of the Depression and the powerful expression of popular will, there was still perceptible the authority of the monopolies, entities that during the years of "prosperity" considered themselves to be "in the saddle." After 1929, in the words of one American business leader, business was "in the doghouse."[46] This decisively weakened the opposition of monopoly capital to progressive social innovations.

Resolving social problems through state socialist methods was accelerated by international conditions and events—signs of the general breakdown of capitalism. The revolutionary practice of socialistic construction in the USSR had a visible influence. The principles of socialist planning, successfully realized in the USSR by fulfilling the first five-year plan, strengthened the position of believers in government regulation of the economy in the United States. Many Americans, not particularly concerned about accurate terminology, drew an analogy between government regulation of the economy and the Soviet experiment in "planning." The social aspects of transformations in the Soviet Union had an even stronger influence on American society. Elimination of unemployment in the USSR together with success in the fields of education and social and health insurance proved convincingly that government responsibility for the fate of each citizen led not to the destruction of individuality, but to improved well-being and to conditions in which individual abilities

1929–1935 (Moscow, 1962); D. G. Nadzhafov, *The People of the United States Against War and Fascism, 1933–1939* (Moscow, 1969); *History of the Workers' Movement in the United States in Recent Times, 1918–1965* (Moscow, 7 1970), vol. 1, chaps. 7–11.

43. *Historical Statistics of the United States,* 98.
44. *Essays on Modern and Contemporary History of the United States* (Moscow, 1960), 2:211.
45. Oral History Collection of Columbia University, "Norman Thomas," 58.
46. E[ric] Johnson, *America Unlimited* (Garden City, 1944), 179.

could be most fully developed. Americans were also influenced from the opposite end of the political spectrum. Spokesmen for world fascism speculated on the inability of traditional parliamentary regimes to resolve social problems, and the false slogans of the fascists about the "final solution" for all problems alienated the masses from bourgeois democracy.

More than anything, the Roosevelt administration had to concern itself with the problem of unemployment. The administration tried to resolve the problem through three basic steps: distribution of monetary subsidies to the unemployed, execution of all possible public works projects, and passage of social insurance legislation. Implementing these measures involved the federal government as well as state and municipal leaders, but the leading role, without doubt, belonged to the federal level. Direct monetary aid was rendered by the Federal Emergency Relief Administration (FERA), founded in 1933 and headed by H[arry L.] Hopkins, whose name came to be connected with aid policy for the unemployed.[47] Public works were the primary means. The form varied from forestry camps for youths to work groups for removing city trash to large capital-intensive construction projects. Works of the first type unfolded under the leadership of the Soil Conservation Service (SCS) and the Works Progress Administration (WPA), which was also headed by Hopkins. The agency headed by Secretary of the Interior H[arold] Ickes, the Public Works Administration (PWA), handled industrial construction projects of social significance.

In contrast to the WPA, the PWA emphasized the economic rather than the social aspect of the problem. Generally speaking, spending so much money on public works and direct aid to the unemployed was for the purpose of "priming the pump," of intensifying economic activity; further, it was a form of social maneuvering aimed at stifling social protest and preventing the unemployed millions from becoming radical. During the lives of the FERA, WPA, and PWA, which continued into World War II, government spent a total of more than $20 billion.[48] If expenditures of all levels of government are counted, including states and municipalities, from 1933 through 1938 more than $25 billion was allotted to overcome unemployment: $18 billion for public works projects, and $7 billion in direct subsidies.[49] For comparison, one can point out that the general military expenditures of the government from 1933 through 1938 amounted to $11 billion, but if one excludes payments to veterans (which to a great degree also should be considered aid to the unemployed), military spending was only $5 billion.[50]

One of the most important laws of the New Deal created a system of social insur-

47. Malkov, "Harry Hopkins: Pages of a Political Biography," *Modern and Contemporary History,* 1979, nos. 2–4.

48. *FDR Public Papers,* 2:241; Georgetown University Library, Special Collection Division, Robert F. Wagner Papers, Box 326, New Deal Agencies, F. Holmes to D. Delman, 2 September 1944, PWA, 1.

49. *Investigation of the Concentration of Economic Power: Hearings Before the Temporary National Economic Committee* (Washington, 1939), pt. 1, 225.

50. *Historical Statistics of the United States,* 719.

ance, which with further development became a skeletal part of the modern "welfare state."[51] The law that passed in 1935 created two types of insurance—old age and unemployment. Both types excluded large categories of labor (agricultural workers, house servants, government servants, and others), provided low payments, and operated inside an entirely undemocratic system. But there were important differences between old age and unemployment insurance as well. The old age insurance plan was operated completely by the federal government and was financed by taxes on both workers and employers. Unemployment compensation, however, was based on federal and state collaboration. The federal law did establish the tax, which only employers paid, to finance the program. But the size of the awards, eligibility to receive them, and length of payment were determined in cooperation with each state. The old age pension scheme (for those sixty-five and older) limited the payment to $85 a month. On the average, the unemployment stipend by the end of the 1930s could be paid a maximum of 9.4 weeks a year at $11 a week, an amount equal to 36.6 percent of the worker's wage.[52]

The New Deal reforms created a foundation for government labor regulation and for cooperation between organized workers and entrepreneurs. This was first established through Section 7(a) of the NIRA, and then more clearly and in greater detail in a number of special statutes. Section 7(a) of the NIRA set forth in general terms the right of workers to create unions and obligated the employers "to observe the maximum work day, minimum wage, and other conditions of labor approved or assigned by the president" (all this was fixed in the "codes of fair competition"). Because these codes were created by monopolists and, as a rule, without real participation by unions, their provisions seemed disadvantageous to the workers. Nevertheless, in summer 1933 the government believed it had made significant concessions to labor and planned no further legislation on labor relations.

However, in 1935 the entire social policy of the New Deal began shifting to the left as a result of class conflict. The shift was most perceptible in the government's labor policies.[53] For the first time in United States history, the right of the workers to create unions was embodied into law. Passed in July 1935, this law was best known as the Wagner Act, after the senator who initiated it.[54] A special administrative agency, the National Labor Relations Board, had full power to suppress specified "unfair labor practices" on the part of employers and to conduct elections that chose labors' representatives to conduct collective bargaining. The elected representatives were considered to be spokespersons for all workers in the unit that elected them. Employers did not have the right to refuse to bargain with them in good faith. For the most part,

51. M. Z. Shkundin, *On the History of the State-Monopolistic Social Policies of the United States, 1929–1939* (Moscow, 1980).

52. *Documents of American History,* 2:505–14; *Historical Statistics of the United States,* 198–99.

53. Malkov, "Workers' Policies of F. Roosevelt (1933–1940)," *Questions of History,* 1965, no. 9.

54. See further A. A. Popov, *The United States: Government and the Trade Unions* (Moscow, 1974), 41–66; N. V. Sivachev, *Legal Regulation of Labor Relations in the United States* (Moscow, 1972), 111–25.

employers and their associations opposed the Wagner Act, and after its passage they immediately organized a campaign to have the law declared unconstitutional. The liberal social reformation was nowhere more completely embodied than in the Wagner Act. The law reflected the strong desires of New Dealers to prevent the working class from taking up an independent political course and to reduce class conflict through concessions. The law bespoke the conclusion that the best model for regulating collective bargaining was one which fully involved the bourgeois government. And although the right to strike was not restricted, the lawmakers projected an image of strikes as undesirable.

When the NIRA was invalidated in 1935, direct regulation of labor conditions by the federal government temporarily ended. But by 1936 Congress had passed a law on minimum wages and maximum hours for employees of businesses that filled orders from the federal government.[55] By 1937 there was increased support for government regulation in all private businesses connected with interstate commerce. In June 1938 Roosevelt signed the Fair Labor Standards Act and thereby established a minimum wage of twenty-five cents an hour. In 1945 it was raised to forty cents. Strictly speaking, the law did not establish a maximum work week, but required only that labor receive time-and-a-half after forty-four hours; from October 1940, overtime had to be paid after forty hours. It was more profitable for employers to pay time-and-a-half than to hire new workers, train them, and pay toward their social insurance and other benefits that were subject to collective bargaining. The Fair Labor Standards Act of 1938, although it did limit child labor and although it would create considerable conflict among the working class in the future, affected a very narrow sphere for many years. In 1938 it covered only eleven million workers.[56]

The social policy of the New Deal embraced not only workers and farmers, but also the urban middle classes and intellectuals. Its goal was to maintain the allegiance of these groups to revitalized bourgeois values, to prevent them from being carried away with revolutionary ideas or from swinging too far to the right. New Dealers did more than a little to preserve "one-story America" through a program of financial aid to those homeowners who wallowed in mortgage debts. The special Home Owners Loan Corporation, created in 1933, guaranteed something on the order of $3 billion to sustain more than a million home owners during the three years of its existence.[57] Accepting the office of president for a second term, Roosevelt uttered a memorable phrase: "I see one-third of a nation ill-housed, ill-clad, ill-nourished."[58] It was, of course, a fair lot of political rhetoric, but it was not without foundation. All the same, the Roosevelt administration had undertaken far-reaching measures, discussed above, for deepening the social reformation. Government housing construction for low-income families even expanded toward the end of the decade: 1937

55. *Monthly Labor Review* (August 1936): 368–69.
56. Franklin D. Roosevelt Library, Official File 3295, Wage and Hour Division, "An Explanation of the Fair Labor Standards Act of 1933," 6–7; E. Andrews to the President, 28 December 1938.
57. *FDR Public Papers,* 2:223–37.
58. Ibid., 1937, 5.

brought appropriations of $500 million for that purpose, and 1938, as the economic crisis deepened, $300 million more.[59]

The New Deal brought no notable positive change in the lives of blacks, the main (but not only) victims of racism in the United States. B[arton] Bernstein has observed correctly that "the New Deal left intact the race relations of America."[60] Yet, it is impossible to say that New Deal social measures did not touch unemployed and homeless blacks. In October 1933, 2,117,000 blacks (17.8 percent of the black population) were receiving government aid; at the time the percentage of whites receiving aid was only 9.5 percent. By the beginning of 1935, 3,500,000 blacks (30 percent) were supported by government subsidies. The various forms of government aid temporarily benefited up to 40 percent of American blacks.[61] These figures also point up the large percentage of blacks who were destitute, as well as the fact that the Democratic administration tried harder to penetrate black society through its social philanthropy. The latter had far-reaching consequences and influenced the political reorientation of blacks who had been (since the Civil War) the Republican party's "own."

Extending material aid to blacks in no way infringed on racism in the social sphere. The passivity and spinelessness of the New Deal in matters involving race were illustrated graphically by the administration's stance on efforts to pass a law against lynching. The reported number of incidents involving lynching rose from thirty-eight in 1930–1932 to fifty-seven in 1933–1935.[62] At the end of 1933 the National Association for the Advancement of Colored People drafted a law that would punish officials who did not take decisive action to stop lynchings and bring the law to bear on violators. This proposed law, in fact, was a very timid measure. It stipulated the intervention of federal officials only after a month had passed from the commission of the crime—after it was clear that state investigating agencies would be taking no action. A similar bill was introduced in 1934 in the Senate by R[obert] Wagner and E[dward] Costigan, but the White House did not support it. All the efforts of black leaders to induce the president to make some kind of statement in support of antilynching legislation came to nothing. After long delay, the House of Representatives passed a bill on 10 January 1940, but the Senate buried it.[63]

The reforms of the New Deal and the conflicts that accompanied them called for certain changes in the functioning of government institutions, in ideology, and in the two-party system. In each area there were marks left by the terrible crisis of 1929–1933 and the aftermath that lasted until World War II. Change resulted from

59. Ibid., 465–72.

60. Bernstein, *Towards a New Past*, 279.

61. *A Documentary History of the Negro People in the United States, 1933–1945*, ed. Herbert Aptheker (Secaucus, N.Y., 1974), 168; *The New Deal*, ed. Braeman, 1:188.

62. *Eight Negro Bibliographies*, comp. D. T. Williams (New York, 1970), no. 7, "The Lynching Records of Tuskegee Institute," 10.

63. *The Negro in the Depression and War: Prelude to Revolution, 1930–1945*, ed. Bernard Sternsher (Chicago, 1969), 181–92.

sharp class and political conflict, which in turn deepened social antagonisms. This dynamic caused the New Deal period to be one of the stormiest in United States history.

At the beginning of the New Deal, during the "hundred days" (the period of the special session of the Seventy-third Congress, 9 March to 16 June 1933), laws were passed usually without discussion and, by American standards, at a fantastic speed. Although petty skirmishes arose over individual bills, on the whole congressmen from both the majority and minority parties obediently endorsed the initiatives that seemed to pour from some legislative cornucopia in the White House. There seemed to be an atmosphere of "national unity" for a time, although in fact it was only a temporary muting of traditional interparty conflict. When the spirit of national unity disintegrated, there were several consequences. Foremost among them was the fact that New Dealers did not pull the economy out of crisis or end the outbreaks of social protest. When the initial response proved so ineffective, Roosevelt's circle was pushed into new experimentation, but that prompted simultaneous opposition from the traditionalists. Having been forced to adjust to the feverish activity of the "hundred days," they now saw the New Deal's shortcomings. And when government became active in matters that were traditionally the province of private enterprise, some considered it threateningly close to "socialism." The rise of the workers' and democratic movements—the main reasons for the New Deal's shift to the left— intensified ideopolitical conflict inside the ruling class. Some in these groups came to believe that New Dealers indulged the masses in order to grab power and to achieve "dictatorial" goals. Such feelings deepened the opposition of business to economic regulatory measures.

At the same time, Roosevelt's reforms were criticized by leftists, including the Communists. But all the heaviest attacks came from the right, from the reactionary-conservative camp. During 1933 and 1934 the tactics of the opponents of the New Deal were not to repeal the laws passed during the "hundred days"; rather, they aimed to strengthen the position of business through government aid, stop additional reform, and win in the 1934 congressional election, after which they would consider self-serving legislation. They entertained the prospect of returning a Republican to the White House in 1936, or at least a more standard Democrat. By the 1934 election, the DuPont-Morgan financial circle had forged an interparty, anti-Roosevelt group under the name of "The American Liberty League."[64] Because it appeared to be the main source and distributor of reactionary ideas, the Liberty League could never count on broad support. The task of tearing the masses away from the New Deal and organizing national dissatisfaction into a reactionary political channel fell to two other forces, neither of which can be called movements in the sense of the Liberty League. Heading these forces were H[uey P.] Long and [Father] C[harles] Coughlin—demagogic and reactionary leaders with strong convictions about "knowing"

64. G[eorge] Wolfskill, *Revolt of the Conservatives: The American Liberty League, 1933–1940* (Boston, 1962).

how to resolve social questions and being "able" to speak the "national" language.[65] However, the 1934 election, and particularly the 1936 presidential election (in which Roosevelt carried every state except Vermont and Maine), showed that there was almost no prospect of convincing the people to put a stop to New Deal reforms.

After the 1934 election, opponents of reform put their hope in the United States Supreme Court, the last stronghold of tradition in the system. It must be said that when the New Deal shifted to the left, the majority of the ruling class did not embrace the Liberty League or fascist demagogues. They supported traditional conservatives, who were particularly strong in the judiciary and reasonably influential in Congress, and reasonably strong in both political parties, especially the Republican. The Supreme Court in 1935 and 1936 raised hopes in the rightist camp by annulling twelve New Deal laws, among them two of the most important passed during the "hundred days"—the NIRA and the act to regulate agricultural production. The NIRA was unanimously declared unconstitutional for two reasons: there was an improper transfer of legislative power to the executive branch, and the federal government undertook regulation of commerce over which it lacked jurisdiction.[66] The acts of suppression, of active government interference in socioeconomic relations, of banning concessions to the workers, were based on those rationales. That is to say, the court decisions were in conflict with the liberal state socialism of the New Dealers.

Thus the courts were severely tested during the Depression; their very existence, in fact, was threatened by efforts of Roosevelt's government to strengthen the bourgeoisie. The ruling class itself seemed deeply split over questions of political strategy. Roosevelt found support for his socioeconomic policies among some major capitalists. Among others, such business leaders as H[y] Harriman, M[yron] Taylor, [A. P.] Giannini, W[alter] Teagle, G[erard] Swope, W[inthrop] Aldrich, A[verell] Harriman, and T[homas] Watson went along with Roosevelt. But the highest monopolistic circles totally opposed his reforms. Nonetheless, this opposition did not bring about liquidation of the New Deal, nor did it even avert a shift in social policy to the left. In the middle 1930s, New Dealers seemed politically stronger than a simple arithmetic calculation of supporters and opponents among the ruling class would seem to warrant. This additional power, so to speak, of the New Deal was the result of broad support among the masses and their realization that here was a political rationale for realizing the demands of the lower classes and for reforming traditional ideas about private property. Roosevelt was not afraid to move, in his words, "a little to the left of center,"[67] for he understood that in the final analysis this served to strengthen those supporters who formerly had misunderstood or for political reasons had opposed him.

If, after the shattering defeat of the Republicans and the whole reactionary bunch

65. Malkov, *The New Deal in the United States,* 144–52.
66. *Documents of American History,* 2:458–63.
67. Perkins, *The Roosevelt I Knew,* 333.

in the 1936 election, the Supreme Court had invalidated the highly important social legislation passed during 1935 (as well it might have in light of its recent performance), there could have been extremely dangerous social outbursts with unpredictable results. The president fully realized that he was mandated to fight for those laws. However, a decision to confront the Supreme Court openly was not easy, for in the United States the image of the Court had long been one of a judicial Olympus of unquestionable authority. Instead, the situation called for plotting a blow to forestall the Supreme Court—something to deter the Court from rashly liquidating the laws passed in 1935 that had found such favor among the masses. The noisy campaign in 1937 to reform the courts should be viewed in this light.[68] Inasmuch as his plan for judicial reform was never enacted, Roosevelt was defeated. But the very debates over the plan played a role in reorienting the Supreme Court—and that was Roosevelt's main objective. Even as the heated political arguments continued, the Supreme Court favorably reviewed three exceptionally important cases—the Wagner Act, the law on social insurance, and state laws to regulate industrial working conditions. These decisions weakened the attacks against the Supreme Court and in many ways warded off a congressional decision to impose unwanted changes.

Contemporaries and, later, bourgeois historiography showed not a few misunderstandings about events and the debates over judicial reform. Roosevelt's opponents clearly exaggerated the extent of his defeat. They lost sight of something more essential—the fact that this campaign helped "reeducate" the judicial body and facilitated the approval of New Deal enactments. Roosevelt's supporters, and some of his opponents, exaggerated another way. They vastly overcredited the 1937 reform campaign with forcing a change in the Court's positions. In so doing, they ignored or underestimated the power of the mass movement for progressive social reform. In its decisions during 1937, the Supreme Court broadly applied socioeconomic arguments and repudiated the legalism of the reactionary Right that permeated its earlier opinions. It was a victory for the ideas of the rightist sociological school, a position to which O[liver] W[endell] Holmes, member of the Supreme Court from 1902 to 1932, had made a great contribution. To the sociological school, formal-legal logic was not of paramount importance; the facts of real socioeconomic life were. Only at the end of the 1930s did Holmes's classical formula receive recognition: "The life of the law has not been logic; it has been experience." He had first put the idea forward in 1881 in a book, *The Common Law*.[69] The United States judicial system henceforth stood solidly on the course of state-monopoly, the course set by the socioeconomic measures of the New Deal, the course to which the executive and legislative branches of government already had adapted themselves.

Understanding that saving capitalism as a system demanded repudiation of "rugged individualism" created state-socialist, state-monopolistic ideology. This doctrine was developed from roots that grew in American soil in the last quarter of the

68. Malkov and Nadzhafov, *America at the Crossroads* (Moscow, 1967), 159–70.
69. Holmes, *The Common Law* (Boston, 1963), 5.

nineteenth century. The traditional liberalism of the New Deal years completed the evolution[70] begun at the end of the nineteenth century from a negative view of strong government in socioeconomic processes to a positive view. Thus Manchester liberalism was turned into a new, state-monopolistic ideology—neo-liberalism. Asked to provide an alternative to socialism from one side and to extreme reaction from the other, "neo-liberalism looked for a means of combining individualistic traditions with the concepts of a regulated economy and reformist social theory."[71]

Neo-liberalism was a left-central variant of state-monopolistic ideology that found institutional and political refuge in government agencies run by New Dealers and in the Roosevelt wing of the Democratic party. Mass movements encouraged the formation of neo-liberalism as left-central bourgeois state socialism. Although no "Roosevelt revolution" occurred, the New Deal, as a declaration of the American Communist party put it in December 1962, was "one of the most progressive chapters" in the history of the United States.[72] The pace of reform was so swift that many American ideologues could not keep up. They remained preoccupied with the dogma of "rugged individualism" and with the myth of the downfall of the "old order." In fact, they were experiencing the transformation, the broad and all-encompassing transformation, of the "old order" to the spirit of state-monopolistic capitalism and to neo-liberal forms.

During the New Deal a change occurred in the power relationship between America's two main bourgeois parties. A fundamental realignment occurred, and a new stage was opened in the history of the two-party system.[73] In the configuration of parties that resulted from the Civil War and Reconstruction, the Republican party led a two-party system with Republicans dominant over Democrats. This conservative and dynamic political combination was unable to resolve the problems that accompanied the general crisis of capitalism. Also unable to overcome the dogma of individualism, the combination suffered its deepest crisis at the beginning of the 1930s. The ideopolitical catastrophe particularly affected the Republican party. The Democratic party assumed first place in the two-party system from the middle of the 1930s, and thereafter the system functioned as a configuration of Democrats dominant over Republicans. Changes in its social base, primarily the urbanization of its electorate, rendered the Democratic party most capable of understanding the ideas of bourgeois collectivism and social maneuvering. The overwhelming majority of workers (particularly those in unions), farmers, the middle class, and intellectuals crossed to the Democratic camp. The black community broke away from the Republicans, and ethnic and religious minorities rallied to Roosevelt's party.[74] The

70. V. V. Sogrin, *Origins of Modern Bourgeois Ideology in the United States* (Moscow, 1975).

71. Malkov, *The New Deal in the United States,* 178.

72. *Political Affairs* (December 1962): 11.

73. I. P. Dementiev et al., "On the Question of Periodization of the Two-Party System of the United States," in *Questions of Methodology and History of Historical Science* (Moscow, 1978).

74. R[ichard P.] Jensen, "Party Coalitions and Search for Modern Values, 1820–1970," in *Emerging Coalitions in American Politics* (San Francisco, 1978).

result was an amorphous political union known as the "Roosevelt coalition."[75] Roosevelt himself played an enormous role in this evolution; he was the strongest U.S. government official and political party functionary in the twentieth century.[76]

Questions about farming were at the forefront of reform movements at the end of the nineteenth century. And even during the "progressive era," for all the emphasis on the urban problems of social insurance, recognition of unions, and regulation of labor conditions, these issues still were not central—although they were rightly on the agenda. The crash of 1929–1933 clearly showed that however deep the social problems of the working and urban middle classes, the need for agricultural reform was not lessened. It became clear, as well, that no reform was possible without the active and constant involvement of the federal government in the process of modifying or forming social structures. The Republicans could not abide the idea of state socialism or the idea of social maneuvering as an instrument of change. Democrats were able to use both. The reasons lay in the nature of their constituency and their traditions as well as in the fact that they had been in the opposition during the speculative prosperity of the 1920s. The Democrats were therefore capable of crafting schemes to battle the economic crisis and to retain the loyalty of the masses—all within the context of a bourgeois world outlook. The result was a division in the degree to which each party influenced society that is rare in the history of the two-party system. They were excessively remote from each other. The balance of consensus and alternative that is important to the functioning of the American two-party system was at risk.

Republican leaders did not immediately understand that their loss of power in 1932 was not insignificant and not an accident. Nor did they understand that it was they—and not the Democrats—who had to fight for votes. But even when they understood all this, the Republican leadership proved unable to offer a realistic alternative to the Democratic program or to enter a consensus with the Democrats concerning innovations. The stability of the two-party system was truly threatened—a dangerous phenomenon for the ruling class. At first the Republicans countered the Democrats' neoliberalism with outworn slogans about "rugged individualism." But Republican ideologues and political leaders had to confront the fact that their decaying dogmas were ineffective and unattractive, and they began an agonizing search for ways to refurbish their ideological baggage. After their shattering defeat in 1936, and after that seemingly inaccessible stronghold of reactionary individualism, the Supreme Court, cracked in 1937, the idea became much more attractive of generating a realistic alternative to the New Deal that recognized the positive aspects of state socialism.[77]

Republicans were unexpectedly successful in the 1938 election. Of course, they could not hope to achieve a congressional majority, but they substantially improved

75. V. O. Pechatnov, *The Democratic Party in the United States: Voters and Policies* (Moscow, 1980), 40.

76. N. N. Yakovlev, *Franklin Roosevelt—Man and Politician* (Moscow, 1965).

77. A. S. Manykin, "The Republican Party of the United States in Search of an Alternative to the New Deal," *Herald of Moscow State University*, History series, 1978, no. 5.

their position. The Republican success is explained not so much by inclusion of state socialism in the party's ideology as by the undermining effect of the economic crisis of 1937–1938 on the Democrats, particularly on their left-central wing. But it must be said that beginning in 1937 the Republican opposition to the New Deal was somewhat different; they repudiated their extreme positions of 1933 to 1936. This created points of contiguity between the Republicans and the right-central wing of the Democrats, primarily the Southerners. Between 1937 and 1939 a conservative coalition of Republicans and Southern Democrats (Dixiecrats) formed in Congress.[78] Analogous coalitions, even stronger, were formed on the state level.

The party alignment of the 1930s took place within the bounds of the traditional parties: the power balance between them was changed, and there were basic changes in the ideopolitical foundations of each. The Democrats had crossed the line to neo-liberalism by the end of the 1930s, and the Republicans had begun to master the principles of neo-conservatism. Neo-conservatism was a right-central variation of state-monopolistic ideology and policy. It differed from the left-central neo-liberal system primarily in that, although it acknowledged the positive aspects of state socialism, it was less active than neo-liberalism in instilling the principles of governmentalization. The major exception to this generalization was that the neo-conservatives used the increased role of government against the laboring masses to a significantly larger degree than did the neo-liberals. As the Republicans developed neo-conservatism, the major contribution was made by a group of new leaders who came to prominence in the party at the end of the decade—W[endell] Willkie, T[homas] Dewey, R[obert] Taft, H[arold] Stassen, and J[ohn D.] Hamilton. The tenets of right-central state socialism reverberated through the party's election campaign in 1940. By visibly stretching the definition, one can speak of the "neo-conservative character of the Republican platform."[79]

If the New Deal is examined as two integral processes—the development of state-monopolistic regulation and the implementation of major social reforms demanded by the masses—it can be considered ended in 1939. After the election of 1938, according to assessments by the bourgeois press, the Roosevelt camp seemed "confused over the next phase of the New Deal."[80] The president was "inclined to move cautiously" and to show "moderation" in his dealings with Congress.[81] Newspapers unanimously considered that the White House had proposed nothing essential to the lawmakers who convened a new legislative session in January 1939. In contemplating the work before the Seventy-sixth Congress, the Speaker of the House of Representatives, conservative Alabama Democrat W[illiam] Bankhead, declared that the

78. J[ames T.] Patterson, *Congressional Conservatism and the New Deal: The Growth of the Conservative Coalition in Congress, 1933–1939* (Lexington, 1967).

79. A. A. Kreder, "American Monopolistic Bourgeoisie and the New Deal of F. D. Roosevelt (1932–1940)," *American Annual, 1979* (Moscow, 1979), 148.

80. *Kansas City Times*, 1 December 1938.

81. *Philadelphia Inquirer*, 14 December 1938.

main goals of the New Deal "have been practically completed" and that the necessity of further reform was less urgent.[82] In his annual State of the Union message on 4 January 1939, Roosevelt proposed no reforms. New Dealers made significant concessions to the rightists by accepting lower appropriations for social programs and the end of some experimental projects. Then the president officially proclaimed an end to the "period of internal conflict in the launching of our program of social reform."[83] The purveyors of bourgeois propaganda applauded this signal of retreat.

But this turn of events did not mean the dismantling of the New Deal. New Deal socioeconomic legislation lasted and, more importantly, state socialism, state-monopolistic structures and principles, became an organic part of American society. The transition to state-monopoly achieved during the New Deal appears irreversible, although as a result of World War II it has taken other, more conservative forms. Government regulation of the economy and the social infrastructure was the most important legacy of the New Deal. To a lesser degree it contributed to the capacity of American capitalism to adapt to modern conditions. However, the "brokers" already had managed to show their inability to offset the blows dealt them by capitalism's ever-deepening crisis. The economic shocks of the following decade confirmed their helplessness.

82. *New York Herald Tribune*, 8 January 1939.
83. *State of the Union Messages of the Presidents, 1790–1966* (New York, 1967), 3:2846.

William E. Leuchtenburg

Comment on "The New Deal of F. Roosevelt," by N. V. Sivachev

One cannot take up the assignment of responding to Nikolai Sivachev without an ineluctable sense of melancholy. I recall his presence as a research student at Columbia University when I was a member of its history faculty, and I remember even more vividly a number of exchanges of ideas in Moscow at the time of the Historical Sciences Congress in 1970—especially a leisurely afternoon when, at his invitation because he wanted to provide an opportunity for us to be alone together, we lunched at Moscow State University and then walked about for a long time looking down at the spires of the city and talking of matters of mutual concern. I regret keenly that, because of Nikolai's premature death, my comments on his essay will draw no rejoinder, and that a fruitful colloquy can no longer be carried on.

Professor Sivachev made an exceptional contribution to the effort to create a sense of community among scholars in America and the USSR—an altogether worthwhile enterprise but also one fraught with difficulty, as Sivachev's own career, and indeed the essay in this volume, indicate. It may be doubted that any Soviet historian has done more to promote discourse between scholars in the United States and in Russia about the New Deal and to encourage interest within the USSR in the age of Franklin D. Roosevelt. In these respects, he has truly been a magisterial figure.

Yet it is no less true that Sivachev was a forthright critic both of the New Deal and of the historians who wrote about it. Anyone who has conversed with him knows that, in private exchanges, he showed himself to be not unsympathetic to American institutions and not insensitive to certain shortcomings of his own land. However, in his public commentary he was often bluntly censorious. In Moscow in 1970, he delivered a rebuttal to a superb paper by Frank Freidel of Harvard University on the emergence of the national state in twentieth-century America that was altogether disapproving, and in the essay on New Deal historiography for this book, his final statement, he is, at times, even more acerbic. Sivachev's essay, indeed, raises a direct challenge to American historians of the New Deal to recognize the flaws in their work and to accept the superior insights of a historian in Moscow.

The first question an American historian of the New Deal will ask of Sivachev's essay is: What is the basis for this critique? The answer is clearly not that he has unearthed new sources of information that American or other scholars have neglected. He makes only fleeting reference to manuscript collections. To be sure, it is difficult for Russian scholars to consult sources in a country so far distant, though Sivachev did, in fact, manage a number of trips to America. It should also be noted that when scholars of the USSR do come to the United States, they find the papers of the Roosevelt administration much more open to them than are the archives of the Soviet regime of the 1930s to American scholars. Historians in the United States would warmly welcome an influx of researchers from Russia, and it is to be hoped that the USSR will step up its efforts to make such visits increasingly possible and will allocate funds for the acquisition of microfilms of American documents along the lines of the program of the Roosevelt Study Center in the Netherlands.

Sivachev's contribution in this instance rests not on fresh original research but on the conviction that American historians have approached their subject from the wrong perspective. In particular, he contends that "Leninist analysis" exposes both the shallowness of liberal historians and "the dogmatism of radical historians" in the United States. Perhaps so. But in assessing the salience of that claim, the historian of the New Deal will want to see whether Leninist analysis does, in fact, deepen our understanding.

We may begin that inquiry by asking if Sivachev's account of historiography in America is accurate, and the answer to that question is, for the most part, not affirmative. Sivachev accuses "the most visible leaders of liberal historiography" of having "virtually sanctified the New Deal," when in fact there is considerably more diversity among the writers he brackets as liberals than he recognizes, and their estimates of the New Deal are decidedly more discriminating than he acknowledges. For example, sanctification hardly characterizes the widely read and highly influential essay by Sivachev's former teacher Richard Hofstadter in *The American Political Tradition and the Men Who Made It.* Its very title, "Franklin D. Roosevelt—The Patrician as Opportunist," suggests the irreverent mood of the piece. A member of the Communist party in the 1930s, Hofstadter has been referred to as "one of the foremost popularizers of Marxist categories among historical circles," and though, by the time he published this essay, he had dropped out of the party, he continued to reflect the opinion of the Left in lamenting FDR's reliance on improvisation rather than a "systematic conception" and in alluding to "the political bankruptcy of the New Deal."

Sanctification may serve better to encapsulate my own work, for my verdict on the New Deal is, on balance, favorable, but I have again and again spotlighted its deficiencies. In *Franklin D. Roosevelt and the New Deal, 1932–1940,* I called the much-admired Social Security Act "an astonishingly inept and conservative piece of legislation"; pointed out that "the New Deal's showplace communities were Jim Crow towns"; and described the Fair Labor Standards Act as "a highly unsatisfactory law." In "The New Deal and the Analogue of War," I concluded that only World War II "rescued the New Deal from some of its dilemmas." Sivachev's essay antedates my more recent writing, but it might be noted that in *In the Shadow of FDR* I observe that "it was in FDR's presidency that Japanese-Americans were herded into internment camps and European Jews were all but abandoned to their fate." There may be examples in Russian historiography of scholars who are as outspoken about current and recent Soviet leaders, but they do not readily come to mind.

There is serious reason to question, too, whether the author of this essay, well-steeped though he was in American historiography, always fully understood the hypotheses with which scholars began their work. He states, "Liberal historians deliberately set for themselves an easy task: they asked whether the New Deal was a revolution, and then easily justified a negative answer." I do not know of any "liberal historian" who set that task. The question of whether the New Deal was a "revolution" was one that was raised by conservative opponents of FDR's policies, but serious scholars never supposed it was a revolution in the sense that it was comparable to the French Revolution or the Bolshevik Revolution. The question raised was a quite different one—whether the New Deal was a "watershed." That is, does the evidence suggest that there was greater continuity or discontinuity between America before and after the changes wrought by the New Deal, and, more particularly, were the New Dealers more like or unlike their predecessors, the Progressives? And on those questions, historians who might be regarded as "liberal" differed sharply. Some of Sivachev's other contentions are truly hard to fathom. What does it mean, for example, to say that "bourgeois historians ignored the process of governmentalization that underlay Roosevelt's reforms"?

Though most of Sivachev's arrows are aimed at "liberal historians" or "bourgeois historians"—the terms seem to be interchangeable—he also targets "radical historians," while crediting them with coming closer to "an understanding of the class character of the New Deal," whatever that may be. "The critical potential of radical historians," he maintains, "was weakened by the absence of a dialectical approach to the historical process. Their vision of the history of the 1930s was inadequate to the extent that they did not understand the complexity of American capitalism's state-monopolistic development." Radical historians may be excused for not understanding what these charges signify. It would indeed be interesting to learn precisely how a Soviet historian finds the work of an American historian of the radical persuasion "inadequate," but surely something less opaque is required. Nor is it correct to say that New Left historians concluded that "there was a continuity of conservatism . . . based on the fact that both Hooverites and New Dealers served the monopolists." On the contrary, some radical scholars took pains to resurrect the reputation of Herbert Hoover by presenting him as an insightful leader who warned against the drift toward bureaucratic centralism which the New Left, with its faith in participatory democracy, so much deplored in the era of Vietnam and the Great Society.

Sivachev encounters even greater difficulty when he moves from historiography to the actual subject matter of the New Deal. When he maintains that the "deep institutional reforms" of the New Deal and deficit spending "prompted the private monopolies that formed the economic base to show sympathy for the idea of state-monopoly," one wonders what evidence can be adduced for such a statement. Similarly, what does it mean to say that the Public Utility Holding Company Act of 1935 was "not antimonopolistic, but state-monopolistic"? The mind boggles at the notion that breaking up holding companies fosters state monopoly. Nor is it at all easy to puzzle out what is intended by the pronouncement, "While the New Deal economy was evolving into state-monopolism, the approach to resolving social problems was becoming that of state socialism," or to grasp the implications of the ensuing assertion, "In the United States state socialism was particularly liberal."

Curiously, Sivachev advances the extraordinary claim that "for the first time in American history social policy was consistent with needs." Not even the most credulous "bourgeois" historian would make that assessment, which credits the Roosevelt administration with a measure of success that few, if any, governments have ever achieved. Furthermore, we are not informed as to how Leninist analysis accounts for such enlightened behavior in a society in which "private monopolies" are said to exert so much power.

Professor Sivachev is especially fond of the rubric "state-monopolistic capitalism," which sometimes obscures more than it elucidates. True, there were efforts by the New Deal, of which the National Industrial Recovery Act is the most conspicuous example, to further cartelization, and "state-monopolistic capitalism" is not wholly unsatisfactory to describe such developments. But the term is altogether inappropriate when used indiscriminately to characterize all of the political economy of the 1930s, and indeed what preceded it and what followed it. "Monopolistic" is particularly inapposite to categorize highly competitive industries such as coal and textiles.

If the discussion of economic issues is problematic, the treatment of Constitutional questions is downright mistaken. Professor Sivachev scolds "bourgeois historiography" for losing sight of the way that the Court fight of 1937 produced a shift of attitude by the Supreme Court; in fact, there is no history of the period that does not mention what scholars commonly refer to as "the Constitutional Revolution of 1937." He goes on to say, contradictorily, that historians, whom he has just reproved for failing to realize the changes wrought in 1937, have erred by "vastly" overcrediting the 1937 struggle for transforming the Court's behavior. Their mistake came, he maintains, from not perceiving "the power of the mass movement for progressive social reform," though there is not a shred of evidence of any influence of a mass movement on the justices. Finally, he explains that this transformation, ostensibly brought about in good part by a mass movement, was "a victory for the ideas of the rightist sociological school." Not a word is offered to elucidate how a mass movement achieved victory for the Right, quite apart from the fact that the Constitutional Revolution was not in the least a triumph of the Right.

The discussion of even more fundamental Constitutional matters does not lessen the confusion. It is asserted that in the New Deal era there were "acts of suppression" which were based on certain "rationales," but there is no way of knowing what presumed acts of suppression are alluded to, or what rationales the author has in mind. Sivachev makes his point much more clearly when he states that the courts' "very existence . . . was threatened by efforts of Roosevelt's government to strengthen the bourgeoisie." Alas, in this instance clarity is gained at the expense of accuracy; at no moment in the 1930s, or at any other time, was the existence of the courts remotely in jeopardy.

This imputation to Roosevelt of a desire "to strengthen the bourgeoisie" points up the fundamental question of whether Leninist analysis helps us to comprehend the relation of class to the state. How does one square the notion of FDR as a promoter of the bourgeoisie with the idea that there were marked social advances in the 1930s? Sivachev acknowledges that New Deal reforms "increased the role of government and reduced the prerogatives of bankers," but he does not analyze how that happened. In a class-based society, with a government catering to the bourgeoisie, how do bankers come to lose prerogatives? Who are the people who reduce their prerogatives, and what is their class base? How do they accrue enough power to be able to diminish the authority of financiers?

Though Sivachev never answers these questions directly, he does indicate what his point of departure would be—that the United States in the 1930s developed a "particularly liberal" variant of state socialism because of "the broad and deep maneuvering of the masses in behalf of a number of urgent demands." He contends that "the workers' and democratic movement" launched "a militant offensive in support of broad sociopolitical goals," including recognition of collective bargaining, guarantees of civil rights, and a halt to the spread of fascism. More than once, he rebukes "bourgeois historians" (sometimes called "consensus historians") for having "underestimated the role of the working class in bringing about progressive social reform."

"Bourgeois historians," though, may remain unpersuaded by this argument not because they have not thought of it, or are predisposed to reject it, but because the evidence does not sustain it. Ever since Werner Sombart raised his famous question, "Warum gibt's in der Vereinigten Staaten keinen Sozialismus?," radicals had anticipated that when there were no longer shoals of apple pie in America, the workers would turn to socialism. But when in 1929 the capitalist system did collapse, as Marxist critics had predicted, there were only sporadic outbursts of working-class protest. In 1932, the year workers had their first opportunity since the Crash to express their sentiments in a national election, the vote for radical parties was pitiful. Moreover, on the eve of the New Deal, "the masses" in the United States had not yet developed the institutions that served as vehicles of protest in other countries; almost no factory worker belonged to a union or any other kind of economic organization. Not until 1934, after the rising expectations of the First Hundred Days, was there any measurable radical activity, and it was of brief duration. A general strike in San Francisco disintegrated after four days. To be sure, as numbers of historians have pointed out, the insurgency of 1934 did help in some respect to create an atmosphere conducive to the social legislation of 1935. But the Second Hundred Days was the result less of a conflict between workers and the government than of the determination of New Dealers and liberal congressmen to take advantage of the altered mood of the country to push through reforms.

American historians are not much more likely to find fully acceptable Professor Sivachev's formulation of the impact of the Soviet Union on the New Deal. "The revolutionary practice of socialistic construction in the USSR had a visible influence," he contends. "The principles of socialist planning, successfully realized in the USSR by fulfilling the first five-year plan, strengthened the position of believers in government regulation of the economy in the United States." To a degree, that statement is correct—but only to a small degree, and even to that extent it must be sharply qualified. There was undeniably considerable interest in America in "the Soviet experiment," and that interest was one of many elements that contributed to greater hospitality to the idea of planning. Without doubt, too, the USSR served as a model for American Communists. But Communists had a negligible part in the Roosevelt administration, and the reform tradition in the United States was far more important than the Russian example as a source of the New Deal. Furthermore, there were aspects of the Soviet experience in these years—the dreadful toll taken by collectivization, the Stalin cult, the Moscow trials, the savage political executions, the brutal slave-labor camps—that caused the USSR to be seen not as an inspiration but as a dire warning of power carried to excess.

Professor Sivachev's article ends with some sentences on the demise of capitalism that only those who already share his outlook will find plausible. The "brokers" of the New Deal, he concludes, "already had managed to show their inability to offset the blows dealt them by capitalism's ever-deepening crisis. The economic shocks of the following decade confirmed their helplessness." We need only think for a moment about the actual condition of the American economy in the next decade— full employment, the impressive growth of national income, and the development of a consumer society that was the envy of most of the rest of the world—to recognize how inapt a term like "helplessness" is, and the ensuing years were to draw enough sharp contrasts between the economic performances of the West and of the Socialist bloc (as in the piping prosperity of capitalist West Berlin versus the drabness of Socialist East Berlin) to suggest that such language ought to be used with greater discretion.

In sum, this essay suggests that even the best-intended attempts by the most dedicated scholars to create a common discourse about topics such as the New Deal may run aground. Such an outcome would be regrettable, for American historians have much to gain from the effort by scholars of other lands to examine the 1930s from their own angle of vision. Since Soviet writers, in particular, approach a phenomenon such as the Great Depression with a very different perspective not only from that of Americans but from that of scholars in other capitalist societies, their viewpoint could conceivably serve to liberate historians in the United States from the often unarticulated preconceptions with which they approach a familiar society.

But for that to happen, and for intellectual exchange to be rewarding, it is essential not only that American scholars be hospitable to new challenges, but also that Soviet scholars immerse themselves in the often intractable data of the period; make an effort to communicate in a vocabulary that is comprehensible to those who do not share their assumptions; demonstrate that they are prepared to cope with evidence that runs contrary to their hypotheses; and, above all, offer well-founded, well-reasoned interpretations that Americans cannot readily dismiss and cannot afford to ignore.

V. L. Malkov

2 "A LITTLE LEFT OF CENTER": GENERAL AND SPECIFIC FEATURES IN F. ROOSEVELT'S SOCIAL POLICIES

During the past decade in the United States several studies have been published that reflect the continuing interest of modern American historians in the New Deal, particularly its social aspects. Even so, the legacy of F[ranklin] Roosevelt (meaning, broadly, his governmental and diplomatic activities plus his political style) has never been so sharply disputed as during the last two or three years. It was not by chance that an article in *Time* magazine on the one hundredth anniversary of Roosevelt's birth traced the origins of the contemporary political setting in the United States to events fifty years past. By that time, the magazine said, the differences in the two parties' approaches to resolving national problems had become apparent.[1]

If the editors of the magazine had pressed further, they would have recognized that a more serious and deeper conflict was obscured by the quarrel over whether the New Deal was a bad imitation of Western European models or an admirable effort of American bourgeois liberalism to make a prosperous and happy society. The deeper conflict involved the collision of two conceptions of economic and social regulation in a state monopoly. These conceptions condition the acute crisis that American capitalism suffers today. The first is the pseudo-traditional concept incarnate in Reagan's "Revolution." It is pregnant with nostalgia for a free-market economy and is both religiously moralistic and politically ultraconservative. The other resembles Keynes's half-and-half prescription, but with populist overtones.

American non-Marxist historiography on the New Deal should concern itself with this dispute. But American historians agree on only one point: that it is not yet time to make a final judgment. Questions raised during the prewar decade when capitalism experienced such economic and social shocks have not yet been answered by a new generation of American historians who were brought up on the legend of consensus in historiography and who have been disillusioned. They must begin their own studies of the New Deal. These studies should reevaluate the premises of the apologetic literature and the speculative argument that a "Roosevelt revolution" was real, ostensibly a radical change in the nature and image of American capitalism. Many studies have called for a reevaluation of the past,[2] but most ask whether the Roosevelt administration achieved its socioeconomic goals and, if not, why plans failed to achieve a

1. *Time*, 1 February 1982, 20–43. This essay by V. L. Malkov was first published in *American Annual, 1983* (Moscow, 1983), 31–60. This English translation is by Brenda Kay Weddle.

2. J[ohn] Braeman and R[obert] H. Bremner, eds., *The New Deal: The National Level*, intro. D[avid] Brody (Columbus, Ohio, 1975).

stable economy, liquidate poverty, eliminate the gulf between haves and have-nots, and end other inequalities.

The present article examines the dialectic of the general direction and the specific political developments of the New Deal years. It exposes the methods of bourgeois liberalism for preserving proprietary power at a time when internal and external events fostered instability and crisis. The present article also deals with the core issues of class conditions and relationships among the classes.

The decade-long sequence of socioeconomic reforms usually connected with Franklin D. Roosevelt's name has become known in United States history as the era of the New Deal.[3] However, there was nothing fundamentally new in what Roosevelt originally planned.

V. I. Lenin said, "In the affairs of the bourgeoisie in all countries two systems of government inevitably arise, two methods of battling for their interests and advocating their supremacy; these two methods first replace one another, then become entangled together in different combinations. First of all there is the method of coercion, of refusing to make any concessions to the workers' movement, of supporting all the old and absolute institutions, of irreconcilably opposing reform . . . . The second method is the method of 'liberalism,' of steps toward development of political rights, toward reform, concessions, and so forth."[4] Lenin's general theory provides insights into a number of special factors. For example, as a result of historical forces (objective and subjective), partial reforms were enacted that have the mark of the existing social structure, the dynamics of class conflict, the numbers of participants, and other conditions, the most important of which were the internal and international political settings.

Marxism's well-known premise that reform occurs as a result of class conflict is entirely consistent within the course of United States history in the imperialist era. It is clear that bourgeois reformism as an ideopolitical course first appeared on American soil in a significant way as a direct consequence of the rise of the working-class struggle and the upsurge of democratic movements among the petty and middle-class bourgeoisie at the end of the nineteenth and the beginning of the twentieth centuries. It was radicalism in the rural populist movement and the rebellious mood of the workers' movement and its rapprochement with socialism[5] that caused the phenomenon that surrounded [William Jennings] Bryan. Bryanism was an effort to

3. In Soviet studies of America, examples of productive attempts to deepen our understanding of the strategy and tactics of the ruling class of the United States in its economic and social maneuvering during the general crisis of capitalism are: N. V. Sivachev, "On Certain Problems of State-Monopolistic Capitalism," *Modern and Contemporary History*, 1980, no. 3; Sivachev, "The New Deal of Franklin Roosevelt," *Questions of History*, 1981, no. 9; and V. O. Pechatnov, *The Democratic Party of the United States: Voters and Policies* (Moscow, 1980).

4. V. I. Lenin, *Complete Collected Works*, 20:67.

5. *The United States: Political Thought and History* (Moscow, 1976), 305–19; I. A. Beliavskaya, *Theodore Roosevelt and the Socio-Political Life of the United States* (Moscow, 1978), 66–72; V. D. Kozenko, "Progressivism in the Democratic Party," *From the History of the Inter-Political Conflict and Social Thought of the United States* (Kubyshev, 1981), 81–100.

eliminate social protest, distract workers from class struggle, and keep workers inside the two-party system. At the same time, it is very important to note that adherents of Bryanism had an ability to interpret the mind-set of the masses, particularly the elementary democratic views among the petty-bourgeois classes. Without breaking with the Democratic party machine, Bryan decided on his own to risk proposing a substitute for the Democrats' left-central platform, one that combined early populist ideas with anti-imperalism and pacifism.

Without going into detail, one notes that as a variety of bourgeois progressivism, Bryanism (built primarily on the lower classes who traditionally supported the Democratic party) was typical of the desire to compromise. The classes who supported Bryan were filled with hatred toward large property, plutocracy, war, corruption, and expansionist foreign policy. They were antagonistic toward both the reigning predators in American society and disfranchisement of the needy classes. It was not by chance that Bryan only briefly abandoned the idea of turning the Democratic party into a party that supported municipal ownership of property and advocated nationalization of the railroads.[6] It is also well known that he was critical of efforts to make the United States the "world policeman."[7]

Against the background of an increasingly expansionist foreign policy at the beginning of the twentieth century on the one side, and the growth of anti-imperialist, antiwar sentiments among the laboring masses on the other, Bryan's position made a strong impression on the general public, and it could not but have had a positive influence. Exposing monopolies, responding sympathetically to union demands, and asserting his loyalty to pacifism ensured the "Great Commoner" the sympathies of workers,[8] the urban middle classes, petty farmers, radical intelligentsia, and youth. Thus, by easy concessions to the radical mood, Bryanism won the votes of many tentative Socialist supporters and fellow travelers. Bryanism prompted a realignment among the constituents of the Democratic party and thereby enabled the Democrats to acquire a reputation as a truly national party.

Subsequently, application of ordinary liberalism to change among the social classes became a political tradition in the Democratic party, despite the fact that it sometimes caused internal discord. At the dawn of his long political career, Roosevelt acknowledged the advantage of the Democrats' ability to transform themselves— a distinguishing feature of the party since that noteworthy convention in Chicago (1896).[9] However, Roosevelt opposed Bryan's positions on money issues, calling them disreputable, harebrained, and as dangerous as playing with fire.

6. Library of Congress, Louis Freeland Post Papers, box 1, William J. Bryan to Post, 12 November 1904.

7. R[obert] Griffith, "Old Progressives and the Cold War," *Journal of American History* 66 (September 1979): 336.

8. Library of Congress, Louis Freeland Post Papers, box 1, Post to William J. Bryan, 8 November 1908.

9. I. P. Dementiev and V. V. Sogrin, "On the Role of Ideology in the History of the Two-Party System of the United States," *Modern and Contemporary History,* 1980, no. 6, 64–79.

Franklin Roosevelt's ideology was another, more moderate variety of bourgeois reformism. By 1912 it had crystallized in the political philosophy of Theodore Roosevelt and Woodrow Wilson. Roosevelt's ideology consisted of ideas about government intervention in economic life, about modernized labor-management relations, and about the system of social relations that resulted from runaway capitalism. As agricultural radicalism weakened as an opponent of bourgeois society, the conflict between labor and capital intensified. By the beginning of World War I, liberals were predisposed to accent the resolution of workers' problems.

Having experienced the "progressive era's liberal character," Franklin Roosevelt initially copied the pragmatic ideas advanced by bourgeois reformers at the beginning of the twentieth century. His goals can be summed up as follows: first, recognition of the priority of social problems; and second, assumption by bourgeois government of the thesis that it had limited but real social responsibilities, particularly when "harmonious" relations were disrupted between labor and capital.

The economic crisis of 1929–1933 revealed the deep class conflict in the country and "radicalized" political thought among bourgeois liberals. The "Great Depression" forced leading figures of the New Deal, including the president, to give the problems of labor a central place in their new programs.[10] Events forced Roosevelt and his advisors to take up this deep and serious problem in earnest. Roosevelt's close advisor S[amuel] Rosenman noted in winter 1932 that the future president already was concerned about ways of projecting himself to simple people as a man of progressive convictions, as a supporter of change.[11]

Thanks to a well-planned intelligence service that operated during the election campaign of 1932, the new president and his "brain trust" were informed of the mood in the industrial and farming centers that had been staggered by the crisis. There could be no doubt—a rebellious spirit penetrated the consciousness of working America. Lorena Hickok, an experienced and observant journalist, traveled the country far and wide, east to west and north to south. In her regularly dispatched reports to [Harry L.] Hopkins and the president in Washington, she did not conceal the internal tensions. She described the tragedy, the destitution and poverty into which the country was ever more deeply submerged.[12] In every stroke of her distinctive portrait of the era, one idea showed through: social tensions had reached dangerous levels even where the vast majority of working people had long been characterized as "100 percent patriotic," politically conservative, and intensely religious.

Hickok was overwhelmed by the material degradation of thousands of families

10. F[rances] Perkins, *The Roosevelt I Knew* (New York, 1946), 31, 325; W[illiam] E. Leuchtenburg, *Franklin D. Roosevelt and the New Deal, 1932–1940* (New York, 1963), 32; M[ilton] Derber, "Labor and the New Deal," in *The New Deal,* ed. Braeman, 111.

11. Franklin Delano Roosevelt Library (hereafter FDRL), S. Rosenman Papers, General Correspondence, box 2, Rosenman to L. Howe, 27 January 1932.

12. D[oris] Faber, *The Life of Lorena Hickok: E. R.'s Friend* (New York, 1980), 137–52.

who, because of unemployment and leadership's inactivity, remained without means to sustain themselves. She emphasized that further deterioration in their situation might shortly bring unstoppable armed confrontation. The accumulation of weapons (particularly in mining settlements) had taken on threatening dimensions. Any moment all these guns and revolvers might "begin to talk." One had the impression, Hickok wrote, that only physical exhaustion kept their owners from decisive action.[13]

From the beginning it was easy to be deceived by the display of apathy by the large masses of people who were destitute and living on occasional charity. Hickock, however, could see behind this external indifference an internal readiness, moving further to the left than usual, to support democratic reforms. The most disturbing symptoms, in Hickok's opinion, were discernible among youth. There was a heightened interest in socialism as an alternative to capitalism. With the increased interest in socialism, she noted in one of her reports, the name *Lenin* was on everyone's lips.[14]

Another feature of Hickok's secret reports was her recognition that laborers wanted government to take the levers of economic management into its hands, to initiate various social programs, and also to become an employer in view of the fact that efforts by private enterprise to resolve the problem of unemployment were an obvious fiasco.

Hopkins, whose pragmatic, sober, calculating nature and insight Roosevelt valued highly, in many ways based his perception of social conditions on Hickok's information. In spring 1938 Hopkins noted: "In 1932 approximately fifteen million men and women were unemployed. People were talking about economic collapse and about political revolution. Fear and fright dominated the American scene."[15] Political functionaries could not deny that the masses, the largest democratic classes in society, were disappointed in capitalism as a system and that they found socialist ideals increasingly attractive.[16] Growing interest in the "Soviet experiment" and the popularity of the "Russian theme" in the periodical press testified to the trend.[17]

Having clearly perceived the commitment of millions to broad reform, Roosevelt took a step, or more precisely, half-step, toward meeting their expectations. He verbally unfurled a banner of national political reform. At the time, nothing further could be said that was concrete about the changes. Walter Lippmann, one of the best-known political commentators in America at that time, was dismayed by Roosevelt's

13. FDRL, L. Hickok Papers, box 2, Hickok to H. L. Hopkins, 31 August–3 September 1933.

14. Ibid., Hickok to H. L. Hopkins, March–April 1934.

15. Ibid., personal letters in the Papers of Harry L. Hopkins, 1930–1946, roll 17, "WPA Looks Forward" (23 May 1938).

16. Library of Congress, W[illiam] Borah Papers, box 325, Borah to Harry G. Thayer, 11 April 1931; box 371, R. Robins to Borah, 22 August 1933.

17. New York Public Library (hereafter NYPL), Norman Thomas Papers, box 3, Editor of *Harper's Magazine* to Thomas, 1 March 1933.

program for change as it was laid out in the 1932 election campaign. The Democratic candidate's conviction, said Lippmann, lacked certainty and logic.[18] Lippmann did not exaggerate: Roosevelt's program was glaringly insipid. But Lippmann clearly underestimated Roosevelt's tactical ability (striking even to those who knew him closely) to respond quickly to changing situations· and to prepare his new course secretly. The famed jurist F[elix] Frankfurter wrote to Lippmann that he failed to take into account Roosevelt's ability to change positions with lightning speed and Roosevelt's inclination to plan unexpected approaches in secret.[19]

Frankfurter was right. When Roosevelt advanced to the presidency, he found himself face to face with the working and farming populations, and with the possibility of a national crisis because the banking system had collapsed and caused outbreaks of panic. In March 1933, Roosevelt ordered the convocation of a special conference on labor under the aegis of the new secretary of labor, Frances Perkins. The conference was called to discuss two basic concerns: special measures required by the catastrophic employment situation, and tasks connected with the long-term "improvement of labor . . . in the United States."[20] The agenda included items that went beyond the Democratic party's election promises, and in effect laid out the position of the president himself. For example, the agenda provided for discussion of a broad program of labor legislation to ensure not only improved labor conditions, but also restoration of "normal employment." The president wanted representatives of the labor movement, i.e., unions, to attend the meeting. He considered their participation as junior partners an important element in the "reconstruction of the industrial system."

In many ways the program of the Washington meeting anticipated the labor legislation of the New Deal. It also created a certain likeness of a deliberative unit in the Department of Labor composed of specialists and representatives of the unions. This was the prototype of the Advisory Council on Labor of the National Recovery Administration and its successors, the National Labor Board and the National Labor Relations Board (NLRB).[21] In all previous platforms of the Democratic party, there had been no such proposals. And no one, not even in Roosevelt's most intimate circle, suspected that the president would make such a sharp turn toward recognizing the role of unions in the regulation of labor relations, and that simultaneously he would assume for government such power to support the "industrial world."

Apparently there were few who remembered that even during his days as an aide in the Navy Department during the Wilson administration, F. Roosevelt had participated in drawing up new labor policies based on state-monopolistic principles for

18. Library of Congress, Felix Frankfurter Papers, box 78, Walter Lippmann to Frankfurter, 14 September 1932. Roosevelt's election campaign did not make even those who were sympathetic to him ecstatic. But, as one of them said, "at least he has recognized the existence of the common man" (ibid., box 74, Harold Laski to Frankfurter, 29 October 1932).

19. Ibid., box 78, Frankfurter to W. Lippmann, 13 October 1932.

20. Ibid., box 150, Frances Perkins to Frankfurter, 22 March 1933.

21. Sivachev, *The United States: Government and the Working Class* (Moscow, 1982), 233.

regulating labor relations.[22] The important idea was to attract leaders of the union movement into a "partnership" in which they were predestined to play a subordinate and entirely independent role from business and the government.

Consistent with this idea, in March 1933 Roosevelt invited leaders of reform-oriented unions to sit at the same table with the secretary of labor and leaders of the business community to draw up a program for overcoming the crises of production, employment, and welfare. Many union leaders crossed the threshold of the White House for the first time to attend the meeting. The meeting seemed casual and even confidential.[23] Many union leaders looked upon the changing of the guard in Washington with hope and offered optimistic predictions. Sidney Hillman, president of the Amalgamated Clothing Workers of America, was charmed by the manner and manners of the president. After Roosevelt implemented the National Industrial Recovery Act (NIRA), Hillman said he was like a "dream come true."[24] And after Roosevelt managed to ward off a complete financial collapse during the first days of his term and became a national hero, no one wanted to hear warnings from the naively deluded about the fate of the money bosses whom the president promised to drive from the "temple." Sober voices were drowned out by cheers of approval.[25]

The nearly unanimous approval of the "forgotten people" of America for the first New Deal laws alarmed the bourgeoisie. They were also uneasy about the presidential couple's new rituals; the pronounced egalitarianism and commonality of Franklin and Eleanor Roosevelt contrasted sharply with the indifference to the suffering of the masses and the haughtiness of the retired heads of the Republican "government of millionaires." Many aristocratic "money bags" were shocked to learn that the president was "on friendly terms" with union leaders they suspected had connections with the Socialists. Bourgeois circles indignantly rejected Eleanor Roosevelt's efforts to gain sympathy for change by circulating Hickok's report on poverty among the masses.[26] Appeals to compassion were no more in favor among capitalists than were calls for reserve and caution in resolving labor conflicts. They considered that such admonitions would encourage violence against authority by workers.

Irritation among business leaders mounted as Roosevelt tried to attune himself to the popular mood. He devoted a segment of his Sunday radio programs, heard by millions of eager listeners, to the immorality and irresponsibility of "big business." In many ways his manner resembled Bryan's—extolling the strength of the "common man" and blaming industrial magnates for using merciless methods to profit from

22. Ibid., 74; R[obert] D. Cuff, "The Politics of Labor Administration During World War I," *Labor History* 21 (Fall 1980): 557–58.

23. M[atthew] Josephson, *Sidney Hillman: Statesman of American Labor* (Garden City, 1952), 360, 361.

24. Ibid., 362.

25. Left-radical circles in the United States feared that Roosevelt's rhetoric, which the masses accepted on faith, could blind those masses and create a false impression that action could only be taken in Washington. See NYPL, N[orman] Thomas Papers, box 3, Ernest Gruening to Thomas, 9 March 1933.

26. J[oseph] P. Lash, *Eleanor and Franklin* (New York, 1973), 509.

human labor, for glaring hostility, intolerance, and arrogance or for hardheartedness and treachery in their dealings with workers and unions. Roosevelt purposely chose the most blunt and precise words possible. It is not surprising that employers responded with hostility: they rebuked him as soft and indecisive and servile to the destitute classes. They even charged that he secretly hoped to "Sovietize" America. By the end of 1933, the bourgeois press had begun to print articles containing these charges and claiming that Roosevelt was on the verge of inciting revolution.[27]

The White House found itself in an awkward situation. There had been no plan to quarrel with major capital. Trying not to make the situation worse, Roosevelt contended that the tension arose from the obstinate refusal of monopolists to accept the reality and meaning of the "new approach" to the labor issue. In all fairness it should be noted that Roosevelt had explained his position in a speech on 2 July 1932 at the Democratic party convention in Chicago. Roosevelt was convinced that an appeal to force in a struggle against American workers, that use of police repression (without extreme need) during times of strain, could result in unforeseen consequences for the two-party system. Roosevelt's speech clearly responded to the polemics of people who wanted harsh reprisals against any expression of social insubordination, different thought, socialism, or communism. Such people included John [Nance] Garner, even though he became Roosevelt's running mate on the Democratic slate. Against the background of the Hoover administration's numerous punitive expeditions directed toward the uprising of farmers and the unemployed, in the face of advice to use weapons to crush them, Roosevelt's message was a warning to advocates of "order at any cost." By all indications, they had begun already to lose their heads.

This, of course, did not mean that Roosevelt refused to use police repression, particularly the FBI, as a means of controlling union activities, left-radical political organizations, the Communist Party of the United States, and so forth. On the contrary, the administration of the New Deal broadened secret surveillance of its political opposition.[28] However, in his effort to strengthen the social base of the New Deal, Roosevelt restrained the zealous supporters of harsh measures right up to the beginning of World War II. He decided to deal with growing radicalism by "killing it with kindness"—in combination with rhetoric and his ability to convince people that the government stood above class interests and was prepared to pursue social justice and harmony in every quarter. The president's spouse, whose influence was considerable on the new administration's social schemes, helped develop these motifs. She gave them a form familiar to the many followers of the social-utopian Edward Bellamy. Some of Bellamy's zealous admirers (Upton Sinclair included) mistakenly believed they had an influential compatriot in the White House.[29]

27. A. A. Kreder, "The American Monopolistic Bourgeoisie and the New Deal of F. R. Roosevelt (1932–1940)," in *American Annual, 1979* (Moscow, 1979), 129.

28. R[obert] J. Goldstein, *Political Repression in Modern America from 1870 to the Present* (Cambridge, 1978), 213–16.

29. Lash, *Eleanor and Franklin,* 510–12.

Roosevelt gave particular attention to creating a new image of the federal government and the White House as model institutions in a system of "general prosperity." He believed that small efforts that required little financial outlay could have large psychological effects and political advantage for the Democratic party. The reader is reminded of the large special mailings the White House used to influence attitudes in the "hottest" sections of the country, where discontent was extreme amid deteriorated economic conditions and inactive local leaders. L. Hickok was struck by the impact of White House letters or other (most often, propagandistic) gestures of the president on the imaginations and emotions of the recipients, by how the president's letters gave them a reprieve from crisis, destitution, and hunger. Despite the solemn nature of most routine White House correspondence, Hickok believed Roosevelt engendered hope that problems could be resolved by influencing the mood of the people "from the top." The protest movement did fizzle out.

An excerpt from a report Hickok sent to Hopkins on 8 April 1934 is testimony. She wrote about Roosevelt's skillful manipulation of the naive perceptions of the masses through specially crafted rhetoric. "It's funny," she wrote, "but people down here [the mining settlements of Alabama] all seem to think they know the President personally! It comes in part, I imagine, from their having heard him speak . . . over the radio, and in such a friendly, man-to-man fashion. They feel he is talking to each one of them personally! And, of course, they don't always understand exactly what he means, are inclined to read into what he says what they themselves want him to mean. Another funny thing is the number of letters you see around over the President's and Mrs. Roosevelt's signature. They are seldom anything more than the briefest and most formal acknowledgement of a letter, usually a letter of complaint or an appeal for help. But I doubt if any other president or his wife has ever been so punctilious about acknowledging letters. And these people take them all very seriously, as establishing a personal relationship. In one way it's a darned good thing. It's made them both very strong with the people. A lot of these people who used to look up that way to their paternalistic landlords and employers have now switched to the President and Mrs. Roosevelt! They just expect them to take care of them!"[30]

It is impossible to underestimate the consequences of the methods Rooseveltian liberals used for political seduction. They helped the White House periodically intervene to "establish peace" in the mean, bloody battle to legalize the right to organize unions during the so-called "first hundred days." The president managed to establish the tone of an "honest broker," of an impartial arbitrator. He created the illusion that he functioned as a disinterested party among the pressure groups in the area of labor relations. For this reason many of labor's rank and file missed the real meaning of events. They perceived that concessions (the right to organize unions, establishment of a minimum wage, etc.) resulted from the kindness of federal powers or from a combination of federal and labor efforts, when in fact workers had torn them from

30. FDRL, L. Hickok Papers, box 2, Hickok to H. L. Hopkins, 8 April 1934.

industrial magnates by force or threat of force.[31] The government considered it an obligation to foster such false ideas and did so with considerable skill. Events in fall 1936 and spring 1937, when New Dealers found themselves facing their most difficult decisions, particularly brought out this tactic.

"Sit-down strikes" in the automobile industry during those months caused serious instability. The country seemed on the verge of social disorder unprecedented in both scale and intensity. The correspondence of Michigan governor Frank Murphy shows how passionately corporate proprietors, police, and conservative politicians in both bourgeois parties wanted revenge against striking workers who had seized factories and, in bourgeois minds, struck the sacred right of property a serious blow and encroached on its inviolability.[32] Bourgeois circles first charged that Murphy was unforgivably sluggish in responding; then they charged him with disrespect for the law, and finally with secret sympathy for Communism. In March 1937 there was a movement among the bourgeoisie to throw him out as governor. With devastating irony Carl Sandburg noted in a private letter that Michigan's financial-industrial oligarchy had inspired a slanderous campaign against A[braham] Lincoln (this "tyrant" and "fool") during the Civil War.[33]

Meanwhile, no one saw better than bourgeois reformers (to which Murphy belonged) that the blind fury of those who supported order at any price could lend chaos to the very foundations of the two-party system and the existing power structure. Among Rooseveltian liberals hope glimmered that pressures from radical workers and other broad protest movements could be resisted, unless there was *extreme need*, without resort to the violence, political terror, and arrests that marked the well-remembered "Red Scare" of 1918–1920 or the slaughter in Washington during summer 1932. The document that stands out as the monument to the social component of liberal philosophy during the New Deal, it seems to this writer, is Murphy's explanation of his motives for action. In a letter to [P. H.] Callaghan on 25 May 1937, the governor of Michigan, under fire from his own people for complicity in socialist schemes, acknowledged that all his concessions to workers were a measure of need: they were dictated exclusively by the unprecedented character of the brewing crisis and the desire to ward off a general strike.[34]

Both President Roosevelt and Secretary of Labor Perkins were in an analogous situation, but on the national level. They did justice to the tactic of maneuvering by congratulating Murphy (with both writing on the same day) for the way he handled

31. J[ames] P. Johnson, "Drafting the NRA Code of Fair Competition for the Bituminous Coal Industry," *Journal of American History* 53 (December 1966): 357.

32. Michigan Historical Collection (hereafter MHC), Bently Historical Library, Frank Murphy Papers, box 15, E. C. Jouston to O. G. Olander, 5 January 1937; O. G. Olander to Murphy, 12 January 1937; J. S. Bersey to Murphy, 12 January 1937; box 16, A. H. Vandenberg to Murphy, 15 February 1937; H. C. Pratt to Murphy, 20 February 1937; box 17, W. L. Smith to Murphy, 17 March 1937; McHugh to Murphy, 24 March 1937; B. E. Hutchinson to Murphy, 16 June 1937.

33. Ibid., box 17, C. Sandburg to Murphy, 29 March 1937.

34. Ibid., Murphy to P. H. Callahan, 25 May 1937.

the conflict, which, as the president put it, "threatened serious disorder and disloca-tion."[35] In his many official statements Roosevelt asked that new preventive mea-sures be put in place to avert revolutionary upheavals.[36] The rectilinear and sharp-tongued Hopkins said that opponents of reform had pushed capitalism straight onto the scaffold.[37]

Thus, the reforms of the New Deal were not acts of mercy nor tributes to Christian goodwill. They were the result of the struggle between workers and employers, unions and corporations, lower classes and upper classes. The working class was not passive, not afraid of sacrifices and deprivation. It was able to take the counteroffen-sive, literally imposing its will on the leaders.

In speaking of the origins of New Deal social reforms, it is also very important to consider the foreign factor (yet another specialized topic)—particularly the influence (direct and indirect) of the attractive achievements of real socialism in the USSR. Soviet socialism eliminated unemployment and ensured orderly implementation of broad social programs in the areas of health insurance, education, housing construc-tion, protection of labor, maternity and infancy, etc. But as is well known, apologetic historiography looks at the labor legislation of the New Deal as a gift of the presi-dent, as evidence of the boundless sympathy and compassion the Roosevelt admin-istration allegedly felt for unions.[38] The facts were somewhat different, and the early measures in this area (widely reported by the press) exposed the narrow-mindedness of liberal reform.

Analysis begins from this: that numerous reservations and shortcomings in the sections on labor in the law to achieve industrial recovery (passed in June 1933) were proposed by employers and corporations who often used those shortcomings to their own advantage. Under pressure of big business, General [Hugh] Johnson, head of the National Recovery Administration, conducted himself from the beginning as if no change had occurred in the status of unions.[39] To crown it all, Roosevelt dealt unions a blow by defending the "closed shop" and by endorsing in August 1933 the so-called merit clause in the code of the automobile industry. The government

35. Ibid., box 16, Franklin Delano Roosevelt to Murphy, 11 February 1937; F. Perkins to Mur-phy, 11 February 1937.

36. T[homas] H. Greer, *What Roosevelt Thought: The Social and Political Ideas of Franklin D. Roosevelt* (East Lansing, Mich., 1958), 38.

37. *Principal Speeches of Harry L. Hopkins, Works Progress Administrator,* "Address by Harry L. Hopkins before the United States Conference of Mayors, 17 November 1936."

38. P[hilip] Taft, *The A. F. of L. from the Death of Gompers to the Merger* (New York, 1959), 45; J[ames] M. Burns, *Roosevelt: The Lion and the Fox* (New York, 1956), 217, 218. Rosenman, who engaged in polemics with several authors after the war, denounced their attempts to portray Roosevelt as a politician who calculatingly thought out every step and followed some kind of firm and unwaver-ing plan. He was convinced that the president was a political opportunist who acted most often "depending on circumstances." In general Rosenman thought Roosevelt was not distinguished by either great thought or forthrightness. See FDRL, S. Rosenman Papers, Rosenman to Jay J. M. Scandrett, 25 July 1950.

39. Library of Congress, F. Frankfurter Papers, box 150, Charles E. Wysanski, Jr., to Frank-furter, 13 September 1933.

thereby sanctified hiring and firing in that industry based on the worker's perceived "individual merit" without consideration for whether or not he was a member of a union. Capital's fierce resistance to attempts by laborers to exercise their rights as set out in the NIRA, together with Washington's stance as a detached onlooker, came as an unpleasant surprise to the majority of unionists.[40] Those who wanted to see proof of a particular government disposition toward unions in the NIRA provisions for labor would have been interested in a remark the president made in 1934. It was to the effect that if workers desired to use Section 7a [of the NIRA], he was totally indifferent as to whether they chose a union or the Royal Geographic Society.[41] Careless and obstructive was how the well-known American historian D[avid] Brody characterized Roosevelt's reaction to labor's demand for the right of collective defense against the tyranny of employers.[42]

However, the interest of the masses of workers in unionizing was so intense that for some time they simply did not notice the NIRA or the vacillation and evasiveness of the White House. The workers possessed the enthusiasm of converts. They spread the infamous words: "The president wants you to organize!" Not many knew that this was not Roosevelt's desire when the NIRA was undergoing its final editing in May 1933. Section 7a might have been lost were it not for Senator [Robert] Wagner. Recognizing the unions' determination to include Section 7a, he demanded that representatives of the National Association of Manufacturers stop blocking the section, and he pressured the president to take a neutral position.[43]

In summer 1933, Johnson assured employers that the NIRA could not be used "to defend the interests of trade unions."[44] In March 1934, the president of the United States himself, in league with the automobile magnates, thwarted the threat of a general strike of automobile workers in behalf of the right to organize unions. And, after rejecting the AFL's feeble attempt to write a code for the automobile industry, the president literally thrust conditions on the auto workers that were dictated by the monopolists.[45]

Sidney Fine, well-known scholar of American labor history during the 1930s, concluded, "The history of the adoption of the code of the automobile industry, despite all the talk of partnership of the government, industrialists, and workers in carrying out the NIRA, clearly illustrated the fact that the organized workers' move-

40. New York State School of Industrial and Labor Relations Library, International Union of Mine, Mill and Smelter Workers (L. McLenegan Papers), L. McLenegan to Ch. Whiteley, 23 April 1934; National Archives, General Records of the Department of Labor, 167/2505–167/2585, box 162, R. B. Stuart to F. Perkins, 20 November 1933, etc.

41. S[amuel] I. Rosenman, compiler and collector, *Public Papers and Addresses of Franklin D. Roosevelt,* 13 vols. (New York, 1938–1950), 1:301.

42. Brody, *Workers in Industrial America: Essays on the Twentieth-Century Struggle* (New York, 1981), 145, 146.

43. J. J[oseph] Huthmacher, *Senator Robert F. Wagner and the Rise of Urban Liberalism* (New York, 1968), 147.

44. Sidney Fine, "President Roosevelt and the Automobile Code," *Mississippi Valley Historical Review* 45 (June 1958): 25.

45. Ibid., 26.

ment, wherever it lacked sufficient power to challenge the unions of employers, was, even in the best of cases, a partner with limited rights. From the moment the draft of the automobile code was drawn up, and until its expiration, President Roosevelt would, in the course of any conflict arising between workers and management of an enterprise, lean to the side of the employers. Acting in such a way, he revealed, perhaps in exaggerated form, something substantive in the nature of the National Recovery Administration and the so-called first New Deal."[46]

One could add that during the latter Roosevelt avoided taking the initiative in social reform and in the advancement of political measures that would clear the way for progressive legislation. Waiting and maneuvering were more characteristic of his tactics. In many instances when he was opposed (particularly after 1938), the president-reformer, despite everything including his personal reputation, preferred retreat to open confrontation.[47] Advisors and political supporters could never sway the president's ideas about balancing the right and left flanks of the party or his caution about proposed social transformation, citizens rights, and so forth.[48]

Roosevelt could move a little to the left of the line he considered most efficient if he were forced to do so by national circumstances. In other words, the social reforms of the New Deal and their magnitude depended on the strength of "outside pressure." Without the pressure of a mass movement, not one liberal law, not one program would have been passed or implemented. At the same time, the mass movement was weakened by the hope that "friends" in the White House and Congress would effect changes automatically. This dulling of the political activity of the masses delayed passage of many reforms or took them off the agenda altogether.

Examination of New Deal activity in the area of employment is important to understanding both Roosevelt's social policies and his use of natural and labor resources.

The problem of unemployment was primary and most intense. In 1930 and 1931, in an act of rare unanimity, the labor movement supported the demand of its left wing that a broad public works system be erected to provide employment. During the 1932 election campaign, Roosevelt, as usual, remained evasive about what concrete measures he would take in the event he attained power. Nevertheless, he did consider the issue, together with questions of how to inculcate the principle of government regulation of economic life, how to use and conserve natural resources nationally, and how to construct socially useful projects—electric power stations, roads and waterworks, and so forth—under the aegis of government.[49]

46. Ibid., 50.
47. FDRL, A. Williams Papers, box 4, Harry L. Hopkins to Franklin D. Roosevelt, 11 September 1935.
48. A. C[lash] Koeniger, "The New Deal and the States: Roosevelt versus the Byrd Organization in Virginia," *Journal of American History* 68 (March 1982): 876–96.
49. A[rthur] M. Schlesinger, Jr., *The Age of Roosevelt, Vol. 1: The Crisis of the Old Order, 1919–1933* (London, 1957), 468–70; O[tis L.] Graham, Jr., *Toward a Planned Society: From Franklin D. Roosevelt to Richard Nixon* (New York, 1976); F[rank] Freidel, *Launching the New Deal* (Boston, 1973); M. Z. Shkundin, *On the History of the State-Monopolistic Social Politics of the United States, 1929–1939* (Moscow, 1980), 98.

Roosevelt took a first step at the beginning of April 1933 when he created the Civilian Conservation Corps (CCC), a network of labor camps for unemployed youth. The Public Works Administration (PWA), headed by H[arold] Ickes, was created later as a consequence of the NIRA. Although PWA received a great deal of money ($3.3 billion), it offered employment on only a few comparatively large projects—mostly road, military, and hydroelectric construction. Neither the CCC nor the PWA resolved, nor could resolve, the employment problem, although the administration widely cited both as examples of performing its public duty.

Even in spring 1933 Roosevelt himself remained aloof from discussions of a long-term employment program, a fact that made everyone uneasy who had pinned their hopes for decisive action on him.[50] Growing dissatisfaction among the people, along with the death threat that the coming of winter posed for thousands, forced the president to change his position. In November 1933 the Civil Works Administration (CWA) was created quickly. It was the invention of Hopkins, and it was one of the most popular, although short-lived, offspring of the New Deal. On the eve of the hungry winter of 1933–1934, the goal of this organization was to ensure work for four million unemployed. Despite expectations, the president and Congress had agreed to Hopkins's project without delay or vacillation. Explaining this unprecedented flexibility, Hopkins said in 1937, "Many leaders of the business world, when the winter of 1933–1934 advanced, came tearing into Washington and tearfully prayed for additional appropriations."[51]

Thus, in an effort to stave off hunger riots, and amid mass indignation, the federal powers began a social experiment truly unique in the United States. All told, approximately four hundred thousand CWA projects were initiated[52] under the direction of government officials and the army. CWA encouraged the creation of several kinds of local cooperatives. These functioned (quite successfully) during the beginnings of workers' self-government. The larger project did provide jobs and assured the subsistence of millions of unemployed people in the most diverse professions—from loggers to writers and artists. They were paid no less than people working in private enterprise. This was a surprise in bourgeois circles, and it became the grounds for their malicious attacks on the CWA. It was clear, however, that the real apprehensions in bourgeois circles were for preservation of their competitive advantages. They viewed the CWA as the prototype of a government sector that would exist parallel to and separate from private business. And this meant that the question of whether or not the CWA should exist became primarily political.

Reminiscent of the way the Parisian bourgeoisie after February 1848 artificially restructured opinion in France and Europe about national workshops, the bourgeois press of the United States happily set out to disgrace and pillory CWA's social proj-

50. Library of Congress, F. Frankfurter Papers, box 74, Robert M. La Follette, Jr., to Frankfurter, 4 April 1933; box 150, Frankfurter to Frances Perkins, 4 April, 2 May 1933.

51. *Principal Speeches of Harry L. Hopkins, Works Progress Administrator,* Address of Harry L. Hopkins at Babson Institute, 12 June 1937.

52. Schlesinger, *The Age of Roosevelt, Vol. 2: The Coming of the New Deal* (London, 1960), 262.

ects, often referring to them as a "Trojan Horse" in the bosom of capitalism. Because events had taken such an unexpected turn, the president considered it necessary to intervene. Taking advantage of the fact that by spring 1934 social tensions had somewhat lessened because of new legislation and a better economy,[53] Roosevelt hastened to end the defiant activities that caused such negative reaction among the bourgeoisie.[54]

The Works Progress Administration (WPA), created in spring 1935 as a "national plan for granting work," clearly was stripped of all characteristics that would make it look like a challenge to the private capitalist economy. Indeed, capital was reconciled by the creation of the WPA, particularly after Roosevelt and Hopkins placated Congress with promises to allot the lion's share of appropriations to military construction and to establish lower pay scales than in the private sector for labor on WPA projects.[55] The public works program under the aegis of WPA existed until 1943, and although it did not solve the problem of employment,[56] in some years it provided work for three-and-a-half to four million people.

Unions and the organized unemployed recognized the great significance of public works and determinedly insisted on their expansion and planned development. Many influential members of the administration shared this view, believing that if the capitalist system was to accommodate to changing conditions new initiatives were essential. For example, Hopkins remarked in Seattle in September 1938 that he foresaw a "great program of federal social works" that would last twenty years and more. The inevitability of such a prospect, he believed, went without saying. "I look to such a program, plus unemployment insurance," he said, "as the only way to take care of our classes of permanently unemployed."[57] Ickes also insisted on the need for an ongoing system of public works as an adjunct to the private economy: the public works would be a measure and a stimulator of economic growth.[58]

Roosevelt always had been apprehensive about such attitudes, but in spring 1933 he was convinced that the country's economic development would be served by

53. FDRL, L. Hickok Papers, box 2, Hickok to H. L. Hopkins, 11 April 1934.

54. W[illiam] W. Bremer, "Along the 'American Way': The New Deal's Work Relief Programs for the Unemployed," *Journal of American History* 62 (June 1975): 642, 643.

55. Malkov, "Harry Hopkins: Pages of a Political Biography," *Modern and Contemporary History,* 1979, no. 2, 138–39, 141.

56. Aubrey Williams, the right hand of Hopkins, self-critically acknowledged that in comparison to the true extent of the tragedy very little had been done by the government to aid the unemployed. See FDRL, A. Williams Papers, box 5, Williams to Mrs. Isaac P. Witter, 1 October 1934.

57. *Tacoma News Tribune,* 17 September 1938.

58. Library of Congress, H[arold] Ickes Papers, box 161, Ickes to Hiram W. Johnson, 21 September 1935. In drafts of various documents created by Hopkins, there are passages that make it appear that, in the event mass unemployment continued, he did not exclude the possibility that government might include gradually private capitalist enterprises. To avoid such a result, undesirable for the bourgeoisie, he believed that capital could only cooperate with the government and be flexible enough to adapt its strategy to changing conditions. See FDRL, personal letters in the Papers of Harry L. Hopkins, 1930–1946, roll 17, "What Price Recovery."

creating a special agency, attached to the PWA, for the purpose of making recommendations about planning, distribution, and rational use of a public works system. The result was the Natural Resources Planning Board (NRPB),[59] an agency that occupied itself, often at its peril, with studying issues connected with economic planning, primarily in the fields of employment and the use of natural resources.

In retrospect, it seems that at one time the NRPB could have played an important role in forming economic policy and determining national priorities (after 1939 when it became an integral part of the administrative structure of the White House and was directly answerable to the president). However, the projects of its founders broke up under the strain of impregnable opposition by monopolists. They objected sharply to NRPB's small encroachments on their privileges in determining economic strategy, and they forced the president to stop the "radical expansion" of plans to systematize the economy, regulate social development, and strengthen federal control over the use of natural resources.

In only one area of social policy did Roosevelt volunteer a worthy plan. The writer has in mind the protection of natural resources. In his personal thinking about a "balanced civilization" and the scientific use of natural resources, Roosevelt had something in common with people who wanted to increase the regulatory role of government to limit the destructive consequences of private competition. In Roosevelt's opinion, the rational use of the country's natural resources was the most important determinant of the nation's economic well-being, and their use justified government efforts on a massive scale. In the name of the well-being of future generations of Americans, Roosevelt proposed to expand government acquisition of deserted lands and forests located in private hands and to instill in people the principle of social regulation of private enterprises involved in exploiting natural resources.[60]

Having surrounded himself with a great many energetic reformers, Roosevelt counterbalanced their political influence by preserving his strong connections with conservative circles—with leaders of the financial-industrial world (B[ernard] Baruch, J[oseph] Kennedy, and others), Southern politicians, local political bosses, and so forth. He extinguished the ardor for reform among several highly opinionated New Dealers by screening their ideas and projects through the sieve of slow-moving conciliation/arbitration commissions and through a skillful game of setting opposing opinions against each other. He used stalling tactics to alleviate acute problems. Even the strongest admirers of the New Deal feared there was no future for all this maneuvering and drifting without a compass in the sea of eclectic ideas. It was not acceptable to talk about it openly, but forebodings of the unreliability of the president's efforts to restore prosperity through concealed plans and occasional fiery outbreaks haunted his closest supporters.

For example, in 1940 Ickes wrote, "Of course, I know as well as you that the New

59. B[arry] D. Karl, *Executive Reorganization and Reform in the New Deal* (Cambridge, 1963), and *Charles E. Merriam and the Study of Politics* (Chicago, 1974).
60. MHC, F. Murphy Papers, box 19, Franklin D. Roosevelt to Murphy, 15 March 1938.

Deal does not represent perfectibility any more than any other political program. It is undoubtedly defective both as to its objective and as to its execution to date. However, time will cure its defect—that is, if we have enough time . . . But I am beginning to fear that we are not going to have enough time to put our house in reasonable order."[61]

Becoming acquainted with the political machinery of the liberals was a bitter experience for the lower classes. Government statements continued to echo optimism, yet, if the economic situation and social status of the great mass of the laboring population (women, Afro-Americans, petty farmers, etc.) changed for the better, it was only within limits. Many important demands of the working class were not satisfied. Thus, after two years of Roosevelt's administration the matter of a legislative proposal for unemployment and old age insurance hardly had moved. It would be a mistake, however, to explain this solely as Roosevelt's apprehension about colliding with impenetrable opposition in Congress.[62] The government hindered the reform of social insurance on its own initiative. During the "first hundred days" (1933) it was not considered possible to discuss the subject in Congress. After that Roosevelt showed that he saw no urgency about drawing up social insurance legislation.[63]

The messages the president sent to Congress in January 1935 were noted for moderation,[64] although they did mention the need for significant appropriations to expand public works and recommended passage of a law on social insurance. It was characteristic, however, that having at last come forth with these long-awaited proposals, the government found itself arguing with the progressive bloc in Congress, which considered the proposals relatively unsatisfying. The progressives criticized the government for infringing on the interests of workers by its numerous concessions to the bourgeois reaction. Languid congressional hearings occurred against a background of almost no government activity.[65] Then, the House Committee on Labor unexpectedly approved a social insurance bill submitted by House member E[rnest] Lundeen from the farm-labor state of Minnesota. This forced the government to come up quickly with a proposal of its own that could win a majority in both houses of Congress. The administration's bill differed greatly from Lundeen's bill, and the differences worsened the division.[66]

61. Library of Congress, H[arold L.] Ickes Papers, box 160, Ickes to Chester A. Braman, 22 January 1940.

62. In that period, Roosevelt declared that the opposition in Congress "is not a very serious thing. It always happens every year, but it can always be handled by devoting a certain amount of time to it." *New Deal Mosaic: Roosevelt Confers with His National Emergency Council 1933–1936* (Eugene, Ore., 1963), 449.

63. Huthmacher, *Senator Robert F. Wagner*, 175–76; Library of Congress, F. Frankfurter Papers, box 49, Thomas G. Corcoran to Frankfurter, 18 June 1934.

64. Huthmacher, *Senator Robert F. Wagner*, 182.

65. M. Z. Shkundin, *On the History of the State-Monopolistic Social Policy of the United States, 1929–1939*, 142, 143.

66. Sivachev, *The United States: The Government and the Working Class*, 212, 213. The Lundeen bill dealt with workers' control over the administration of unemployment compensation.

Although it was assured of an overwhelming majority in both the House and the Senate in spring 1935, the president watched the second passage of the Wagner Act in attentive silence. [Labor Secretary] Perkins wrote that Roosevelt had never considered the Wagner Act a component of his own program. Moreover, the administration (and Perkins herself) had done all they could to stop the bill.[67] Senator Wagner was so frightened by this cold reception that he weakened his own bill, refusing to expand its provisions to cover agricultural workers. Justifying himself in April 1935, Wagner wrote that the threat of the bill's total defeat made him receptive to pressure.[68] He did not exaggerate; the bill's movement through Congress was precarious. On the eve of the decisive Senate vote on 15 May 1935, Roosevelt declared at a press conference that he had no position on the Wagner Act.[69] This meant that the most disastrous result, presidential veto, was a possibility.

And then, suddenly, from contemplation and delay there was an abrupt about-face; the president loyally supported (what Tugwell called)[70] "orthodox" progressivism and actively encouraged the most radical social legislation in the history of American government—including bills on social insurance, labor relations, taxes on large fortunes, and so forth. The president's rhetoric also changed considerably. Accusations in the spirit of Populists of an earlier era such as Bryan and [Robert] La Follette to the effect that monopolists were predators and boundlessly greedy were accompanied by affirmation that the needs of the impoverished classes would be included in the government's policy of "national reconstruction." The annals of the American presidency, it seems, had never known such a drastic zigzag.

In his annual message to Congress in January 1935, Roosevelt had declared that he did not want to change the existing tax system, and at a press conference on 7 June he said he was not concerned with a tax problem. But on 19 June the president sent a message to Congress proposing a progressive tax on large fortunes and corporation profits. The opposition screamed that the president had "tricked" them, that he had usurped the causes of left and right extremists such as H[uey] Long, C[harles] Coughlin, and others. Nonetheless, the White House won congressional approval of the legislative proposal, even if in greatly modified form. On 5 July 1935 Roosevelt signed the Wagner Act. It confirmed and strengthened the right of workers to organize into unions and to bargain collectively that had been set out in Section 7a of the NIRA. On 14 August 1935, Roosevelt signed the bill on social insurance.

Thus, suddenly, during the hot summer months of 1935 and after protracted digression and waiting, Roosevelt's administration again acquired a taste for social reform. Reflecting on the reasons for this metamorphosis, many bourgeois historians have lost themselves in conjecture. [William E.] Leuchtenburg, for example, has written that Roosevelt changed for "reasons that are not wholly clear" and that, in

67. Perkins, *The Roosevelt I Knew,* 239. See also Pechatnov, *The Democratic Party of the United States: Voters and Policy,* 16; Brody, *Workers in Industrial America,* 144.
68. NYPL, N[orman] Thomas Papers, box 8, Robert F. Wagner to N. Thomas, 1 April 1935.
69. Huthmacher, *Senator Robert F. Wagner,* 197.
70. R[exford] G. Tugwell, *The Democratic Roosevelt* (Garden City, N.J., 1957), 341.

turn, Congress, by voting for administration-supported bills (which the White House had cold-shouldered in the recent past), acted in a way that "no one, then or later, fully understood."[71] Of course, the program was not entirely dictated by electoral considerations. Roosevelt's desire to work out a general strategy for bourgeois progressivism during capitalism's greatest crisis had evolved over the course of the New Deal. So, in fact, had Roosevelt's desire to subordinate the masses to himself and to transform the lower-class organizations begot by him into an "extended arm" of the political system of bourgeois supremacy.

Evaluating the situation in summer 1935, Secretary of the Interior Ickes expressed the opinion that "the country is more radical than the administration or any of us."[72] The movement of the unemployed rose to a new level after unification of the many organizations that comprised that movement was outlined and then achieved under the aegis of the Communists and Socialists. A wave of strikes occurred in basic industry. The movement to organize the masses in unions spontaneously broadened from below. In most instances, the effort was headed by militantly inclined labor leaders.[73]

Still, the working class was not united in its notions about the current reality or its own aspirations. This could be explained in part by the influx of a petty bourgeois element that advocated social protest movements that were broad, not singular, in character, and that often pursued different, if not entirely opposite, goals. This brought serious confusion into the situation. In a number of instances it aroused feelings that enabled the reactionaries to play on racial prejudice and political bias and to make antiradical and antiliberal propaganda.[74] The weakest links in the New Deal coalition were the petty bourgeois masses in the South, Midwest, and far West and part of the urban middle classes (particularly those under the influence of the Catholic Church). These groups were subject to the greatest oscillation; they transferred it to the proletariat, whose own political experience was too limited to resist it.[75]

In light of the contrasts and contradictions in the sociopolitical situation, Roosevelt

71. *Franklin D. Roosevelt and the New Deal, 1932–1940,* 151.

72. Wisconsin State Historical Society Library, R. Robins Papers, box 27, H. L. Ickes to Robins, 19 August 1933. Ickes was not the only person bothered by the schism between bourgeois liberals and the masses who had moved to the left. It is impossible to ignore the astute observation of New York mayor F[iorello] La Guardia in a letter to a friend. In April 1938 he wrote that many of his political colleagues "feared I was a little too radical." But he thought subsequent events had convinced them that "I was 'guessing right' at the time" (New York City Archives, F. H. La Guardia Personal File, location 2675, La Guardia to E. M. Elciott, 4 April 1938).

73. FDRL, L. Hickok Papers, box 2, Hickok to H. L. Hopkins, 1 June 1935; Hickok to A. Williams, 15 August 1934.

74. Ibid., 10 October 1935.

75. FDRL, A. Williams Papers, box 2, E. C. Lindeman to Williams, 26 March 1937; box 4, Williams to Eleanor Roosevelt, 18 August 1939; Papers of Harry L. Hopkins, Confidential Political File, 1938–1940, box 120, Samuel C. Cleland to Daniel C. Roper, 14 November 1938; Pechatnov, "The Democratic Party and Its Electorate in the Years of the New Deal," *American Annual, 1980* (Moscow, 1981), 83, 84.

looked for a pretext to refuse to enunciate the government's responsibilities for social policy—the contours and prospects of which remained diffused and undefined. Moreover, Roosevelt had promised the bourgeoisie more than once that the era of liberal reform would not last forever. As early as fall 1935, to the chagrin of its supporters, the administration announced that there would be a "respite." The presidential election year of 1936 confirmed that the leader of the Democratic party wanted to turn the truce with capital into a durable peace at the cost of playing down the social aspects of the administration's activity. From time to time Roosevelt came down on the "economic royalists" who were "robbing other people," but nothing concrete or particularly reassuring about improving, increasing, or expanding social legislation was said. And even less was done.

The president remained deaf to appeals that he support the campaign to pass the Wagner bill for government housing construction, a proposal of interest to the impoverished classes in overpopulated industrial centers. The White House informed the public that it did not consider recommendations to construct government housing for the poor a "priority" measure.[76]

Roosevelt also refused to support the Wagner–Van Nuys–Gavagan bill that made lynching a criminal offense under the jurisdiction of the federal courts. The Southern Democratic bloc, Huthmacher has written, was so effective that Roosevelt could not lift a finger to defend the victims of terrorism against blacks.[77] The negative attitude of the president also predetermined defeat for a government health-insurance system even though, as its opponents admitted, the great masses of the people favored it.[78]

By 1936, the opposition had made an impression on the Democratic party platform. Many of Roosevelt's advisors suggested the platform should deny any intention of carrying social reform further. However, Roosevelt did not change a single word in the document presented by the special committee selected to write it. It is worthy of note that Senator Wagner headed that committee. Wagner should have symbolized Democratic readiness to advance the cause of reform: however, the senator himself was pessimistic about what had been attained and what was attainable.[79]

Meanwhile, a significant part of the public became more sensitive to the need for drastic change.[80] The growth of the labor movement itself became a factor, a force in

76. Huthmacher, *Senator Robert F. Wagner,* 213–16.

77. Ibid., 238–43.

78. NYPL, F. La Guardia Papers, 1939 (Good-Gray), Frank Gannett to F. La Guardia, 4 March 1939; Lash, *Eleanor and Franklin,* 611.

79. Library of Congress, F. Frankfurter Papers, box 109, Robert F. Wagner to Frankfurter, 25 June 1937.

80. Many in Roosevelt's circle recognized the discrepancy between what was desired and what was achieved. In spring 1937, Secretary of Agriculture Henry Wallace, appearing at the Economic Club of New York, acknowledged that "four years of heroic efforts" had not ended the impasse in American society that had caused the collision "between the different economic groups," the conflict between poverty and wealth, the pursuit of profit at any cost, and the realistic disenfranchisement of "the other half of our population," having created bitter economic anarchy and outrageously underestimated social responsibility of the government leadership. See FDRL, A. Williams Papers,

favor of such change. The steady raising of the level of working-class consciousness also showed that labor had critically evaluated what had been occurring. This was most evident in the avant-garde forces of the labor movement—the auto workers, metallurgists, miners, chemists, etc., who had achieved, qualitatively, a new level of understanding of class and of political arrangements in society.

The higher level of working-class consciousness (primarily in mass production industries), the American historian D[avid] Montgomery has noted, also manifested itself in a stronger effort to improve community controls over the activities of private enterprises[81] and in a stronger preference for independent political action to create an anticapitalistic program and for creation and expansion of a nationalized sector as a way out of the crisis. Even AFL leaders believed the "Great Depression" was an unavoidable result of "fatal defects" in the country's economy: among the defects was the absence of mechanisms to coordinate production or to develop a financial-credit system, spheres of distribution, and so forth.[82] Of course, Gompersists did not say it publicly, but the AFL executive council told both bourgeois parties that government needed to create an ongoing public works system.[83]

The unions of the Congress of Industrial Organizations (CIO),many of which were obliged to the Communists and the left wing for their creation, showed an intense interest in government activism and the implementation of social reforms. These unions saw as their immediate tasks the guiding of laws through Congress on minimum wages and the right to organize, and the broadening of workers' participation in making government policy.[84] The spirit and practice of the "new trade unionism" showed that its social ideals transcended purely economic matters. Len De Caux, one of the CIO leaders, remembered that organization as an "ambitious, practical, crusading movement to organize American working people for the betterment of their immediate conditions, without setting limits to the aspirations which a well-organized, militant, and intelligently led working class should have for the eventual transformation of society."[85]

At its first national conference, held in October 1937 in Atlantic City, the CIO drew up a list of proposed legislation that would satisfy most members of the American union movement. The emphasis was on the "fundamental demand" that the right to work be fixed in legislation. One proposal was to enforce strict observance of labor's rights by New Deal legislation. Another proposal demanded introduction of

---

box 5, Address by Secretary Wallace before the Economic Club of New York, 3 February 1937. In the culminating moment of reformatory activity of the New Dealers, Senator Wagner wrote Frankfurter, "I feel we have done a minimum of what we should have" (Library of Congress, F. Frankfurter Papers, box 109, Robert F. Wagner to Frankfurter, 25 June 1937).

81. *Workers' Control in America: Studies in the History of Work, Technology, and Labor Struggles* (New York, 1979), 164.

82. Library of Congress, John P. Frey Papers, box 12, folder "Notes and Memoranda (2)."

83. Taft, *The A. F. of L.*, 305.

84. Josephson, *Sidney Hillman,* 401–3.

85. W[alter] Reuther Library, Labor History Archives, Oral History, interview of Len De Caux, 4, 5.

federal legislation to regulate hours and minimum wages. There were high hopes for this measure, particularly for increased employment. Yet another proposal was for amendments to the social security law—to make it more compatible with the changing times, more democratic (i.e., under workers' control), and to expand coverage to all workers without exception.[86]

The problem of resolving unemployment and assuring millions of unfortunates a minimum standard of living remained unresolved. Despite every effort, the unemployment rate had not been lowered significantly. At a meeting of the Special Economic Council that Roosevelt attended in late December 1935, Department of Labor representatives cited twelve million unemployed, only two million fewer than in 1933.[87] Meanwhile, the index of industrial production reached ninety points higher than its level in 1929. The new economic recession that occurred in 1936 became the sore spot in relations between the government and the labor movement. The Workers' Alliance (an organization of the unemployed headed by Communists and leftists) aggressively criticized the government for ignoring the best solutions to the problem.[88]

The unions agreed with this criticism. Hopkins and other leaders of the Democratic party, recognizing the growing importance of the organized unemployed and their influence on politics,[89] repeatedly advised the president to avoid a serious confrontation.

The course of events presented the labor movement with a dilemma—whether to go further in the direction of bourgeois progressivism or, without breaking with it completely, to move decisively toward political independence and then shift to the left.[90] The idea of controlling bourgeois democracy and creating a broad political movement around the CIO as the first step toward schism with the tradition of *khvostism* [a Leninist term that translates literally as "tail-enders," i.e., those who postpone dealing with a problem, or who follow far behind the vanguard of political events] shows up in many documents left by participants in the "new trade-unionism."[91] The support by unions of locally created farm-labor parties also bespeaks unionist feeling.

Without a reevaluation of the extent to which the labor movement was radicalized during these years, it is impossible to measure its achievements. No one could say, if there was a reevaluation, that the movement's small size was insignificant in the balance of social forces or that it was unable to stand up for itself. Therefore, the demand for a decisive review of the situation in which the working class and the labor movement were not represented on all levels of government leadership—a demand

86. Committee for Industrial Organization, *The Program of the C.I.O.* (Washington, 1937), 12, 13.

87. *New Deal Mosaic*, 496.

88. *People's Press*, 31 October 1936.

89. FDRL, A. Williams Papers, box 4, H. L. Hopkins to FDR, 11 September 1935; Williams to E. Roosevelt, 18 August 1939; Papers of Harry L. Hopkins, Confidential Political File, 1938–1940, box 121, B. Sperling to James A. Farley, 4 November 1937.

90. W[alter] Reuther Library, Labor History Archives, H. Kraus Collection, box 6, radio broadcast, Mr. Arthur Green, 4 July 1936.

91. Ibid., Walter P. Reuther Papers, document "New America and Labor" (1938?).

that echoed in the ears of union leaders and in union documents of the 1930s—was interpreted by the liberals in both bourgeois parties as a challenge to the reigning political system, as a signal to break with it.

Roosevelt was uneasy about the stability of the two-party system. He took public sympathy for the labor movement seriously, and he took steps to eliminate the potential for crisis and disintegration. From a political point of view the question was resolved simply: following Bryanist traditions, the president told Democratic leaders to absorb local farm-labor parties as a part of the vast "historic bloc" that had sworn allegiance to the New Deal. Roosevelt considered this tactic completely justified, particularly after the Republican success in the midterm election of 1938 caused such internal conflict in his party.[92] But in an ideological sense, New Dealers faced a complicated problem. Rapprochement with socio-reformist parties (like the Farm-Labor party of Minnesota or the American Workers' party of New York State) and with the unions and the movement of the unemployed, together with an influx of democratic forces (Southern sharecroppers and organizations of blacks, women, youth, and others that strengthened the social base of the New Deal coalition), could not occur without affecting the social doctrine of the Democratic party.[93] One consequence was the appearance of the term *national capitalism* in the party's doctrine. The growth of the labor movement at the end of the 1930s, in combination with the success of national front movements in Europe and America, forced Roosevelt and his congressional supporters to resume the struggle against poverty and under that flag to support other progressive proposals in Congress. Tensions between the labor movement and the administration lessened during 1937.

In his effort to take advantage of an opportunity to tie the labor movement more closely to political liberalism, Roosevelt again resorted to patronage and a different sort of reorganization. The government took a reasonably tough antitrust position; it advocated an expanded public works program; and it accepted "emergency" aid measures for families of workers in industrial centers.[94] On 1 September 1937 Roosevelt signed the Wagner-Steagall bill, which created the Federal Housing Administration and authorized government assistance in the construction of housing for the impoverished classes. The agency's financial capacity was not large, but the significance of the principle that had been established cannot be underestimated. Roosevelt's agreement to support a bill on fair hiring practices was yet another landmark in the process of "rehabilitating" the government's labor policies.

The labor movement's support of the bill on minimum wages and maximum hours,

92. Pechatnov, *The Democratic Party of the United States: Voters and Policy,* 22–24.

93. Many "regular" Democrats—Roosevelt supporters—were not satisfied with the digression, as they put it, from the original program of the New Deal, the program of moderate liberalism. The appearance of sociodemocratic factions inside state Democratic party organizations and the diminished role of party machines in communities distressed them. See FDRL, Papers of Harry L. Hopkins, Confidential Political File, 1938–1940, box 121, Frank Tierney to Hopkins, 2 October 1939; Tierney to L. Mellett, 3 October 1939.

94. Ibid., A. Williams Papers, box 4, Franklin D. Roosevelt to Harry Hopkins and Williams, 17 May 1938.

as has been shown, was a part of the search for a means of softening the anarchy of capitalistic production, which created chronic mass unemployment. The Democrats did not sidestep this issue in their 1936 platform.[95] That year, for the first time, the administration played an appropriately active role in putting together a legislative proposal that would prohibit child labor and prevent employers from using various antiunion practices. But then, when the National Association of Manufacturers and the majority of Southern employers (who widely used cheap, unskilled black labor in order to compete with Northern industrialists) reacted negatively to the bill, the administration allowed events to run their course. This weakened the position of the administration's supporters in Congress. At the end of 1937, it seemed there was no chance the regular congressional session would examine this bill.[96]

One could argue that the political results of the 1938 election served Roosevelt by forcing him to take a new look at social policy. The dividing line between progressives and conservatives in the Democratic party was taking on a more distinct contour at this time because of their dissimilar evaluations of events inside and outside the United States. Because of the party schism and the withdrawal of the left wing in anticipation of a conservative victory at the party convention in 1940, the entire affair appeared to be nearly resolved. Information flowing into the White House from throughout the country testified to serious disagreement over whether there could be a popular third party based on unions and the unemployed.[97] Roosevelt's sharp turn away from the conservatives and his renewed support for a bill on fair hiring practices should be seen in that context. Having once made his decision, Roosevelt acted quite energetically and ingeniously. Ignoring threats from the right, he literally forced Congress to vote for the Black-Connery bill.

Many argue convincingly that this event symbolized the end of the New Deal, but one can hardly agree without reservations. True, by 1939 the White House secretly had begun to mend its relations with the conservative opposition. And the growth of the military danger in Europe, together with the desire to see the Democratic party united, forced Roosevelt to give up his confrontations with his rightist opponents. But continuation of the reform era did not depend solely on the subjective desire of the president. The moving force behind the process of liberation that began in 1933 was, and remained, the nation's masses, primarily the working class. It was the independent, instigative role of the masses in events that assured so many democratic changes. Testimony that this was true took the form of increased numbers of new progressive coalitions in local legislatures and the selection and appointment of progressive and even radical functionaries to important posts. And although these changes seldom corresponded with Roosevelt's plans or those of his supporters, the administration's own political interests required it to acknowledge the new forces and even use them to pressure the conservative opposition.

    95. P[aul] H. Douglas and J[oseph] Hackman, "The Fair Labor Standards Act of 1938," *Political Science Quarterly* (December 1938): 492.
    96. Ibid., 511.
    97. FDRL, Papers of Harry L. Hopkins, Confidential Political File, 1938–1940, box 120, W. Evjue to James A. Farley, 12 December 1938.

It must be recognized, at the same time, that the situation in the working-class movement was extremely complicated on the eve of the war. A sharp conflict between two tendencies—radical and moderately conservative, to mention only the major categories—was in process. Bourgeois reactionaries feverishly mobilized allies and the methods for cultivating national public opinion in behalf of "American traditions," antiradicalism, and anti-Communism. This circumstance created great disorder in the ranks of the workers' democracy and its supporters, and it was unclear which of the two tendencies won out. Therefore, after 1939, as Roosevelt tried to preserve the broad social base on which his administration had leaned for many years, he chose to act in the spirit of "progressive liberalism." Not one New Dealer, however, either then or later could (or wanted to) explain precisely what this term meant.[98] Nevertheless, the desire to stick to a course that had justified itself is undeniable.

As New Dealers prepared for the 1940 Democratic party convention, their motto was to keep the most important instruments of power in their own hands.[99] And they viewed their success in the 1940 fall election as a guarantee that the New Deal coalition would be preserved. Hopkins wrote in several letters that the election results were a victory for the Democrats and for the nation, and Frankfurter made the special point that Roosevelt, again in the presidential post, was full of messianic spirit.[100]

However, the course of events did not justify these optimistic prognoses. By the end of Roosevelt's third term, reaction and the counterreform movement had gathered strength. One reason was that New Deal liberalism, subordinate as a whole to the class interests of the bourgeoisie, bore a superior, elite character. Spontaneity and inconsistency were its distinguishing traits, and fear of the initiative of the masses its birthmark. Outside the aspirations of individual New Dealers, the social policy of the New Deal was, as a whole, subordinate to one task—saving capitalism as a system. Inevitably, this stimulated the internal contradictions that are inherent in American society.

---

98. Many prominent functionaries close to Roosevelt understood that the inability of liberalism to formulate a well-thought-out and sound program of progressive development was fraught with difficult and far-reaching consequences not only for the development of internal events, but also for the role of the United States on the world scene. They expressed misgivings that if the New Deal stopped at what had been achieved, it would signify capitulation to the reaction, and subsequently would have an adverse effect on the position of the United States in world affairs. Chester Bowles, for example (then head of the Office of Price Administration), wrote S. Rosenman in 1943, "In my opinion, the failure to develop a liberal program in the near future may result in a breakdown of our democracy and the development of an aggressive American nationalism which would be even more dangerous to world peace than our past isolationism" (FDRL, S. Rosenman Papers, box 1, General Correspondence, Chester Bowles to Rosenman, 23 December 1943).

99. FDRL, Papers of Harry L. Hopkins, Confidential Political File, 1938–1940, box 120, Memoranda, 23 May 1939; Lash, *Eleanor and Franklin,* 7, 96, 811.

100. FDRL, Papers of Harry L. Hopkins, Confidential Political File, 1938–1940, box 120, Hopkins to L. Moore, 18 November 1940; Library of Congress, F. Frankfurter Papers, box 74, Frankfurter to Laski, 27 November 1940.

Theda Skocpol

Comment on "The New Deal of F. Roosevelt," by N. V. Sivachev, and " 'A Little Left of Center': General and Specific Features in F. Roosevelt's Social Policies," by V. L. Malkov

V. L. Malkov and N. V. Sivachev offer insightful overviews of the New Deal. "The meaning of what occurred from 1933 to 1939 has become an integral part of American political and intellectual life," Sivachev rightly observes. Characterization of those years is apparently also fundamental to Soviet scholarship about the contemporary United States. To this end, V. L. Malkov portrays the New Deal as "bourgeois liberalism . . . preserving proprietary power" at a time of crisis. He focuses on the tactics used by a cautious President Franklin Delano Roosevelt to deal with—and ultimately defuse—the rising strength of the industrial working class. N. V. Sivachev also invokes pressures from below by the "workers' and democratic movement," yet spends more time exploring the nature of the changes wrought by the New Deal. "Government regulation of the economy and the social infrastructure was," he concludes, "the most important legacy."

My own recent work on the development of economic and social policies in the twentieth-century United States has also prompted me to try to characterize the overall transformations of the New Deal and to grasp the political forces at work in this period. Thus I found it enjoyable and fruitful to read these kindred efforts by Soviet scholars. Drawing on my own research, and on my sense of the recent American historiography, let me suggest some additional interpretive emphases that can help to make sense of the events Malkov and Sivachev present.[1] My remarks are organized under two headings: the administrative weakness of the U.S. national state, and the role of local and congressional forces. Attention to the ways in which U.S. political institutions channeled political forces and class interests can, I believe, improve our analyses of what occurred—and what failed to occur—during this watershed period in modern U.S. history.

1. The works of my own that serve as background for this comment include "Political Response to Capitalist Crisis: Neo-Marxist Theories of the State and the Case of the New Deal," *Politics and Society* 10 (1980): 155–201; "State Capacity and Economic Intervention in the Early New Deal" (co-authored with Kenneth Finegold), *Political Science Quarterly* 97 (1982): 255–78; "The Political Formation of the American Welfare State in Historical and Comparative Perspective" (co-authored with John Ikenberry), *Comparative Social Research* 6 (1983): 87–148; "Did Capitalists Shape Social Security?" (co-authored with Edwin Amenta), *American Sociological Review* 50 (August 1985): 572–75; and "Redefining the New Deal: World War II and the Development of Social Provision in the United States" (with Edwin Amenta), in *The Politics of Social Policy in the United States,* ed. Margaret Weir, Ann Shola Orloff, and Theda Skocpol (Princeton, 1988), pp. 81–122.

THE ADMINISTRATIVE WEAKNESS OF THE U.S. NATIONAL STATE

The New Deal brought unprecedented increases in federal government interventions into the workings of the American economy and society; virtually all scholars agree on this. At the same time, there were sharp political shifts during the 1930s. Both Malkov and Sivachev treat 1935 as a major turning point, a time when Roosevelt quarreled with business and placed more emphasis on economic and social reforms. Such political turning points are analyzed by Malkov and Sivachev primarily in terms of class struggles between capitalists, on the one hand, and working-class and popular-democratic forces, on the other. The assumption seems to be that, at each phase of the New Deal, President Roosevelt and the federal executive did what existing balances of class forces required of them.

However, the administrative institutions of the U.S. national state also need to be brought into the picture if we are to better understand how New Deal leaders designed their interventions in relation to the political shifts that occurred during the 1930s. When we bring governmental institutions into the analysis, we learn that more was at work in shaping the New Deal than class struggles.

To begin with an important episode, it is not adequate to characterize the NRA as an instance of a monopolistic state creating industrial cartels that uniformly favored the interests of large, oligopolistic corporations. While the early Roosevelt administration and business spokesmen did agree that anarchic market competition had to be regulated in order to promote recovery, the U.S. federal government had little preexisting administrative capacity to plan for industrial production.[2] The NRA was set up very quickly, and in the absence of a strong civil service with experience in industrial regulation, authority to regulate each industry was basically delegated to hundreds of private trade associations.[3] In some industries, those associations were dominated by large, technically progressive firms; but in other industries, smaller firms gained much leverage through trade associations to protect themselves from larger competitors. Moreover, the hundreds of separate associations could not easily settle disputes across industries.

Consequently, the NRA soon became a battleground for bigger versus smaller firms and for firms from different industries. Quarrels among businessmen became politicized, and the national economy as a whole was not at all rationally planned, or even stably cartelized.[4] National economic recovery failed to materialize. Therefore,

2. On the prior administrative development of those parts of the U.S. federal executive dealing with business, see Stephen L. Skowronek, *Building a New American State: The Expansion of National Administrative Capacities, 1877–1920* (Cambridge and New York, 1982); Robert D. Cuff, *The War Industries Board: Business-Government Relations during World War I* (Baltimore, 1973); and Ellis W. Hawley, "Herbert Hoover, the Commerce Secretariat, and the Vision of an 'Associative State,' 1921–1928," *Journal of American History* 61 (June 1974): 116–40.

3. Ellis W. Hawley, *The New Deal and the Problem of Monopoly* (Princeton, 1966), pt. 1; and Louis Galambos, *Competition and Cooperation* (Baltimore, 1966), chaps. 8–11.

4. Ibid.; and Bernard Bellush, *The Failure of the NRA* (New York, 1975).

by 1934–1935 most American capitalists had turned against "government regulation" and were becoming politically opposed to the New Deal. Even before the
Supreme Court found the NRA unconstitutional in 1935, the Roosevelt administration was looking for a new approach to promote national economic recovery.
Between mid–1934 and mid–1935, the president changed his mind and agreed to
support Senator Robert Wagner's National Labor Relations Act, which business bitterly opposed because it would promote the organization of independent labor
unions. The Wagner Act did not gain Roosevelt's support because strikes were on the
rise; they actually declined in this period.[5] Rather, Roosevelt was persuaded by
liberal congressmen and some of his advisors that the Wagner Act could help promote national economic recovery, in place of the defunct National Recovery
Administration.[6]

The NRA, in short, failed to achieve its original goals of "stabilizing business," in
large part because the U.S. national state was too administratively weak to control
major industries. The United States did not get "state-monopoly capitalism" in
1933–1935 (or at any later point). If it had, probably the break between Roosevelt and
big business would not have occurred, the "turn to the left" in 1935–1936 would not
have followed, and legislation legalizing independent American trade unions would
not have been passed.

THE ROLE OF LOCAL AND CONGRESSIONAL FORCES

During the course of the New Deal, the reach of the U.S. federal government
extended deep into the American economy and social life. At the same time, government agencies proliferated, and government expenditures more than doubled as a
percent of national income between 1929 and 1939.[7] Even so, much less centralization of governmental activities occurred than one might have expected; and the subsequent national mobilization for World War II also failed to bring permanent
centralization of many U.S. governmental functions.

New Deal liberals made repeated attempts to strengthen the role of the federal
executive and to increase the authority of the national government over the states and
localities. Yet often their efforts failed. Thus attempts to reorganize cabinet departments and strengthen the president's capacities to plan the economy and control
public expenditures largely came to nought between 1937 and 1939.[8] During and

5. See the figure in Skocpol, "Political Response to Capitalist Crises," *Politics and Society* 10
(1980): 188.

6. David Jerome Shyrock, "Business Performance and Public Policy: The Formation of the Reve-
nue Act of 1935 and the National Labor Relations Act" (unpublished Honors thesis, Harvard Col-
lege, 1980), 67–69, 88–89.

7. G. Warren Nutter, *Growth of Government in the West* (Washington, D.C., 1978), 13–14.

8. Richard Polenberg, *Reorganizing Roosevelt's Government, 1936–1939: The Controversy over
Executive Reorganization* (Cambridge, 1966); and Barry D. Karl, *The Uneasy State: The United
States from 1915 to 1945* (Chicago, 1983), chap. 8.

after World War II, moreover, the National Resources Planning Board (NRPB), an advisory agency reporting to President Roosevelt, attempted to "complete" the liberal reform agenda of the New Deal. Yet NRPB proposals for nationalized social programs, for Keynesian management of the economy through increased levels of public social spending, and for a commitment by the federal government to guarantee jobs for all Americans who wanted to work, all failed. And the NRPB itself was dismantled in 1943.[9]

To understand the limits of New Deal reforms, it is essential to grasp why efforts such as these to enhance the federal executive's role in national economic planning and social provision were not successful. Invoking the opposition of monopoly capitalists is not sufficient. Big businessmen were not always opposed to nationalizing reforms; they preferred nationally uniform unemployment insurance policies, for example.[10] Moreover, many New Deal measures passed despite concerted business opposition. The social groups that most fiercely and effectively opposed nationalizing reforms were commercial farmers organized into the American Farm Bureau Federation, local business interests associated in the Chamber of Commerce, and private medical practitioners organized by the American Medical Association. What all these organized privilege groups had in common was their presence across many local communities in the vast American nation, and their consequent ability to register opinions with many congressional representatives across the country. Organized labor and large-scale business, by contrast, were not organized in nearly as many local political arenas.

For all that the New Deal (and the subsequent World War) strengthened the role of the government in Washington, the U.S. polity remained substantially decentralized, and Congress continued to play a central role, arbitrating all legislative changes. Local and state political interests were strongly represented in Congress and tended to favor limiting the direct reach of the national government into local affairs. Moreover, Congress itself had an institutional interest in limiting the power of the presidency over such fundamental matters as setting budget priorities and dispersing public funds.

These institutional "givens" of U.S. federalism and the division of powers within the national government were not abolished by the New Deal. They help us to understand the success enjoyed by the coalitions that formed to limit the nationalizing economic and social reforms favored by liberal New Deal planners. The Committee on Economic Security (CES) in 1934–1935 proposed federal rather than national unemployment insurance in anticipation of congressional opposition to the latter.[11] The CES omitted health insurance from the proposed Social Security bill because it feared the opposition of the American Medical Association in Congress, opposition

9. Philip W. Warken, *A History of the National Resources Planning Board, 1933–1943,* ed. Frank Freidel (New York, 1979).

10. See Skocpol and Ikenberry, "Political Formation of the American Welfare State," *Comparative Social Research* 6 (1983): 128–29.

11. Ibid.

that did in fact help to defeat later proposals for such insurance, despite widespread public support.[12] Congressional liberals and conservatives alike joined forces to defeat most proposals for government reorganization in the late 1930s, fearing that Congress would lose prerogatives to the presidency if the proposals were accepted.[13] And most important, from the later 1930s to the late 1940s, conservative coalitions in Congress, urged on by midwestern farmers, local businessmen, and Southern planters, defeated Keynesian social spending and full employment proposals, blocked the nationalization of social insurance, and eliminated the National Resources Planning Board by cutting off its funding.[14]

Pinpointing institutional leverage through Congress helps us to make sense of the special role of the South in modern American public policymaking—a regional role that certainly rivals that of either capitalists or the industrial working class. To be sure, the South's role is not without class dimensions; southern interests cannot be understood without underlining the class structure of cotton agriculture as a landlord-dominated sharecropper system from the late nineteenth century through the 1930s.[15] Nor could we possibly ignore the explicit racism that ensured minority white dominance over black majorities in all sectors of economic and social life. Yet the South was militarily defeated in the Civil War, and by the 1930s this region was not very weighty in the national economy as a whole; nor were its social mores typical of the nation. Thus socioeconomic factors and generalized references to racism will not alone tell us why Southern politicians had so much leverage during the New Deal that they could take a leading role in congressional alliances opposed to national welfare standards and any strong federal presence in economic planning.

The influence of Southern agricultural interests in the New Deal depended on the insertion of their class power as landlords and their social power as white racial oligarchs into federal political arrangements that from the 1890s to the 1960s allowed an undemocratized single-party South to coexist with competitive two-party democracy in the rest of the national polity. Above all, Southern leverage was registered through a congressionally centered legislative process in Washington that allowed key committee chairmen from "safe" districts to arbitrate precise legislative details and outcomes. From the New Deal onward the "national" Democratic party used congressional committees to broker the internal divisions between its Southern and

12. Daniel S. Hirshfield, *The Lost Reform: The Campaign for Compulsory Health Insurance in the United States from 1932 to 1943* (Cambridge, 1970).

13. Polenberg, *Reorganizing Roosevelt's Government*.

14. See James T. Patterson, *Congressional Conservatism and the New Deal* (Lexington, Ky., 1967), especially chap. 9; Stephen Bailey, *Congress Makes a Law* (New York, 1950); Warken, *History of the National Resources Planning Board;* and Amenta and Skocpol, "Redefining the New Deal."

15. See Lee J. Alston and Joseph P. Ferrie, "Labor Costs, Paternalism, and Loyalty in Southern Agriculture: A Constraint on the Growth of the Welfare State," *Journal of Economic History* 65 (1985): 95–117; and "Resisting the Welfare State: Southern Opposition to the Farm Security Administration," in *The Emergence of the Modern Political Economy*, ed. Robert Higgs (Greenwich, Conn., 1985), pp. 88–120.

urban-liberal Northern wings.[16] This prevented the often contradictory orientations of the two wings from tearing the national party apart, but at the price of allowing the enactment of only those social policies that did not bring the national state into direct confrontation with the South's nondemocratic politics and racially embedded systems of repressive labor control.

***

In sum, many features of the New Deal can only be understood by moving beyond the analysis of class struggles between labor and capital. The administrative weaknesses of the U.S. national state at the start of the New Deal helped to ensure that a simple business–New Deal alliance could not quickly bring economic recovery, and opened the way for pro-union measures as a way to boost popular spending power. To understand the full development of New Deal reforms after 1934, moreover, we need to pinpoint the social interests and political alliances that were able to gain leverage through the longstanding federal and congressional institutions of the U.S. state. The New Deal certainly brought policy innovators to the fore through the newly active federal executive. It also energized urban-liberal forces and created new possibilities for political alliances through the electorally strengthened and partially realigned Democratic Party. Nevertheless, in the end, America's federal state and regionally uneven democracy placed severe limits on the political alliances and policies that could prevail as the foundations were laid for nationwide social provision and economic regulation in the United States.

The result of the New Deal was *not* centralized state-monopoly capitalism. Social benefits remained regionally uneven and incomplete in the postwar United States. And the role of the national government in managing the economy, although unquestionably much greater than before the 1930s, nevertheless remained limited in comparison to many of the capitalist welfare states of Europe. Soviet scholarship on America's New Deal, just like U.S. scholarship, can benefit from greater attention to political variations *within* the bounds of capitalist development.

---

16. In addition to Patterson, *Congressional Conservatism,* see Richard Franklin Bensel, *Sectionalism and American Political Development, 1880–1980* (Madison, Wis., 1984), especially chap. 7.

A. A. Popov

3 ON THE NATIONAL LABOR RELATIONS BOARD IN THE UNITED STATES IN THE 1930s

Regulation of labor relations in state-monopolistic capitalism has its own history, its own nature, and, of special importance, its own mechanism. Investigation of this mechanism with its complicated hierarchy of institutions, dry formulation of laws, and frequently hidden functions is not some narrow, specialized undertaking—it is necessary to understanding the nature of modern capitalism.

Bourgeois politicians and the leadership of the American Federation of Labor-Congress of Industrial Organizations (AFL-CIO) present regulation of relations between employers and employees as one of the exemplary models of American democracy. Dozens of studies written on this topic have the aim of proving that the procedure for negotiation insures equal rights for both sides, and that the government plays the role of a neutral and good-natured middleman in helping to settle disputes. However, study of the mechanism of regulation allows one to show the true role of the government. Government has to make concessions to the labor movement, but primarily it aims to control the unions in defense of the capitalistic system.

The era of the New Deal was critical in establishing the relationship between the ruling classes of the United States and the organizations of industrial workers. From policies of repression, the government changed to policies that helped establish and support unions of a reformist character. Although government had attempted some intervention since the end of the nineteenth century, and particularly during World War I, it was precisely during the New Deal, during the rapid transition from monopolistic capitalism to state-monopolistic capitalism, that the modern principles for regulating industrial disputes were established.

The new policy found expression in the Wagner Act of 1935. That law created a regulatory mechanism in the form of the National Labor Relations Board (NLRB). Somewhat modified by the Taft-Hartley Act, the NLRB is a primary tool in the government's system for intervening in labor relations even now.

The structure of the NLRB is distinguished by its centralization, a feature designed to insure fast and direct intervention in labor disputes throughout the country. The board was headed by three men (a chairman and two members) named by the president and approved by the Senate. A comparatively small central bureaucracy was created in Washington. It was divided into five departments (judicial, administrative, investigative, economic, and publishing) and a number of subdepartments to help carry out board decisions. Regional divisions of the board (there were twenty-one) also were distinguished by comparatively simple arrangements that allowed leadership to be concentrated in a few hands.

During its first two years, the NLRB staff did not exceed three hundred people, although it grew to one thousand in subsequent years.[1] The smallness of the organiza-

1. H[arry A.] Millis and E[mily Clark] Brown, *From the Wagner Act to Taft-Hartley* (Chicago,

72

tion reflected its meager funding, a condition the board accepted unwillingly as a consequence of right-wing criticism in Congress.[2]

The tasks of the board flowed from the intent of its creators—to prevent strikes by working out concessions informally, to create unions it could control, to direct the labor movement toward reform. These goals clearly were implicit in the Wagner Act, and they emanated from the necessity of eradicating conditions that provoked "strikes and other forms of civil strife in industry."[3] As Senator [Pat] Harrison said, he was for the bill as a safety measure because "I regard organized labor in this country as our chief bulwark against communism and other revolutionary movements."[4]

Accordingly, the functions of the NLRB were twofold: intervention in conflicts in which it had clear jurisdiction because of "unfair labor practices" by employers or their failure to conclude collective agreements; and control over formation of unions—the right to determine exactly how many representatives of a union would be "recognized" and empowered to conduct negotiations and sign agreements with management.

The Wagner Act restricted antiunion activities, which were called "unfair labor practices," on the part of employers. Section 8 on "unfair labor practices" was central in the law, and it represented the most significant achievement of American workers in the entire history of the labor movement. It forbade factory owners to persecute workers' organizations, and it provoked fierce opposition from employers.

Related to "unfair labor practices" were attempts by employers to create so-called "company unions," i.e., a false "representative of workers" that existed at the behest of an industrialist and depended on him for everything. This practice was widespread throughout American industry in the mid–1930s. Employers also could not threaten or intimidate workers with "force or violence" when they organized unions. The law prohibited other methods in vogue with industrialists at the time, such as dismissal of union agitators and activists, composition of blacklists, spying, assault on pickets, and dispersal of peaceful demonstrations.

Industrial managers were forbidden to demand that a worker not be a member of a union as a condition of employment (in other words, so-called "yellow dog contracts" were not allowed). At the same time, unions had the right to conclude agreements with management that required all employees of a firm to join a union (the so-called "closed shop").

Employers could not refuse to enter collective bargaining with representatives of their work force who had been selected in a prescribed manner. Thus the law and its implementation encouraged collective agreements and the creation of reform-oriented unions that favored "peaceful relations" with management.

1950), 41, 61. This article by A. A. Popov first appeared in the Soviet journal *Modern and Contemporary History*, 1971, no. 2, 169–74. This English translation is by Brenda Kay Weddle.

2. *Congressional Record*, vol. 80, pt. 1, 1936, 959; pt. 2, 1356; pt. 7, 7455; pt. 8, 9113, 9186; vol. 83, pt. 3, 1938, 2454–57; pt. 7, 7224, 7918.

3. M[ilton] Handler, *Cases and Materials on Labor Law* (St. Paul, 1944), 719.

4. A[rthur M.] Schlesinger, Jr., *The Age of Roosevelt, Vol. 2: The Coming of the New Deal* (New York, 1959), 404.

Any workers, group of workers, or union could lodge a complaint with the board about an employer's "unfair labor practice." If a complaint seemed justified after a preliminary investigation, the board could propose unofficially to the head of the enterprise that the injustice be rectified. If the employer refused to settle in this unofficial way, then the NLRB issued a so-called "stop order" against the employer's antiunion activities. The board also could require that workers who had been dismissed for participating in "legitimate forms of union activity," including strikes, be restored to their jobs and compensated for lost wages.[5]

If management of an industry refused to obey the order, the board could turn to a circuit appellate court for enforcement. The court confirmed or rejected the order; however, it did not investigate anew the evidence of the case. The court accepted the version of the NLRB as final. Both the board and the employers could dispute the circuit court's decision and appeal to the Supreme Court, the ultimate recourse. After the Supreme Court handed down its verdict, the matter returned to the circuit appellate court, and the employer was subject to punishment for contempt of court. The measure of punishment was determined by that circuit court.[6]

Thus the procedure for compelling management to make changes was lengthy and expensive. Basically preserved even today, it is evidence that ruling circles tried to give business every privilege and make government intervention as little onerous as possible.

The other responsibility of the NLRB was overseeing the selection of labors' representatives to negotiate with employers. Such a practice, in actuality, signified official recognition of the union. After receiving application from one or several (competing) unions, the board, as a rule, conducted the elections. The workers' organization that received the majority of votes was promptly established as the sole representative of the work force in negotiations with management; the other unions received no rights.[7] This procedure, although directed against creation of the "company unions" that had provoked great indignation among workers, simultaneously placed the formation of unions in general under government control.

The size of the sector of an industry that won the right of collective bargaining (in American terminology, the "bargaining unit") had great significance. Such a "unit" could be a shop, a factory, a group of factories owned by one company, or even an entire branch of an industry. Several collective agreements might be concluded in one factory with several (as a rule, craft) unions; and yet a single collective agreement might be concluded for several dozen factories by one (as a rule, industrial) union. The determination of the nature of the "bargaining unit" rested completely with the board. The bigger the "unit," the greater the advantage to the workers, inasmuch as it was easier for an employer to impose conditions on a collective of fifty craftsmen than on one hundred thousand workers united in a powerful union. The selection of a

5. Handler, *Cases and Materials on Labor Law*, 727–28.
6. Ibid., 725–26.
7. Ibid., 723–24.

"unit" actually influenced the outcome of competition between two or more feuding unions. The craft unions of the AFL, as a rule, were fragmented into smaller units than the massive industrial unions of the CIO. Therefore, if the board conducted elections to determine the bargaining unit at the level of the shop, the victor often was the AFL; but if elections occurred at the factory level or among a group of enterprises, the CIO almost surely won.[8] Thus, much depended on NLRB decisions.

In general, this method of determining "bargaining units" encouraged unionization. "The Board usually approved the broadest unit, as far as this agreed with the clearly expressed desire of the workers and the commonality of their interests, and if this was justified by the form of the business's organization and was allowed by the articles of the law," former employees of the NLRB reported.[9] The statement was consistent with reality. In mid-1937, agreements at the company level were concluded in steel, automobile, rubber, electric, shipbuilding, and other fields of industry. However, it is important to stress that agreements typically followed major strikes. And the board's services to unions that wanted company-wide agreements consisted more of moral support than of effective action against the companies.

What was the extent and character of this mediating organ's activity? Statistical reports of the board look impressive. During the first twelve years of its existence (1935–1947), it reviewed 45,649 charges of "unfair labor practices" and 59,692 issues involving representation; it conducted 36,969 elections in which 7,677,135 workers participated; it restored to work 76,268 union activists, of which 40,691 received $12,418,000 in compensation; and it restored work to 226,488 strikers.[10]

On the basis of these figures, one might conclude that the board successfully enforced the Wagner Act. However, more careful examination of its reports makes clear that statistics do not reflect the complete picture. While the number of conflicts examined by the board is important, so is the character of their resolution. Were the interests of employers restricted, and was there favoritism toward the "communistic" CIO, as the bourgeois press charged? Of course, some employees of the board were outraged by the employers' unseemly campaigns and their often-belligerent behavior. This, however, could not change the nature of the board as an organ of bourgeois government that directed its efforts primarily at reconciling and smoothing out conflicts, at establishing "class harmony in industry." In full conformity with goals set out in the Wagner Act, the NLRB strived for compromise in the issues that came before it and pressured workers to make goodwill concessions. Board officials were proud when they succeeded in persuading unions to compromise before a case went beyond the preliminary investigation. Their strategy was to make as few so-called "formal decisions"—i.e., use of their official power against employers—as possible.

For the 1935–1936 fiscal year, the board received 1,068 complaints and petitions

---

8. *American Federationist,* 1937, no. 10, 1090.

9. Millis and Brown, *From the Wagner Act to Taft-Hartley,* 147.

10. NLRB, *Twelfth Annual Report* (Washington, D.C., 1947), 83, 88, 89.

affecting the interests of 240,865 workers. Of these, 865 related to alleged "unfair labor practices" by employers, and 203 to matters of representation.[11] In the second year's report, the corresponding figures were 4,068 cases (1,398,282 workers), of which 2,895 concerned "unfair labor practices" and 1,173 representation.[12] During the first year, 201 cases, i.e., 27.2 percent of those considered closed, were returned to the unions after employers compromised as a result of unofficial negotiations. The board simply returned 15.3 percent (113) because regional directors found the complaints without basis. The board considered 331 cases or 44.9 percent settled.[13] This meant that after both sides presented their positions in the informal investigation and negotiated with each other, the employer had made some concession to the union, but did not fulfill all its demands. For example, one employer agreed to recognize the union, but refused to rehire dismissed workers; in another case, an employer restored work to some but declined to take back the most active "agitators and rebels." Although the unions did not withdraw their complaints, the board considered such cases resolved and closed them without going to the next stage. The large percentage of such cases testified to the board's effort to satisfy employers at the expense of workers at the slightest opportunity.

During the second year, 69 percent (1,429) of the cases were settled, 22.9 percent (599) of the cases were recalled, and 10.8 percent (254) of the cases were rejected.[14] Thus the tendency strengthened.

In only 1 incident out of 20 did the board force changes on the employers. In 1938 the NLRB issued a total of 56 "formal decisions," and during all the years it existed the board forced change on employers in only 6.7 percent of the cases concerning "unfair labor practices" and 22.4 percent of those concerning representation.[15] Thus, only under certain conditions, as when employers proved unwilling to make any concessions, did the board set its full machinery in motion and act as a coercive agent.

Basically, most large monopolies did not want to compromise with workers. Not one major corporation yielded to the NLRB before 1937—that is, not until the moment the Supreme Court recognized the constitutionality of the Wagner Act. Several companies, General Motors, for example, paralyzed the board by obtaining "restraining orders" against it. Others simply did not recognize the legitimacy of the NLRB, ignoring hearings, recalling their advocates, proclaiming that the board operated without constitutional authority, and so on. The board encountered this position in its dealings with Remington Rand, Mackay Radio and Telegraph, Globe Mail Service, Chrysler Corporation, Associated Press, Jones and Laughlin Steel,[16] and others.

In 1935–1937, there were flagrant instances of reprisals by management against

11. NLRB, *First Annual Report* (Washington, D.C., 1936), 29.

12. NLRB, *Second Annual Report* (Washington, D.C., 1937), 13; *Twelfth Annual Report*, 83.

13. NLRB, *First Annual Report*, 30.

14. NLRB, *Second Annual Report*, 15.

15. NLRB, *Twelfth Annual Report*, 86, 87.

16. NLRB, *Decisions and Order,* vol. 2 (Washington, D.C., 1937), 626, 500, 610; vol. 1 (Washington, D.C., 1936), 164, 788, 503.

union members. Thus in "bloody Harlan" (a mining county in the state of Kentucky, where, as one journalist put it, they lacked only medieval castles and drawbridges to complete the feudal image[17]), acknowledgment by a miner that he belonged to a union was tantamount to suicide. According to the press, "Nobody knows exactly how many miners have been killed, either by secret assassination or in pitched battles with the mine owners' imported thugs, but the number is certainly large."[18] A special Senate subcommittee, headed by R[obert M.] La Follette, Jr., examined conditions in Harlan and established that intimidation, beatings, terrorization of wives and children, torture of adolescents, and murder of union activists were common occurrences. (There was a saying that "death from a bullet in Harlan is considered death from natural causes.") The subcommittee also established that the county sheriff chose his underlings primarily from hardened criminals, that the entire police force consisted of company men, and that not one union leader could enter the county unimpeded and rent a room in a hotel.[19] Eyewitnesses wrote that the situation in the county was reminiscent of Dante's Hell and that law and civilization simply were forgotten there.[20]

Another example of reprisal by monopolists against unions, documented in the records of the board, occurred in Illinois, where Remington Rand suppressed strikes in its factories. In their tyrannical defense of Remington Rand, the owners flooded the town with armed men who patrolled the streets and completely isolated the workers from the outside world. Situations such as these illustrated the weakness of the NLRB.[21] One could continue with a long list of similar examples.

While the board's authority and power often sufficed to force small and middling entrepreneurs to make concessions to their workers, it was rendered helpless against the major corporations that were the main enemies of the Wagner Act. The monopolies ignored the board and continued to suppress workers' organizations with impunity. Nevertheless, there was enormous opposition from monopolies toward the agency that implemented the hated Wagner Act. As one contemporary testified, "Almost every sin, from the time God created man, is attributed to the Board." It was depicted as the harbinger of a victorious proletariat and of approaching doom for the profit system and the middle class. The law was attacked as an "instrument of communism."[22] Its opponents contended that intervention in labor disputes expanded the law's defects. The board was blamed for bureaucratization and characterized as "social enemy No. 1" and the "American inquisition."[23] In the face of these attacks, the NLRB changed the character of its activities—it cooperated even

17. J[erald] S. Auerbach, *Labor and Liberty* (New York, 1966), 115.

18. *New Republic,* 5 May 1937.

19. U.S. Senate, *Hearing before the Subcommittee of the Committee on Education and Labor: Violations of Free Speech and Rights of Labor* (Washington, D.C., 1941), pt. 10, 3448, 3450.

20. *New York Times,* 25 November 1936; *New Republic,* 24 December 1937; *Congressional Digest,* May 1937, 133.

21. NLRB, *Decisions and Orders,* 2:626.

22. J[ohn] H. Mariano, *The Wagner Act* (New York, 1940), 29–30.

23. R[obert] R. Brooks, *Unions of Their Own Choosing* (New Haven, 1939), 203.

more with capital and less decisively upheld the law and battled its violators. Two former prominent officers in the NLRB, [Harry A.] Millis and [Emily Clark] Brown, have written, "It is not an oversimplification to speak of three different boards, under the three chairmen." The first board under the chairmanship of J. W. Maddon was distinguished by the most energy and decisiveness in the execution of the law in comparison with the second and third.[24]

Another, more powerful force was necessary to restrain the monopolists, to force them to recognize the principle of collective bargaining, and, to the extent it did so, to define the future of the NLRB. That force was the American working class, which had won important victories in the mid–1930s. The second half of the 1930s was noted, as is well known, for the rapid growth of unions in fields where labor organizations previously had been pitifully weak. Of major concern were the steel, oil, rubber, automobile, and electric industries. The membership in labor unions grew from 3,728,000 in 1935 to 7,218,000 in 1937, and to 8,980,000 in 1939—i.e., by two-and-a-half times.[25] Unions had achieved stability.

"Sit-down" strikes in the rubber industry in Akron, Ohio, in February 1936; in the electric industry in Camden, New Jersey, in summer 1937; demonstrations of steel workers in May 1937 in Chicago; and particularly the "sit-down" strikes at General Motors from December 1936 to February 1937, and at Chrysler in April–May 1937, forced employers at the cost of blood and heavy sacrifices to sign collective agreements with industrial unions.

This state of affairs could not be ignored even by the United States Supreme Court—the very Supreme Court that from January 1935 to July 1936 declared eleven acts of Congress unconstitutional, including several that embodied the fundamental reforms of the New Deal. On 12 April 1937, the Supreme Court—influenced by the workers' victories—changed course and upheld the constitutionality of the Wagner Act and consequently the legality of the NLRB. Through their actions, workers had not only won the battle for unions, but also had defended the liberal legislation of the New Deal.

The strike for reform, for integration of the unions, encountered the most fierce opposition of big business during the 1930s. As they established dictatorship over various industries, major corporations did not want labor organizations or even a capitalistic government to limit their control in any way. Hence their loud complaints about union "dictatorship in industry."

However, the supporters of "rugged individualism" and uncontrolled management of the monopolies were doomed to failure. Supporters of state-monopolistic regulation won. Big business was forced to accept state-monopolistic regulation as the only possibility, although the fight over the "extent and type of concessions," over the scale and tempo of regulation, did not end immediately. A modified board, created by the Taft-Hartley Act, not only continues to exist, but has served as the

24. *From the Wagner Act to Taft-Hartley,* 235.
25. *Historical Statistics of the United States* (Washington, D.C., 1960), 97–98.

primary instrument for government intervention in labor relations to the present time. Although the character of regulation, compared to the liberal spirit of the New Deal, sharply changed and acquired a conservative and even reactionary coloring, the principles of government regulation and control have remained unchanged. Furthermore, experts do not foresee a substantial change in NLRB functions for the next ten to fifteen years.

In evaluating the results of the board's activity, it should be kept in mind that the process of government regulation in general was contradictory. Policies of integration, which ruling circles in the United States pursued through the mechanism of the NLRB, did not abolish or replace the struggle of the working class. As has been shown, even during an era of liberalism the board did not always capably defend workers' rights. However, it is impossible to underestimate the consequences of government intervention, and it would be an error to disregard the tremendous efforts in behalf of integration that took place in the course of thirty years. The elite of the union gladly established a rapprochement with the government and received significant advantages in return for their cooperation. The union elite even succeeded in captivating many among the unionized masses. Nevertheless, the quantity and intensity of strikes today testify that the major reason for creating a regulatory system—to eliminate strikes in favor of regulation from above—was not fulfilled.

V. I. Borisiuk

4 FROM THE WAGNER ACT TO THE TAFT-HARTLEY ACT: A TURN TO REACTION IN LABOR LEGISLATION IN THE UNITED STATES, 1935–1947

From the perspective of employers in the United States, the end of World War II in fall 1945 came too soon. The war years had constituted a period of definite "prosperity" for American business. Capitalizing on the slogan "national unity for the sake of victory over our enemies" and using the tools of the government's executive agencies to prevent labor conflicts, monopolies had made the country's economic machinery function smoothly. As the monopolies steadily regained their former power in the country, people who wanted to alter the New Deal spoke out more loudly. (The necessity of observing requirements set out in [Franklin D.] Roosevelt's socioeconomic reforms did effectively restrict employers.) In the early postwar years, American political life centered on the very different views of supporters and opponents of the New Deal and the ideopolitical battle that those differing views engendered.

The strongest passions raged around the Wagner Act, "the most radical act" of the 1930s.[1] The intensity of the "anti-Wagner" campaign was caused by conflict between stronger tendencies toward state-monopoly as American capitalism matured and the traditions of private enterprise. Conflict between the growing power of labor unions and the traditions of private enterprise also played a part. More precisely, ideological arguments and political conflicts in the United States during the first years of peace centered on defining the role of government in regulating the country's economic life and on the legal status of American labor unions. Any review of the social legislation of the New Deal should answer not only the question of how the rights of labor organizations changed, but also the question of whether heightened government involvement during the 1930s represented anything more than a whim of neo-liberals.

A historically accurate analysis of the basic provisions of the Wagner Act and the product of its revision, the Taft-Hartley Act, permits one to present clearly the character, direction, and result of the ideopolitical battle in the United States during and immediately after the war.

The battle to repeal or amend (at times these two concepts were the same) the Wagner Act began almost from the day the bill passed. That battle, which ended in

1. See V. L. Malkov and D. G. Nadzhafov, *America at the Crossroads: An Essay on the Socio-Political History of the New Deal in the United States* (Moscow, 1967), 11. This article by V. I. Borisiuk was originally published in *Herald of Moscow State University,* History series, 1971, no. 5, 15–31. This English translation is by Brenda Kay Weddle.

1947 with the passage of the Taft-Hartley Act, is clearly divided into three phases: the prewar years (1935–1941), the period of American participation in the war (1941–1945), and the postwar years (1945–1947). Each phase of the "anti-Wagner" battle differed from the others in its intensity and scale as well as its methods and character.

One should add to the basic causes for the violent campaign to repeal the Wagner Act the dissatisfaction of employers with provisions of the statute that violated their immediate interests. They resented the fact that the government openly defended workers' rights to organize and bargain collectively. When he signed the bill, President Roosevelt had stressed that it guaranteed "the right of self-organization of employees in industry for the purpose of collective bargaining, and provides methods by which the government can safeguard that legal right."[2] Section 7 of the law stated that "employees shall have the right to self-organization, to form, join or assist labor organizations, to bargain collectively through representatives of their own choosing."[3]

Nonrecognition of these rights by employers was considered an "unfair labor practice." This term also included interference by employers in the organization of trade unions, financing or otherwise supporting workers' organizations, attempts to influence union membership through discriminatory hiring or firing policies, refusal to bargain with representatives of the workers, and a number of other activities.[4]

The National Labor Relations Board was created to guarantee the rights enumerated in the law. The board had original jurisdiction over the Wagner Act. Although the right to review NLRB decisions was reserved for the courts, the first investigation of alleged "unfair labor practices" was the responsibility of the board. This provision of the law displeased employers primarily because the decisions of the NLRB showed disregard for the truly inexhaustible variety of methods for restricting labor that had come from more than one hundred years of experience. So far as the NLRB was concerned, guilt was determined solely by whether the law's provisions or the board's own order had been violated. And by conducting elections to determine the nature of union representation among workers, the NLRB constantly reaffirmed the right of collective bargaining. Before and after the passage of the Wagner Act, employers considered that determining the criteria for hiring was their privilege alone. The law required employers to accept collective bargaining, but it did not obligate them to accept without change the conditions proposed by workers. More important, the law did not obligate workers to accept proposals initiated by employers. Not a word in this law that legalized the right of workers to organize was said about prohibiting strikes by the unions. In fact, Section 13 of the Wagner Act specifically recognized the legitimacy of strikes ("nothing in the present law shall be construed as an obstacle or limit in any form whatsoever of the right to strike"). Considering that the provision on "unfair labor practices" in the Wagner Act applied

2. National Labor Relations Board (NLRB), *First Annual Report* (Washington, D.C., 1936), 9.
3. For the text of the Wagner Act, see *Compilation of Laws Relating to Mediation, Conciliation and Arbitration Between Employers and Employees,* comp. Lewis (Washington, 1937), 225.
4. National Labor Relations Act, Section 8, in ibid., 228–29.

only to employers, it is not difficult to understand why employers immediately christened the new law a "prolabor" law. (This was reinforced by the fact that during the first few months—by 30 June 1936—the NLRB and its regional branches had received 1,065 petitions from workers' organizations that accused employers of "unfair labor practices" or demanded elections to determine representatives for collective bargaining.)[5]

The Wagner Act significantly accelerated the growth of union membership and increased labor's organizational and contractual opportunities.[6] Both supporters and critics recognized its impact.[7] Also, the increased number of elections to determine representation could not have occurred without a corresponding increase in the membership of American unions.[8]

In discussing the causes of dissatisfaction among employers with the Wagner Act, it is impossible to omit its ideological foundation. Two opposite strands of bourgeois social thought collided over the Wagner Act, one supported by adherents of the theory of "rugged individualism" and the other by people who believed government should participate actively in regulating the country's economy.

The first volleys in the ideological war between followers of these two variations of American bourgeois ideology had sounded by the end of the nineteenth century. At that time, the rapid growth of monopolies and the extraordinary rate of business consolidation forced people to ask whether government should massively and immediately intervene in economic life.[9] However, during those years the people who opposed the ideology of rugged individualism and nonintervention seemed to be visionaries more than anything else. Their arsenal of arguments contained no more than personal conviction of the truth and logic of their ideas and, at most, reference to the broad philosophy of positivism.

Adherents of this visionary antitraditionalism—the neo-liberals of the 1920s–1940s—profited by the obvious failure of the theory of nonintervention during the

5. NLRB, *First Annual Report*, 29.

6. The following figures show the growth of the two major unions in the United States—the American Federation of Labor (AFL) and Congress of Industrial Organizations (CIO). Even for the period 1935–1937, when employers tried every method of sabotaging the enforcement of the Wagner Act, membership in the AFL grew to 3,400,000; and the membership of the newly created CIO by December 1937 reached 3,700,000. In ten years, by 1945, these figures nearly doubled: members of the AFL numbered 6,931,221, and the CIO 6,300,000. Labor Research Association, *Labor Fact Book* (New York, 1947), 107–9.

7. M[eyer] Jacobstein and H[arold G.] Moulton in their research on the influence of the defense program on prices, wages, and profits note that wage increases in the prewar years occurred largely as a result of "effective collective bargaining encouraged by the government." *Effects of the Defense Program on Prices, Wages, and Profits* (Washington, 1941), 41.

8. In 1936 the NLRB conducted only 203 elections to determine union representation. In 1937 it conducted 1,173; in 1938, 3,623. In 1939, 1940, and 1941, the NLRB conducted, respectively, 2,286, 2,243, and 4,334 elections (NLRB, *Tenth Annual Report*, 6).

9. See the regulations and materials of the first congress (1885) of the American Economic Association; *Palgrave's Dictionary of Political Economy*, 1:808–10; R[ichard] Hofstadter, *Social Darwinism in American Thought* (New York, 1959).

first year of the Great Depression. Given the circumstances under which the liberal-reformist wave of the New Deal developed, the views of the neo-liberals seemed indisputable. "Truly the old methods will never return, they simply cannot return," exclaimed C[arl] Magruder in 1937.[10] J[ohn R.] Commons and his followers, who offered a comprehensive theory in 1936 of the development of government intervention in labor relations, were convinced that neo-liberals had achieved the final victory.[11]

Evidence that neo-liberals had too quickly ruled out the durability of nonintervention ideology appeared in 1941 in the form of an anthology edited by J[asper V.] Garland, *Federal Regulation of Labor Unions*.[12] A number of articles in the collection challenged the expediency of most New Deal measures and questioned the ideas that inspired their creators. The articles also cast doubt on the worthiness of the Wagner Act.

Conflict over this law began with its enactment. The opponents of the new statute, having convinced themselves of its unconstitutionality, awaited the decision of the Supreme Court as a cure-all. On 5 September 1935, exactly two months after the law was passed, the American Liberty League published a special report written by its lawyers that concluded the law clearly was unconstitutional.[13] It was characteristic of the times that, for practical purposes, the law was not yet in effect; the NLRB did not even have a full staff.[14]

As a shield to their unshakable belief that the new law was illegal, employers ignored the Wagner Act for two years. Almost all American analysts agree that the force of the law did not come into full effect until the Supreme Court passed favorably on it in April 1937.[15] That opinion was accepted also by the authors of the NLRB's second annual report, who admitted that during its first two years the Wagner Act "has not represented the law of the land."[16] The employers' tactic of ignoring the Wagner Act during 1935–1937 did not mean they were inactive while they awaited the Supreme Court's decision. Before 1936, employers filed nearly 8,080 petitions[17] with various judicial bodies of the country for orders that would prohibit any activity by the NLRB whatsoever. Such practices were nothing new in

10. Magruder, "A Half Century of Legal Influence Upon the Development of Collective Bargaining," *Harvard Law Review* 50 (1937): 1071.

11. Commons and J[ohn B.] Andrews, *Principles of Labor Legislation* (New York, 1936).

12. Published in New York.

13. National Lawyers Committee of the American Liberty League, "Report of the Constitutionality of the Wagner Act," cited in *From the Wagner Act to Taft-Hartley,* ed. H[arry A.] Millis and E[mily Clark] Brown (Chicago, 1950), 36.

14. The first annual report of the NLRB described the American Liberty League's document of 5 September 1935 as a "deliberate and concerted effort by a large group of well-known lawyers to undermine public confidence in the statute . . . , to assist attorneys generally in attacks on the statute, and perhaps to influence the courts" (p. 47).

15. H[enry] Pelling, *American Labor* (Chicago, 1960), 161.

16. *Second Annual Report*, 6.

17. NLRB, *First Annual Report*, 1.

American history. In the U.S. Constitution the courts have an unlimited right to interpret laws and pass judgment on the extent to which each is legal. The magnitude of employers' activities against the government's new administrative agency drew attention as, to prevent recognition of the NLRB, the number of requests for judicial orders against the board grew like a "rolling snowball."[18]

Once the constitutionality of the Wagner Act was confirmed, petitions to the NLRB and its regional branches increased by almost 1,000 percent.[19] Reaction from conservatives in the Congress was instantaneous. In 1937 Senator A[rthur H.] Vandenberg introduced several amendments to the Wagner Act, some provisions of which were embodied in Taft-Hartley ten years later.[20] As though making up for lost time, the Wagner Act's opponents in the national capital launched fevered action. Such was their impatience that Representative [Edward E.] Cox proposed to suspend traditional procedures for introducing new legislation "until Gabriel blows his horn."[21] On Cox's recommendation, H[oward W.] Smith, his colleague on the House Judicial Committee, began an investigation of NLRB activity in July 1938. The "research" of the Smith Commission was fully endorsed by reactionary senators [Carter] Glass, [Harry F.] Byrd, [Josiah W.] Bailey, and [Walter R.] McCarran, who referred to the Wagner Act in their speeches as evidence of "Communist influence" in labor policy. By March 1940, the Smith Commission had prepared seven amendments to the Wagner Act.[22] Other members of the Congress attacked the law with maniacal persistence. Representative [Clare E.] Hoffman introduced amendments to the law in every session of Congress from 1939 to 1947, relaxing only after the Taft-Hartley Act became law. He achieved sad notoriety by asking his legislative colleagues to consider thirty-four proposals. Smith, second only to Hoffman, introduced nine bills, not counting numerous amendments to the law. The apparent weakness and small number of conservative opponents in Congress before the war does not truly illustrate the scale of the opposition movement. It does not follow that the majority of congressmen would oppose the labor law during the years in which the most important measures of the New Deal were being passed in Congress. The small number of conservative opponents in Congress[23] resulted from the general decline of business influence during the Depression, the unsubsiding class war fought by American workers, and the powerful antimonopolistic sentiment across the spectrum of American society. During these years even the anti-Wagner programs of large organized business—the National Association of Manufacturers

18. Ibid., 48.

19. NLRB, *Second Annual Report*, 1.

20. On the significance of Vandenberg's amendment, see Garland, *Federal Regulation of Labor Unions*, 12–20.

21. If people had to wait for proposed amendments to come down from the Labor Committee of the House of Representatives, in Cox's opinion, they would be there "until Gabriel blows his horn" (J[ames] T. Patterson, *Congressional Conservatism and the New Deal* [Lexington, Ky., 1967], 317).

22. *Congressional Record*, vol. 86, pt. 3, 1940, 2501–2.

23. The opponents of the Wagner Act did not number a third of the members of each house of Congress: there were 30–35 in the Senate, and as many as 70–78 in the House.

(NAM) and the U.S. Chamber of Commerce—reflected the necessity of reconciliation to changed circumstances. Although both the National Association of Manufacturers and the Chamber of Commerce had come out in favor of repealing the Wagner Act in 1935, one comes across documents issued over the next several years in which they propose only partial changes and advise employers on how to live with it. These documents contain demands for "egalitarian" treatment, which the Wagner Act allegedly denied them, and extensive recommendations, tinged with despair, on how to live with the NLRB.[24]

Almost no leaders of the American Federation of Labor (AFL) opposed the Wagner Act during the prewar years. But in 1939–1940 the leadership of the AFL came out in support of the Smith Commission's inquiry into NLRB activity, expressed dissatisfaction with individual provisions of the Wagner Act, and proposed their own amendments. Although NLRB decisions were by no means always "pro-worker" (as right-wing critics endlessly proclaimed), it is unlikely that AFL charges against the law were made because of concern for the well-being of the labor movement.[25] During these years leaders of the AFL were so busy fighting the Congress of Industrial Organizations (CIO) that they assigned no particular significance to the fact that their anti-Wagner pronouncements in essence allied them with the most reactionary forces inside and outside the Congress.

In discussing the Wagner Act's opponents during the prewar years, it is necessary to take into account the predominance of "Hoover-type" conservative traditions in their ideological foundations. According to such thinking, increased government intervention in labor relations regulation was objectionable. The strongest attacks from 1935 to 1941 were directed not so much against legal recognition of the workers' right to organize as against the creation and functioning of the NLRB. Analysis of congressional documents shows that in 1939 and 1940 alone, fifteen legislative proposals were submitted to limit jurisdiction of the NLRB. The activity of the board was investigated by the Smith Commission and was an issue in most of the legislative proposals authored by the infamous Hoffman. The minority in the House of Representatives issued a special declaration in 1940 that addressed the problems of the NLRB.[26] Many authors of New Deal social reforms regarded the reforms as bitter pills to be swallowed in order to avoid a grave illness.[27]

24. U.S. Congress, Senate, Subcommittee of the Committee on Education and Labor, *La Follette Committee Report*, 75th Congress, 3d sess., 7624–28; 76th Congress, 1st sess., 14071–76.

25. For additional detail on the position of the AFL, see American Federation of Labor, *Report of the Proceedings of the 63rd Annual Convention* (Washington, 1943), 68–69.

26. "Fair or not," said the House declaration, "but public opinion is convinced that the Board is far from impartial in its decisions, its prejudice is evident, the public blames it not only in its misuse of power which was never given to it, but also in the injustice and unfairness of its judgements" (Committee on Labor, Minority Report, 76th Congress, 3rd sess., 10).

27. For example, D[onald] Richberg, contributing author to a number of laws (including railroad legislation in 1936 and the NIRA in 1933), after the war published a book that was sharply antiunion and critical of the majority of the New Deal measures: *Labor Union Monopoly: A Clear and Present Danger* (Chicago, 1957).

The factor that truly caused employers to vacillate in their adherence to Hoover's "rugged individualism" and to accept a more suitable reality (one characterized by state-monopoly of the neo-conservative sort) was their understanding of labor relations management as handled by the government during the war.

The war significantly strengthened state-monopolistic tendencies and furthered the evolution of American capitalism. This was reflected not only in the growth of the government's regulatory functions over social and economic life, but also in the proper expansion of government into the spheres of economics, government licensing, government contracts, etc. The wartime necessity that industry function smoothly forced the government to invoke every means of preventing labor conflicts and the strikes, lockouts, and boycotts affiliated with them. Between 1941 and 1945 the U.S. government immeasurably expanded its prerogatives in regulating economic life. It pursued a policy "of strict regulation of social relationships, and placed any and all agreements of note between workers and employers under official control."[28] In its relentless appeal to the patriotism of the workers, the government relied on powerful administrative agencies in the executive branch. By invoking the extraordinary conditions of war, the government justified its reactionary measures to regulate labor relations and its renunciation of reforms effected during the prewar period.

Even before 7 December 1941—i.e., during the period of defense—all kinds of departments, institutions, boards, and commissions were created in the United States to control and regulate war production. The National Defense Mediation Board (NDMB) joined the agencies responsible for regulating labor relations, quite apart from the NLRB and the mediation and reconciliation service of the Department of Labor.[29] Jurisdiction of the NDMB extended only to those matters referred to it by the secretary of labor; thus the board considered only labor problems that the mediation service of the Department of Labor was not in a position to settle. The extraordinary character of the NDMB was reflected in its status as the "ultimate authority." Although the president's executive order limited the NDMB's authority to labor disputes that "threatened interruptions to continuous production or transportation of materials essential to national defense,"[30] desire and necessity made it possible to use this wording as authority to take up industrial disputes that were far removed from national defense. To help settle conflicts, the presidential order directed the NDMB to propose good-willed arbitration, to investigate the causes of conflict, and,

28. N. V. Sivachev, "Intervention of the Executive Organs of Power in the United States in Labor Conflicts During World War II," *Herald of Moscow State University,* Law series, 1969, no. 4, 20.

29. *The Termination Report of the National War Labor Board* (hereafter, *Termination Report*), Appendix B-1, 2:48–49.

30. President Roosevelt, unlike presidents before and after him, often used the right of "presidential seizure." Roosevelt used it not only during the war, but also before the official declaration of war—three times in support of the NLRB. During the war years, "presidential seizure" of property was one of the most effective means of stopping labor conflicts. To implement a seizure, only a presidential order and substantiation that "the particular conflict threatens the national interest" was required (J[ohn L.] Blackman, *Presidential Seizure in Labor Disputes* [Cambridge, Mass., 1967]).

finally, to make recommendations to the parties. The NDMB's most extreme means, its "Damocles' Sword," forced the participants of a dispute to agree to NDMB's "good-willed" recommendations or risk possible presidential seizure. Of the 118 cases examined by the NDMB during its existence, three ended in presidential seizure, i.e., the transfer of the enterprise with an unresolved labor dispute to government administration.[31] Despite the fact that the NDMB existed only from 19 March 1941 to 12 January 1942, its importance should be emphasized. The creation of the Mediation Board was one of the first victories for employers. It was not part of the initial Wagner Act; rather, it was a consequence of its enactment. In the problems the NDMB faced, in the unusual nature of the agency, one can see the tendency to protect industry from the growing activity of unions. And this tendency was evident long before defense needs justified the NDMB's creation. The restraint of the union movement during these ten months of NDMB activity was the first real victory for employers since the beginning of the New Deal and the first serious setback to the ideas that underlay the Wagner Act and the union movement.

In discussing the regulation of labor relations in the United States during World War II, it is impossible to ignore the National War Labor Board (NWLB), created by presidential executive order on 12 January 1942.[32] The NWLB was the first administrative body in the history of American labor relations in which decisions were final and not subject to higher review. This meant that decisions in more than seventeen thousand labor disputes settled by the NWLB from 12 January 1942 to 31 December 1945 were made by an instrument of the presidency. All NWLB operations illustrate that the government excluded even the possibility of a challenge to the prescribed solution from either employers or workers. The effectiveness of the NWLB should be noted well—the percentage of unresolved disputes during the war was not great, and, what is more, any of them could have ended with presidential seizure. One should not be misled by the apparent democratic structure of the agencies for controlling labor relations during wartime.[33] The inability of the NDMB or the NWLB to resolve one or another conflict, or the disagreement of either side with the decision, constituted grounds for taking the most peremptory measures. The penalties were determined solely by the president. American employers tried to make the most of the government's conservative policy in regulating labor relations. They wanted to use it as part of an offensive to revise New Deal sociolegal reforms they had challenged unsuc-

31. *Termination Report,* Appendix B-1, 2:49.

32. Ibid., Appendix B-2, 2:49–50. Concerning the functions of American government agencies in regulating labor conflicts, see Sivachev, "Government Regulation of Trade Union Guarantees in Collective Bargaining During the Second World War in the United States," *Herald of Moscow State University,* Law series, 1968, no. 3, 34–44; see also F[red] Witney, *Wartime Experiences of the National Labor Relations Board, 1941–1945* (Urbana, 1949).

33. The NWLB (like the NLRB) included representatives from the trade unions, the "public," and employers. And although they were all established chiefly by the president, the wartime boards were the only ones in the history of the United States with administrative organs including workers' representation. On the composition of the NWLB and the NLRB, see *Termination Report,* Appendix A-1, 2:2–3; Appendix A-3, 5–47.

cessfully during the prewar years. It was precisely these aspirations that brought about the Smith-Connally Act in 1943. This law on "labor disputes in wartime"[34] authorized even greater executive intervention in labor relations and sanctified presidential seizure of enterprises in which a work stoppage threatened damage to a war industry. The law embodied a number of reactionary legislative proposals introduced in Congress in 1940–1941. The law set limits on the right of workers to strike; it placed the very process of declaring a strike under control of the government, prohibited strikes in enterprises under governmental jurisdiction, and, finally, placed restrictions on union political activity.

At first glance, all wartime measures that increased government intervention in labor relations thwarted the aspirations of anti–New Dealers. Indeed, from 1935 until the United States entered the war, critics had taken the position that government influence should be eliminated in the area of labor relations. Government policy during the war, it would seem, should only have heightened dissatisfaction among opponents of intervention. And it should not be forgotten that in nearly half the "presidential seizures" during the war, employers agreed with the orders of the NWLB and the provisions of the Smith-Connally Act that forbade both strikes and lockouts. For all that, there was no continuity in the opposition to government intervention that had characterized business attitudes during the prewar years.

More than that, many opponents of government intervention became its supporters. The same Representative H[oward] Smith who had taken a stand before the war against what seemed to him the extraordinary power of the NLRB became the coauthor of a law during the war that gave the NLRB almost absolute power. The example of Smith in converting to another faith was typical. However, bourgeois historians avoid that paradox in their attention to or talk about patriotic humility, about the submission of business to the will of government for the sake of winning the war.[35] This was not the case. The reactionary methods used by government to regulate labor relations during World War II led some people to reevaluate many prewar concepts, the most basic of which was the ability of the government's executive apparatus to prevent labor conflicts.

Before the New Deal, employers had relied primarily on their own strengths or the arsenals of their legal counsels in the fight against labor unions. Then the war years demonstrated the possibility of achieving nearly conflict-free industrial operation through very strict regulation of all aspects of the union movement by the government's executive branch. Understanding the significance of the NLRB's wartime experience, of "presidential seizure," and of government policies that clashed with the trade union movement led to a neo-conservative trend in bourgeois ideology. This trend was peculiar in that its tenets concerning the role of government in regulating the country's economy (including labor relations) differed not only from those of liberals and neo-liberals, but also from those of traditional conservatives. While the

---

34. For the text of the law see *Congressional Record*, vol. 89, 1943, 6487–88.

35. C[lark] Kerr, "Employer Policies in Industrial Relations 1945 to 1947," in *Labor in Postwar America* (New York, 1949), 44.

conservatives joined liberal-traditionalists to propagate the idea that government should not intervene in labor relations, neo-conservatives wholeheartedly believed in the necessity of government intervention—but by this they meant intervention only against union activity. The government's regulation of labor relations during the war fostered neo-conservatism not only as a trend in bourgeois ideology, but also as a political course—the primary contribution to the revision of New Deal legislation.

It was this theoretical premise of neo-conservatism that had the greatest effect on postwar labor legislation. In the late 1930s and early 1940s important changes also took place in state legislation. State and federal legislation on labor differed a great deal at least in part because the problems of the 1930s were perceived differently at each level. On the state level, where politicians never argued in terms of such concepts as a system, government, or nation, but in terms of shortsighted political ideas that did not leave the boundaries of the state, the necessity of shaking out traditional views was not so keen as on the federal level. The states became the natural reserves of traditionalism. Opposition to the New Deal began in the states and could be seen most clearly in the growth of reactionary anti–trade union legislation. The basic thrust of state legislation between 1937 and 1947 was directed against guarantees to trade unions and against unions in industrial disputes. During this decade thirty-five states passed laws that in one way or another touched on the problem of labor relations.[36] One basic feature of this state legislation was the so-called "right to work law," which completely nullified the concept of "trade union guarantees" and in essence legalized not only the "open shop," but also the antilabor practices of employers. State legislation passed between 1937 and 1947, analysts H[arry A.] Millis and E[mily Clark] Brown concluded, "strengthened the hands of those who desired a comprehensive revision of federal labor policy."[37] At the same time, the pattern of state legislation showed how union conflict would affect a new labor law: the most reactionary laws were passed in states noted for the weakness of the trade union movement (primarily in the South and Southwest of the country).[38] This meant that after the end of the war cooperation between labor and capital would play a paramount role in the formation of a new national labor policy.

Fearing a powerful upheaval in the labor movement after the end of the war, national leaders tried to extend the special wartime agencies for labor relations another two years.[39] The government's apprehensions were not unfounded. The

36. For more detail on state legislation from 1937 to 1947, see S. Cohen, *State Labor Legislation 1937–1947* (Columbus, Ohio, 1948); C. C. Killingsworth, *State Labor Relations Acts* (Chicago, 1948); *Monthly Labor Review* 63 (1946): 754–59; *Harvard Law Review* 61 (1948): 840–50.

37. Millis and Brown, *From the Wagner Act to Taft-Hartley,* 332.

38. Supporters of strong antiunion legislative measures explained that they were battling "gigantic unions," which were "monopolies of labor." The true purpose of these individuals becomes evident when one considers that the most reactionary laws were passed in the states with the weakest union movements, in states where any "giganticism" or "monopoly of labor" was out of the question (D. Ziskind, "Countermarch in Labor Legislation," in *Labor in Postwar America,* 313–35).

39. According to the provisions of the Smith-Connally Act, it should have remained in force until six months after the day the U.S. government proclaimed the cessation of war activities. The end of war was proclaimed 31 December 1946: therefore, the Smith-Connally Act ceased to have effect on

American labor movement confronted a mass of complicated problems, most of them related to the demilitarization of industry and reconversion of the economy to peacetime operation. American union leaders worried most about postwar levels of employment and wages and about retaining guarantees made to the unions. It was clear that the number of jobs industry could offer would not equal the demand.[40] Curtailing the defense production that had absorbed such a significant part of the work force, on the one hand, and demobilizing large numbers of workers in the army to add to those in need of work, on the other, threatened to increase unemployment drastically. (Out of fear that they would not find jobs, this army of returning workers was prepared to accept working conditions below union standards.)[41] Everything American unions won through strikes during the early postwar years merely preserved their achievements during the war and the prewar years. Nearly 50 percent of all strikes of 1944–1946 arose from the refusal of employers to satisfy demands for increased wages.[42] Unions did not consider such demands "intentionally aggressive acts," as the bourgeois press called them. They simply occurred as a natural response to the planned offensive of employers,[43] for whom the end of the wartime emergency signaled the start of a raucous antiunion campaign. Although the unions won sizable increases in wages as a result of strikes in 1946, the end of government price controls reduced these gains to practically nothing since "real purchasing power fell with every increase in prices."[44] Both large union organizations in the United States, the AFL and CIO, confronted the times with similar demands: an increase in wages without an increase in prices.[45] The difference between them was that the AFL relied more on its own capabilities to achieve the goal[46] while the unions of the CIO counted on sympathetic action by the government. During the reconver-

---

1 July 1947.

40. The preliminary estimate of the number of people who needed work was twelve million. The situation was so serious that Secretary of Labor Lewis B. Schwellenbach was pleased to receive any suggestion for decreasing unemployment—even such ephemeral ones as "the desire of many soldiers to spend some time at home before returning to work" (*34th Annual Report of the Secretary of Labor* [Washington, D.C., 1947], 4–6).

41. Because of the curtailment of wartime production, nearly 20 percent of men and 37 percent of women lost their jobs during the winter of 1945–1946 (ibid., 6–8).

42. According to data given in the *Monthly Labor Review,* 104 million workdays were lost because of strikes in the first year after the war. Disputes over wages and the length of the workday accounted for 77 percent of the strikes and 88 percent of the lost time. *Monthly Labor Review* 63 (1946): 886; 62 (1946): 280, 304, 343; 64 (1947): 983–96; 66 (1948): 483.

43. A month before the end of the war with Japan, in July 1945, the average weekly wage in industry was $45.45, and the average hourly wage was $1.03. In the words of the secretary of labor, these wages "dropped immediately" after the war. In September 1945 the average weekly wage was $40.87, and the average hourly wage was $.99. *45th Annual Report of the Secretary of Labor* (Washington, D.C., 1947), 10.

44. *American Federationist,* February 1947, 13.

45. *CIO News,* 8 December 1947, 1, 3.

46. During the postwar years, AFL leaders repeatedly spoke against government intervention in labor relations; see, for example, *American Federationist,* October 1946, 8; March 1947, 3.

sion from war to peacetime operations, strikes reached a level unprecedented in the history of the United States—in 1946 more than 4,650,000 workers struck.[47]

The persistence of conflict between employers and unions is noteworthy: the number of strikes in 1946 and 1945 was nearly the same—4,700 and 4,750 respectively—but on the average, strikes in 1946 lasted three times longer than strikes in 1945 (in 1946, 113 million work days were lost in strikes, and in 1945, 38 million work days).[48] The strike movement lasted because of a distinctive "psychological" factor. In strikes and negotiations over wages, the loss or acquisition by the union of an extra cent in any single dispute was perceived as a gauge of the unions' weakness or strength. Employers also evaluated their strength or weakness in terms of negotiated successes or concessions.[49] The pitch of battle was so fevered that a number of strikes ended in presidential seizure (in its foresight the government had not hurried to announce the end of wartime conditions and to relinquish its special wartime powers).[50]

The employers' postwar offensive against the rights of American unions took the form of a many-faceted plan involving both an economic attack on the working class and an expanded ideological battle on the proper role of government. It involved a political campaign to overthrow the fifteen-year supremacy of the Democratic party and a legislative battle in the Congress. This offensive by employers was accompanied by constant appeals to public opinion. In the press, radio broadcasts, special publications, and personal appearances, employers depicted the unions as the sole cause of all postwar problems, including inflation, high prices, and irregularities in supplies. In January 1947, when strikes had reached their zenith, the NAM launched a newspaper war. It began with full pages of antiunion material in 73 daily newspapers. In April and May, NAM antiunion pamphlets—composed in slogan form, devoid of any real reasoning, and with frequent mention of the "public interest"—appeared in 287 daily newspapers. Of these, 193 circulated in major industrial centers and were intended for 38 million readers.[51] For ten years, from 1936 to 1946, the Congress coped with more than 200 antilabor proposals to revise New Deal legislation.[52] Of this number, more than 60 bills were directed against striking workers and guarantees to trade unions.

47. Labor Research Association, *Labor Fact Book* (New York, 1947), 152.

48. *34th Annual Report of the Secretary of Labor* (1947), 8.

49. Kerr, "Employer Policies in Industrial Relations 1945 to 1947," 46–47.

50. On strikes during the postwar years, see V. A. Korolkov and A. P. Medvedev, *Workers' and Trade Union Movement in the United States after the Second World War* (Moscow, 1954); V. A. Nikitin, "The Offensive on the Democratic Conquests of the Working Class in Labor Legislation in the United States in 1945–1947," in *The Workers' and National-Liberation Movement in the Countries of America* (Moscow, 1966).

51. The antilabor campaign mounted by employers during 1945–1947 was fought under the battle flag of the "public" interest. In bourgeois propaganda, business was portrayed as the good-willed defender of the "public" against the encroachment of "monopolistic unions." This tactic certainly did not fail: all the reactionary measures of the 79th and 80th Congresses passed as a "mandate of the nation" (E[dward W.] Bakke, "The Public Interest in Labor-Management Relations," in *Unions, Management, and the Public: Readings and Text,* ed. Bakke et al. [New York, 1949], 897–903).

52. Millis and Brown, *From the Wagner Act to Taft-Hartley,* 333.

If the ostentation of all such slogans as "legislative equality," "social interests," and so on is cast aside, the true intent of opponents of the Wagner Act did not change much after 1935, although their demands in the postwar years were extreme. "The Wagner Act created a monopoly of trade unions and should therefore be repealed," J[ohn W.] Scoville categorically declared in 1946.[53] Scoville was a leading economist of the Chrysler Corporation and author of the postwar pamphlet-bible of ordinary employers, *Labor Monopolies or Freedom*? A Republican gubernatorial candidate in Oklahoma, O[lney F.] Flynn, plastered the state with placards from which Republicans rhetorically asked, "Haven't You Had Enough?" The entire Republican party adopted this slogan in the election campaign. In 1946 I[ra] Mosher, president of the NAM, demanded no more and no less than the "establishment of truly free collective bargaining relations" and the elimination of all controls in this area.[54] Of the ten-point "Full Recovery Program" presented to Congress by R[obert R.] Wason, the chairman of the NAM's Council for Reconversion, the first two called for a speedy curtailment of the government's wartime controls and the restoration of free collective bargaining.[55] Although by the end of the war the neo-conservatives already had made themselves well known, their messages sometimes were lost in the outlandish agitation in behalf of traditionalism, which took nearly every conceivable form, from religious sermons to satirical vaudeville songs.

To draw a clear distinction between neo-conservatives and "traditionalists" of the time is a difficult task. It is complicated primarily by the fact that in the postwar years, in contrast to the prewar years, propaganda for noninterference by government contained a certain element of rhetoric, and neo-conservatives did not hesitate to use "traditional" terminology. To publicly renounce the ideals of "rugged individualism" would have been considered un-American. One can cite numerous examples of the eclectic interweaving of the two strands of bourgeois ideology. F[red A.] Hartley, Jr., who believed that "big government is a drain upon the resources of the nation,"[56] talked endlessly about noninterference; nevertheless, his variant of a new labor-relations law stipulated greater government intervention.[57] Analogous discrepancies exist between the statements of R[obert A.] Taft and his legislative proposal. President [Harry S.] Truman charged in his veto message on the Taft-Hartley Act that "the new act appears to be contrary to the national policy of economic freedom. It demands that government become an unwarranted participant at every bargaining table."[58] However, in the same document he contended that the law gave the government insufficient power in "extraordinary circumstances." There is little reason to doubt that in 1945–1947 employers at many levels seriously considered breaking

53. *Labor Monopolies or Freedom?* (New York, 1946), xv.
54. Kerr, "Employer Policies in Industrial Relations 1945 to 1947," 48–49.
55. Ibid., 49.
56. *Our New National Labor Policy* (New York, 1948), 192.
57. For the text of Hartley's proposal, see *The Legislative History of the Labor Management Relations Act . . . 1947* (Washington, 1947–1948), 1:31–38.
58. "The New Labor Law: Special Analytical Report," in ibid., Appendix F, 2.

with all "New Dealer" innovations and returning to the golden era of free (including free from government control) competition. This not-so-complicated political position was based on a solid ideological foundation. In 1944 F[riedrick von] Hayek issued an apology for economic doctrines of a hundred years standing and became a major figure of the postwar decade.[59]

W[illiam W.] Leiserson echoed him, citing entire pages of A[dam] Smith with the assurance that "this sounds exceptionally modern."[60] A number of well-known scholars, union representatives, and employers who rallied around the Twentieth Century Fund in 1945 came out against the future growth of the "omniscient power of the government."[61]

The existence of so much right-wing criticism of the Taft-Hartley Act in the latter 1940s and early 1950s to the effect that even after 1947 the government possessed too much control over industry was evidence that the conflict between adherents and opponents of government expansion involved much more than simple rhetoric.[62] The "traditionalist" movement absorbed a very diverse group—from the reactionary conservative J. W. Scoville to the moderate liberal G[eorge W.] Taylor. Although Taylor emphasized the reactionary methods of intervention dictated by the Taft-Hartley Act in his speeches against government involvement in labor relations, his "ideal" labor-relations law for the times inclined in the direction of laissez-faire. For Taylor this was the only positive form of protest against the Taft-Hartley Act.[63]

With the "virus of traditionalism" engulfing America, the unmistakable victory of Republicans in the congressional election of 1946 was considered by the conservative camp a "popular mandate," as Senator Taft put it, "to cast out a great many chapters of the New Deal, if not the whole book."[64] A comparison of elements of political realism in the positions of "traditionalists" and neo-conservatives shows those in the neo-conservative position to be preferable, for they stood more solidly on

59. "Both competition and central direction become poor and inefficient tools if they are incomplete; they are alternative principles used to solve the same problem, and a mixture of the two means that neither will really work and that the result will be worse than if either system had been consistently relied upon" (*The Road to Serfdom* [Chicago, 1944], 42).

60. "The Rise of Government in Industrial Relations," in *Unions, Management, and the Public*, 866.

61. S[amuel T.] Williamson and H[erbert] Harris, *Trends in Collective Bargaining* (New York, 1945).

62. Even in 1949, when traditional agitation was incomparably weak compared to 1945–1947, the reactionary *Labor Law Journal* published an article comparing the battle of the employers against government intervention in labor-relations regulation with the battle of Parliament against King Charles in the time of Cromwell. The *Journal* did not hesitate to extend the historical analysis, remembering that Parliament beheaded the king. *Labor Law Journal* 1 (1949): 76.

63. Taylor's ideal of government regulation of labor relations was not quite believable. He considered the best form of regulation to be self-regulation that did not require governmental control. Collective bargaining should result in the "good-willed repudiation" by all parties of strikes, lockouts, etc. (the principles of "voluntarism"). *Government Regulation of Industrial Relations* (New York, 1948), 4–8.

64. W[illiam] S. White, *The Taft Story* (New York, 1954), 57.

the socioeconomic foundation of postwar realities. Their ideas more fully satisfied the ruling class, while the "traditionalist" movement, despite its widespread appeal, depended mainly on memories and illusions of the 1920s.

The day the Taft-Hartley Act was passed—23 June 1947—marked an end to the ideological quarrel and established a landmark in the twelve-year struggle to revise New Deal labor legislation. The revision had occurred. The new law was a triumph of neo-conservative ideas. At its base lay the principle of direct government regulation of labor relations. One should have expected nothing else at the time state-monopoly capitalism became a reality in the United States.

In the Taft-Hartley Act[65] the principle of government responsibility for preserving peace between employers and unions was hyperbolized to such a degree that government functioned as a chancellor in charge of labor affairs. The desire to "incorporate" the unions—that is, to destroy their superficial independence, turn them into a department of the government, and make them responsible for the slightest violation of government orders—was reflected in nearly every phrase of the law. The creators of the new act addressed this ambition in two ways: first, all union activity, from participation in collective bargaining to organization of union pension funds, would conform to a "code of behavior" written by the creators themselves; and second, all relations between employers and unions would pass into the hands of the government.

In discussing the reactionary "code of behavior" in the Taft-Hartley Act, it is necessary to emphasize the "list of unfair labor practices" that did not exist under the Wagner Act. The "unfair" category included the following forms of union activity: refusing to bargain collectively, conducting a secondary boycott, attempting to force employers to negotiate with organizations not recognized by the NLRB, participating in jurisdictional strikes, striking in violation of a contract, levying excessively high initiation fees, coercing employers to pay for services never performed (the principle of "featherbedding"), attempting to limit the "free speech" of employers, refusing to sign certificates of nonmembership in the Communist party, and a number of other activities. The "code of behavior" forbade "closed shop" contracts and prescribed the terms of a "union shop." The code forbade strikes by government employees. Permissible strikes had to be preceded by a number of conditions. For example, the law required unions to give notice of their intent to strike and required them to accept unchanged labor conditions during a "cooling-off period." Failure to observe these conditions deprived the unions of legal protection. Analyses of the law by well-known union lawyers showed that the statute's obfuscated legal language admitted still more reactionary practices.[66]

The authors of the Taft-Hartley Act wanted direct control of labor organizations. The NLRB would not have to conduct votes or investigations of "unfair labor practices," nor would it have to determine whether this or that union would be the repre-

65. For the text of the Taft-Hartley Act, see *The Legislative History of the Labor Management Relations Act . . .* , 1:1–30.

66. *American Federationist,* August 1947, 4–5.

sentative in collective bargaining if, before the NLRB took other measures, each union filed a proper report with the secretary of labor. The union was required in this report to disclose the name of the organization and the place of its activity; the names, position, and wages of the three top leaders; the wage scale for union functionaries who received more than five thousand dollars a year; the manner by which the union's leaders received their positions—election, appointment, or other means; the range of initiation fees and membership dues; the organizational structure of the union; and the rules and by-laws that regulated its internal operations. Unions were obligated to file an annual financial report and affirm their compliance with all the other obligations placed on them by the many subpoints of the law. Even a cursory analysis of the Taft-Hartley Act proves that after 1947 government intervention in labor relations became all-embracing in form and reactionary in content. The law stipulated how collective bargaining should occur, what form a rejection of old collective agreements should take, who to inform and how regarding the desire to negotiate a new collective agreement, and what demands the unions should address once collective bargaining had begun.

As head of state and principal in the entire apparatus for regulating labor relations, the president received extraordinary powers, including the use of court orders against unions in disputes that threatened the "national interest." It was up to the president to determine in each instance whether the national interest was involved.

The government limited the political activity of unions and took upon itself the responsibility for ideological "purity" in the ranks. Each year it required union leaders to submit a signed statement that they were not members of the Communist party.

The government created a new administrative arm to resolve troublesome issues between employers and unions. The Federal Mediation and Reconciliation Service (which functioned much like the National Defense Mediation Board) became an independent agency with authority to act for the "preservation of peace in industry" at the request of a participant or on its own initiative. The law led to changes in state legislation, most of it for the purpose of achieving greater conformity with federal labor policy.

The Taft-Hartley Act reflected the intention of binding the courts more tightly to government policy on regulation of labor relations. Centripetal features of the Taft-Hartley Act increased the significance of government machinery for regulating labor and "harnessed" that machinery to a united and centralized end.

All this permits one to regard the Taft-Hartley Act, which "inflicted on the American workers' movement the most intense blow of the entire legislative history of this country,"[67] as the beginning of a new era in labor legislation in the United States. Liberal methods of regulating labor relations had been exchanged for reactionary principles of government regulation.

67. *Political Affairs* 8 (1947): 702.

David Brody

Comment on "On the National Labor Relations Board in the United States in the 1930s," by A. A. Popov, and "From the Wagner Act to the Taft-Hartley Act: A Turn to Reaction in Labor Legislation in the United States, 1935–1947," by V. I. Borisiuk

The New Deal poses very special problems for the Soviet historian. If, as every Marxist-Leninist knows, economic crisis is inherent in the contradictions of capitalist production, ever deepening and leading inevitably to systemic collapse, how are Soviet scholars to account for the recovery of monopoly capitalism from the Great Depression? In theoretical terms, an answer was quickly forthcoming and, by the early 1950s, incorporated into Soviet doctrine. The 1930s signaled, as A. A. Popov says in his essay, "the rapid transition from monopolistic capitalism to state-monopolistic capitalism."[1] For it was, of course, the bourgeois state that revealed itself as the one agency capable of rising to the crisis of the Great Depression. Popov and his colleague V. I. Borisiuk explicitly affirm the correctness of state-monopoly capitalism as a theoretical position. Their task, as Soviet historians, is to give it concrete reality, to reveal the actual historical processes by which, on the central issue of working-class insurgency, the New Deal fashioned an effective response. Hence Popov's opening remark about the "special importance" of studying the "mechanism" of state-regulated labor relations: "Investigation of this mechanism with its complicated hierarchy of institutions, dry formulations of laws, and frequently hidden functions is not some narrow, specialized undertaking—it is necessary to understanding the nature of modern capitalism."

Naturally, such an inquiry provokes the interest of a bourgeois historian of liberal persuasion like myself. It would perhaps seem ungenerous to satisfy one's curiosity without giving something in return. As it happens, there is some basis for reciprocation. Popov's and Borisiuk's essays rely almost entirely on government documents and contemporary commentary. It would be useful, certainly, to square their analyses up against American scholarship on New Deal labor policy. What adds spice to the comparison is a shift in American historiography roughly contemporaneous with the appearance of these Soviet essays in 1971.

At that time, it would probably be fair to say, a wall of incomprehension stood between such Marxist-Leninist authors and the prevailing liberal school of American scholarship. What could liberals who conceived of the New Deal in terms of the "broker state" have to say to Soviets who saw it as a manifestation of state-monopoly capitalism? But the dominant liberal school then came under increasing challenge

1. For a brief account of state-monopoly capitalism in Soviet thought, see the entry in Tom Bottomore, ed., *A Dictionary of Marxist Thought* (Cambridge, Mass., 1983), 468–69.

from American historians on the Left who, while they would scarcely have placed themselves in the Marxist-Leninist camp, did in fact define the central problem of the New Deal very much as had Popov and Borisiuk—that is to say, they assumed that what needed above all to be explained was the resiliency of the standing order in the face of deep crisis. This radical scholarship has been characterized by a great deal of diversity; certainly no consensus has emerged among corporate-liberal exponents, New Left celebrants of rank-and-file militancy, critical legal studies scholars, and other less classifiable critics of the New Deal. What is clear, however, is that the liberal scholarship that uniformly confronted Soviet historians twenty years ago has been seriously challenged—although by no means routed—and in ways conducive to a greater degree of dialogue between hitherto wholly alien worlds of scholarship. In what follows, I propose to explore how state-monopoly capitalism as official Soviet doctrine translates into a specific historical analysis of New Deal labor policy, with a counterpoint of commentary drawn selectively from the full range of current American scholarship on the subject.

Neither Popov nor Borisiuk has much to say about the central event in any capitalist crisis—the rising of the working class. Because their essays begin with the passage of the Wagner Act, they offer no estimate of the scope or nature of the class forces that brought the labor-reform program into being. Popov takes up the story with the struggle to put the law into effect between 1935 and 1937. The force that defeated business resistance, says Popov, "was the American working class, which had won important victories in the mid-1930s." But these victories are put in terms of union growth and battles for recognition entirely consonant with, for example, Irving Bernstein's treatment in *The Turbulent Years: A History of the American Worker, 1933–1941* (Boston, 1970). Likewise, Borisiuk sees the 1945–1946 strike wave in very much the same terms of postwar collective-bargaining reaction as does Joel Seidman in *American Labor from Defense to Reconversion* (Chicago, 1953). Borisiuk does make passing reference to "the unsubsiding class war fought by American workers," but in concrete terms this does not, for either Soviet scholar, amount to much beyond what might be found in the liberal American writings of their day.

American scholarship has since then explored much more fully the character of working-class activity during the 1930s. New Left scholars have stressed its radical potential, with a particular twist in the direction of rank-and-file control of the union and shop floor. Their critics have noted the limited participation in the sit-down strikes, the conservatism of immigrant workers, the shallow and sectional character of the shop-floor movements.[2] One is hard put to know precisely how our Soviet scholars might have negotiated their way through this thicket of disputed history. While they would have found much to support their sense of revolutionary potential, the syndicalist cast which American radical historians have given to the industrial struggles of the 1930s would have been hard to square with Marxist-Leninist

2. For an assessment of the literature on this issue, see my "The CIO After 50 Years: A Historical Reckoning," *Dissent* (Fall 1985): 457–72.

advocacy of the revolutionary vanguard. The Soviet scholars would certainly have had to step gingerly past those historians critical of the Communist role at the time for being, in Martin Glaberman's words, bureaucratic, tending "to substitute the power of officials and institutions for the direct power of the rank and file," and stemming from the Marxist-Leninist identification of "the motive power of historical development as being the Party rather than the class."[3] On the relationship of the Communist party to the working class, of course, Popov and Borisiuk themselves are silent.

The specifics of working-class unrest are, in any case, less consequential to them than the response it elicited from the state. Neither Soviet scholar suggests that labor reform occurred at the behest of American capital. On the contrary, writes Popov, it "encountered the most fierce opposition of big business . . . . Major corporations did not want labor organizations or even a capitalistic government to limit their control in any way." On this key point, Soviet and current American scholarship are in agreement. The argument of the corporate-liberal school has not been sustained by empirical research: big business may have been progressive on other issues, but not on one deemed, as the Wagner Act was, to threaten its managerial prerogatives.[4] The bourgeois state is thus conceded to be, as western neo-Marxist theorists would soon put it, "relatively autonomous."[5]

That, in turn, raises the problem of agency: who are the people instrumental in bringing about New Deal reform? On this point, Borisiuk is explicit. New Deal labor policy is the achievement of the "neo-liberals"—"people who believed government should participate actively in regulating the country's economy"—finally triumphant against the conservatives in an ideological war that went back to the late nineteenth century. There is much in American scholarship to amplify Borisiuk's treatment of the agents of reform. Liberal historians, of course, are predisposed to this line of inquiry by their conception of the New Deal as a stage of American progressivism. A case in point would be J. Joseph Huthmacher's treatment of labor policy as part of the reform agenda of the principal champion of New Deal labor policy in *Senator Robert F. Wagner and the Rise of Urban Liberalism* (New York, 1971). For their part, radical critics of the New Deal have been equally fascinated by the architects of public intervention into the hitherto free sphere of American labor relations. These "indus-

3. "Vanguard to Rearguard," in *Political Power and Social Theory: A Research Annual 4* (Greenwich, Conn., 1984), 44, 59.

4. The classic statement of the corporate-liberal position is Ronald Radosh, "The Corporate Ideology of American Labor from Gompers to Hillman," in James Weinstein and David W. Eakins, eds., *For a New America: Essays . . . from "Studies on the Left"* (New York, 1970), 125–52. The fullest critique is Stanley Vittoz, "The Economic Foundations of Industrial Politics in the United States and the Emerging Structural Theory of the State in Capitalist Society: The Case of New Deal Labor Policy," *Amerikastudien* 27 (1982): 365–412.

5. A key evaluation that tests theory against New Deal history is Theda Skocpol, "Political Response to Capitalist Crisis: Neo-Marxist Theories of the State and the Case of the New Deal," *Politics and Society* 10 (1980): 155–201. See also, for a more general, historically grounded analysis, Fred Block, "The Ruling Class Does Not Rule: Notes on the Marxist Theory of the State," *Socialist Revolution* (May-June 1977): 6–28.

trial pluralists" are, for example, a central concern of Christopher L. Tomlins in his *The State and the Unions: Labor Relations, Law, and the Organized Labor Movement in America* (New York, 1985).

Can the capitalist state, then, act against the interests of capital? No, says Popov. "Government has to make concessions to the labor movement, but primarily it aims to control the unions in defense of the capitalistic system." Under the New Deal, the state shifted "from policies of repression . . . to policies that helped establish and support unions of a reformist character" and sought thereby the "integration" of the American working class. Popov is not especially successful at elaborating this argument. His analysis of the law is too cursory, his treatment of the NLRB somewhat sidetracked by his desire to stress its conciliatory approach to business. But the thrust of his argument in fact prefigures the current emphasis in American radical scholarship on the co-optive character of New Deal labor policy. It was designed, writes Christopher Tomlins, to transform militantly independent trade unions into "quasi-public instrumentalities whose function was to bargain within the parameters of a model of labor relations defined by a state agency . . . ."[6] The impact on rank-and-file control has been especially stressed, as in the critical legal scholar Karl Klare's analysis of the evolution—his own word is "deradicalization"—of the Wagner Act through the process of conservative legal interpretation.[7] The mastery of a militant rank-and-file by the union bureaucracy is similarly the focus of Nelson Lichtenstein's study of the CIO during World War II.[8] So that, should a Soviet scholar pick up where Popov's essay leaves off, he or she would find ample support in recent American scholarship.

If business resistance seems essentially misguided to Popov, quite the opposite is the case with Borisiuk. We have come to a quite remarkable parting of the ways between the two Soviet scholars. "The necessity of observing requirements . . . did effectively restrict employers," Borisiuk writes. They pressed for the repeal of the Wagner Act because its provisions "violated their immediate interests. They resented the fact that the government openly defended workers' rights to organize and bargain collectively." And they especially resented the NLRB, for its decisions "showed disregard for the truly inexhaustible variety of methods for restricting labor that had come from more than one hundred years of experience." Their defeat on labor policy was very real, and it reflected the larger defeat of American conservativism. Borisiuk clearly sees the New Deal in terms of genuine political struggle, in which a neo-

6. Tomlins, *The State and the Unions,* 147.

7. Karl E. Klare, "Judicial Deradicalization of the Wagner Act and the Origins of Modern Legal Consciousness, 1937–1941," *Minnesota Law Review* 62 (March 1978): 265–339. For important critiques, see Matthew W. Finkin, "Revisionism in Labor Law," *Maryland Law Review* 43 (1984): 23–92; and, from a less legalist perspective, Howell Harris, "The Snares of Liberalism? Politicians, Bureaucrats, and the Shaping of Federal Labour Relations Policy in the U.S., ca. 1915–1947," in *Shop Floor Bargaining and the State,* ed. Steven Tolliday and Jonathan Zeitlin (Cambridge, Eng., 1985), 148–91.

8. *Labor's War at Home: The CIO in World War II* (New York, 1982).

liberal victory "resulted from the general decline of business influence during the Depression, the unsubsiding class war fought by American workers, and the powerful antimonopolistic sentiment across the spectrum of American society." Nor was this victory necessarily transient. At the end of the 1930s, there remained "the question of whether heightened government involvement . . . represented anything more than a whim of neo-liberals." Borisiuk's remark, oddly phrased as it seems, in fact reflects the critical ideological juncture he has come to. If neo-liberalism as he defines it should prevail, then state intervention can only be a "whim" and not a new stage of capitalist development. Only through alignment with the interests of capital can state intervention be said to signal state-monopoly capitalism.

The bulk of Borisiuk's essay is devoted to an account of the unfolding of that process. World War II is the decisive moment for him. In the wartime reaction, the conservatives regained the political initiative that they had lost in the Great Depression. More important, out of the war experience there emerged an alternative to their discredited individualism. The emergency controls imposed on labor revealed to them the double edge of state intervention: it could be used against organized labor as well as in its favor. A new conservative formation appeared—neo-conservatism—that "wholeheartedly believed in the necessity of government intervention—but by this they meant intervention only against union activity." Under the provisions of the Taft-Hartley Act (1947), the apotheosis of neoconservatism, "government functioned as a chancellor in charge of labor affairs. The desire to 'incorporate' the unions—that is, to destroy their superficial independence, turn them into a department of the government, and make them responsible for the slightest violation of government orders—was reflected in nearly every phrase of the law." After 1947, concludes Borisiuk, "government intervention in labor relations became all-embracing in form and reactionary in content."

For the first time in this reading of Soviet essays, one is at a loss to find any common ground with American scholarship. Not even his own colleague Popov accepts Borisiuk's characterization of the 1947 amendments to the Wagner Act. Popov speaks of the NLRB as "somewhat modified by the Taft-Hartley Act" and elsewhere of the fact that, while the "liberal spirit" of the New Deal gave way to "a conservative and even reactionary coloring, the principles of government regulation and control have remained unchanged." No authority that I know of would characterize Taft-Hartley in Borisiuk's terms as serving to turn the labor movement "into a department of the government." The added intrusiveness of government—by the reporting requirements and non-Communist affidavit, by the regulation of union pension funds and political contributions, and by the limitations on strikes deemed to be national emergencies—pale by comparison to the changes designed to modify or limit labor's rights under the law to organize and bargaining collectively. Taft-Hartley was directed not at labor-state relations, but at labor-management relations. The impact on the trade unions was serious—although, at least in the short run, less so than they had at first feared—but in the collective-bargaining terms already well established under New Deal labor policy.

The prevailing radical view, indeed, is to minimize Taft-Hartley in favor of the continuities of a system of industrial pluralism that already served effectively, in Katherine Stone's words, "as vehicle for the manipulation of employee discontent and for the legitimation of existing inequalities of power in the workplace." She argues, in a major critical legal statement on American labor law, that the key development of the postwar period was the insulation of the collective-bargaining relationship from public scrutiny so that its inherent inequities would not be called into question.[9] The rival liberal interpretation advanced in a detailed study by James A. Gross sees the Wagner Act as a continuing source of conflict, but, unlike Borisiuk, locates the battle at the administrative level and dates the conservative triumph well before Taft-Hartley. The emasculated NLRB, concludes Gross, was by the early 1940s transformed "from an expert administrative agency which played the major role in formulation of labor policy into a conservative, insecure, politically sensitive agency preoccupied with its own survival and reduced to deciding essentially marginal issues using legal tools of analysis exclusively."[10]

The book that meets Borisiuk's neo-conservative interpretation on its own grounds is Howell Harris's *The Right to Manage: Industrial Relations Policies of American Business in the 1940s* (Madison, 1982). There is little in Harris's book to sustain Borisiuk's notions about the impact of war experience on conservative thinking. It is true that, insofar as the disciplining of labor under the government's war powers did occur, this was welcomed by businessmen. But, on balance, they felt themselves more victims than beneficiaries of the wartime control of labor relations, which enforced union-security provisions and stable contractual relationships they bitterly opposed. The policies of the National War Labor Board, writes Harris, "made businessmen increasingly and understandably anxious about the strengthening of labor power and the entrenchment of labor unions." Nor, in a detailed survey of what businessmen thought, does he discover Borisiuk's strain of neo-conservatism. They defined their labor problems above all in terms of the erosion of their managerial authority. Insofar as they sought a solution from the state, it was, as one businessman put it, by "the provision of more equitable rules of the game." And this was not the primary thing in any case. Harris quotes from an NAM report on "lukewarm" business attitudes toward the recently passed Taft-Hartley Act that probably best sums up his own assessment: ". . . the status of their relationships with their employees did not depend upon legislation, and they were not expecting any set of laws to work new miracles in their labor relations."[11] Harris entitles his two key chapters "Recovery of the Initiative." Employers saw this as primarily their own

9. "The Post-War Paradigm in American Labor Law," *Yale Law Journal* 90 (June 1981): 1509–80 (the quotation appears on 1517).
10. *The Reshaping of the National Labor Relations Board: National Labor Policy in Transition, 1937–1947* (Albany, N.Y., 1981), 267. See also his previous volume, equally authoritative on the first phase of the NLRB history: *The Making of the National Labor Relations Board . . . 1933–1937* (Albany, N.Y., 1974).
11. *The Right to Manage*, 56, 126.

task, not that of the state. Neo-conservatism as Borisiuk defines it has little meaning within the industrial battlefield of postwar America.

What bears emphasis, however, is the boldness of Professor Borisiuk's attack. It is a fascinating instance of the interplay between Marxist-Leninist theory and empirical historical practice. Having fallen into a liberalist treatment of New Deal labor policy, Borisiuk must employ heroic measures to pull his analysis back into line—that is to say, he must posit a neo-conservative reaction to a neo-liberal advance. One does not suppose that the tension between Soviet doctrine and historical practice has lessened in the years since Popov and Borisiuk published their essays on New Deal labor policy. But scholarship on the subject has certainly advanced. And the recent breakdown of the postwar labor-management accord has dramatically altered the context for interpreting the labor history of the past half-century. It would be a matter of great interest to know what Soviet historians today would have to say about New Deal labor policy.

Response by A. A. Popov and V. I. Borisiuk

We are sincerely grateful to Professor B. Brody for the various comments and observations he has addressed to us. A study of a problem from the perspective of different points of view, its analysis from different methodological positions, makes it possible to increase one's understanding of it and to subject many of its aspects to comprehensive analysis. Therein, in our opinion, lies the rationale for such exchanges of views between Soviet and American historians on problems of U.S. history and for maintaining and further developing such contacts.

We found Professor Brody's method of comparing the views and conclusions of Soviet historians with the conceptions, methodological principles, and observations of U.S. scholars and, in particular, of historians of the liberal, neo-Marxist, and radical tendencies most useful and productive for our understanding of the position adopted by the reviewer and the range of subjects examined in our articles. The views of these authors on the meaning of the New Deal, the causes that brought it about, the role of the administration, business, and labor unions in the formulation of Roosevelt's legislative proposals, enable us to cast a critical eye on our own articles and the conclusions they contain. It must be stressed that these two studies were written quite a long time ago. Had we undertaken an analysis of the problems of the New Deal today, many of the sections in the article might have looked different: there might have been a less categorical ring to them; they might have contained more evidence and a greater number of facts, and facts of different kinds might have been adduced; references to a wider range of American authors might have been made. It is possible that today our approach to these problems would have borne greater resemblance to the research principles of the "new political history" in American historiography, would have been more interdisciplinary in character and have employed the methods of sociology, social psychology, and other disciplines. But we are convinced that in everything that relates to the appraisal of the causes and content of the New Deal and its place in American history, to the significance of the struggle of the working class during that period, and to the nature of the postwar policy of the U.S. administration, our views and approach would have remained the same.

In conclusion, we should like to express our hope for further collaboration between Soviet and American historians in the study of a wide range of problems in U.S. history.

V. L. Malkov

5 THE CRISIS OF GOMPERSISM AND THE FOUNDATION OF THE CIO: IDEOLOGICAL AND POLITICAL ASPECTS

Bourgeois historiography of the labor movement in the United States has long characterized the events of the 1930s that gave birth to the Congress of Industrial Organizations (CIO) as a phenomenon that could never be repeated, one that arose from a unique congruence of circumstances. Today these events are only of academic interest. Twenty- or twenty-five-year-old facts are considered only peripherally relevant to present-day realities. In the inflexible and detached manner of the chronicler, bourgeois authors impose on their readers the idea that the provocation of the American proletariat to class activism—quite normal during the world crisis and Depression of the thirties—is as unrepeatable as the "episode" in which hundreds of thousands of Americans cast votes for the socialist E[ugene V.] Debs in the 1912 presidential election. The split in the American Federation of Labor (AFL) has been explained as a happenstance, and the progressive characteristics of the CIO are considered a fad that passed without leaving a mark.

However, the renewed outbreak of social conflict in the United States during the 1960s and early 1970s, in addition to the quantitative and qualitative growth of the labor movement that resulted from the spread of economic conflict, pointed to strong historical parallels in rank-and-file activism and in dissent over questions of domestic and foreign policy. Bourgeois authors, therefore, have been pressured to take a fresh look at the history of the New Deal—which now seems less distant.

It is now accepted that many recent developments in the labor movement closely resemble conditions that existed during the New Deal, despite the fact that until recently the latter were perceived by bourgeois historians as ancient and irrelevant to the present. The Communist Party of the United States has described the common features of the two eras quite poignantly:

In many ways the situation today is comparable to the situation in the mid–30s. Then, too, there was a mighty rank-and-file upsurge and a mass unemployed movement in which the Communists and the Left played a decisive role. Then, too, there was a crisis of class-collaborationist labor leadership which had proved its bankruptcy. It was in such circumstances that a number of labor leaders led by John L. Lewis stepped forward to form the CIO and make a break with the discredited policies of the old craft union leadership. A new chapter was opened in American labor history. Its achievements are a matter of history, although it never realized its full potential for reasons which have been thoroughly analyzed in the writings of William Z. Foster, Gus Hall, and others.[1]

1. J. West, "Crisis of Collaborationist Labor Leadership," *Political Affairs* (November 1970): 39, 40. This article by V. L. Malkov was first published in *American Annual, 1971* (Moscow, 1971), 44–88. This English translation is by Brenda Kay Weddle.

It is obvious that recent events in the American labor movement cannot be understood outside the context of the historical battle against collaboration policies and quests for favors that reformist leaders from [Samuel] Gompers to [George] Meany have imposed on the union movement. This necessarily brings the analyst back to the question of class and the ideological content of the tradition that surged so strongly in the past.

The American Federation of Labor was the result of the merger of three trade unions that were linked to the bourgeoisie and its parties ideologically, politically, and, to a certain degree, materially. During the years of economic crisis (1929–1933), the AFL clearly revealed not only its reactionary character, but also all the signs of degradation. There were indications of the crisis to come. Political ideas improved in quality and became more intense; slogans containing those ideas attracted millions of unorganized workers into unions; and important unions grew up in areas of basic industry where previously there were practically none at all. This proved sufficient (to use the words of F[riedrich] Engels) to propel the working-class movement into the forefront of contemporary politics.[2]

The reconstruction of the union movement in the United States began in 1932 and 1933. It resembled the renewal of the English working-class movement at the end of the 1890s that opened the era of "new unionism" and saw the founding of a labor party. In both cases, the real need to improve material conditions and the shattering of archaic labor laws were the immediate causes of activity among the masses. And similarly, just as their English counterparts had difficulties in seeing beyond the obvious, American researchers have not discerned the existential changes necessary to sustain a union movement, changes that lead toward high levels of conscious class politics.[3] By the same token, the majority of observers did not begin to understand the organizational consolidation and restructuring of the working-class movement in the United States as the core of contemporary events, directions, or perspectives. At the end of 1933 the journal *Political Quarterly* wrote: "There seems to be at least a chance [in the area of labor—V. M.] of something resembling the 1890 movement in England. But nobody would dare to prophesy, for nobody now could guess what the outcome of the New Deal will be."[4]

Today, the course of events is well known. But though the events have been described in many places, the meaning of the massive struggle to unionize remains unclear. This issue was addressed by W[illiam Z.] Foster in one of his last articles, one addressed specifically to Soviet readers.[5] The meaning is not to be found on the

---

2. See Marx and Engels, *Collected Works*, 19:127.

3. See V. I. Lenin, *Complete Collected Works*, 17:237.

4. H. A. Marquand, "American Trade Unionism and the Roosevelt Regime," *Political Quarterly* (October-December 1933): 502.

5. "The Struggle for the Creation of Industrial Trade Unions in the United States," *Contemporary and Modern History* 4 (1960): 3–10.

surface, and despite the abundance of literature on the history of the "great schism" in the American union movement, the picture is far from complete.[6]

One should keep in mind that bourgeois historiography in the United States perpetuates an elaborate and reactionary idea, the very heart and substance of which is hostile to Marxist understanding of the dynamics of social progress. This is despite the fact that Marxists possess a substantial arsenal. In their compassionless descriptions of the thirties, bourgeois researchers invariably include the working class, but they do so in such a way that, to use Engels's words, "the working class appears as a passive mass, unable to help itself and not even making any attempts to strive toward its aims. All attempts to pull the working class out of its dulling destitution originate from the outside or above."[7] Credit for "educating their feelings" and raising the material, social, and civil status of industrial workers has been reserved exclusively for Roosevelt and other bourgeois reformers. Were it not for them, supposedly, the labor movement would have remained dormant. Supposedly the new order forced labor to make a historical move.[8] Bourgeois historians perceive the crux of the problem in the labor movement to be the existence of two incompatible ideas about organizational structure. The dilemma centered on differences between craft and industrial unions. According to the various interpreters, all contradictions and conflicts converged on these differences, and the differences defined not only the mood of the times, but also its hidden agenda. No one in bourgeois science has disputed this postulate, even though it has never seemed very well founded.[9]

These two characteristics of bourgeois historiography are related and complementary. The idea that the New Deal was full with messianic mission has been used to dispel doubts about the origin of the split in the labor union movement of the thirties and the resulting formation of the CIO. If the edicts of a friendly government removed the main obstacles in the way of labor's emancipation and political influence, what occasioned the fights among the two factions of the union movement other than minor differences and misunderstandings among individuals? Discord could then have been occasioned only by petty differences over the constitutional and jurisdictional structure of unionism. The fact that there were no substantive grounds for a clash made it possible to explain the conflict, explicitly or implicitly, as the manifestation of personal antipathies and the egotistic designs of some people in the highest ranks to succeed at the expense of others.[10]

6. The well-known American historian D[avid] Brody wrote in his recently published work that the stormy rise of trade unionism became the main factor of United States political life in the 1930s. "Yet," he continues, "we lack a precise understanding of how this labor achievement came about. Recent labor history has still to be examined" (*The Butcher Workmen: A Study of Unionization* [Cambridge, Mass., 1964], ix).

7. Marx and Engels, *Collected Works*, 37:35–36.

8. P[hilip A.] Taft, *The A. F. of L. from the Death of Gompers to the Merger* (New York, 1959), 45, 46.

9. W[alter] Galenson, *Rival Unionism in the United States* (New York, 1940), 18.

10. J[ames O.] Morris, *Conflict within the AFL: A Study of Craft versus Industrial Unionism, 1901–1938* (Ithaca, N.Y., 1958), 262; J[oel I.] Seidman, "Efforts Toward Merger; 1935–1955,"

The relationship between the reforms of the New Deal and the labor movement of the thirties has been mentioned above with a comment about which retains primacy and which has come to be secondary and what gave unions such freedom of action.[11] It need only be added that the people from below supplied the initiative. They experienced all the hardships of the economic crisis. They tasted the bitter fruit of disorganization in the labor movement, and they were demoralized by half-witted fights between factions that sprang up among the followers of [Samuel] Gompers. During the years 1930 to 1933 it was the movement of the unemployed workers that did most to educate American laborers.

The claim that domestic factors were much stronger than foreign factors does not explain the union movement. Even so, this claim is representative of the mediocrity of the commonly held views. Quite a few bourgeois authors are inclined to attribute little importance to Roosevelt's personal role. Instead, they emphasize a "solid core of indisputable facts," by which they usually mean changes in modern industry and the structure of the working class at the beginning of the twentieth century. All considerations about the effects of the past on the American labor movement during the 1930s is reduced to a dull conclusion based solely on the "material" evidence. According to such historians, technological changes and the consolidation of industry are the main factors that divided craftsmen and caused the schism in the AFL.

However, deeper reflection makes clear that these facts by themselves do not raise all the relevant questions. The questions remain: why did those "indisputable facts," which were obvious to everyone, begin to be important only at a precise time? Why did such polemics, dispute, and dissension arise from a clear situation? Why did these developments take on the character of a historic global movement precisely when they did? These questions deserve the closest attention because they bear on economic, social, and political developments in the United States.

Soviet literature has focused on the fact that these problems, which existed before the 1930s, were not caused by the rigid separation of craft and industrial unions.[12] To argue that they were is to oversimplify the picture. Partisans of this explanation completely ignore ideological differences inside the union movement. Still, with all that said, one should not minimize the importance of conditions as they were, of changes in the economic structure, of technological innovation, of the consolidation of firms, and so forth. Indisputably, all of these created the conditions needed by the industrial union movement; all these developments made the union movement an inescapable feature of the times and an important agent of social progress. Karl Marx has written in *Capital* that contemporary industry "incessantly causes upheavals in

Industrial and Labor Relations Review 9 (April 1956): 358; S[elig] Perlman, "Labor and the New Deal in Historical Perspective," in *Labor and the New Deal,* eds. M[ilton] Derber and E[dwin] Young (Madison, Wis., 1957), 361–73.

11. See *Questions of History,* 1965, no. 9, 88–101; see also V. L. Malkov and D. G. Nadzhakov, *America at the Crossroads: Essays on the Socio-Political History of the New Deal in the United States* (Moscow, 1967).

12. *Essays on Modern and Contemporary History of the United States* (Moscow, 1960), 2:598.

the technical basis of the production process and at the same time in the function of the workers and in societal combinations in the work process."[13] Unions must adapt to these changes. However, in capitalism the process breaks down in clashes between contending forces in the class struggle; inevitably there are ideological contradictions among these forces—often they are irreconcilable.

Thus, by taking into account changes in the "technical understructure of production" when analyzing the union movement of the 1930s, one should see the underlying ideological cause of the conflict. Bourgeois historiography is silent on the last point. That is because conscientious research would uncover the fallacy of the traditional wisdom that American workers were boundlessly pragmatic and lacked spirit.

Until the 1930s, mass production industries were dominated by the open shop system. This situation was changed by the spontaneous formation of local unions, a phenomenon that released energy among lower-level workers. The new unions had an orientation to national problems that differed from the approach leaders of the Gompers school had imposed for years. AFL president W[illiam] Green was forced to admit that there was a "new spirit" in the work place, one that attracted millions of people to the banner of organized labor. "The recent stirrings of unorganized labor reported from all sections of the country suggest that something like a 'labor psychology' may take the place of the old beliefs," wrote the *Political Quarterly* in 1933.[14] At the very least, it is known that the leaders of the AFL went along with this swelling mass emotion of social protest and with labor's demand for social change.

The old leaders stated that they always had been and always would be on the side of the "clashing, fighting and active" unions. Green even invoked the heroic past of the United Mine Workers to show that he identified with those who self-sacrificingly stood up for the "exploited" (as if to say, "I came from such an organization myself").[15] His pretty words in behalf of solidarity cannot be explained except as a liar's attempt to save face.

The rank-and-file movement continued to develop strength. Although they retained the ability to assess the situation accurately, the leaders of the AFL began to lose real control over the masses. A crisis began to ripen. That was not solely because the executive council of the AFL declined to accept a passive role; nor was it solely because the rank and file, in their effort to establish industrial unions, often transgressed in spheres long dominated by the old craft unions. The pretensions and disputes over jurisdictional boundaries, by themselves, were hardly sufficient to confound the leadership of the industrial and craft unions. They had learned to coexist under the same roof; and this was not the first year they had "clarified their mutual relations." However, intervention from below—whether in the form of polemics or in the form of action—did constitute an unusual situation. The new unionists

13. Marx and Engels, *Collected Works*, 23:498.

14. Marquand, "American Trade Unionism," 502.

15. See Green's appearance at the eighteenth biannual convention of the International Hatters Union (October 1933). *Cloth Hat, Cap and Millinery Workers International Union Proceedings*, 16–23 October 1933, 93.

rejected the idea of separated, isolated trade unions from the very beginning. That was not all, however, that distinguished them from the old unionists. Many observers noted their unusually rebellious activities and their adoption of higher ideals than were embodied in the wisdom of Gompers. The ideological dogmas and canonical rules that had pervaded the old AFL unions could not flourish in this environment. The new atmosphere was incompatible with routine, stagnation, defeatism, and spiritual pettiness—all of which had consumed the majority of the old trade unions.

In discussing the ideological maturing of the "new unionism," one should not dismiss the problem of leadership, which always was, and still remains, extremely acute in the American case. The rise of the labor movement in the mid-thirties pushed the leadership issue to the forefront of its concerns. Changes inside the unions drew attention in government circles and among diverse bourgeois analysts, all of whom watched nervously to see who would be brought to the surface by the powerful current that had undermined the old leaders.[16] One eyewitness to these events wrote: "The industrial movement has thrown to the front a corps of rank-and-file leaders who are clearheaded and wary, who have an eye to the future. They hope to produce in actuality that which now exists only in theory: a government in America by the majority of Americans."[17] It can be assumed that the author meant to include bourgeois Democrats when talking about the "governing power of the majority of Americans."

However, there was, indisputably, another dimension. The young CIO activists, uplifted by the enthusiasm of ordinary workers, rejected the strategy of defeating evil by peaceful methods. They chose class solidarity, assertiveness, and conflict as their tools.[18] The memory of the first decades of the twentieth century and the maturing of the International Labor Organization was fresh in their minds.

In many ways the Communist party played a decisive role in founding the industrial unions and in shaping their political and ideological orientation. The influence of the party increased because of the selflessness of Communists and their fearlessness during the fight to unify the workers as well as their unselfish interest in the success of workers' initiatives. These interests ranged from those that advanced "inch by inch," to more sweeping concerns (such as shaping national labor law and social policies, elimination of racketeering, attracting blacks into unions, and the like), and finally to the art of planning ahead. All this strengthened the Communist party's popularity and authority. Furthermore, as the big centralized unions were

16. Taft, "Some Problems of the New Unionism in the United States," *American Economic Review* (June 1939): 313–24.

17. C[ecil] Carnes, *John L. Lewis: Leader of Labor* (New York, 1936), 303.

18. There is an interesting document in the archives of Norman Thomas, former presidential candidate in the United States for the Socialist party. The mayor of Anderson, Indiana, wrote to ask Thomas to influence somehow young CIO leaders who then belonged to the Socialist party so that they would not foster the "spirit of antagonism" among the workers, would not flout local authorities, and would conform to the "tenor of the community" (New York Public Library [hereafter NYPL], N[orman] Thomas Papers, Harry R. Baldwin to Thomas, 23 February 1937).

organizing in the basic industries, workers showed they trusted the Communists by selecting them for leadership posts.[19] In a number of states the labor movement developed to such an extent that its enemies consciously avoided hostilities, afraid that their involvement would hurt their own popularity. An editor of a socialist newspaper in Wisconsin wrote to Norman Thomas, "I think it would be a serious error for our party to make a frontal attack [on the growing influence of the Communist party in the movement to establish industrial unions in Wisconsin—V. M.] . . . . Furthermore it must be recognized that . . . a large number of Communists have done indispensable work in building many of the new unions. Before we are in a position to attack this record, we will have to do better ourselves."[20]

One of the most important reasons for the success of the Communist party was that in the process of encouraging workers to take the initiative it also worked to preserve and strengthen the unity of the movement and to discourage discord and factionalism. This is documented by letters from local Socialists to the leaders of the Socialist party. The information can be considered trustworthy since the relationship between Socialists and Communists was known to be quite hostile.[21]

American unions seemed particularly intent on maintaining ideological autonomy and on building new and stronger foundations. The ordinary masses who participated wanted new leaders who understood their needs and who could express them in slogans and in the strategic and tactical conduct of the movement. As V. I. Lenin said, the working masses who brought the movement to life were not without character.[22] In making their decisions about the theories and abilities of their leaders, the working masses listened most attentively to those for whom the fight against capitalist exploitation and the lack of social justice was an inner conviction, not a matter of fashion—those for whom the fight was part of the framework of their philosophy of life, not a momentary passion.[23]

The rightists and centrists of the Socialist party of the United States were neither the first nor the last people to understand that the Communists and leftist Socialists had been strengthened by deep currents that stirred the lower masses. This stirring occurred despite the fact that even today the lower masses have not entirely decided where they fit in the labor movement. But the devaluation of Gompers's moral and political tenets, to which the renaissance and growth of the left wing testified, forced many old AFL leaders to reflect sadly. They also began to study how, despite years of suppression, opposition to them had gained strength and attracted hundreds of thousands of workers. A wave of dramatic change was sweeping over vast numbers of

19. W[ellington] Roe, *Juggernaut: American Labor in Action* (New York, 1948), 116; Seidman, *American Labor from Defense to Reconversion* (Chicago, 1953), 10.

20. NYPL, N. Thomas Papers, Editor of *The Kenosha Labor* to Thomas, 6 October 1937.

21. NYPL, N. Thomas Papers, T. Smith to Thomas, 8 October 1937; F. Winn to L. Stark, 5 December 1937; B. Fisher to A. McDowell, 8 December 1937.

22. See Lenin, *Complete Collected Works,* 34:415.

23. W[illiam Z.] Foster, "The Struggle for the Creation of Industrial Trade Unions in the United States," *Modern and Contemporary History,* 1960, no. 4, 8–9.

craft unions, i.e., the citadel of conservatism in the labor movement. The old unions were in the process of fragmenting. In one after another, internal opposition groups sharply criticized the local leadership's obedient implementation of orders from the AFL executive committee. Workers wanted their trade unions to intervene in "big politics." Workers decidedly wanted New Deal reforms that were in their own interests. They wanted the laws to be more than a safety net for capitalists. Expanding democratic rights, reigning in tyrannical monopolists, and thwarting the influence of special interests on social life and the government were the concerns of the day. "All branches of labor are in earnest in wanting a big change for the better. They all realize they're getting but the barest subsistence at this time, and I think all are in the mood to go to the mat." So claimed an officer of a local miners' union in Butte.[24]

The secret yet obvious sympathy for the leftists by workers who were organized into unions, together with the support of people who merely went along with the majority, provoked a growing estrangement between those workers and the governing apparatus of the AFL. That was because the latter was passive in its action and conservative in its rhetoric.

Although it was unnoted, a surge among the rank and file from 1933 to 1935 was a direct precursor of the CIO, and in many respects it anticipated the CIO ideologically. Unfortunately, this instructive phase of the CIO's history has not been researched. However, currently available sources enable one to see that the rank and file were ideologically radicalized very rapidly. The search for its own position brought out the idea that the working class could be liberated if it accepted a program that opposed the structure of union governance. As it turned out, this program failed to stabilize the movement, and its slogans and plans were eclectic. Nonetheless, the program marked progress, a step toward breaking with Gompersism and bourgeois politics.

The ideological influence of the left and of progressive forces was set against a deeply ingrained system determined to counter it. However, logic would triumph eventually. All this was recognized by AFL leaders such as Charles P. Howard, John L. Lewis, and Sidney Hillman. They and others reluctantly accepted the executive committee's efforts to eliminate ideological revolt through reprimands, orders, expulsions, exclusions, and similar processes. Would such a course work? Would it not lead to mass purges in the union movement like those carried out by Gompers at the beginning of the 1920s? Would it not bring results diametrically opposite those desired?

Through pressure from below, the working class in the United States found itself on course with what Lenin called the political consciousness movement of the masses.[25] This would occur through mass struggle and take such forms as strikes, demonstrations, hunger marches, and demonstrations of solidarity. It would involve

24. New York State School of Industrial and Labor Relations Library (hereafter NYSSILRL), International Union of Mine, Mill and Smelter Workers (hereafter Lew McLenegan Papers), L. McLenegan to J. R. Robinson, 10 March 1934.

25. See Lenin, *Complete Collected Works,* 16:119.

denial of unprincipled deals between unions and entrepreneurs, and refusal to trade mass obedience for concessions made through compromising methods of bargaining.

The facts show that the aspirations, conviction, and ability of participants to struggle surpassed the assessments even of those who were most capable of assessing union leadership. At first timidly, then with a growing assertiveness in order not to lag irreversibly behind events, G[us] Hall wrote, "Most of the leadership and the structure of the CIO appeared on the scene only after it was obvious to everyone that the workers in the basic industries were going to build new forms and pursue new policies of militant struggle. This is the really meaningful history of the CIO. The history of most of the leaders was one of years of resistance to organization of new unions, years of wavering and hesitation, maneuvering and compromising."[26] Lewis, Hillman, D[avid] Dubinsky, and their supporters—people whose names are connected with the founding of the CIO—did not understand immediately the viability of the movement and that inevitably they would become part of it. It is generally recognized that during 1933 and the first half of 1934 they expressed no significant interest in seeing the movement mature and triumph.[27]

The emergence of a "new" Lewis in the political arena during early autumn 1934 coincided with the AFL convention in San Francisco. Lewis's biographer, Saul Alinsky, has written that an acrid declaration by workers from Toledo, Minneapolis, and San Francisco during summer 1934 furnished the impetus. The conference resembled a prelude to civil war. Other urban strikes followed, then a general strike of textile workers in September 1934 opened a new phase in the evolution of class conflict. The proletariat turned from defense to offense.

Conference meetings of San Francisco's trade union leaders would hardly have left a mark on the labor movement had events outside the conference room been of an everyday character. In keeping with the executive committee's scenario, stifling and repetitious ceremony alternated with lengthy disputation. Suddenly, these proceedings were interrupted by the spirit of the streets, echoes from the docks and unrest in the working districts. The idea of organizing workers according to basic industries became the center of attention. After long debate, a compromise was reached between those who favored equality between industrial unions and craft unions and those who would preserve the privileges of the craft unions.[28] Lewis, representing the first group, and Frey, representing the second, were satisfied that the resolution they drafted (and which the San Francisco convention unanimously adopted) allowed people to interpret the document according to his/her own point of view.[29] There was a feeling of relief in the AFL executive committee. Collusion at the highest level promised to relieve tensions and restore peace in the federation.

26. "The Rank-and-File Upsurge: A New Page in Working Class History," *Political Affairs* (August 1970): 3–4.

27. Galenson, *Rival Unionism,* 195, 208.

28. *AFL Proceedings,* 1934, 586–87.

29. Taft, *The A. F. of L.,* 91; Morris, *Conflict within the AFL,* 198, 199; *Industrial and Labor Relations Review,* 1960, no. 3, 458.

Lenin wrote that "historical events should be judged by class movements and not by the frame of mind of individuals and groups."[30] The inevitable crisis in the highest ranks of the AFL had been temporarily averted, and the position of the two leadership factions seemed appreciably closer. The situation was different, however, among the working masses. They continued to rage, angered by the standstill and the obvious sabotage of progress toward the establishment of unions in the basic industries. The first evidence of this growing wave of discontent could be seen in the automobile industry.[31] In the eyes of the auto workers, the AFL executive committee had compromised itself. It had tried to impose its will on the leadership of the United Auto Workers and then had been cowardly in warding off the antilabor activities of the automobile magnates. The magnates had convinced themselves that the AFL position was weak and quite harmless.[32] By the beginning of 1935 a number of the large federated unions of the auto industry had come to the conclusion that the AFL executive committee was working singlemindedly to stop the implementation of the mandate it had received at the San Francisco convention.[33]

Tired of waiting, workers took the initiative into their own hands. Methods for recruiting new members resulted in the spontaneous organization of many union cells in the automobile companies. Many thousands of people attended organized meetings as well as improvised conferences. The primary topics of these meetings were how to force the big corporations to recognize the workers' right of organizing labor unions, to offer acceptable working conditions and salary, and to respect workers as human beings. The words *general strike* were on everyone's lips. AFL leaders were unable to control this rebellion, and they were fearful of the workers' inclination to use the press to promote a general strike if the corporations rejected their demands.[34]

Sometime in mid-January 1935, Lewis received an invitation to address workers in Cleveland's automobile industry. His speech to the Cleveland workers was among the first in a series that marked the end of the armistice achieved in San Francisco. The president of the United Mine Workers understood only too well what those who assembled to hear him wanted to hear. He began by expressing his "great sorrow" and pain that the federal government and "the shortsighted opposition of some of the powerful groups in the recognized labor movement" had failed to understand the aspirations of union people. He emphasized that unionizing workers in the basic industries would transform the American labor movement into a "really significant factor in the economic and political life of the nation." Then followed a passage that one member of the AFL executive committee said sounded like "sedition." Lewis declared that "political action by organized labor will also be increasingly necessary

30. *Complete Collected Works,* 22:85.
31. Morris, *Conflict within the AFL,* 202–3.
32. *Mississippi Valley Historical Review* 45 (June 1958): 23–50.
33. Wisconsin State Historical Society Library (hereafter WSHSL), AFL Papers, file C, box 1, W. Green Papers, 1934–1936.
34. *Detroit Labor News,* 11 and 18 January 1935.

for two reasons: first, to safeguard the fundamental principles and rights of industrial democracy; and second, in order to secure legislative and perhaps constitutional sanctions for its economic program." Success of the campaign would give the workers political clout and enable them to deliver a smashing blow to the "industrial and financial dictatorship" that ruled America. Lewis concluded with a call to end "industrial autocracy."[35]

Quite a few people were stunned by this effusive expression of resentment against the tyranny of moneybags, by the promise to lead the labor movement beyond the narrow limits of traditional economics, and by this declaration of egalitarianism. (Only ten years before, Lewis had declared the similarity and legitimacy of both workers' and capitalists' aspiration to enjoy material prosperity and gain.)[36] Contemporaries were at a loss to explain this metamorphosis; it was unfathomable in a leader of the AFL. From whence came Lewis's passionate appeal for political self-determination of the labor movement, his anger toward the monopolistic oligarchy, and his great democratism? What was it? Was it merely faddish, a specialized "plate du jour"? Could the entire situation be the result of something as ephemeral as Lewis's oratorical style?

There was something to the contention that Lewis was wont to use gaudy phraseology and speak for effect in his radical orations. However, his declarations were not as much for dramatic effect as for adapting his policies to the democratic socioeconomic outlook, the hopes and aspirations of the masses. "To Them [the uprising American miners—V. M.], whose servant I am, I express my pride in their courage and loyalty. They are the household troops of the great movement for industrial democracy and from their collective sentiment and crystallized power I derive my strength," Lewis stated in a radio speech on 6 June 1936.[37]

Lewis resolved to follow certain principles: not to complain, no matter how dangerous a situation became; to try to stay in rhythm with the movement without losing his influence among the masses who were moving to the left; and to establish control over the masses rather than save the privileges of the old unions. "You cannot deny that the American Federation of Labor has frittered away two years of valuable time," Lewis wrote to Green in 1936. "Your lament is that I will not join you in a policy of anxious inertia. Candidly, I am temperamentally incapable of sitting with you in sackcloth and ashes, endlessly entoning 'O, tempora!, O, mores! . . . .' You will make your own decisions. For myself I prefer to err on the side of America's underprivileged and exploited millions, if erring it be . . . ." Lewis did not understand how one could awaken these awesome social forces and at the same time hope to control them.[38]

35. WSHSL, AFL Papers, file C, box 1, W. Green Papers, 1934–1936. Lewis's popularity grew quickly. National unions frequently asked him to appear at their meetings (*Detroit Labor News,* 8 March 1935).

36. Lewis, *The Miners Fight for American Standards* (Indianapolis, 1925).

37. H[oward] Zinn, ed., *New Deal Thought* (Indianapolis–New York, 1966), 206.

38. WSHSL, AFL Papers, file C, box 1, W. Green Papers, J. Lewis to Green, 6 June 1936; J. Lewis to Green, 7 June 1936.

Lewis had no plans to accelerate the new labor movement; at the same time he knew it could not be stopped. As he said again in 1937, the labor movement in the United States "is under new inspirations" and was characterized by enthusiasm; "I have no desire to interrupt that march . . . ."[39]

While Green, Wall, and others remained passive, Lewis decided not to remain aloof during the strikes initiated by the masses. As a rule, he did not argue the point that presumably interested him and his opponents the most: namely, the organizational structure of the union movement. More often and more confidently his speeches portrayed the basic problem as a clash of ideas. One idea was that the labor movement in the United States was a congealed mass that could develop no further. The other was that there were new stimuli. It held that the masses had discovered hidden possibilities for organized struggle against the monopolies at the same time they developed a sense of social responsibility and took up problems that had presented themselves during the recent critical period.[40]

The "peculiarities" of Lewis's logic reflected reality. In time, dissension over the status of industrial unions faded inside the AFL.[41] Nonetheless, conflict itself did not level out; it intensified. This illustrated one of the laws observed by Lenin. As he expressed it: "After there is lengthy, decided, and ardent struggle, the central and basic points of controversy usually start to outlive themselves. The final outcome of the campaign then depends on how these are resolved, and the minor episodes in the fight increasingly recede into the background compared with these controversial points."[42]

Strictly speaking, it was during the AFL convention in Atlantic City (1935) that a political group inside the executive core of the AFL broke with official policy. Both main factions at the convention (to a varying degree, of course) wanted to make the

---

39. International Ladies Garment Workers' Union (hereafter ILGWU), *Proceedings, 1937,* 300.

40. Lewis stated his position to the AFL executive committee in his letter of 21 July 1936. See further *Proceedings of the Executive Council of the American Federation of Labor in the Matter of Charges Filed by the Metal Trades Department Against the CIO* (Washington, D.C., 3 August 1936).

41. Toward the end of the decade, when everything had fallen into place, the sense of the crisis was more convincing. For example, one speaker at the Hatters' Union convention in 1939 said, "While originally the division of the ranks of labor into two camps had come about through a serious difference of opinion on the principle of 'industrial unionism against craft unionism,' the historian of the labor movement will record that conflict in principle is no longer the issue which divides the American labor movement . . . . That issue alone could be easily adjusted . . . . Unfortunately other issues sprang up" (*United Hatters, Cap and Millinery Workers International Union Proceedings, 1939,* 309, 310). In 1960 W. Foster wrote, "The CIO organization's campaigns, which began in 1936, were mostly successful. The AFL trade unions were also growing rapidly. The leaders of the latter understood that their persistent attempts at upholding narrow craft-unionism were doomed to failure. They started to enlarge their unions. The Federation began to accept workers, students, and many others, who had close ties to the basic working professions and who did take an active part in the defense of their interests at that time. In fact, while not recognizing the principle of industrial trade unionism, to a certain degree the AFL trade unions turned into a kind of semi-industrial organization" (W. Z. Foster, "The Struggle for Creation of Industrial Trade Unions in the United States," *Modern and Contemporary History,* 1960, no. 4, 8).

42. *Complete Collected Works,* 8:187.

structure of the AFL more flexible. According to a majority resolution (by Green, Frey, Wall, and others) the jurisdiction of industrial unions was limited to unskilled and semi-skilled workers. The minority stood for a more radical solution. They proposed to extend the jurisdiction of industrial unions to all workers in the major industries. This disagreement, however, was not considered unresolvable. Witness the fact that most labor federations on the state level, the majority of central committees among urban craft unions, and the overwhelming majority of federal unions stood behind the minority resolution, i.e., they believed craft and industrial unions could coexist. In keeping with suggestions from Lewis, Howard, Dubinsky, and others, they ruled out anything that would have seriously restricted the craft unions.[43] Leaders of the new unions acted responsibly when they refrained from suggesting that craft unions be transformed into industrial unions, or that they be liquidated.[44]

Large trade unions organized on the principle of local branches had supported the conservative line of the AFL executive committee. Soon they were holding back or departing from the official line on various issues. Such was the case with the International Ladies' Garment Workers' Union, the United Hatters, and a number of others. Their example was followed by the leadership of the Amalgamated Meat Cutters, a fact that caused a split among the members. Dissatisfied with their leadership's activities, a good half of the workers in the meatpacking industry rallied to the CIO's organization campaign in their industry in February 1937. Thereafter there were two unions among meatpackers, each extremely unfriendly to the other.[45] The typographers' union, one of the founders of the CIO, withdrew in 1938 after the death of its president, Charles Howard. A group led by Dubinsky and [Max] Zaritsky that played a significant role in the founding and early history of the CIO was very hostile to the inclusion of leftists and Communists in the leadership of many industrial trade unions. They quickly tied the Ladies Garment Workers and Hatters unions to the

43. *AFL Proceedings, 1935,* 574, 575. The following statement is included in the report of the executive committee of the ACWA for the organization's twelfth convention: "Many AFL unions completely ignore the rule that they should remain within the limits of the traditional craft organizations. They accept workers into their ranks who were organized according to the industrial principle and who would not agree to join when craft unions were first organized" (*Report of the General Executive Board to the Twelfth Biennial Convention of the ACWA* [Atlantic City, 1938], 49).

44. WSHSL, AFL Papers, file C, box 2, W. Green Papers, 1934–1936; *Proceedings of the Executive Council of the American Federation of Labor in the Matter of Charges Filed by the Metal Trades Department Against the CIO, August 3, 1936;* Committee for Industrial Organization, *The Case for Industrial Organization* (Washington, 1936), 38. During the drive to organize the automobile industry, labor leaders wrote to John Frey: "Let us forget jurisdictional quarrels. We are all brothers in the great common cause. The benefit of one cannot help being beneficial to the other and the hurt of one will inevitably be detrimental to the rest . . . with this understanding we ask your cooperation in our drive. Help us spread unionism among the . . . exploited auto workers. Help us make Cleveland a union town by organizing Fisher Body!" (Library of Congress, John P. Frey Papers, W. Mortimer and others to Frey, 27 November 1935).

45. T[heodore V.] Purcell, *The Worker Speaks His Mind on Company and Union* (Cambridge, Mass., 1953), 52, 53.

moorings of the AFL.[46] Ideological discords clearly caused complications through-out organized labor.

Roughly speaking, the labor movement in 1929 was considered to be divided as follows. On the left were the partisans and members of the industrial unions; and on the right the craft workers, conservative and bourgeoislike to the end. The facts, however, do not support this view of the division. The CIO called for a "renewed and progressive labor movement"[47] as a means of breaking through the confusion of ideological orientations. That confusion was interfering with the formation of the foundation a vibrant working class needed to define its horizons. This call was echoed among the workers where the AFL was considered to have a stronghold.[48] "You may be surprised to know of the number of state and local union bodies that are veering towards the Lewis thought," wrote a Milwaukee friend of AFL vice-presi-dent John Frey. "They may be timid for the present in venturing forth but nev-ertheless at heart they are for Lewis. . . . The Wisconsin and Milwaukee move-ments, with rare exceptions, have stood for that thought . . . ."[49] Frey responded that this was not news to him. He expressed the opinion that the only positive result might be closer collaboration between the AFL and the entrepreneurs who would come to see eventually where their mistreatment of the AFL was leading.[50]

Once more, these events illustrate that not only the structure of the labor move-ment, but also the ideological and political values espoused by Gompers had become the object of criticism. Ideological positions and suggested social ends had come to the forefront, not organizational principles. Obviously, there was not a single state federation of labor or important urban union that was not caught in the conflict between the masses and the "top." In most cases, observed V[ictor A.] Olander, treasurer-secretary of the Illinois Federation of Labor, the former supported the "new trade-unionism"; the latter obediently, though not always willingly, carried out the orders of the AFL executive committee. Even in his home state of Illinois, Olander could not guarantee the old leadership that their seats were safe.[51] In Sep-tember 1936 the AFL executive committee decided to exclude unions that joined the CIO from the federation. The headquarters of the federation immediately received an enormous number of protests from state labor federations and large craft unions as

46. Taft, "David Dubinsky and the Labor Movement," *Labor History,* special supplement, 9 (Spring 1968): 34.

47. Thus John Lewis summarily characterized the aims and tasks of the CIO in his speech at the convention of the ladies garment workers in 1937 (*International Ladies Garment Workers' Union, 23rd Convention,* 297).

48. G[eoge H.] Soule, "The Trade-union Movement," *Political Quarterly* (October-December 1937): 560.

49. Library of Congress, J. P. Frey Papers, Correspondence, file N 1-A, W. B. Rubin to Frey, 5 December 1935.

50. Library of Congress, J. P. Frey Papers, Correspondence, file N 1-A, Frey to W. B. Rubin, 30 November 1935, Frey to W. B. Rubin, 9 December 1935.

51. Library of Congress, J. P. Frey Papers, Material, file N 1-C, V. A. Olander to Frey, 14 Au-gust 1936.

well as from united urban trade unions.[52] The resolutions and letters opposing the exclusion of the CIO argued that this split in the labor movement would set back its progress, not to mention that the executive committee's rationale was incompatible with, and in contradiction to, the AFL constitution.[53] The AFL executive committee recognized clearly that it could not play off one professional organization's scheme against another. Thus, the AFL committee tried to establish credibility for the position that lack of obedience, "partisan" action, and the lawless pretensions of aggressive industrial unions forced it to take disciplinary action. The executive committee weighted its pronouncements with footnotes about jurisdiction and procedure—in effect, battle cries to conscienceless schismatics trying to usurp federation power for rapacious gain. The miscreants supposedly disregarded the will of the overwhelming majority of the membership, among other things. The extraordinary sanctions imposed by the executive committee were presented as temporary, a punitive measure made necessary by the wrongful actions of a group of arrogant and fraudulent people—that is, by Lewis, Hillman, and others. In reality, by the end of 1935 the top level of the AFL had consciously decided to break with all factions sympathetic to the new course. The move toward a break began in the name of stopping two structures from emerging among unions, but it became a complex intrigue against the CIO. The fight, by the end of 1935, had gone beyond any dispute about structure, although neither hostile leadership group wished to advertise this fact widely. Those in strategic command of the dramatic hostilities knew full well where the conflict centered, just as they knew full well why it set off passion, debate, and sometimes, among other things, small wars.[54]

52. The archives of W[illiam] Green, housed in the library of the Wisconsin Historical Society, contain a great number of similar resolutions, private letters, etc. WSHSL, AFL Papers, file C, box 2, W. Green Papers, 1935–1936; see also *ILGWU Proceedings, 1937,* 215, 216; *Minnesota State Federation of Labor Proceedings, 1936,* 71; Taft, *The A. F. of L.,* 179.

53. WSHSL, AFL Papers, file C, box 2, W. Green Papers, 1935–1936, P. L. Glatzert to Green, 3 July 1936; W. C. Steward to Green, 9 August and 28 August 1936. A great many ordinary members of the big craft unions definitely opposed a split and demanded a referendum. A typographic worker from Texas wrote to Frey in September 1936: "I don't have any respect for you, nor Morrison, nor Hutcheson, nor Wall. The whole pack of you would do the labor movement the greatest service you ever rendered if you'd get out lock, stock and barrel. You always have been an enemy of democratic principles in the union movement. You are and always [have] been of the opinion that the rank and file don't have enough sense to do anything except to vote as told by top leadership . . . . I am by no means alone. Many, many thousands among the rank and file feel the same way, and many of them are in the unions which are identified on your side of this issue. After all, the rank and file pays your fat salary. After all, the rank and file keeps you on your job. Why not let them vote on this matter in a referendum vote?" (Library of Congress, John P. Frey Papers, A. D. Covin to Frey, 30 September 1936).

54. Publicly, Green, Frey, Wall, and others tried to give the impression that they were only fulfilling the will of the majority of union members and were strangling the unlawful uprising by an unrepresentative minority faction. In private, though, they admitted that the dividing line cut through the middle of working-class America, touching its heart. It touched everyone except those who did not work and those who did not care. Green wrote to one of his closest collaborators, "Men who were friends for years are now bitter enemies. Families and communities are divided because of the crea-

This conflict, which had long fermented beneath the surface, was caused by ideological differences. Like a red scare, this awareness ran through the correspondence of AFL legal consultant Charlton Ogburn, one of the architects of the AFL's "clever" system for legal reprisals. According to him, the opposition movement canceled out the AFL executive committee's campaign plans and their orders.[55] Frey wrote in March 1936, "There is much more to the internal controversy over so-called craft unions and industrial unions within the AFL which lies below the surface, much that does not appear in the records or can be found in the statements made by both sides at the recent convention of the AFofL [in Atlantic City—V. M.]." In this transparent statement Frey was getting at the essence of the political mind that guided AFL leadership. The aim of AFL leaders, he continued, was to raise a wall against new ideological trends, and they intended to do so in the name of saving the labor movement in the United States from enslavement by political radicalism.[56] Frey and his colleagues on the AFL executive committee defended Gompers's backward doctrine on organizational principles as well as those on functions and ideology.

On the eve of the historic convention in Tampa (November 1936), when conflict inside the AFL was most intense, Green reaffirmed in confidential letters to Ogburn that the problem of coexistence of different types of professional organizations within the framework of a united federation seemed to the executive council *ipso facto* to have been solved. The details of working together under the new circumstances were delegated quietly to the executive committee. The convention in Tampa temporarily stopped the AFL from expelling unions that joined the CIO—at least until a ruling could be made on disputed points.[57]

Later, in 1938, Frey, reminiscing and reflecting on the origin of the split, remarked in his notebook that disputes over organizational form before the CIO was founded were of no particular importance to anyone.[58]

Statements on the issue by leaders of the new trade unions—Lewis, Hillman, and Howard—became increasingly direct. The essence of what they said was that their split from the majority of the AFL executive committee mainly was due to different perceptions of political momentum in the labor movement and in the country and what this difficult political orientation would mean. By the by, Charles Howard was among those who saw that no one much wanted to end the polemics. As Howard saw it, the stakes were too high to pretend that only such things as the organizational structure of unions were in dispute. In November 1935, he wrote: "During recent years we have heard much of radicalism. Many of our people believe American ideals

tion of the dual, rival, rebel movement called the 'C.I.O.' " (WSHSL, AFL Papers, file C, box 3, W. Green Papers, 1936–1942, Green to M. F. Tighe, 17 May 1938).

55. WSHSL, AFL Papers, file C, box 2, W. Green Papers, 1934–1936, Charlton Ogburn to Green, 29 May 1936.

56. Library of Congress, John P. Frey Papers, Frey to Fred Carr, 10 March 1936.

57. WSHSL, AFL Papers, file C, box 2, W. Green Papers, 1934–1936, Green to Charlton Ogburn, 3 June 1936.

58. Library of Congress, John P. Frey Papers, Miscellaneous, Notes and Articles, 10 March 1938.

and institutions are endangered by '-isms' imported from foreign countries. It was the conditions of the great mass of wage workers that brought Communism to Russia . . . . To permit millions of industrial workers to remain unorganized in this country invites a condition which will become a national menace. To permit them to organize under a leadership opposed to the policies and philosophy of cooperative trade-unionism, would constitute a greater menace."[59] The motives that forced Howard to reconcile himself to initiatives from below are clear. It was no one's ill will that transformed the psychology of the struggling masses; it was the conditions in which they lived. It was dangerous and shortsighted to speak hostilely of such people, to condemn their aspirations, to oppose them. Howard, as president of the oldest craft union, stood for a flexible strategy. He believed that the political demands and aspirations of the masses should in some way be met.

Appeals to be realistic had no effect. Conversely, every clarification of motives led to an ever-increasing polarization of opinion. What had been caution was replaced by estrangement; what had been efforts to find common ground were replaced by refusals to consider rapprochement.

Three factors contributed to the growing alienation of the AFL executive committee from the new unions. First, political radicalism increased in the labor movement. Second, new methods of struggle were unfamiliar to the Gompersists; the committee found them unacceptable because they went against tradition. Finally, there was the labor movement's frightening inclination to merge its economic struggle with its political actions. Because almost every step taken by the new unions was paralleled by an attempt to free themselves from rigid control by the AFL, AFL leaders saw these acts as movements toward Communism.[60]

On the eve of the AFL convention in Tampa, federation leaders perceived the "new unions" as a simple analogy to European unions under the influence of the Social Democrats. Frey wrote in August 1936: "One result not hard to visualize is the existence of two trade union movements, one representing the practical, constructive, international unions influenced in their activities by American institutions, and the other composed of groups who more or less favor the leftists' policies which are so prominent in many of the European labor movements."[61]

Frey categorically opposed any talks predicated on equality between the two. In a series of speeches during September he constantly referred to the ideological divergence of two, already distinct, labor movements. Predictably, he demanded complete separation of the AFL and CIO. If allowed to freely develop and consolidate, the radicalism of the latter would undermine faith in "free institutions" in the United States (i.e., bourgeois institutions) and would lead to victory for the socialist world view, said Frey. "To continue talk about craft-unionism versus industrial trade-unionism," Frey thought, would "be more stupid."[62]

59. WSHSL, Charles P. Howard Papers, box 2 (text of his presentation at Wesleyan University).
60. Library of Congress, John P. Frey Papers (see the notes of J. Frey, dated May 1936).
61. Library of Congress, John P. Frey Papers, Frey to Hiram Brown, 14 August 1936.
62. Library of Congress, John P. Frey Papers, Speech on the Convention of Structural Iron Work-

Frey became one of the most active "red hunters," although he tried, unsuccessfully, to deny the charge. He deliberately perverted facts, claimed the new trade unions were a Trojan horse for a socialist revolution, and changed that CIO activists and leaders took their orders directly from the Communist party in Moscow.[63] However, "nothing helps more to clarify the essence of political events than their assessment by the opposition (as long as the adversaries are not desperately stupid people)," said Lenin.[64] And Frey was not stupid. More than the minutes of AFL executive committee meetings, Frey's behavior reflected the anxieties of the Gompersists. A significant part of the labor movement had shown its displeasure with the federation's opportunistic politics, cowardly strategy, capitulations, lack of principles, and other extremes. Now, Frey and some other AFL leaders were obsessed with preventing a higher consciousness from evolving out of the current spontaneity and ideological vagueness. The majority of the AFL executive committee considered it a catastrophe to find themselves in league with people who had declared industrial unions an anachronism. According to conservatives at the top of the AFL, it was possible that the "exclusions" [of industrial unions] would bring undecided numbers back to their senses and isolate the progressive forces. Such AFL leaders justified the risk of losing influence over a good half of the working class on grounds that if left alone these people might become a part of the political mainstream. (As Green expressed it, judging by its aim, "the opposition's course was much more political than economic.")[65]

Here, then, one can see both the economic and political dimensions of the "new unionism." The issues raised are of key importance; however, they have been misinterpreted or superficially explained in the historiographic literature. Typically, solid bourgeois works assert that manifestations of a new ideology among workers were ephemeral. Such works treat a single aspect of the topic, i.e., the infiltration of leading posts in the CIO by Communists.[66] This is an example of falsification in the transmission of facts and circumstances, or, as Marx said, lies "in the concrete sense of the word."[67] In form and essence, this treatment is akin to the defensive demagoguery of the Gompersists. After they had collided with the crisis of their doctrine

---

ers, St. Louis, 21 September 1936; Frey to I. Feinberg, 27 October 1936; WSHSL, AFL Papers, file C, box 2, W. Green Papers, 1935–1936, Labor Day 1936, Address by John P. Frey.

63. Library of Congress, John P. Frey Papers, Frey to Thomas J. Ramsey, 10 June 1937; Thomas J. Ramsey to Frey, 16 June 1937; Frey to Arthur H. Vandenberg, 2 July 1937; Arthur H. Vandenberg to Frey, 3 July 1937; Frey to Joseph Tumulty, 15 July 1937. Frey did not act independently. AFL president Green himself encouraged this "diplomacy" to undermine the influence of the CIO (WSHSL, AFL Papers, file C, box 3, W. Green Papers, 1936–1942, B. V. Sheehan to Green, 15 March 1937; Clare G. Fenerty to Green, 11 June 1937; Green to Clare G. Fenerty, 25 June 1937).

64. *Complete Collected Works,* 12:117.

65. WSHSL, AFL Papers, file C, box 3, W. Green Papers, 1936–1942, Green to C. G. Fenerty, 25 June 1937.

66. Such an approach characterized a well-known collaborative work of bourgeois historians, M. Derber and E. Young, eds., *Labor and the New Deal* (Madison, Wis., 1957).

67. Marx and Engels, *Collected Works,* 1:171.

during the 1930s, they attempted to explain it away as merely the crafty machinations of the Comintern operating through the leftists.

G. V. Plekhanov has written: "There is not a single historical fact that would not be preceded or accompanied and followed by a certain degree of consciousness."[68] However, changes in the consciousness of the masses cannot be induced by some-one's tyrannical rule, nor by blazing slogans or inflammatory exultations. Much more is necessary. A lasting interest on the part of the masses in a hopeful or, at least, discernible alternative to the old world view is critical. The inevitability of a crisis within Gompersism was proven by the fact that belief in the original dogma was lost not only by deprived, unskilled, and immigrant workers who were susceptible to leftist agitation, but also by the majority at the top levels of the working class—such as the highly skilled workers who constituted the backbone of most AFL unions. "When John L. Lewis hit him (Bill Hutchison) and knocked him down it was too bad that he didn't break his neck . . . . The principle of the CIO is right and the principle of the AFL is wrong from the bottom up and has always been wrong . . . . I told Samuel Gompers many times that the principles underlying the AFofL were wrong which time and events would prove. The last time I told him was in 1906 . . . . The AFofL will become a body of scabs. These are hard words, but they are true."[69] This was written by a skilled workman, a longtime member of a Chicago local of the carpenters' union, the union that "Big Bill" Hutchison served as president. The masses were engaged in a difficult search for new ideological values. Inescapably there was inner conflict, criticism of previous ideas, and, finally, gradual rejection of those ideas. Although it was slow, progressive change in the social consciousness of the working class did occur. However, a declaration of this transformation contributes little to understanding the direction of change.

It is well known that Marxist-Leninist research methodologies are particularly concerned with the historical experience of the masses. Lenin wrote that "it is necessary to make an all-out effort to collect, study, and learn the true facts connected with the action and moods of the masses, not of individuals or groups."[70] This is the task of the present writer as well. Although the literature on the history of the labor movement in the United States during the 1930s is being constantly revised as a result of new research, a description of the movement's external functioning and its meaning, to use Lenin's expression,[71] clearly should be included in a study of basic concerns of the working class.

That this is still needed does not result simply from a lack of inquisitiveness. Overcoming inertia in scientific thinking always takes time—not to mention a certain reorientation. There is very little coverage of the function and meaning of the ideological dialectics in American sociopolitical practices during the 1930s even in specialized international literature. And what there is, is superficially researched (this

68. *Selected Philosophical Works* (Moscow, 1956), 11:247–48.
69. Library of Congress, John P. Frey Papers, Henry Hansen to Frey, 26 January 1937.
70. *Complete Collected Works*, 25:245.
71. See ibid., 29:199.

includes the development of proletarian consciousness). One is strongly aware of the lack of data about the attitudes and feelings and views of workers; in a word, about the true state of consciousness[72] of the central figure in the events, the ordinary workers. Scientific studies are based on extremely selective materials (including local letters that have accumulated in American archives). Bourgeois researchers accord local materials a second- or third-rate importance. They put the colorful leader or union boss on the highest plane. He speaks, disputes, decides, abandons the interests of his union during the negotiations with the industrialists, etcetera.[73]

Despite this, even a cursory knowledge of these sometimes-troubling documents makes it possible to comment on the growth of individual and collective consciousness among workers. The documents make it possible to feel the charged atmosphere of the 1930s, the workers' passion to implement rights they already had proclaimed and their desire for still more. The atmosphere bespoke class solidarity, a feeling of strength and confidence among workers that resulted from the success of their concerted actions. It seemed, suddenly, that people had been gifted with speech—and they felt the need to talk. Even people in God-forsaken, out-of-the-way places were caught up in a self-assured, eye-opening political enlightenment. All of this constituted a break with the past and led people to think about the omnipotence of business and the sacred idea of "individual success." Even the South, the bastion of conservatism, experienced a crisis over traditional wisdom. In March 1936, one ordinary worker in Alabama wrote Republican senator W[illiam] Borah: "I live in the midst of people who know next to nothing about radicalism. But they are slowly approaching a state of extreme agitation which surrounds us and are becoming fully available subjects for the propagandists of 'isms' . . . . What a damned thing hangs over us. There is no alternative, the material conditions of life inspire despair. People wish for only one thing, to shatter the hated shackles in which we are chained."[74]

A better understanding of the antagonisms between classes enabled workers to see more clearly how they were dependent on the capitalists. At the same time, it gave them a better understanding of the need to limit, weaken, even rid themselves of that dependence. On 5 February 1935, Frey wrote a secret memorandum: "Industry and labor are separated into more or less hostile camps animated by suspicion and therefore by antagonism."[75] Protests were having an effect. And workers were coming to understand that various strivings for improvement within the limits of their shops or enterprises were ineffectual. Outcomes, they determined, resulted from control over social mechanisms and participation (so far only participation) in governing.

72. See ibid., 41:42.

73. E[li] Ginsberg and H[yman] Berman, *The American Worker in the Twentieth Century: A History Through Autobiographies* (London, 1936), 3, 4; S[idney M.] Peck, *The Rank and File Leader* (New Haven, Conn., 1936), 38.

74. Library of Congress, William E. Borah Papers, container 606, Homer Owens to Borah, 25 March 1936.

75. Library of Congress, John P. Frey Papers, Correspondence, 1903–1951, folders 161–78, John P. Frey's Memorandum, 5 February 1935.

Increasingly serious differences between New Dealers and many influential bourgeoisie made the workers' reaction even stronger. This reaction enhanced Roosevelt's popularity, but it also fostered efforts to limit the political autocracy of an individual.

Antimonopoly feelings became the most important element in the new consciousness. In the eyes of millions of ordinary workers, big financiers and industrial capitalists were less and less the "great creative force." The myth crumbled as former enterprising geniuses acquired the look of "robber barons." Exposition of basic class conflicts and its incorporation into criticism of the egotistical interests of the monopolistic bourgeoisie made it possible for the majority to grasp the movement's special class character. The rhetoric of labor leaders such as Hillman and Lewis reflected the anger of workers over the uncontrolled power of major capital. In his previously mentioned speech in Cleveland (January 1935), Lewis spoke of the longstanding industrial and financial tyranny over American affairs that "should be destroyed immediately" if ever the plans of the labor movement were to be realized.[76]

In January 1936 Lewis arrived in Akron, Ohio, to find the town agitated and tense to the breaking point. Workers in a number of main plants of the Goodyear Corporation, the huge rubber empire, had started a sit-down strike to gain recognition of their right to organize unions. Local forces of "order" were waiting for the signal to attack the strikers. Even the most naive person who attended the meeting that featured Lewis as the main speaker could feel the crowd's hatred for the corporation's owners.[77] Certainly Lewis felt the fast pulse. He chose to talk about how the capitalist system deprived workers of their civil rights and denied them the material well-being to which they were entitled. "We are told," he said, "that labor and capital are partners, and that labor should be patient, and considerate, and not undertake to express its view . . . . Tell them, we are partners aren't we; partners in theory— enemies in fact."[78] The crowd received Lewis's speech enthusiastically. "It was not John L. Lewis's gift for oratory," one chronicler noted appropriately, "that won him overnight top place among Akron rubber workers. His speech and his appearance were remembered because he said what people already knew."[79] Lewis's feelings against monopolies were in harmony with the popular movement that was even more

76. WSHSL, AFL Papers, file C, box 1, W. Green Papers, 1934–1936.

77. In one interesting "memoir" of events in Akron (center of the rubber industry of the United States), it was said that not even the small business press dared to support the financiers and entrepreneurs. Further, "the class lines were drawn, for the first time in the history of the city, during the bank panic. And forever afterwards people in Akron would speak of the 'little fellow' not with, but against, 'the big fellow' " (R[uth] McKenney, *Industrial Valley* [New York, 1939], 82). The open admission that people were sensitive to class distinctions and that class conflict was becoming more pronounced was reflected in the words of one of Akron's leading merchants. In October 1934, he asked his fellow entrepreneurs not to abandon "brotherly solidarity." "The country cannot be happy if this class idea is promoted," he said. And he volunteered that "money is not important. Business is fun. That's why I gave my life to business, because it was fun, not because of the money" (ibid., 185).

78. Library of Congress, John P. Frey Papers, Speech of J. Lewis, Akron, Ohio, 19 January 1936; McKenney, *Industrial Valley*, 248, 249.

79. McKenney, *Industrial Valley*, 251.

highly developed by fall 1936. The working class, the new trade unions, had become a major force in a broad antimonopolistic coalition. In the consciousness of the masses, concentrated wealth ceased to be synonymous with national greatness and social well-being. People came to believe that when monopolies grabbed up national resources they impoverished the nation and established a base from which to attack its democratic institutions. When commissions headed by Senators J[oseph C.] O'Mahoney and R[obert P.] La Follette exposed the unpatriotic and antilabor attitudes of leading capitalists, antimonopolistic feelings coursed stronger. Long-cultivated sentiments of servility toward so-called enterprising geniuses, the captains of industry, were displaced by suspicion and anger. This was caused by the undisguised egoism and greed of the leading bourgeoisie—people whose only concern was their own well-being (even during the most critical moments in the life of the nation).

The tragic course of events in Italy and Germany exposed the tie between monopolistic capitalists and fascism. A comparison with similar developments in the United States prompted the observation (a correct one) that monopolies were a major danger to constitutional freedoms. When the CIO was formed the International Hatters Union unanimously resolved: "Wealth has become the possession of a few. The small number of corporations and the financial capital to which they are tied, hold within their enterprises many millions of workers and in their hands have a political and economic power that eclipses that of the government. Unaccustomed to obeying the laws except for those they choose to recognize, they are motivated exclusively by their desire to keep the government submissive to their monetary autocracy. In a case of necessity, like the similar forces in other countries, they too are ready to destroy democratic institutions, if those institutions threaten their oligarchal power. They do not hesitate to challenge the government. Every day they are mightier, their structure more autocratic and haughty."[80] The point of the declaration was that organized labor was the only force capable of saving the country from the financial-industrial oligarchy. During the Hatters' convention there was a heated discussion between partisans of the AFL and those of the CIO. However, the portion of the declaration quoted above did not occasion a single quarrel. Cecil Bragg, representative of the Philadelphia local of the United Electrical, Radio and Machine Workers Union (CIO), openly expressed what others well knew. The country's economic structure was in need of radical change. Currently it offered full advantages to a handful of financial and industrial magnates while it facilitated the parasitic exploitation of the destitute majority. Speaking at the convention in 1939, Bragg said: "Today all humanity and the labor movement have the inescapable duty of changing the economic conditions which have given birth to the unemployment of twelve million in our country. Our existing system has something depraved within it, otherwise the conditions which we encounter today would not have arisen . . . . There are steep

80. *United Hatters, Cap and Millinery Workers International Union Proceedings, October 7–11, 1936*, 85.

steps to be taken if we are ever to obtain our share of the wealth produced in our country."[81]

However, the understanding that change was needed did not automatically bring an understanding of the means and methods by which the power of monopolies could be limited. What would it take to defeat the forces that perpetuated class antagonism, that humiliated labor, that kept the material well-being of labor at such a low level? G. V. Plekhanov has written, "The formation of consciousness as a result of experience is a complex process that takes an indeterminate length of time. That is why workers do not always know what is in their own best interests."[82]

In the United States, given so many uniquely American counterarguments, the process was slow and indecisive. Nevertheless, during the stormy decade of the 1930s labor unions came close to becoming a reform movement, however diffuse, with a general idea of what a reasonably organized society should be. In such a rational society, workers would cease to be slaves to endless commands by a handful of financial and industrial magnates who lived sumptuously and cared not about the fate of the millions they exploited.[83] By the 1930s even those union members who had voted so enthusiastically for the AFL's "famous" Portland Manifesto of 1923 did not want to be reminded of its contents. The Portland Manifesto had categorically rejected government intervention in the economy and in dealings between labor and entrepreneurial capital. Then, in 1932, during its convention in Cincinnati, the AFL leadership yielded to pressure from below and declared its support for unemployment compensation. The AFL also supported the National Industrial Recovery Act (NIRA), which ascribed basic regulation of the economy to the government. Green called the NIRA a "great economic experiment" in which government took the only correct position—of intermediary between capital and labor. Green's support of this measure was highly unusual when considered against the background of orthodox Gompersism. But since there was a worsening "national crisis" and society was rapidly approaching collapse, only "constructive efforts" by government could prevent a catastrophe. Green concluded that all the labor movement's hopes depended on the success of the "great economic experiment" and resolved not to allow its enemies to destroy it.[84]

The identification of unions with ideas about a regulated economy and expansion of the government-run sector of the economy forced unions to reconsider their world view. For some the vision was clear, for others it was not. However, the touchstone of the new world view was real-life situations. Conservative groups in the labor movement admittedly feared the New Deal might unleash forces bent on the liquidation of individual enterprise: that is, socialism. One leader of the Steam Stokers and Machinists' Brotherhood wrote in February 1938, "No matter what the policies of

---

81. *United Electrical, Radio and Machine Workers of America Proceedings, 1939*, 43.

82. Plekhanov, *Complete Collected Works*, 12:14.

83. B[enjamin J.] Taylor and F[red] Whitney, "Unionism in the American Society," *Labor Law Journal* 18 (May 1967): 301.

84. *Cloth Hat, Cap and Millinery Workers International Union Proceedings, 1933*, 93, 94.

our union or any other union are, I oppose government ownership of the railroad of any other branches of the economy . . . . I fear that if we allow the government to get too involved in business life we play into the hands of the Communists."[85]

Yet the new unionists supported New Deal reforms and even came to see the need for radical measures beyond the scope of ordinary bourgeois reform. Their criticism was constructive, although it was not always heeded. Their errors and inconsistencies can be explained in large part by contradictions in American politics.[86] Reference is made to the two main orientations within the labor movement; to other movements situated between the two extremes that gravitated toward one or the other; and to movements that represented fewer workers, but were ideologically more clearly defined. Despite the AFL's long tradition of conforming, the organization began to question the natural play of economic forces that Gompersists had defended so ardently. Quietly, the AFL accepted government regulation as the most effective instrument in economic development.[87]

In the case of the CIO, the "new unionism" meant more. The CIO accepted unconditionally an increased government role in national economics. Its propaganda defended more far-reaching reforms. Most of all, the CIO insisted that the social upper-crust stop plundering human labor for their own enrichment and idle lifestyles. The CIO also demanded that business decisions be determined democratically, that the fruits of labor be distributed according to a plan, and that workers have greater participation in all decisions relating to socioeconomic development.[88]

These new political ideas were not always clearly articulated because they were emerging from the masses—people who were backward in matters of theory and who were just taking the first steps to overcome that condition. Also, at higher levels, proposals for structural reform were presented in such a way as to prove once again that the "working class is instinctively and spontaneously Social-Democratic."[89] "Today we do not accept being duped," one speaker told a wildly enthusiastic audience at the ILGWU convention in May 1937. "There are three words which

85. NYSSILRL, Record Group C-8, Frank Columbus Papers, (surname of the letter's author not provided) to Columbus, 14 February 1938.

86. See V. L. Malkov and D. G. Nadzhakov, *America at the Crossroads,* 196–97.

87. A. Henle, "Chronicle of Trade Union Positions on Government Ownership," *Monthly Labor Review* (July 1965): 816.

88. The AFL leaders reacted very nervously to what they considered a nihilistic approach to the sacrosanct right to private ownership. Such nihilism was apparent in the speeches of many advocates of the "new unionism." W[illiam] Green demanded that the AFL stand as a bastion against all "foreign influences" that would undermine capitalistic institutions. Green reaffirmed the traditional pro-bourgeoisie character of the AFL and warned that every concession the CIO extracted from the AFL should be written off as a loss for the defenders of capitalism. "Can it be supposed," he asked, "that the AFL would capitulate before a different type of movement? Is it conceivable that the AFL would abandon its position and be eliminated? Destroy a movement which has recognized the principle of private ownership and supported it already for almost three-quarters of a century? No, this is not conceivable" (*United Hatters, Cap and Millinery Workers International Union Proceedings, May 20–28, 1939,* 223).

89. Lenin, *Complete Collected Works,* 12:86.

begin with the letter 'P' [prices, profits, and politics—V. M.]. We should take specific steps toward these problems. To struggle for higher pay makes no sense if the cost of living grows even faster. To preserve high salaries, we have to fix prices and control inflation. We must convince American capital that it is vain to count on giving us concessions at our own expense. However, to achieve all this, we have to go seriously into the politics of direction and regulation."[90] John Brophy, as spokesperson for the CIO executive committee, told delegates to a special convention of the National Maritime Union of America that the economic upheavals of the 1930s resulted from the alienation of the working class in making economic policy. The main task for organized labor, Brophy declared, was to acquire new status in the economic mechanism for the working class, a status reflective of its power. "Only then will we be able to balance the economy, only when we workers find in ourselves the strength to assume functions within the governing process."[91]

This "idealism" in the CIO, contributed by progressive workers and radical intellectuals, was immensely attractive to many. Workers like Bregg, whose unsophisticated yet eloquent speech has been mentioned, supported the CIO because they considered the "new unionism" better than the AFL. It was not better because it was more *practical*, but because its orientation, in a social sense, was more correct— broader and from a clearer perspective. This segment of the working class welcomed the founding of the CIO and agreed with its criticisms of industrial autocracy and the cruel denials of workers' civil rights. It seemed to some that the variety of unionism espoused by AFL leaders constituted an adaptation to "big business." For all that, these condemnations of the "old order" were not accompanied by a determined effort to generate a program of social reconstruction. Among the illusions hampering reform were misunderstandings of the complex causes of exploitation and the essence of class struggle. The class struggle is a means for gradually improving the material conditions of workers in a capitalist system. It is also the creative force that brings about a radical transformation and lays the basis for a more perfect economic and political society.

The majority of the working class still thought empirically, and not yet in terms of programs. They questioned only whether the labor movement should reject the system that had ruined millions of fellow workers and forced them into idleness. Despite its outer attractiveness, the catchword of the day, "industrial democracy," had little real appeal.[92] It generally was understood to mean an alternative to the semi-feudal

90. *ILGWU Proceedings, 1937*, 207.

91. *National Maritime Union of America Proceedings, 1937*, 214.

92. The battle cry for an industrial democracy did not originate during the 1930s; it had been heard before. During earlier years, its meaning was illusive or different. For Gompers and the majority of his AFL colleagues, the term was almost synonymous with a good-neighbor relationship, structured around collective agreements between trade unions and the entrepreneurs. Capital's magnates perceived industrial democracy as a system of paternalistic relationships within the various enterprises. Some bourgeois analysts and politicians ascribed to the term the notion of "industrial partnership" and an "equal division of rewards" between the workers and capitalists. Such was the

order that then existed in many capitalistic enterprises (especially the industrial empires). Improving labor's position in an individual enterprise was inseparable from a revolutionary solution to socioeconomic and political problems at large. Under existing conditions, it was impossible to limit individual capitalists effectively without restricting oligarchic groups throughout the American economy (and still respect the inviolable principle that labor was subordinate to capital). No scheme to change this situation was ever worked out, and that failure was the main reason the "new unionism" never achieved a higher level of ideological maturity.

There were all sorts of suggestions for economic regulation by the government, for democratizing various enterprises, for labor to hold positions on administrative councils, for labor to have a voice in distribution, for labor to participate in defining policy in specific industries—indeed, for the protection of labor at every level.[93] However, the idea that the fundamental interests of American workers could be served only through fundamental basic economic and political changes was heard much less frequently.

The CIO's official publications, particularly the program adopted in October 1937, generally ignored this issue.[94] The changes in labor law and social relationships advocated in these publications and the speeches of most CIO leaders were little different from those advocated by bourgeois progressives—Senators [Robert] Wagner, [George] Norris, [Robert] La Follette, and others.[95] This conduct by the CIO leadership bespoke their opportunism. They were ardent in explaining the

---

understanding of "industrial democracy" during the 1920s by Herbert Clark Hoover, the idol of industrialists and future president of the United States. Among social reformists, the term meant the gradual elimination of the paid labor system and the establishment of a socialist order through peaceful means. Sometimes the term was perceived as an expression of a tendency toward partial nationalization (R[onald] Radosh, "The Corporate Ideology of American Labor from Gompers to Hillman," *Studies on the Left*, no. 6, 6:70; M[ilton] Derber, *Research in Labor Problems in the United States* [New York, 1967], 33–34). In the 1930s the term *industrial democracy* took on a lesser meaning. It became a part of the growing consciousness that class interests were polar and of the tendency to solve problems within the framework of an enterprise or even some branch of it. A resolution offered automobile workers at the CIO's special convention in Cleveland (April 1938) is revealing. According to the way the auto workers used the word, *industrial democracy* included the demand that corporations abandon the practice of dictating internal operations. The nature of the enterprise's operations should be determined only in agreement with the workers and the unions (*United Automobile Workers of America Proceedings, 1939*, 4). At the 1934 convention of the UAW, there was much discussion about workers' participation in running businesses. The discussion made clear that the term *industrial democracy* in many minds was not limited to labor's participation in determining working conditions and the status of unions. The issue became broader: workers should have a voice in deciding the distribution of profits (ibid., 75). Thus the aims of the labor movement seemed unjustly narrow.

93. See *National Maritime Union of America, Proceedings, 1937*, 217; *United Hatters, Cap and Millinery Workers International Union Proceedings, 1939*, 301–7, 326, 333, 334, and further.

94. CIO, *The Program of the C.I.O.* (Washington, 1937).

95. J[ohn L.] Lewis, *The C.I.O. Crusade* (Washington, 1937), 6; N. V. Kurkov, "From the History of the Struggle of American Miners for Social and Economic Rights in the 1930s," *Workers' and National Movement in the Countries of America* (Moscow, 1966), 84.

rapacity and inhumanity of the monopolists to crowds of workers; but they lost their gifts of speech and lapsed into passivity when called upon to explain their own positions and put them in a program document.

This said, one should not ignore clear efforts to implement social control of production and to find answers about the nature of control over the means of production. Questions on such issues turned up in the correspondence of many top labor leaders during the crisis years of 1929–1933. A vast majority of leftist labor unions led by Communists or left Socialists, unions that previously had joined the League for Industrial Democracy, saw socialization of industry, banking, and trade as the solution to contemporary problems. In one form or another that demand was incorporated into speeches by a great many activists in the middle and lower ranks of the CIO. With increasing frequency, one heard voices raised in behalf of nationalizing idled plants and even entire branches of industry. Such recommendations were heard even at AFL conventions. The Committee on Unemployment of the Labor Federation of Minnesota sent a proposal to the Fifty-First Congress that expansion of individual ownership be restricted and that government control be imposed on all aspects of the private sector. The committee supported the "fundamental principles" of the NIRA; but the members hoped subsequent developments would lead to greater abundance for labor on the one hand and sharper restrictions on private acquisitions on the other. The authors envisioned a gradual transformation in which the blatant exploitation of labor would cease while social well-being would be preserved.[96] The polemics in which these propositions were encased led to serious differences of opinion within the federation. At the 1934 convention, delegates of the United Tailors' Union introduced a resolution concerning efforts of the NIRA to deal with the economic crisis— a crisis caused by flaws at the heart of the capitalistic system. The resolution said the "capitalistic economy is organized in such a way as to enrich the few to the detriment of the material well-being of society as a whole." Then there was the demand that all idle businesses be taken over by the state in order to put the unemployed to work at salaries on which they could support themselves. The [Minnesota] convention passed the resolution.[97] However, subsequent events proved that a majority of the state's AFL leaders remained loyal to the ideologically ill-defined, eclectic position put forward by the executive committee in 1933.

Nonetheless, a minority persisted. As they saw it, continuing unemployment and "all the empty reflections of economics" only strengthened the proposition that "private ownership of industrial plants has proven its inability to provide material security for the worker." This minority submitted their resolution to the federation's convention in 1935. It demanded nationalization of idle enterprises and their transfer to workers' cooperatives. The resolution was filled with angry words directed against the capitalists; and it did not pass.[98] Its proponents, nonetheless, did not abandon hope for a breakthrough.[99]

96. *Minnesota State Federation of Labor Proceedings, 1933*, 50, 51.
97. Ibid., 1934, 49.
98. Ibid., 1935, 65.
99. Ibid., 1938, 83–85.

The idea of nationalizing the means of production (partially or completely) was better received by labor unions in Wisconsin, a state known for its long-standing ties with the Socialist movement. In 1933, among other goals, the state's federation accepted the following: "8. Municipal ownership of all municipal enterprises. (This should be understood as a union of inhabitants within cooperatives and as the liquidation of private monopolies' power over public utilities that gave a minority the capacity to enrich themselves at the expense of the majority.) 9. Nationalization of communication, transportation and natural resources. (All these branches of the economy should be in the hands of the people and function in the national interest. In the case of private citizens, they especially fulfilled an opposing role.) 10. National collective ownership of production and distribution. (This means that when any sector reaches a high degree of concentration and falls under the power of trusts and monopolies, that sector should be turned over to the government, as is demanded by the interests of the nation.)"[100]

Annually, until 1945, these theses remained in the platform of the Wisconsin Federation of Labor. Individual labor unions submitted resolutions at their conventions, making the recommendations more precise, specifying the fields and economic sectors that should be nationalized. And all these resolutions were welcomed by the delegates.[101] Still, a majority of the big AFL unions passed over these issues. The elite among the leadership of the major craft unions seemed to have a knack for leading discussion at their conventions into "safe" and conventional topics. Unlike many well-known CIO leaders, the AFL executive core preferred to speak softly about the sins of American capital, to present them as correctable, not as ruinous. According to these leaders, American society was strong because of cooperation among the classes. "The unity of class aspirations" that supposedly characterized American social relationships was inevitably contrasted with the "purely European phenomenon" of a debilitating class struggle that fostered "totalitarianism." So argued the Gompersists. W[illiam] Green argued in 1939, for example, that the prejudice and social hatred on which fascism fed did not exist in the U.S.[102]

In contrast, speakers at conventions of unions affiliated with the CIO were unrelentingly critical of society. The most opinionated among them realized that palliatives (monetary aid, administrative reforms, etc.) offered only an illusion that dysfunctions in the system had been eliminated. One such leader of anticapitalistic orientation was Michael Quill, president of the International Transport Workers Union. He dedicated a great many speeches to explanations of the need for a new social order. "The old system has had the opportunity to prove itself for 160 years, and now we want changes," he told delegates to the convention of Electrical, Radio and Machine Workers in 1939.[103]

Quill believed the establishment of the new socioeconomical system would be smooth, bloodless, and painless—the further development of democracy and the

100. *Wisconsin State Federation of Labor Proceedings, 1933*, 4.
101. Ibid., 1934, 44, 100; ibid., 1935, 141.
102. *United Hatters, Cap and Millinery Workers International Union Proceedings, 1939*, 220.
103. *United Electrical, Radio and Machine Workers of America, Proceedings, 1939*, 138.

expression of voter sentiment. Representative bodies devoted to the interests of labor would be the result of rational choice. The first measure of the new government would be to assume control of the railroads; then, said Quill, government would accelerate the construction of housing in order to provide working families with inexpensive living quarters. He also believed it was urgent to destroy the control of monopolistic capital over the food industry and, without exception, to strengthen the regulatory role of government in other sectors of the economy.[104]

The influential leader of the millinery union (CIO), Joseph Schlossberg, had different ideas about the necessary conditions for the birth of a new society. In a speech to labor movement activists, later published in *Advance*, the millinery workers' popular periodical, he said: "The primary aim of the working movement consists in working class freedom from the hard work on which the capitalist system rests. This will not happen either automatically, nor suddenly. To accomplish it, a long process of trial and error is necessary . . . . Capitalism can attain a high degree of development, which makes possible the transition to socialism; however, without a forceful, conscious and active workers' movement there is no possibility for socialism . . . . The worker can be set free only as the result of incessant struggle . . . . Can the working movement attain this high aim? Might it be that all that is only a dream, a utopia? No, this is neither a dream, nor a utopia. The working movement is redirecting itself toward this goal."[105]

Even though the majority of union members shared Quill's expectation of a radical economic transformation, it was, to use Lenin's words, as "a dream, and not as an overthrow of the exploiting class government; it had the form of peaceful submission to a minority which understood its duty toward the majority."[106]

Nevertheless, one must admit that the level of political consciousness among the membership of America's labor unions was rising, however immature and utopian its nature. Inside the CIO the dialogues were characterized by equality among the discussants, by democratic procedures, and by freedom to express and to disagree. These conditions were conducive to the development of political consciousness, which in turn prompted countermeasures by the Gompersists. The new ideas were meek in part because the ardent opposition of Gompersists was undiminished and in part because conditions in the United States at the time worked against them. The majority of workers had tied their innermost hopes for resolving national economic problems and ending poverty and mass unemployment to implementation of New Deal reforms. And this implementation was to be attained through traditional methods, from the top, through elections, the result of pressure on "friendly workers," in the context of government institutions, and so on. Many honestly believed that the anarchy that characterized production could be overcome gradually, without any kind of political overthrow. They believed that the private economy, controlled by

104. Ibid.
105. *Advance*, June 1935, 11.
106. *Complete Collected Works*, 33:25.

the government, would achieve permanent stability. Under the influence of the petty bourgeoisie—and of the radicalism and neo-liberalism that was so widespread in the United States at the time—workers were deluded into believing they could bypass a series of developmental phases and not have to endure a fight and the radical reorganization of political power. The influence of the petty bourgeoisie was apparent in the willy-nilly approach to creating something new by compromising and working hand-in-hand with the old order. The rank and file of the CIO were not yet prepared to accept the sober judgments of leaders like Schlossberg.

The CIO program that was accepted at its convention in Atlantic City in 1937 set out the union's position on civil rights and the expansion of democratic institutions. The CIO program reaffirmed that it was the organization's obligation to fight infringements upon civil rights.[107] The CIO considered tragic clashes to be a brutal reality—a characteristic of political conditions in a society in which two hostile camps (capital and labor) confronted each other. Victory for one side necessarily meant defeat for the other. The AFL, unlike the CIO, ascribed all the losses and failures of the labor movement to the "craziness of extremists" or the instigations of radicals. The daring fight of those who supported the "new unionism" against the monolithic bourgeoisie proved that active forms of mass struggle were superior in achieving democracy and right to the declarative methods that hypocritical Gomper-sists strongly favored. In fact, the latter's talk about freedom hid their true anti-democratic feelings. Many CIO leaders voiced fear for the future of democracy in America because of dangers posed by aggressive monopolies. The monopolies were manipulating justifiably discontented people to blame false targets—"instigators," "radicals," and "reds." Preserving the fighting spirit inside the labor movement was clearly the best guarantee that democratic gains would not be lost. In his speech to the convention of the ILGWU in 1937, Hillman said: "Remember that the labor movement should at all times preserve a fighting character; otherwise it will be thrown back. Even if we wanted to, we cannot stand in one place. The forces that we are facing are the same forces with which we clashed during the elections in November of 1936, during the course of the most historically important election campaign of our country. We should not lie to ourselves; the forces did not go away and at the first opportunity they will attempt to install a regime of concentration camps, where they will expel workers and liberals."[108]

Their own grim struggles for survival had shown the new unions the danger on the right. Their experiences taught them (though not always clearly) that the struggle for democracy and the economic and social rights of labor was the same fight as the fight against monopolies and monopoly influences in government.

In 1937, at the first special convention of the National Maritime Union, Joseph Karren declared: "The CIO has become a new face in our country, embodying such a labor movement, which not only defends the purely material interest of workers, but

107. CIO, *The Program of the C.I.O.*, 50, 56.
108. *ILGWU Proceedings*, 1937, 357.

also is quickly becoming one of the main defenders of the democratic institutions and democratic freedoms of the American nation. It has become the bastion of struggle against reactionaries, 'economic royalists,' to use the words of Secretary of the Interior Harold Ickes. We have to unite with the CIO not only because it gives us necessary might, but also in order to facilitate realization of the general principles of the workers' movement."[109] In a gesture of solidarity the Maritime Union unanimously adopted a resolution that characterized "the big industrialists and economic royalists" as the main danger to the American labor movement and society in general.[110] In his address to the Maritime Union convention, John Brophy (executive director of the CIO) tried to sustain the mood by emphasizing the deep political differences between the reactionary bourgeoisie and the new unions.[111]

Maurice Spector, a leader of the Hatters Union, expanded on the aims of the "new unionism" in a rousing speech at his union's convention in 1939. Spector denied that the CIO willfully and consciously provoked situations in which there was danger of bloodshed or danger of forcing public opinion to shift to the right. The actions of the CIO, he insisted, were not only lawful, they were necessary in the struggle to achieve democratic ideals. It was the working masses, he said, who breathed life into the CIO, and in so doing they had offered to sacrifice to keep alight the spirit of a better America. This belief in the future inspired the entire labor movement. In conclusion Spector said: "There is no reason to be nervous about the evolving situation. We are experiencing a painful process, but the birth of a child is also demanding on a woman. The CIO gave life to a new movement. Of course it was not without big sacrifices. Everyone among us hates bloodshed; however, principled people of high ideals never stop before decisive actions . . . . The AFL increased the number of its members in many ways thanks to the existence of the CIO. This is the truth."[112]

The bourgeoisie and leaders of the AFL attempted to scare workers away from the "new unionism" by screaming "socialism!" Many union leaders anticipated the maneuvers of the enemies of unity in the proletarian movement and exposed their tricks. In so doing, they showed whose rapacious interests the self-appointed and jealous guardians of the "American way" were defending. The argument against these critics usually were constructed on two premises: first, enlarging the horizons of the labor movement is a process that is consistent with natural law, and it should not be opposed nor limited according to the decrepit ideas of Gompers; and second, socialism cannot be perceived as an incompatible phenomenon with the ideas inspired by the rise of the lower working class. One cannot fight for a democratic alternative to the old order if one fears socialism.

As Michael Quill told the United Electrical, Radio and Machine Workers in the

109. *National Maritime Union of America Proceedings,* 1937, 80, 81.
110. Ibid., 121. Analogous formulations, textually similar, can be found also in the materials of other major unions in the CIO (see, for example, the *International Union of United Automobile Workers of America, Proceedings, 1939,* 93).
111. *National Maritime Union of America Proceedings, 1937,* 216–17.
112. *United Hatters, Cap and Millinery Workers International Union, Proceedings,* 1939, 454–56.

previously mentioned convention speech in September 1939: "When we speak about government regulation of major industry, they (i.e., the monopolists) go into a panic and attach to it the label of some 'ism' . . . . When we speak about the creation of a public housing fund, about the construction of residential housing with government money, they immediately announce that it injures the competitive capability of big landlords and big construction firms. To them it is an anti-American action which infringes upon private rights . . . . Our task is difficult, since they constantly put sticks in our wheels. In recent years we have heard more and more often about the problem of Communism. Everyone who sticks his head above water, takes into hand the placard of a striker, visits a meeting, or stands for high rates of profits for workers, is called a Communist. The power of possessions could never exist without a scarecrow or trickery . . . . It was so in the 1900s, the 1920s, and in the 1930s. At one time they said that organized working movements followed anarchists. Today they scream about the Communists."[113] At the same convention the executive secretary of the League of Workers, Eli Oliver, said: "When the conservatively inclined congressman says that Americans will not accept socialism, he really means the following: 'We want to continue to exercise our power over the workers and farmers of America, to wring out of them everything they are capable of.' At the same time he says to us that the fight for improvement of our material condition leads directly to socialism . . . . Such is the doctrine of the capitalists. God save you in the attempt to get something to eat, if you do not want to arrive at Socialism! We cannot take a single step in the direction of improving life without being told: 'You are on your way to Socialism and Communism.' In spite of this, we are going to take the necessary steps . . . regardless of all the labels and characterizations which will be put upon our action by conservative Republicans and Democrats in Congress. These steps have to be taken, regardless of everything."[114]

Generally speaking, new industrial unions in the major industries prohibited discrimination based on political conviction or party affiliation (and they embodied those prohibitions in their charters and by-laws). The United Automobile Workers (UAW), to cite but one example, rejected a resolution at their convention in 1936 that proposed closing the doors to Communists. The union then proceeded to admit workers regardless of race, national origin, creed, or party affiliation. Indeed, leftists and Communists played a leading role in organizing the UAW and, for a considerable period, in its direction.[115]

Events in Europe—the advent of fascism in Italy and Germany and the tragic fate of the labor and democratic movements in those countries—placed a new question squarely before the progressive wing of the labor movement in the United States. What should be its role in the fight for democracy and the struggle against internal reactionaries who might see in the Italo-German experiment a blueprint for problem

---

113. *United Electrical, Radio and Machine Workers of America, Proceedings, 1939*, 135.
114. Ibid., 160.
115. *Daily World*, 2 January 1971.

solving? CIO leaders frequently tried to incorporate international considerations in their analysis of emerging conditions. They considered the possibility of a fascist overthrow in the United States a very real threat, and they believed the masses could ward it off. "We have at our disposal a very strong labor movement," declared Brophy to thundering applause at the Automobile Workers convention in 1939. "The movement knows too well its enemy and knows how to fight it."[116]

Of course, not every assessment of these developments was distinguished by balance, depth, or objectivity. However, they were characterized by one common trait: recognition that labor and the fate of the country depended on developing a policy to thwart the international, profascist feelings of the monopolists. Usually leaders of CIO unions directly or obliquely criticized U.S. foreign policy. They stressed Washington's intent to protect imperialist interests while failing to heed simultaneous popular demands for peace and collective security.[117]

As for the AFL, its national conventions and those of the state labor federations inevitably declared themselves against fascism and war. However, they usually ignored questions about their sources and preconditions. As a result, AFL assessments of socioeconomic and political developments outside the United States appeared to be extraneous to their concerns about American domestic life. Analyses of international conditions by the elite of the AFL did not show great concern for eliminating the threat of war. The elite did permit themselves angry statements against Communism and the Soviet Union, together with the opinion that fascism resulted from the imperfections and vices of the human spirit and from flaws in the political organization of this or that country. They presented the United States as the bastion of democratic order, freedom, and justice. The majority of AFL unions (both separate labor unions and state federations) trusted the foreign policy of the White House and State Department. The AFL did not lay out the basis for its analysis. Of course, all this did not mean that AFL members en masse were indifferent to international crises and their domestic consequences. The membership was not homogeneous. There are known instances in which resolutions were proposed and passed by AFL bodies that addressed the problems of war and peace and of fascism and democracy from antimonopolistic and antifascist positions.[118] It should be noted, however, that independent expressions of opinion by AFL unions were the exception and not the rule. The executive committee did not encourage deviation from its assessment of United States foreign policy. For many reasons, unions that joined the federation preferred not to contradict.

116. *United Automobile Workers of America, Proceedings, 1939,* 24; see also Kurkov, "From the History of the Struggle of American Miners for Social and Economic Rights in the 1930s," 105.

117. See, for example, *ACWA Proceedings, 1938,* 360; *United Automobile Workers of America Proceedings, 1939,* 164.

118. See, for example, *Wisconsin State Federation of Labor Proceedings, 1934,* 101–3, 133, 134; *AFL Proceedings, 1935,* 182; *Minnesota State Federation of Labor Proceedings, 1935,* 44; ibid., 1936, 53; ibid., 1937, 88; ibid., 1939, 87, 88; *Wisconsin State Federation of Labor Proceedings, 1939,* 237.

Advocates of the "new unionism" were more forceful and forthcoming in their conclusions about developments in domestic and international life, and they made judgments in the context of class struggle. In contrast, the AFL usually was concerned with cooperation among the classes. The differences were broadened by the CIO's suspicions and skepticism toward bipartisanship and by the large number of CIO members who favored the establishment of a labor party for the masses.[119]

For some time the CIO had developed ideologically and politically. It was markedly different from Gompersism, a movement that had become the living incarnation of all the extremes of bourgeois labor politics. As Lenin wrote, Gompers's policy was aimed always at pressing the working class to forget about "their freedom goals" and to limit themselves to "preoccupation about alliances with one or another bourgeois party in order to obtain imaginary 'improvement' of their slave status."[120] The "new unionism" challenged labor's pitiable subservience to the bourgeoisie. For many years servility had undermined the strength of the working class, although AFL leaders had touted it as absolutely essential—something without which there would be no labor movement. Through its struggles and considerable successes in the area of social policy, the CIO had proved the opposite. In many ways, the strengths and weaknesses of the "new unionism" were reflected in the eclipse of Gompers's heritage in the areas of ideas and actions. The ideas of contemporaries about the future were bound to be affected profoundly by the split between the organization of craft professionals and unions that had broader social aims, naturally inclined to be anti-bourgeois and politically independent. In 1938 the author of an article in an American scientific publication commented on the struggle inside the labor movement: "It is not unlikely that the present rift in the American labor movement is an indication of the transition from the middle-class character of American labor ideology to what may be termed a labor-class ideology. The ultimate outcome of such a rift may be an attempt to give political expression to this new class ideology through the formation of a labor party . . . ."[121]

A number of very serious events, including the war, interfered with this development. The process was cut short. Yet the complex and difficult course of the American labor movement continues to ascend to a new level of ideological maturity. The report of the Central Committee of the Communist Party of the Soviet Union to the Twenty-fourth Party Congress said: "In the United States there is a broad rise of importance of the working class against monopolies in addition to the unusual sharpness of the black people's struggle for equality as well as that of the youth against the war in Vietnam."[122] The day is coming, Gus Hall has emphasized, when labor unions in the United States will follow progressive, militant workers and the Com-

119. See further V. L. Malkov, "F. Engels and the American Workers' Movement" (on the question of creating a third party), *Questions of History* 11 (1970): 18–33.
120. *Complete Collected Works*, 22:232.
121. *American Journal of Sociology* 43 (January 1938): 525.
122. L[eonid I.] Brezhnev, *Report of the Central Committee of the CPSU to the 24th Congress of the Communist Party of the Soviet Union* (Moscow, 1971), 20.

munists. "The history of the working class also develops in a certain direction."[123] It should be remembered that "only through the long struggle and hard work of the most progressive and conscious workers there arose the possibility of purging and separating the proletariat class movement from all kinds of petty bourgeois additions, limitations, narrow-mindedness, and vices."[124]

---

123. Hall, "History Has a Direction," *Political Affairs* (November 1970): 11.
124. Lenin, *Complete Collected Works*, 25:100–101.

Nelson Lichtenstein

Comment on "The Crisis of Gompersism and the Foundation of the CIO: Ideological and Political Aspects," by V. L. Malkov

V. L. Malkov composed his 1971 essay on the origins and character of the early CIO at a critical juncture in the history of American labor scholarship. In the United States, and throughout the West, the influence of the first postwar generation of social scientists and historians had begun to wane. They had found the system of industrial relations that emerged out of the New Deal years a bulwark of pluralist democracy, welfare state capitalism, and limitless economic advance. But the cohort of New Left and neo-Marxist scholars that were now appearing on the scene proved far more critical of the political structures that jelled in the late Depression years. The social democratic tenor of those years proved too pallid for their tastes. Malkov therefore shares with the new generation of labor historians an effort to find an alternative to what he calls the dominant tradition of "bourgeois historiography," although this Soviet scholar seems unaware of even the earliest impact of the American New Left on this problem.

Malkov's "bourgeois historians" include the labor economists Philip Taft, Joel Seidman, and Walter Galenson, and though he fails to mention them by name, such influential historians of the New Deal as Arthur Schlesinger, Jr., Carl Degler, and James McGregor Burns would also fall in this category. Although never particularly systematic about it, Malkov charges these scholars on three grounds: first, in their "compassionless descriptions of the 1930s," the "working class appears as a passive mass" whose fate was largely in the hands of President Roosevelt and other bourgeois reformers. Second, Malkov argues that these labor and political historians have all too often seen the crux of the problem in the labor movement as one of organizational structure (i.e., craft vs. industrial unionism) rather than political and ideological conflict between the new unions and the old Gompersarians. And finally, Malkov puts forth the charge, simultaneously repeated by a generation of social historians, that the history of labor in the 1930s requires an exploration of local materials, a need to search for the attitudes and feelings of workers, "in a word, about the true state of consciousness of the central figure in the events, the ordinary workers."

In many respects the liberal historians and social scientists writing in the 1950s and 1960s did celebrate the New Deal as the great and salutary turning point in the history of industrial America, in which a tight focus on the personality and politics of the president relegated the new union movement of that era to a supporting role, whose importance lay merely in the extent to which it proved an obstacle or spur to federal social reform. To some extent this is even true in one of the finest works of labor scholarship of that era, Sidney Fine's *Sit-Down: The General Motors Strike of 1936–1937*, which puts the role of Michigan's New Deal governor Frank Murphy at the center of events.[1] But Malkov's charge here seems both off the mark and over-stated. It would be hard to characterize the work of Irving Bernstein's 1969 *Turbulent Years* as "passionless," nor are Arthur Schlesinger's chapters on the social move-ments of the Left in his multivolume *Age of Roosevelt* without genuine fire and sympathy.[2] However, it may well be that Malkov's impatience with these scholars arises not so much from their supposed devaluation of the workers' movement of that era, as from their presumption that the radicalism of the New Deal era labor move-ment was but a transitory characteristic, rightly and easily accommodated by the new industrial-relations system the Roosevelt administration put in place. In this context, Malkov rightly emphasizes that the labor movement's internal debate over craft ver-sus industrial organization proved far less important than the political and social thrust of the new unionism, a point first emphasized by labor historians Melvyn Dubofsky and David Brody.[3] Most American historians would agree with Malkov that in the crucial years of the mid–1930s one important difference between the CIO and AFL was simply that of energy and hopefulness. Impressionistically, but not incorrectly, Malkov describes these CIO unions as characterized by "unusually rebellious activities and their adoption of higher ideals than were embodied in the wisdom of Gompers. . . . The new atmosphere was incompatible with routine, stag-nation, defeatism, and spiritual pettiness—all of which had consumed the majority of the old trade unions."

Having granted Malkov this much, it is hard to know what to make of his essay. The usual complaint Western scholars offer Soviet work is that the latter rely too heavily on boiler-plate quotations from the Marxist classics, and indeed there are the usual references here to Marx, Lenin, and even Gus Hall. But these are irritating less because of any straitjacket they put on the author's thinking than because in Malkov's hands they seem simply irrelevant to the issues at hand. For all its Marxist pretense, Malkov's work is disjointed and sentimental. The essay never defines Gompersism in any precise way, except to indicate that it represents pig-headed and retrograde con-servatism. Malkov might, for example, have found in Lenin's work on imperialism and the "aristocracy of labor" a material and organizational basis for AFL insularity and jingoism. Nor does Malkov's work discuss popular consciousness except as a sense of undifferentiated solidarity and militancy in the service of an "anti-monopoly" coalition. Along with Irving Bernstein, Malkov points out that there was much AFL militancy in the National Recovery Administration years (1933–1934) and that later not all AFL locals supported the anti-CIO campaign of federation leaders William Green and John Frey, but this hardly begins to penetrate the multi-layered consciousness of industrial workers during that decade.

1. *Sit-Down: The General Motors Strike of 1936–1937* (Ann Arbor, 1969); and of course Fine went on to write a three-volume biography of Frank Murphy.
2. Bernstein, *The Turbulent Years: A History of the American Worker, 1933–1941* (New York, 1969); Schlesinger, *The Politics of Upheaval, 1935–1936* (New York, 1960).
3. Dubofsky and Warren Van Tine, *John L. Lewis: A Biography* (New York, 1977); Brody, *Work-ers in Industrial America* (New York, 1980).

Moreover, there is virtually nothing on the character of the New Deal state (one could imagine Lenin's sharp comments here) and no curiosity concerning the relationship between rank-and-file workers and the CIO leadership, an issue not ignored in the industrial-relations literature of the 1950s and 1960s. Nor does the essay demonstrate any interest in what happened after the CIO's formative moment in 1936 and 1937. These were the months when the New Deal sounded most radical, when foreign affairs were relatively unimportant, when Socialists, Communists, and Catholic corporatists were most in agreement, and when the AFL, stunned by the CIO secession and success, seemed indeed to have slid into a dustbin of history. But a little perspective here might have gone a long way. Thus as evidence of CIO radicalism Malkov quotes several of the more anticapitalist passages found in the speeches of New York needle trades leaders. Certainly their rhetoric reflected many years of Socialist party experience, but after 1937 the unions of hatters and ladies garment workers would return to the AFL. And under the leadership of Sidney Hillman, the Amalgamated Clothing Workers would raise its traditional policy of "class collaboration" with both employers and New Dealers to such a level of sophistication that the ACW president won the title "labor statesman" for the remaining years of his life.[4]

Since the early 1970s one can find in the work of American historians a rich and largely successful effort to break from the perspectives of "bourgeois historiography" condemned by V. L. Malkov. Not all these scholars would define themselves as Marxist, even in the expansive definition of the term used on the academic left, but all have gravitated toward an analysis that asks the kind of questions posed by traditional Marxist scholarship. In the late 1960s and early 1970s the New Left notion that the Wagner Act and other New Deal reforms simply represented an effort by a far-sighted wing of capital to coopt insurgent forces proved popular, but intensive research in business and governmental archives has rather quickly discarded this once-popular explanation for the failure of Depression-era radicalism to make more of an impact on the character of American trade unions. Except for a tiny and rather uninfluential minority, big business was bitterly hostile to the new labor movement and the legal/administrative reforms that sustained it. This is not to say that the New Deal did not reconstitute and stabilize class relations in the United States, but as Theda Skocpol and Howell Harris have shown, this process could only take place when a combination of popular mobilization from below and state activism from above generated a brief window of opportunity in which a new system of industrial relations could be imposed on a temporarily weakened business community.[5]

---

4. Steve Fraser, "From the 'New Unionism' to the New Deal," *Labor History* 25 (1984): 405–30.

5. The classic New Left statement remains Ronald Radosh, "The Corporate Liberal Ideology of American Labor Leaders from Gompers to Hillman," in *For a New America: Essays in History and Politics from "Studies on the Left," 1959–1967*, ed. James Weinstein and David Eakins (New York, 1970), 125–51. In contrast see Theda Skocpol, "Political Response to Capitalist Crisis: Neo-Marxist Theories of the State and the Case of the New Deal," *Politics and Society* 10 (1980): 155–201; Howell Harris, "The Snares of Liberalism?: Politicians, Bureaucrats, and the Shaping of Federal

Perhaps the main thrust of Malkov's essay is to draw a sharp line between the politics of CIO and AFL leaders, to demonstrate that their differences were hardly ones of mere personality or institutional power, but represented significant ideological visions of how the unions should function in a capitalist society. Although he does indicate that CIO rhetoric sometimes simply replicated that of such liberal Democrats as George Norris and Robert Wagner, Malkov finds CIO denunciations of monopoly far more progressive than that of the insular and self-satisfied AFL. Undoubtedly CIO leaders were able to make use of a more social democratic idiom that captured the aspirations of a generation of immigrant and black Americans who saw the CIO as a vehicle for their participation in and redefinition of mainstream society.

But as the New Deal promise has faded, historians have actually become more critical of the CIO's brand of labor politics, especially its reliance on the state apparatus and the Democratic party, and conversely these same historians have found in the tradition of AFL volunteerism unexpectedly intriguing virtues. Almost all of the CIO's leading figures, including those in the Communist orbit, tied their organization to the politics of the Roosevelt coalition even as the New Deal stumbled rightward after 1938. There was much labor party talk, but after 1936 little action. Of all its major personalities, only John L. Lewis sought to give the CIO an independent political voice, and after 1940 he became an increasingly marginal figure in American politics. Where the CIO did make an effort to bring forward a distinct political program, it tended toward corporatism rather than social democracy. Certainly this was the perspective of Philip Murray and so many others in the CIO's heavily Catholic leadership stratum.[6] And as Steve Fraser has shown, Sidney Hillman and other industrial union leaders in the competitive industrial sector saw a strong union as essential both to rationalize production and discipline radical and/or parochial elements within the working class. In alliance with the New Deal state, Hillman sought to build a sociopolitical foundation for a more stable regime of Keynesian demand management. This would prove a radical break with the undisciplined capitalism of the era from 1870 to 1930, but it hardly represented a step on the road toward socialism.[7]

Historians have also begun to find in the old Gompers AFL some virtues once obscured by the liberal tilt of the New Deal industrial-relations system. As Christopher Tomlins has emphasized (overemphasized actually), the AFL saw state

Labour Relations Policy in the United States, ca. 1915–1947," in *Shop Floor Bargaining and the State: Historical and Comparative Perspectives,* ed. Steven Tolliday and Jonathan Zeitlin (London, 1985), 148–91.

6. Mike Davis, *Prisoners of the American Dream* (London, 1986), 52–101; and Nelson Lichtenstein, *Labor's War at Home: The CIO in World War II* (New York, 1983).

7. Fraser, "Dress Rehearsal for the New Deal: Shop-floor Insurgents, Political Elites, and Industrial Democracy in the Amalgamated Clothing Workers," in *Working-Class America: Essays on Labor, Community, and American Society,* ed. Michael Frisch and Daniel Walkowitz (New York, 1983), 212–55.

control of union-management relations as a threat to its institutional integrity and its historic claim that the construction of an industrial order must lie primarily within the ambit of the union movement itself. The AFL therefore declared its hostility to both the CIO and much of the New Deal labor-relations philosophy.[8] There was much hyperbole in its denunciation of those who would trample on its historic claims, because as Michael Rogin and Michael Kazin have demonstrated, state and city AFL bodies were not above making important alliances with local political parties and government agencies when these proved advantageous. And of course, the AFL was not above the use of some anti-Semitism and a good deal more red-baiting in its efforts to discredit the new industrial-union movement and those elements within the government that helped sustain it.[9]

Since Vietnam and Watergate, AFL fears of a strong state have begun to seem much more plausible to leftist historians. After 1938 the CIO alliance with the Rooseveltian New Deal paid out far fewer dividends than before, in part because such important agencies as the National Labor Relations Board and the wartime wage adjustment agencies bent themselves toward an accommodation with those forces hostile to a strong industrial-union movement. Moreover, a whole school of neo-Marxist legal studies has taken as one of its axioms the cooptive and repressive character of the federal labor law, embodied in even such reformist legislation as the Wagner Act of 1935, not to mention Taft-Hartley twelve years later.[10] Moreover, this latter-day reappreciation of the AFL has also been advanced by the realization that as a trade-union movement the older federation did not do so badly after all. Although Malkov emphasizes the "passive" quality of the AFL, affiliates like the Teamsters, Machinists, and Carpenters quickly adopted elements of the CIO organizational structure and strike tactics, thus enabling the old federation to outpace the new group in almost every year after 1937. This growth partially reflected employers' preference for the conservative AFL over the "red" CIO, but its success also flowed from the AFL's mixed craft-industrial structure, which actually best fit the contours of such long-term economic growth sectors of the economy as transport and retail trade far better than did the CIO's more rigid industrial set-up.[11]

Finally, there is the issue of working-class consciousness in the 1930s, and in recent years historians have brought to its study a number of models of working-class behavior. In the early 1970s New Left historians like Jeremy Brecher and Staughton Lynd celebrated the radical potential of the Depression-era working class in the years just before the emergence of the CIO. But like Malkov, who is also aware of the

8. Tomlins, *Organized Labor, the Law, and National Labor Policy* (Baltimore, 1985).

9. Rogin, "Voluntarism: The Political Functions of an Antipolitical Doctrine," *Industrial and Labor Relations Review* 15 (July 1962): 521–35; and Kazin, *Barons of Labor: The San Francisco Building Trades and Union Power in the Progressive Era* (Urbana, 1987).

10. See for example Karl Klare, "The Judicial Deradicalization of the Wagner Act and the Origins of Modern Legal Consciousness, 1937–1941," *Minnesota Law Review* 62 (1978): 265–339.

11. Tomlins, "AFL Unions in the 1930s: Their Performance in Historical Perspective," *Journal of American History* 65 (1979): 1021–42.

mobilization that took place in 1933 and 1934, these New Left scholar-activists saw this early militancy in largely unambiguous and undifferentiated terms. They were less interested in understanding the internal texture of this militancy than in arguing that a labor-relations system built upon this mobilization might well have proved more accommodative toward a regime of institutionalized workers' power than that eventually engendered by the CIO and the NLRB half a decade later.[12]

In this regard, Malkov occasionally uses the word *spontaneous* to describe worker activism in these years. Such a phrase was also used by the early New Leftists, but in the years after 1975 most radical historians came to think that a reference to "spontaneity" was ahistorical and crude because the phrase distances and objectifies consciousness in a most un-Marxist fashion. At mid-decade Peter Friedlander's pathbreaking work pointed up the extraordinarily mixed character of working-class consciousness as a way of discovering precisely which layers of the working class, indeed which individuals in a particular factory, were responsible for the micro-historical shifts in sentiment and ideology which, taken from a distance, amounted to the seemingly "spontaneous" activism of that era. Friedlander's schema highlighted the ethnocultural dimensions of working-class consciousness and found in the peculiar experience of second-generation East European workers the mass base both for CIO activism and its latter-day bureaucraticism.[13]

His almost anthropological approach was soon appropriated by historians who examined the 1930s working class with particular reference to other of its characteristics, including skill, gender, religion, and ethnicity. Joshua Freeman, Ronald Schatz, Gary Gerstle, and Jacquelyn Hall have also found a pattern of well-differentiated consciousness among such disparate groups as Irish transit workers, Franco-Belgian textile workers, skilled machinists, and Piedmont textile-mill families. This approach has often found that skilled workers of a Northern European background were the most radical and union-conscious workers, although ironically such workers were also the backbone of AFL craftism. Thus skilled auto workers provided much of the plant-level leadership of the UAW in the 1930s, but in the years after 1939 they developed an increasingly craft-conscious mentality that had both radical and reactionary components.[14]

12. Lynd, "The Possibility of Radicalism in the Early 1930s: The Case of Steel," *Radical America* 6 (1972); Brecher, *Strike!* (Greenwich, Conn., 1974), 181–266; and Frances Fox Piven and Richard A. Cloward, *Poor People's Movements: Why They Succeed, How They Fail* (New York, 1977), 41–95.

13. Friedlander, *The Emergence of a UAW Local, 1936–1939: A Study in Class and Culture* (Pittsburgh, 1975).

14. Freeman, *The Transit Workers* (Oxford University Press, 1989); Schatz, *Electrical Workers: A History of Labor at General Electric and Westinghouse, 1923–1960* (Urbana, 1983); Gerstle, "The Mobilization of the Working Class Community: The Independent Textile Union in Woonsocket, 1931–1947," *Radical History Review* 17 (1978): 161–72; Hall et al., *Like a Family: The Making of a Southern Cotton Mill World* (Chapel Hill, 1987); and Steven Babson, "Pointing the Way: The Role of British and Irish Skilled Tradesmen in the Rise of the UAW," *Detroit in Perspective* 7 (1983): 75–96.

If a number of these historians sought to fathom the inner texture of union militancy, still others have become attuned to the broad reaches of working-class conservatism even in a period long characterized as one of upheaval and turbulence. One can sense two sometimes complementary dimensions here. Historians like Robert Zieger, Melvyn Dubofsky, Daniel Nelson, and John Bodnar have often emphasized the episodic and fragmentary quality of union consciousness in the 1930s. Even in cities like Flint, Akron, and Pittsburgh, most workers did not participate in strikes, demonstrations, or union meetings. Among the broad mass of Catholic immigrants and recently urbanized native whites, the values implicit in family, neighborhood, church, and job frequently stood counterposed to the solidarity and cosmopolitan vision embodied in the union movement of that epoch. For a brief moment of crisis these more parochial values were either overcome or enlisted in the union cause, but these bedrock sentiments nevertheless put firm limits on union radicalism in the 1930s and 1940s. [15]

But the very impact of the radical currents that did sweep through the working class in the 1930s provide another dimension that helps explain the state of class consciousness in late New Deal America. The CIO used many of the institutions of the ethnic working class—the International Workers Order, Finnish Halls, Slavic press, and East European church—to mobilize Catholic and Jewish workers and bring to the factory and mine a sense of social cohesion and political participation which had so long eluded these workers in the larger society. The new political symbols and social values advanced by the rise of the CIO's brand of mass unionism—cultural pluralism, populist Americanism, the cult of Roosevelt—therefore helped legitimize for a whole generation of once-marginal workers the elements of a political and economic order largely unchanged by all the reforms of the New Deal. Among Eastern European Catholics especially, the assimilationist patriotism so pervasive in the late New Deal and World War II was easily transmuted into the chauvinistic Cold War posture many American workers—and the CIO itself—adopted in the postwar era. Anti-Communist jingoism had its most dramatic impact and sunk its deepest roots in precisely those sectors of the working class which had been most insulated from patriotic hysteria. Thus the social base for a mass radical movement evaporated in the United States; and even when radical ideas again gained currency thirty years later, the political culture engendered in the Depression era made most members of the white working class impervious to their appeal. [16]

15. Zieger, *Rebuilding the Pulp and Paper Workers' Union, 1933–1941* (Ithaca, 1984); Dubofsky, "Not So Turbulent Years: A New Look at the 1930s," in *Life and Labor: Dimensions of American Working-Class History,* ed. Charles Stephenson and Robert Asher (Albany, 1986), 205–23; Bodnar et al., *Lives of Their Own: Blacks, Italians, and Poles in Pittsburgh, 1900–1960* (Urbana, 1982); and Nelson, *American Rubber Workers and Organized Labor, 1900–1941* (Princeton, 1988).

16. These ideas are discussed in greater detail in Lichtenstein, "The Making of the Postwar Working Class: Cultural Pluralism and Social Structure in World War II," *The Historian* 51 (November 1988): 42–63. This paper was first delivered at the Sixth Soviet-American Historians Colloquium, September 1986, Washington, D.C.

These notes have only begun to reveal the richness and complexity of the CIO scholarship that has emerged in the last two decades.[17] The interest taken in this subject by so many Marxist-oriented historians and social scientists is testimony to the importance of that labor upsurge in the reconstruction of the political economy of mid-twentieth-century American society. However, in the process of understanding why the emergence of the new industrial unions had such a limited impact on the shape of class relations in the United States, these same scholars have found the once easily understood conflict between the AFL and the CIO full of complexity and irony. With welfare states in disrepair and labor movements on the defensive throughout the industrialized West, the whole experience of the American working class in the New Deal era will undoubtedly continue to be the subject of an extended and fruitful analysis.

17. For more see Zieger, "Toward the History of the CIO: A Bibliographical Report," *Labor History* 26 (Fall 1985): 487–516.

Response by V. L. Malkov

I cannot but express my satisfaction with the very competent and instructive analysis of my article carried out by Nelson Lichtenstein. I also cannot but say that, as it appears to me, he shares my belief that the issues raised in it represent important scientific problems (which are still not fully resolved, and therefore are open to discussion). This is my first point.

My second point is that, if one is to ignore several points that largely relate to the personal attitude of Professor Lichtenstein toward the positions of certain representatives of the "first postwar generation" of American historians and sociologists, points which are essentially of secondary importance, it would furthermore appear that N. Lichtenstein does not deny the correctness of the author's general conceptual approach to the research problem posed in his article or reject the ideas regarding matters of principle expressed in it. Of course the critic has something to say about quotations (in some instances) and about matters not discussed in the article, the inclusion of which would have been desirable. The author of the article himself regrets that the limitations imposed by the article format did not allow him to analyze more deeply and exhaustively (in time and space) certain contradictory processes in the history of the American labor movement of the 1930s. Had it been possible to broaden the scope of the article, many of the themes mentioned by N. Lichtenstein would have been discussed, although perhaps in a fashion less categorical than the one employed by my respected critic when writing about them. I hope that the American reader, having read the other article written by me that is being published in this collection, will realize that I do not ignore this important topic's aspects to which my critic has referred.

On the basis of today's new level of knowledge about the complex tendencies and phenomena in the evolution of the ideological and political processes characteristic of the workers' movement in the United States during the last few decades, N. Lichtenstein speaks of the necessity of correcting many of our notions about the past. One cannot but agree with this, although one should also avoid the "transposition" of contemporary politics into the past. All the research techniques we historians employ must be based on the historical method. This universal methodological principle makes it possible for us to assess more objectively, with greater scientific accuracy, the interaction of two processes—the liberal reformism of the period of the "New Deal" and the workers' movement—as well as the evolution of the class consciousness of American workers with reference to the degree of differentiation within it and to the changes in the workers' leaders. Additionally, the concrete historical approach is important not only in the analysis of the phenomena of social existence, but also in the analysis of the history of social thought and historiography. N. Lichtenstein's efforts to show where and how certain American historians went further than the author of the article under review in exploring the problems it raises are both laudable and useful. But one should bear in mind that the overwhelming majority of them published their works in the mid–1970s and the 1980s, that is, subsequent to the appearance of my article in the *American Annual* for 1971. In particular, I highly value the level of scholarship in the works of D. Brody and M. Dubovsky, but N. Lichtenstein's claim that they were the first to stress the political character of the new labor movement is puzzling. The works of these eminent American historians (the titles are given in the notes to the commentary) appeared in 1977 and 1980.

I wish to state, not for purposes of self-advertisement but only to make a further point, that important aspects of the subject I discussed in my 1971 article had been examined by me in a number of studies (including monographs) published as far back as the early 1960s, long before the "New Left" appeared on the scene.[1] But of course it is not the question of priority that matters. What is most important is that, as N. Lichtenstein rightly says, in the light of contemporary problems the historical experience of the struggle of the American working class during the period of the New Deal continues to provide material for deepened scientific analysis.

1. See "The Movement of the Unemployed and the Struggle for Social Insurance in the United States (1929–1933)," *Reports and Communications of the Institute for History of the U.S.S.R. Academy of Sciences*, 1957, no. 2; *The Workers' Movement in the United States during the Period of the World Economic Crisis (1929–1933)* (Moscow, 1969); etc.

N. V. Sivachev

6 REALIGNMENT IN THE TWO-PARTY SYSTEM IN THE YEARS OF THE NEW DEAL

American political parties operate inside a durable system. The two-party system continually changes, and at times its components are substantially and profoundly restructured. These changes lead to the disappearance of some parties, the emergence of others, and also to abrupt shifts in the relationship of forces that constitute the parties. The internal restructuring of a party and its realignment within the two-party mechanism are achieved through a combination of interruption and continuity that has sustained the two-party system as a continually functioning institution for nearly two centuries.

The phenomenon of realignment in the two-party system has been treated by both bourgeois scholars and Marxist historians. However, the studies of Marxists and the works of bourgeois authors offer different interpretations of the causes and meaning of the phenomenon. As a rule, bourgeois scholars see change in the behavior of the electorate as the driving force behind realignment, an explanation that does not reveal the deep roots of change and that reduces the problem to one of "critical elections." For example, a collective study of party realignments led by the well-known American sociologist S[eymour M.] Lipset firmly establishes that "each [was] brought about by a 'critical election,' which altered the previous pattern of partisan loyalties." The authors do not deny the existence of "sharp, polarizing issues which caused large numbers of voters to leave their previous political homes and form new coalitions," but their explanations stress "the emotional force of those realigning issues" and the abstraction, far from historically sound, of "the cyclical nature of this process."[1]

Marxist-Leninist methodology necessitates inquiry into the relationship of party realignment, as political superstructure, to changes in the basis of capitalistic society. This helps one understand that party realignments result from successive stages of development in which a capitalist structure characterized by manufacturing undergoes transformation to state-monopolistic capitalism. The history of the two-party system reveals several party realignments.[2] Each has occurred at an abrupt turning point in history that evoked socioeconomic and ideopolitical changes and aggravated class conflict. "It is all the more clear," wrote V. I. Lenin in 1912, "that the division of any society into political parties happens in a time of profound crises, stunning the

1. Lipset, ed., *Emerging Coalitions in American Politics* (San Francisco, 1978), 4–5. This article by N. V. Sivachev first appeared in *Political Parties of the United States in Contemporary Times* (Moscow, 1982), 67–93. This English translation is by Brenda Kay Weddle.
2. See A. S. Manykin, *History of the Two-Party System in the United States* (Moscow State University Press, 1981).

entire country . . . . The epochs of such crises always determine for many years and even decades the party alignment of the social forces of the given country."[3]

The economic crisis of 1929–1933 and the stormy years of the New Deal that followed constituted such a critical period.[4] This crisis era brought about a major party realignment and determined the new configuration of the two-party system for a decade. The two-party system of Republicans and Democrats, formed as a result of the Civil War and Reconstruction, proved incapable of resolving the socioeconomic problems which were caused by the general crisis of capitalism and which the crisis of 1929–1933 made clear. The ideology of "rugged individualism," staunchly maintained by the Republican party, was a major feature of the two-party mechanism before the New Deal, and it endured the Crash. Nonetheless, the development of state-monopolistic tendencies, the influence of the Great October Socialist Revolution, and then the demonstrable successes of socialist reconstruction in the USSR forced the bourgeoisie of the United States to use government as a means of achieving more acceptable socioeconomic conditions.

During the crisis of both the economic system and the two-party system, realignment began to take place around the core issue of using government to resolve socioeconomic problems. It was by no means accidental that the Democratic party came to play the more important role in this process. The "prosperity" of the middle and latter years of the 1920s obscured the inability of the Republican party to keep the working class in its sphere of influence. Between 1865 and 1929 nearly thirty-two million immigrants arrived in the United States.[5] Immigrants and first- and second-generation Americans concentrated primarily in the urban centers of the northeast. As they became more active politically, they were decidedly less inclined to affiliate with the Republican party than with the Democratic. Republicans were more conservative and valued the maintenance of the party's status quo. They had a reputation for strong chauvinism and anti-Catholicism. The latter is impossible to overemphasize because Catholics dominated immigration into the United States from the end of the nineteenth century. In the absence of an influential workers' party and in light of the dependence of trade unions on bourgeois ideology, the resolution of social problems was left to the Democrats. Liberal-urbanites like New York's immigrant senator Robert Wagner[6] existed among Democrats even before 1929, and the tendency of the urban lower classes to support candidates of the Democratic party was apparent as

3. *Complete Collected Works*, 21:276.

4. See E. F. Yazkov, *The Strike Movement of the Agricultural Proletariat in the United States from 1929 to 1935* (Moscow, 1962); N. N. Yakovlev, *Franklin Roosevelt—Man and Politics* (Moscow, 1965); V. L. Malkov and D. G. Nadzhafov, *America at the Crossroads 1929–1938* (Moscow, 1967); V. P. Zolotukhin, *Farmers and Washington* (Moscow, 1968); *History of the Worker's Movement in the United States in Recent Times in Two Volumes* (Moscow, 1970–1971); Malkov, *The New Deal in the United States* (Moscow, 1973); M. Z. Shkundin, *The History of the State-Monopolistic Social Politics of the United States, 1929–1939* (Moscow, 1980).

5. *Historical Statistics of the United States: Colonial Times to 1957* (Washington, 1961), 60–61.

6. J[oseph J.] Huthmacher, *Senator Robert F. Wagner and the Rise of Urban Liberalism* (New York, 1968).

early as the 1920s. Beginning with the 1922 election, the number of Democrats in Congress elected by urban constituencies increased significantly.[7] In the 1928 presidential election, the urban-Catholic standard bearer of the Democratic party, Alfred Smith, won a majority of votes in the twelve major cities of the country.[8]

But as the Democratic party's platforms during the 1920s and the policies of its officeholders show, its leaders and functionaries proposed no significant alternative to the Republicans on the vital problems of socioeconomic life. Party members wrangled among themselves along the periphery of these problems and thereby retarded party realignment before the upheaval of 1929–1933. The painful, negative experience of the administration of [Herbert] Hoover proved convincingly that any significant reform required a national approach, active involvement of the federal government, and restriction—if not of the interests, at least of the prerogatives—of the employers. The two-party system of Republicans and Democrats could not fashion an effective anticrisis remedy. Even after a relatively long time, when the economic crisis and social upheaval had peaked, the natural and politically logical mass exodus from the bankrupt Republican party to the Democratic party was hampered by the fact that the latter, in essence, did not propose anything new.

The contours of a party restructuring began to form against a background of socioeconomic and political crisis. Although that process occurred slowly during Hoover's administration, it was settled by the election of 1932. Democrats ascended to power at the pinnacle of economic crisis, bewilderment of leaders, and ominous discontent among the lower social classes. Thereafter, realignment occurred rapidly. After a lengthy period of negative consensus, alternative ideas had emerged. Before 1929, consensus was maintained by avoiding vital problems. Beginning with 1933, however, consensus was disrupted sharply by a clear alternative proposed by the Democratic party.

The alternative grew out of feverish activity, the essence of which was an unprecedented activation of government in behalf of liberal reform in socioeconomic life. This was the basic feature of the New Deal. Thanks to neo-liberalism,[9] the Democratic party was able to devise a scheme for government regulation of the economy and to set out a plan to redress social grievances. This made it more suitable than the Republican party for effecting the will of the bourgeoisie. Meanwhile, the Republican party held to the fringes of reactionary individualism.

The movement of the Democrats in the direction of state socialism, together with the leftward shift of their social policies, made that party the leader in the two-party system. Largely because the overwhelming majority of workers came to support it, the Democratic party was transformed quickly into a broad and amorphous coalition

7. V. O. Pechatnov, *The Democratic Party in the United States: Voters and Politics* (Moscow, 1980), 8.

8. *Political Parties in American History*, gen. ed. M[orton] Borden, 3 vols. (New York, 1974), 3:1110.

9. On the neo-liberalism of the New Deal see Malkov, *The New Deal in the United States*, 166, 168, 176, 187.

of forces. From 1936 to 1968 an average of 63 percent of the industrial workers ("blue collars" in the terminology of an American sociologist) in the northeast voted for Democratic candidates in federal elections. Among this group, "blue collars" of Catholic origin cast 76 percent of their votes for Democrats; those of Protestant origin, 52 percent.[10]

The 1936 presidential election took place at the moment of greatest displacement of voters from one component of the two-party system to the other, and the election results reflected the extent of the realignment. Having been the minority for seventy years, Democrats in 1936 received 27,753,000 votes of 45,643,000 cast, whereas Republicans received only 16,675,000. Of those who voted, 60.8 percent chose Roosevelt.[11] The Democratic victory in 1936 showed that the Republican loss in 1932 was not accidental and that the Democratic majority had stabilized. According to data published by the American Institute of Public Opinion, 42 percent of the people at the top of the social ladder voted for Franklin Roosevelt in 1936, as did 60 percent of those in the middle and 76 percent at the bottom. Some 84 percent of those who had received unemployment aid voted for the Democrat. The fact that Roosevelt won 47 percent of the businessmen to his party illustrated support for the New Deal inside ruling-class circles and the preference of powerful Republicans for a different world. Roosevelt's supporters included the farmers, 61 percent of the "white collars," 65 percent of the skilled, 74 percent of the semiskilled, and 81 percent of the nonskilled workers.[12] In 1932, despite unbelievable conditions of poverty, Roosevelt had been unable to win in eleven cities of over 100,000 people in the Northern industrial states. Four years later he won even those localities; and from then until the beginning of the 1950s those cities, except for one, sided with the Democrats.[13]

The shifts, so important in the evolution of the two-party system, included the transition of the black population from the party of A[braham] Lincoln to the party of F[ranklin] Roosevelt. Although there were no special measures for blacks, the reforms of the New Deal, particularly unemployment aid and regulation of labor conditions, did have a certain practical, positive impact on their lot. In 1936, 76 percent of black Americans who were permitted to vote supported Democratic candidates.[14] The fact that the conservative whites of the South and blacks in all regions of the country supported the same party gave rise to substantial problems.

The acuity of these problems, however, was dulled for many years by the fact that blacks in the Southern states were without the right to vote. The party orientation of the Jewish community also changed substantially. Before the New Deal the majority of Jews were oriented toward Republicans; in the elections of 1936 and 1940, 85 percent of them supported Democrats.[15]

10. Lipset, *Emerging Coalitions*, 33–35.
11. *Historical Statistics of the United States*, 686.
12. *Public Opinion Quarterly*, September 1940, 467–68.
13. S[amuel] Lubell, *The Future of American Politics* (New York, 1962), 49.
14. *Public Opinion Quarterly*, September 1940, 467–68.
15. E[verett C.] Ladd, *Transformations of the American Party System: Political Coalitions from the New Deal to the 1970s* (New York, 1978), 61.

Before the crisis of 1929–1933 and the New Deal, the influence of geographic sections in political parties was blatantly obvious. This was particularly true for Democrats. The accelerated development of state-monopolistic capitalism, which led to government resolution of fundamental socioeconomic problems, weakened sectional differences and strengthened the state socialism of the parties. The Democrats became a more national party, their dominance extending into all regions of the country. In 1936 Roosevelt won 54 percent of the votes in New England, 59 percent in the east central states, 60 percent in the mid-Atlantic states, 61 percent in the west central states, 68 percent in the western states, and 76 percent in the Southern states. Having lost the majority in both houses of Congress in 1918, Democrats were the minority in the House of Representatives until 1930 and in the Senate until 1932. From the beginning of the 1930s, the situation began to change, and the party of Roosevelt won the majority in all congressional elections with the exception of 1946, 1952, and 1980.[16] In 1932 the Democrats won 71.3 percent of the seats in the lower house and 62.5 percent in the upper; two years later they held 73.3 percent and 71.9 percent. This was particularly important in that midterm elections usually weakened the ruling party. After 1936 the ratio of Democrats to Republicans in the House of Representatives[17] was 331:89 and in the Senate 76:16. An analogous situation could be found in the state organs of power. From the time of Reconstruction to the crisis of 1929–1933, the two-party mechanism had functioned as a combination of Republicans and Democrats; from the New Deal until 1981, it worked as a system of Democrats and Republicans.

Having become the party of the majority, armed with neo-liberal ideology, the Democratic party underwent significant internal changes. Weakening the role of the Southern wing was one change. From 1920 to 1928 Southerners comprised 56–72 percent of the Democratic faction in the House of Representatives and 55–70 percent in the Senate. In 1930, however, they lost the majority in both units (37.4 percent and 43.3 percent). They reached the nadir of their influence in the 1936 election—35 percent and 34.2 percent.[18] This also explains why the Democratic party convention of 1936 changed the rule, in effect since 1844, that required a two-thirds majority of convention delegates to nominate the party's candidates for president and vice-president. The change severely diminished the influence of Southerners in deciding these candidates.

A study of the two-party system undertaken shortly after World War II by a special committee of the American Political Science Association noted, "The Democratic party is today almost a new creation, produced since 1932."[19] However, this committee did not say what it truly meant. Primarily it meant that the party had found a

16. In the 1980 elections the Democrats preserved the majority in the House of Representatives, but lost the Senate to the Republicans.

17. *Historical Statistics of the United States*, 691.

18. R[alph M.] Goldman, *Search for Consensus: The Story of the Democratic Party* (Philadelphia, 1979), 173.

19. *Toward a More Responsible Two-Party System: A Report of the Committee on Political Parties* (New York, 1950), 25.

state-socialist ideology, had moved to the left ("a little to the left of center"[20] in Roosevelt's words) under pressure from the labor and democratic movements, had incorporated in its political tenets many of the demands of the masses, and thus "gave shelter to the simple people."[21] It turned into a broad coalition in which the leading role unequivocally "belonged to the bourgeoisie, more precisely, its liberal wing."[22] Within the party, professional functionaries and party machines had less influence. The transition from voluntarism to state socialism, accompanied by a shift to the left, greatly strengthened the Democratic party in the two-party combination and increased its importance in the eyes of the ruling class.

But this transition also involved costs—of both an inner- and inter-party character. Vastly expanded by strengthening the left wing, the party sustained losses on the right flank and, after the 1936 election, collided with the right-center of the spectrum. The "uprising" of the right wing led to the creation in 1934 of the reactionary Liberty League[23] and in 1936 to the withdrawal of "Jeffersonian Democrats" headed by A[lfred E.] Smith. Although the Liberty League and the "Jeffersonian Democrats" lacked a popular base, the Democratic senator from Louisiana, Huey Long, enticed a large number of poor whites in the Southern states with his demagogic "Share-Our-Wealth" program and posed a serious threat to the national leadership of the party. Only the Louisiana dictator's assassination in September 1935 removed this problem for Roosevelt.

Dealing with the powerful right-center core in the party leadership was more complicated. This group consisted of powerful professional politicians, particularly Southern congressmen, and masses of "recruits" (organized and unorganized) that suddenly joined the Roosevelt coalition. The acknowledged leaders of the right-center conservatives were visible congressional leaders, some of Roosevelt's cabinet members, and Vice-President J[ohn N.] Garner (Texas). The congressional leaders were Senators J[oseph T.] Robinson (Arkansas), J[ames F.] Byrnes (South Carolina), P[at] Harrison (Mississippi), C[arter] Glass (Virginia), and A[lben W.] Barkley (Kentucky) and Representatives W[illiam B.] Bankhead (Alabama), S[am] Rayburn (Texas), and R[obert L.] Doughton (North Carolina). The cabinet members were Secretaries C[ordell] Hull and J[ames A.] Farley.

But due to the upsurge in democratic thinking and the shift of the New Deal to the left, party leadership was affected greatly by luminaries of the left-center wing— Senators Wagner, H[ugo L.] Black, D[avid I.] Walsh, E[lmer] Thomas; members of the Cabinet, Democrats F[rances] Perkins and H[arry L.] Hopkins and the progressive Republicans H[arold L.] Ickes and H[enry A.] Wallace, who had converted to the Democratic camp; as well as the governor of New York, millionaire H[erbert H.] Lehman. At their head stood the president himself; and to them were handed the reins of government.

20. F[rances] Perkins, *The Roosevelt I Knew* (New York, 1946), 333.
21. N. N. Yakovlev, ed., *The United States: Political Thought and History* (Moscow, 1976), 301.
22. Malkov, *The New Deal in the United States*, 232.
23. G[eorge] Wolfskill, *The Revolt of Conservatives: American Liberty League, 1934–1940* (Boston, 1962).

Although the chairman of the party's National Committee, J[ames A.] Farley, had adjusted the party apparatus at both the national and state levels, the outcome of the 1936 election was predetermined by the action of the masses. For them it was a battle to preserve and expand the social reforms associated with the name of the president elected in 1932. From 1933 to 1936 Roosevelt preferred not to flaunt his party membership. He consciously blurred the dividing lines between the liberal and conservative views of the inner-party and, more generally, of the two-party spectrum. In a letter to Col. E[dward A.] Hays in March 1934, he explained to the old Wisconsin Democrat that for the time being it was especially important for the president to be seen as representing "all parties." He even prohibited publication of a National Committee survey that emphasized the role of the Democrats in the revival of the economy. His decision not to participate in the party's traditional spring rally that accompanied T[homas] Jefferson's birthday was conditioned partly by his ambition to win over bewildered Republicans.[24] None of this was well received by leaders and functionaries of the right-center, who numerically dominated the ruling circles of the party. For a time they had no choice but to endure, for Roosevelt's methods were working and bringing valuable political dividends to the bourgeoisie and the entire Democratic leadership.

Even greater distortion occurred in the two-party mechanism. In the first phase of realignment, which concluded with the 1936 election, there was, for all intents and purposes, only one active participant—the Democratic party. By the mid-1930s it was clear the two parties differed greatly in influence, an unusual phenomenon in the history of the two-party system. More importantly, they had become extremely polarized. A dangerous schism had formed in the center of the political spectrum that jeopardized the future ability of Republicans and Democrats to function within the bounds of a two-party system.

The change in the Democratic party, which basically constituted the first phase of the realignment, had more than one significance. It greatly benefited the ruling circles and the entire dominating class. Roosevelt's party had proved its capacity for social maneuvering and had become, in that critical time, the most reliable political support group of major capital. The American bourgeoisie worried that the new leaders had moved too far to the left, and the destabilization of the two-party system concerned them. The second phase of realignment, which began after the 1936 election, involved two equally active participants—the Democratic party and the Republican party. The complexity of this stage involved not only the quest of the Republican party for a more realistic means of combating the New Deal and its initial revisions, but also a second internal restructuring of the Democratic party in which the challenge came not from the left of center but from the center.

Buffeting by the economic crisis and the long-lasting depression reduced the Republican party to minority status. Its leaders did not immediately understand this, but after their catastrophic defeat in the 1936 election, it became clear. Some even

24. E[lliot] Roosevelt, ed., *F.D.R.: His Personal Letters 1928–1945*, 2 vols. (New York, 1950), 1:394.

questioned whether the party would continue to exist. Revival of its influence and the restoration of the two-party mechanism depended on developments in the "Grand Old Party," in the two-party system, and in the nation's entire socioeconomic and political system.

During the first phase of realignment, the Republican party had been unable to offer an effective alternative to the New Deal. It had countered the neo-liberalism of the New Dealers with yesterday's slogans. *The Challenge to Liberty*, Hoover's book published in 1934, testified convincingly to the Republicans' ideopolitical helplessness.[25] Rejection of Roosevelt's course and panic over the approaching end of "freedom" in the United States—by which Hoover meant the foundations of private monopoly—resounded from every page. The leadership of the Republican party clearly expressed the interests of proprietary America, people who still believed that no significant change in the socioeconomic structure was the best medicine for the temporary illness that affected the country. All infringements on the interests of private entrepreneurs—taxes to aid the unemployed, regulation of production, restriction of employers' prerogatives through recognition of trade unions, and others—were declared steps toward "socialism."

The nominal head of the party (Hoover), leaders of the congressional faction (C[harles L.] McNary in the Senate, B[ertrand H.] Snell in the House of Representatives), and the National Committee headed by H[enry P.] Fletcher continued to lead the party along the old reactionary, individualistic course. The Old Guard steadfastly held the party in its grip. Individual efforts toward party renewal brought nothing healthy to party ideology or practice. Hoover's former secretary of the treasury, O[gden L.] Mills, tried to organize certain centrists outside the party hierarchy. In his words they "purported to see that America shall go ahead upon American lines." But his group of "Republican Builders" consisted only of a few socially elite residents of New York State, and they did not breathe fresh strength into Republican ranks. Analogous efforts in Ohio by the little-known functionary of a well-known family, R[obert A.] Taft, also ended without notable effect.[26]

On the heels of the 1934 defeat, the Republican senator from Michigan, A[rthur H.] Vandenberg, proposed the creation of a two-party coalition government. The Democrats never seriously discussed it. Senate Democratic leader Robinson announced that his party would not refuse Republican support, but he feared Republicans would be weak and unreliable allies. He reminded Vandenberg that the negative response to his initiative was promoted by his own consistent votes against New Deal measures.[27] Republicans themselves viewed New Dealers with too much hostility to contemplate a coalition. In a speech on 31 January 1935, Fletcher said: "While we are rebuilding and re-enforcing our party lines, we must remember that if the two-

25. *The Challenge to Liberty* (New York, 1934).

26. J[oseph] Boskin, "Politics of an Opposition Party: The Republican Party in the New Deal Period, 1936–1940" (Ph.D. diss., University of Minnesota, 1959), 63–64.

27. Franklin D. Roosevelt Library, Records of the Democratic National Committee 1928–1948, container 1196, DNC Release, 18 November 1934.

party system is to survive in this country we must not shirk our plain duty and responsibility as a party of opposition." Reasoning clearly, the chairman of the Republican National Committee understood the task of his party to draw up an alternative to the New Deal based on principles deeply interwoven in the fabric of American society. But he could not propose the substance of such an alternative. What he offered was a condemnation of "demagogic radicalism" and the affirmation that "the New Deal has sown and is sowing the wind of socialism." "All we need do," he maintained, "is to apply to present-day problems and conditions the same devotion to economic freedom and social progress which has characterized the Republican party through these years."[28]

In a speech in June 1935, Col. F[rank] Knox reiterated the obligation of Republicans to play the role of the opposition and reaffirmed their inability to propose realistic alternatives. He declared that the "minority party" should "serve as the party of opposition." He added that "the Republican party in the present crisis is not satisfied with mere opposition. It does have an alternative program."[29] But the "alternative program" he proffered was no more than expletives addressed to the New Deal.

Naturally, the question arose of the role of the progressive Republicans in the party transformation. Progressive Republicans had occupied a comparatively visible place in the party from the beginning of the twentieth century. With the coming of the economic crisis in 1929, it seemed these Republicans were destined to become the initiators of socioeconomic reform. In part, they fulfilled the mission. The campaign of Senator G[eorge W.] Norris for a government hydroelectric plant in the Tennessee Valley, the progressive Norris–La Guardia act on limiting the arbitrary rule of the courts in labor disputes, the act of Senator R[obert] La Follette for unemployment relief, the endless agitation of Senator W[illiam E.] Borah for recognition of the USSR—all these testified to significant and positive potential in the ranks of progressive Republicans. But, on the whole, they were unable to lead the process of reform because they ceded the initiative to the left-center wing of the Democratic party. The most important reason was their lack of wide support in the urban centers where the main socioeconomic problems existed. The fact that progressive Republicans sometimes appeared excessively devoted to individualism—although in a democratic, farmer, petty-bourgeois variant—also played its role. Even though progressive Republicans promoted programs of socioeconomic reform, under the circumstances their state socialism seemed too radical and at the same time clearly antimonopolistic. Their thinking did not blend with either the traditional conservative views of Republicans or the state-monopolistic structure of the New Deal. In future years isolationism among progressive Republicans, which alienated the most active antifascist groups from them, also would serve as a drawback. During the New Deal, progressives contributed significantly to reforms, but only insofar as they broke with

28. *Vital Speeches of the Day,* 25 February 1935, 350.
29. Ibid., 1 July 1935, 639.

their own party and joined the Roosevelt camp or organized third parties to the left of the New Deal at the state level.

Of course, some individual Republicans initiated efforts to modernize the ideology of "rugged individualism" during the first phase of the two-party realignment. One correspondent of an influential Baltimore newspaper complained in 1933 that "the old conservatism, in a word—failed us and failed wretchedly in the depressed days of the past three years."[30] In 1934 the old conservatism was subjected to tough scrutiny in a book by the well-known Republican intellectual G[lenn] Frank, who had been removed as president of the University of Wisconsin by the progressive governor [Philip] La Follette. Frank reached a conclusion that was important to Republicans: "The circumstances of the age demand a new relationship between government and private enterprise . . . . Some measure of statism is not only inevitable but desirable."[31]

But in the mid–1930s, social enlightenment in the Republican party remained as before. "When the Republicans gathered at Cleveland in 1936 for their national convention, atavistic thoughts were the order of the day," wrote C[onrad] Joyner.[32] At the very beginning of the convention its temporary chairman, Senator F[rederick] Steiwer from Oregon, talked about the approaches of both parties to resolving important problems: "The ideals of both the great political parties have always had to do with finding ways and means to make that system work more perfectly. Our parties have differed as to these ways and means, but never until March 1933 has an administration elected to preserve and develop the American system tried, by the autocratic abuse of its executive power, to abolish the very system that it had sworn to conserve."[33] Republicans had not altered their reactionary, individualist views in the least. They categorically opposed government regulation of the economy and liberal social legislation. The Republican platform promised Americans to preserve "their political liberty, their individual opportunity and their character as free citizens, which today for the first time are threatened by government itself."[34] The spirit of Hoover still hovered over Republican leaders, even though they chose the governor of Kansas, A[lfred M.] Landon, as their candidate instead of the ex-president.

After the catastrophic defeat of the Republican party in the 1936 election, the press widely discussed its future and its place in the two-party system. Most evaluations and prognoses were pessimistic. One of the party's primary ideologues, Columbia University president N[icholas M.] Butler, concluded, for example, that "there isn't any Republican party any more, and there hasn't been a Republican

30. W[illiam E.] Leuchtenburg, ed., *The New Deal: A Documentary History* (Columbia, S.C., 1968), 30.

31. *America's Hour of Decision: Crisis Point in National Policy* (New York, 1934), 77.

32. *The Republican Dilemma: Conservatism or Progressivism* (Tucson, Ariz., 1963), 33.

33. *Official Report of the Proceedings of the Twenty-First Republican National Convention Held in Cleveland, Ohio, June 9–12, 1936* (Washington, 1936), 33.

34. D[onald B.] Johnson and K[irk H.] Porter, comps., *National Party Platforms* (Urbana, Ill., 1973), 365.

party for some time." He continued, "I expect to see a realignment, which will be composed of two new parties—a liberal party, built upon the Constitution of the United States and the lessons of history, and a reactionary-radical party which doesn't care about the Constitution or anything else."[35]

Hoover, recognizing weaknesses in the party and noting that "it is in part from these weaknesses that there is some discussion over the country of new party alignment,"[36] spoke in more optimistic tones. He discussed three propositions, each of which could significantly change the fate of the Republicans: creation of a new party, changing the name of the Republican party, and forming a coalition with "Jeffersonian Democrats" in the next presidential election. Hoover led convincing arguments against all these variants of restructuring and realignment. He pointed out that the existing Republican national organization could not be dismantled with a single wave of the hand; that changing the party's name would be resisted by Republican functionaries and would require extensive changes in state laws that concerned the party; and that only the least influential group in the Democratic camp would consider changing its party loyalty. He took care to dispel the illusion that Southerners might withdraw from the Democratic party. He saw the Southern intent "to recapture their party from the New Deal or to modify its course."[37]

Very soon discussions about creating a new party—in union with conservative Democrats or without them—and about changing the name of the Republican party died down. In their place were discussions about how to increase the effectiveness of Republican opposition in the two-party system. Hamilton, elected in 1936 as chairman of the National Committee, on 1 May 1937 broadcast an important speech on the role of Republicans as the opposition. By that time Roosevelt already had met strong opposition within the ranks of his own party over reform of the Supreme Court and the problem of "sit-down strikes." Republican chances for enhancing their political role immediately had increased. Hamilton described the broad purpose of opposition: "The task of the opposition is not a single task. It has in reality many tasks. Some are negative. Some are positive. All are legitimate. All are essential." He tried to persuade the country that the "Republican party is not a party of negation" and to draw a positive picture.[38] Promising that Republicans "will not be merely a party of opposition, but also a party of proposal," the chairman of the National Committee nonetheless showed himself the captive of individualist abstraction when he tried to explicate these "proposals."[39]

The economic crisis of 1937–1938 came in very handy for the Republicans; it gave them a real trump in the contest with the Democrats. By that time, in addition, Republicans had begun to accept some kinds of government regulation. In part this was because they had seen even the strongest anti-Roosevelt citadel in the govern-

35. *New York Times*, 2 April 1937.
36. "The Crisis and the Political Parties," *Atlantic Monthly*, September 1937, 264.
37. Ibid., 264–66.
38. *Vital Speeches of the Day*, 1 June 1937, 502.
39. Ibid., 505, 502.

ment structure—the Supreme Court—recognize the rationale of state socialism in solving social problems. "The Roosevelt recession," as Republicans immediately christened the crisis in retaliation for the label "Hoover depression" that Democrats had used widely in 1929, was the occasion for a more convincing verbal attack on New Dealers. And without rejecting governmental interference 100 percent (that was too dangerous), Republicans also used the opportunity to declare that government regulation should be used only after careful consideration of the "proven" methods of "free enterprise." Infringing on these proven methods, they explained, had caused the 1937 recession.

Knox, the Republican nominee for vice-president in 1936, declared on 11 January 1938 that "a people, seriously alarmed over the swift return of depression conditions, will not listen patiently to explanations of why this is so. They want to know the way out. If the Republican Party can point the way back to good times, the voters will restore our party to power. If we content ourselves with nothing but indictments of the New Deal, which has admittedly failed to find a way out and has merely plunged the country into a new kind of depression, they will turn elsewhere." He challenged the party to devise a positive alternative to the New Deal. "Unless it can become 'positive' again, its service is ended and the party will die." To prevent this and to return to power, "it is imperative that Republican leadership address itself to the formulation of a progressive, forward-looking, economically-sound program—a program that will recall to its support the popular following that gave the party almost continuous domination in national affairs through three successive generations of American life."[40]

It must be said that Knox's speech contained a fairly concrete program of economic and social policies. His proposals were the result of new realities, which in turn resulted from the crisis of 1929–1933 and Roosevelt's reforms. He obviously "Republicanized" a good many New Deal measures, verbally tying them to Republican traditions while at the same time modernizing those very traditions. Knox helped begin the political philosophy of "we too"; that is, of the unavoidable adaptation by the Republican party, enlightened to state socialism in its own way, of the actions of the Democrats. Landon and Knox thus had sinned to some extent in the campaign of 1936. By the election of 1938, the altered Republican stance in the two-party system was much clearer. In the course of an intense political battle over vital socioeconomic problems, the Republican party took the first steps toward an alternative to the New Deal based on a modernized conservatism.[41] Neo-conservatism developed as a right-center variant of state-monopolistic ideology and politics. Neo-conservatives accepted a state-socialist platform roughly similar to that of the neo-liberals, but they accented traditional individualist values and were less sympathetic to the demands "of the streets."

40. Ibid., 1 February 1938, 243.
41. See Manykin, "The Republican Party of the United States in Search of an Alternative to the New Deal," *Annual Studies of Moscow State University,* 1978, no. 5.

The position of "rugged individualists" headed by Hoover significantly weakened from 1937 to 1938. More voices in the party said that "salvation lay in the acceptance of the New Deal welfare program,"[42] even though they still espoused such traditional Republican values as a balanced budget and the importance of private initiative. Republican conservatism was adopted also by Democrats and comprised part of their ideological restructuring—the defense of "states' rights," which became a "footbridge" between the "Grand Old Party" and the Dixiecrats. The tempo of activity among professional Republicans quickened. In 1937 Hoover proposed a special convention as a prelude to the 1938 and 1940 elections.[43] Moderate Republicans, grasping the rudiments of neo-conservatism, feared a convention would become a forum for Hooverism and buried the idea. As an alternative Hamilton proposed that Glenn Frank head a special commission of 215 people to compose position papers for the party.[44]

In the 1938 election Republicans won unexpected and very convincing victories. They increased their representation in the Senate from 16 seats to 23 and in the lower house from 89 to 163.[45] They also scored large victories in the gubernatorial elections. Apart from the 5 posts they already had, they won 13 more.[46] The Republican party itself offered nothing substantially new through its campaign slogans. In June 1938, congressional leaders McNary and Snell had introduced a ten-point program, but it consisted of nothing more than deteriorating Republican dogma.[47] In August 1938, twenty thousand party activists who attended the "corn conference" on the farm of H[omer E.] Capehart in Indiana turned the event into an anti-Roosevelt brawl.[48] Republicans simply did not adopt in proper measure the substantive and positive slogans of the burgeoning neo-conservative ideology, a fact that was obvious in the utterances of individual party leaders and commentators.

The outcome of the election was determined mostly by circumstances independent of the Republicans. There was a new and perceptibly widening breech in the ranks of the Democratic battalions, and the weaknesses of the Roosevelt coalition were particularly visible against the background of the new economic crisis. In the accompanying conflict, Dixiecrats and some of the Northern Democrats rose in opposition to the new leaders, and thereby opened to the Republicans an important new avenue for two-party intrigue. It was highly evident that the switch of the Democratic party to a neo-liberal platform did not signify a complete realignment of the two-party system. For this phenomenon to occur, the Republican party needed to accept the principles

42. Boskin, "Politics of an Opposition Party," 209.

43. *Atlantic Monthly,* September 1937, 168.

44. P. McGinnis, "Republican Party Resurgence in Congress, 1936–1946" (Ph.D. diss., Tulane University, 1967), 49–50.

45. *Historical Statistics of the United States,* 691.

46. A[rthur M.] Schlesinger, Jr., ed., *History of American Presidential Elections 1789–1968,* 4 vols. (New York, 1971), 4:2919.

47. McGinnis, "Republican Party Resurgence," 49.

48. *New York Times,* 28 August 1938.

of state socialism as well. At the time, consensus about state-monopoly remained unattainable, and Democrats still seemed too "socialist" to their partners. Finally, a full realignment in the mid–1930s could not occur without destroying the uncoordinated movement for the creation of a third party.[49]

At the same time that the Republicans made their first step in the direction of neoconservatism, the Democratic party slackened its ardor for reform and then in January 1939 officially suspended its reform efforts.[50] By so doing, it significantly accelerated realignment in the two-party system. The well-to-do classes in the Roosevelt coalition wanted to conserve what had been achieved and to thwart leftist influence on government policies. Public opinion polls in 1938–1939 showed that 66 to 75 percent of the American people preferred that the Roosevelt administration take a more moderate course.[51] From 1934 to 1936 the left-center had grown stronger in the Democratic party. Then, after the 1936 election, the right wing of the party subjected New Dealers to ever-growing pressure. By 1937 Roosevelt was convinced that an overwhelming majority of Democrats elected to Congress in November 1936 would not help him pass new laws. In several ways this development weakened the united front in support of the New Deal (as the press had forewarned).[52] Democrats weakened in face of the political adversary, and this created favorable conditions for the formation of new blocs among the Democratic factions.

In contrast to 1933 and 1936, Roosevelt's rhetoric became more partylike. On the threshold of the 1938 election he resorted to a lecture, rare in the history of the two-party system, on party discipline and the responsibility of party functionaries for implementing the party program. On 11 August 1938, he delivered the most partisan speech of his entire presidential career. "To carry out my responsibility as President," Roosevelt said, "it is clear that if there is to be success in our government there ought to be cooperation between members of my own party and myself—cooperation, in other words, within the majority party, between one branch of government, the legislative branch, and the head of the other branch, the executive. That is one of the essentials of a party form of government. It has been going on in this country for nearly a century and a half." Further, the leader of the Democratic party proposed criteria to judge how well the activists supported the party line. "The test," he explained, "lies rather in the answer to two questions: first, has the record of the candidate shown, while differing perhaps in details, a constant active fighting attitude in favor of the broad objectives of the party and of the government as they are constituted today; and secondly, does the candidate really, in his heart, deep down in his heart, believe in those objectives?"[53]

49. See Sivachev, "Movement for the Creation of a Third Party in the United States in the Mid-1930s," *Annual Studies of Moscow State University,* 1961, no. 3.

50. F[red L.] Israel, *The State of the Union Messages of the Presidents, 1790–1966,* 3 vols. (New York, 1966), 3:2846.

51. R[ichard] Polenberg, "The Decline of the New Deal, 1937–1940," in *The New Deal,* ed. J[ohn] Braeman, R[obert H.] Bremner, and D[avid] Brody, 2 vols. (Columbus, 1975), 1:254.

52. *New York Times,* 8 November 1936.

53. *Public Papers and Addresses of Franklin D. Roosevelt,* ed. Samuel I. Rosenman, 13 vols.

On this basis Roosevelt openly opposed the reelection of Representative J[ohn J.] O'Connor (New York) and Senators G[uy M.] Gillette (Iowa), W[alter F.] George (Georgia), E[llison D.] Smith (South Carolina), and M[illard E.] Tydings (Maryland). Nothing similar had occurred in party political history. The president's opponents immediately labeled his position a purge and mobilized their forces to fight it. The purge failed; the White House succeeded only in stopping the nomination of O'Connor. This was "an obvious slap in the face" to Roosevelt.[54]

The results of the 1938 election strengthened the centrifugal forces in the Democratic party and pushed it further from the left toward the center. Farley composed a list of reasons for these severe Democratic losses from the correspondence of important supporters. Dissatisfaction with high government spending and the expanded influence of unions, particularly the CIO, figured as the primary reasons.[55] It is possible that Roosevelt came to the same conclusion, but he ignored Farley's analysis and attributed the recent misfortunes to the fact that the party apparatus at the local level had not worked hard enough. He proposed to the chairman of the National Committee that he "begin giving . . . the works" to Republicans elected in 1938 and that he organize pressure on them. He even suggested instigating, "where possible, mass meetings of protest." The latter shocked Farley, and the National Committee, in its turn, ignored the president's proposition.[56]

The 1938 election was important also because both Democrats and Republicans badly hurt the third parties, which until that time had held significant positions in several states. From the very beginning of the New Deal, Democratic leaders had been uncomfortable with the unofficial coalition they were forced to accept with left progressive parties and movements. In 1933 Farley had tried to persuade the citizens of Minnesota: "A third party in this country cannot be but a temporary political expedient, for ours is a two-party government and in the national field there is no room for an independent organization. It has been a two-party government from the beginning."[57] But Roosevelt believed Democratic leaders should be reconciled with the third-party movement, at least for a while, in order not to push it further to the left. Knowing full well Farley's jealousy in matters of party organization, in the course of 1934 Roosevelt nonetheless instructed him, "In Minnesota hands off."[58] In 1936 the third-party movement turned into a campaign for Roosevelt. Two years later the Democrats no longer saw the need to be cautious about the left flank and took a more rigid position on third parties. Democrats kept power in their own hands in Minnesota and Wisconsin, and progressives lost gubernatorial posts in both states. In the U.S. Congress, progressive representation decreased from thirteen seats to

(New York, 1938–1950), 1938 volume, 467–70.

54. *Philadelphia Inquirer,* 18 September 1938.

55. *Jim Farley's Story: The Roosevelt Years* (New York, 1948), 154.

56. Roosevelt, *F.D.R.: His Personal Letters 1928–1945,* 2:829–30, 835–36.

57. Franklin D. Roosevelt Library, Records of the Democratic National Committee, 1928–1948, container 1195, Address of J[ames] Farley, 8 May 1933.

58. Schlesinger, *The Age of Roosevelt,* 3 vols. (Cambridge, 1957–1960), 3:103.

four.[59] In the results of the 1938 election, which were a disappointment to the party, Roosevelt also saw a plus. In a private letter he wrote openly: "As a positive, we eliminated" the threat of a third party in the Northwest. Republicans happily concluded the same thing. Progressives in Wisconsin and Minnesota were replaced, not only by New Dealers, but also by Republicans. Hamilton considered the outcome a contribution to restoration of normal functioning of the two-party system.[60]

From 1938 to 1939 Roosevelt repeatedly mentioned the necessity of an ideological restructuring of the parties in his speeches. One of them should turn to middle-of-the-road conservatism and the other to liberalism—with a greater internal homogeneity in each. In a speech on 25 September 1938 he contrasted the conservatives and reactionaries with liberals and progressives and pointed out that the Democratic party could preserve its majority status only "so long as it remains a liberal party."[61] On 7 January 1939, at the traditional banquet on A[ndrew] Jackson's birthday, Roosevelt welcomed the "return of the Republican Party" to its responsibility for the administration of the country and even suggested that "nominal Democrats" cross to the Republican side.[62] In a letter to Young Democrat clubs on 19 April, the president again urged loyalty to liberal principles and observance of party discipline. "Where men are at variance with the course their party is taking," he declared emphatically, "it seems to me there are only two honorable courses—to join a party that more accurately mirrors their ideas, or to subordinate their prejudices and remain loyal."[63] Finally, in an address to the Young Democrats' convention on 8 August 1939, he once again pointed out the abnormality of the situation when progressives and reactionaries existed in both parties. "Republican and Democratic reactionaries," he warned, "want to undo what we have accomplished in these last few years and return to the unrestricted individualism of the previous century." Roosevelt cautiously predicted that "the Democratic party will fail if it goes conservative next year."[64]

However, New Dealers did not go further than these general, albeit loud, pronouncements. No organized efforts for change followed. None of the political functionaries in the United States—neither conservatives ("reactionaries") in the Republic party, nor liberals ("progressives") in the Democratic party—thought seriously about shaking up the ideological principles of the two-party system. It soon became clear that Roosevelt made all these statements because he was developing the strategy for his third presidential campaign. He had calculated correctly that, in any case, the conservative camp would come out against him. He preferred that they blame him for his liberalism rather than for "dictatorship," "usurpation," or violation of the tradition of serving no more than two presidential terms. He remembered that in 1937 nothing had come of it when some liberals had turned away

59. *Historical Statistics of the United States*, 691.
60. *Vital Speeches of the Day*, 15 February 1939, 283.
61. *Public Papers and Addresses of Franklin D. Roosevelt*, 1938 volume, 512–20.
62. Ibid, 1939 volume, 60–68.
63. Ibid., 232–34.
64. Ibid., 434–37.

because public opinion considered his pressure on the Supreme Court as too high-handed and a violation of the Constitution.

Neo-liberals feared that realignment between ideological poles (even on the part of the spectrum that admitted bourgeois values) would lead to radicalization of the Democratic party. They also feared something else: in the event of such a polar realignment, their opposing partners were not fully prepared to implement moderate state socialism and might degenerate into an ineffectual crowd of reactionary individualists. This would retard the reestablishment of political stability that major capital needed to strengthen itself. According to Roosevelt's thoughts about "liberals" versus "reactionaries," there should have been a "great exodus" of Southern Democrats, but they did not abandon their ancestral seats in the party. They were tenured, and despite some erosion of influence in Washington, they remained powerful. They achieved the suspension of reform by addressing high government spending (by criticizing it and forming blocs with the Republicans when some issue made them uncomfortable). Southern Democrats also prevented any kind of New Deal interference in their racist ancestral lands. Party decentralization also retarded realignment;[65] it did not allow national and state leaders to make the kind of far-reaching political decisions that best served their interests. And one cannot rule out foreign policy. The reactionaries whom Roosevelt had snubbed turned out to be more supportive of the "internationalist" course the White House pursued than moderate and even progressive Republicans.

The 1938 election was an important milestone in the restructuring of parties during the 1930s in that it strengthened the Republican party and hastened its evolution in a neo-conservative direction. A new group of Republican leaders had emerged—Senator Taft, Governor H[arold E.] Stassen, Governor L[everett] Saltonstall, and the young public prosecutor T[homas E.] Dewey, who won nomination but not election for New York's gubernatorial post. These individuals, together with Senators Vandenberg, H[enry Cabot] Lodge, Jr., and S[tiles] Bridges, comprised the primary cohort of party functionaries who relegated Hoover's "old guard" to the background and formulated and adopted the principles of neo-conservatism. Hamilton, of course, exaggerated when he declared in January 1939 that "the Republican party has been restored to a place of approximate equal footing with the Democratic party on the national scene." The Democrats had sustained appreciable losses, but they preserved more than sufficient strength to maintain an undisputed first place in the two-party mechanism. This was very important because it showed retrospectively how pervasive the shift to the left had been in 1936. In 1938 the return to the Republican camp of people who thought they had acted impetuously two years before did not undermine the majority status Democrats had achieved through New Deal reforms. Nor can one agree without reservation with Hamilton's other assessments, particularly his contention that "our traditional bipartisan system remains substan-

65. See Manykin, "The Evolution of the Organized Structure of the Bourgeois Parties," in *The United States: Economics, Politics, Ideology,* 1978, no. 10.

tially intact."[66] Both parties had changed significantly, and the configuration of their relationship was different.

The fundamental change was that both parties had accepted the ideopolitical tenets of state socialism at a time state-monopolistic capitalism was developing rapidly. The change occurred at a different tempo in each party and with substantial differences in the character and depth of the process. Although it incorporated fewer expectations of government in its ideological baggage as World War II approached, the Republican party was substantially different from what it had been in the mid–1930s. Even the important business component of the Republican party gradually took a more positive view of the expanded role of government. Conservative believers in state socialism supported and cultivated that view through energetic propaganda. One of the leaders in promoting a new outlook by business was R[aymond] Moley, the former head of Roosevelt's brain trust who broke with New Dealers when they moved to the left. Appearing at the congress of the National Association of Manufacturers in December 1938, he preached that "business must realize that, when we talk of a conservative drift, the word 'conservative' must be interpreted to mean a position distinctly to the left of 1929. Business can honestly hope for relief from some of the more oppressive forms of regulation of the past three years, but it should not hope for a reaction that will sweep away the earlier and sounder reforms of the New Deal."[67] Little by little, business came to understand this neo-conservative wisdom that was so important to strengthening the position of the Republican party.

The ideology of American bourgeois parties always has been noted for "pragmatism, conditionality of the concrete, and, frequently, unexpected and changing expectations of the leaders."[68] Republican leaders at the end of the 1930s were in the process of creating "modern Republicanism."[69] They were guided by the demands of the day and armed with a right-center variation of state-monopolistic ideology— neo-conservatism. This turn of events drew both parties together. The balance of consensus and alternative was restored, but it was in the context of a new state-monopolistic platform. The journal *Review of Politics*, first published in 1939, wrote that the functioning of the two-party system demanded "unity of fundamentals." "That this is not mere theory," it said further, "the recent elections have once more demonstrated. So far as the Republicans were concerned, they knew that after their successive defeats they would have to do something in order to catch step again with the electorate and to regain the millions of voters which they needed in order to make another successful bid for power. All observers agree, however, that the Republicans tried hard in order to adjust themselves to the new mood of the electorate. In past elections already they had eliminated from their leading ranks all the members of the

66. *Vital Speeches of the Day,* 15 February 1939, 283.

67. Ibid., 1 January 1939, 179.

68. I. P. Dementiev and V. V. Sogrin, "On the Role of Ideology in the History of the Two-Party System of the United States," *New and Recent History,* 1980, no. 6, 78.

69. M[ilton] Plesur, "The Republican Congressional Comeback of 1938," in *Political Parties in American History,* 3:1184.

so-called 'Old Guard,' no matter whether these were really 'reactionary' or not. In 1938 this tendency was carried further than ever."[70]

The result, one mouthpiece of the business world wrote with delight, was "perhaps the most exciting phenomenon in contemporary politics: the reemergence of the GOP from apparent extinction to a functioning role in the traditional two-party system."[71] When the Republicans knocked progressives in Minnesota and Wisconsin out of gubernatorial posts, Governors Stassen and J[ulius] Heil showed how neo-conservatism worked on the state level. They accepted the spending policies of the New Deal as their starting point. They continued the programs for unemployment relief and preserved the right of collective bargaining. However, they changed state labor-relations laws in order to diminish a long list of trade-union rights. "Stassen," wrote *Fortune* magazine, "has tried to steer a wary course between the varying brands of conservatism desired by his farmer-business wing and his A.F.of L. supporters."[72]

The shift to neo-conservatism also affected the conduct of Republican leaders on the national level. This was apparent in "A Declaration of Republican Principles" that Taft presented in March 1939.[73] Taft opened himself to criticism in this document, in a series of thirteen debates with Democratic representative T. V. Smith (a liberal progressive from the University of Chicago) on national radio between 21 February and 16 May 1939,[74] and in a number of other appearances. He combined biting criticism of the New Deal—little different from Hoover's tirades—with semi-recognition of many elements of state socialism, albeit in reactionary interpretation. Dewey seemed even more accommodating to the New Deal. Like Taft, Dewey was promoting his own candidacy for the presidency. Americans "will give to the New Deal generous credit for sponsoring much-needed liberal legislation,"[75] he said. But at that point he turned to what he considered the mass of defects in the necessary legislation. Republicans, he insisted, would be better and more diligent administrators. The philosophy of "me too" was quite evident here. Not without reason, Farley referred to neo-conservative Republicans as a "diluted brand" of Democrats.[76]

In 1939 Republican leadership changed in the House of Representatives. Congressman J[oseph W.] Martin from Massachusetts became minority leader. In his memoirs Martin wrote that in 1939 "there was a far different brand of Republicans in the House from any that the country had known since the Hoover administration." They were perceived as having a "reasonably liberal leadership." He placed himself

70. *Review of Politics*, March 1939, 207.

71. *Fortune*, August 1939, 33.

72. Ibid., 101.

73. *Vital Speeches of the Day*, 1 April 1939, 381–84.

74. Materials of these debates were published in a book, *Foundations of Democracy* (New York, 1939).

75. Dewey, *The Case Against the New Deal* (New York, 1940), vii-viii.

76. Franklin D. Roosevelt Library, Records of the Democratic National Committee, 1928–1948, container 1209, Address of J[ames] Farley, 19 April 1939.

"at-least-near . . . the center of the Republican spectrum."[77] Of course, there were some fresh ideas among Republicans in the House of Representatives. For instance, the newly elected congressman from Ohio, G[eorge H.] Bender, argued, "Today our task is to form a program to consolidate the reforms of the past few years. The Republican party must not adopt an obstructionist attitude, but must see to it that the people have some of the social reforms they are entitled to."[78] Martin, as Republican leader in the House, concentrated his energies more on combating Roosevelt's policies than on drawing up alternatives. The twelve-point program he unveiled in spring 1939 was by no means a "broad policy of constructive cooperation [by] the minority party in the House," as he would have liked to present.[79] It was of greater significance that the new leader had breathed new confidence into the enlarged Republican minority and made them believe they could force the Democrats to take the opposition seriously.

In the process of party realignment during the prewar years, Republicans managed to stand solidly on their own two feet, but they could not devise a clear alternative to the New Deal. Serious internal contradictions in the Democratic camp, as has been pointed out, helped consolidate Republican positions. As early as 1937–1938 a conservative anti-Roosevelt coalition of Republicans and right-wing Southern Democrats had formed in Congress.[80] It was not, however, a formal bloc. It was united only by opposition to continuation of the New Deal. Its formation was stimulated by a declaration that Democratic senator Bailey wrote and distributed to members of Congress in December 1937.[81] The main points of this document boiled down to promoting investment of private capital at a time when government spending had diminished, reducing taxes on corporations, balancing the budget, and defending states' rights. As he read it, Bailey appealed passionately, "But, in God's name, do not do nothing while America drifts down to the inevitable gulf of collectivism."[82] Twenty years later, an analysis of the conservative coalition showed that as early as 1937 Republicans and Southern Democrats in the House had united against the Democratic majority[83] in 10 percent of the roll-call votes. After the 1938 elections Martin concluded that Republicans in the lower house "put us in a position for the first time to offer formidable opposition to the New Deal."[84] Republicans often left the initiative of attacking Roosevelt's proposals to the Democrats themselves and thereby expanded the opposition front. Although it was short-lived, this tactic and

77. Martin, *My First Fifty Years in Politics* (New York, 1960), 82–83.
78. *New York Times*, 30 November 1938.
79. *Vital Speeches of the Day*, 1 June 1939, 489–92.
80. J[ames T.] Patterson, *Congressional Conservatism and the New Deal: The Growth of the Conservative Coalition in Congress, 1933–1939* (Lexington, Ky., 1967).
81. *Congressional Record*, vol. 82, pt. 2, 1937–38.
82. Ibid., 1940.
83. Ibid., vol. 106, pt. 2, 1441–42.
84. Martin, *My First Fifty Years*, 82.

better party discipline enabled Republicans in the House of Representatives to defeat the ruling party in nineteen roll-call votes.[85]

Neither Republicans nor Southern Democrats took steps to organize beyond the informal blocs that defeated neo-liberal legislative proposals, but the tactic of blockade used by the conservative coalition in Congress did contribute to realignment in the two-party system. The seeming consensus between the Republican party and a faction of the Democratic party prompted the latter to adopt a more moderate facade. Dulling the sharp corners on the Democratic left flank, the coalition conditioned the party to free itself of "leftist misconceptions." And this interaction with Republicans was conducive to consensus in the two-party system. "If the Republicans had taken a considerable step in order to meet their opponents half-way," wrote a contributor to the *Review of Politics* in March 1939, "the Democrats had done likewise."[86] This weakened the "polarization of the electorate"[87] and opened a broader field in which the surviving components of the two-party system—changed and reversed in their power relationship—could operate on the basis of consensus, but with alternative methods.

The Democratic party zigzagged in its evolution. At first it veered to the left; then from 1937 to 1939 it moved to center; and then it shifted to the right during World War II. All of this was part of the realignment of the two-party system. The evolution of the Republican party was slower and more straightforward—from reactionary individualism to neo-conservativism. This is not to say, however, that analysis of this change is easier. The main difficulty here lies in determining the degree to which Republicans remained devoted to Hooverism and the extent to which they shifted to a right-center variation of state socialism as an alternative to the New Deal. This difficulty springs from the ambivalent, deeply contradictory reaction of the Republican party to the realities of state-monopolistic development. Events during the 1940 election campaign revealed that ambivalence.

The Frank Commission had prepared and published its report by the beginning of the election campaign.[88] It criticized the New Deal harshly for giving rise to "unworkable economics." It also acknowledged the rationale for many New Deal principles, although the more conservative Republicans recommended that these principles be attacked. The authors of the report "accepted most of the New Deal, but with slight camouflage."[89] The report of the Frank Commission, for all its ideological vagueness, was one of the first Republican documents to be written in the spirit of neo-conservatism. Its content did not affect the provisions of the party's platform as one might have expected. The convention bosses still were afraid to stray

85. Ibid., 83.
86. *Review of Politics,* March 1939, 207.
87. J[ames L.] Sundquist, *Dynamics of the Party System: Alignment and Realignment of Political Parties in the United States* (Washington, 1973), 217.
88. *New York Times,* 19 February 1940.
89. Joyner, *Republican Dilemma,* 5.

far from tradition and appear to be "non-Republicans." The platform blasted the New Deal for sowing "class hatred" and undermining "the traditional American spirit."[90] However, in many ways such remarks now were simply party rhetoric designed to help the electorate differentiate between Democrats and Republicans. They did not necessarily reflect the true views of the Republican leadership. Therefore, one can speak of the neo-conservative character of the Republican platform in 1940.[91]

And still the Republican party remained at an ideological crossroads. It was not accidental that no candidate for the presidency emerged from among its own leaders and that the party nominated a former Democrat, the businessman W[endell L.] Willkie. Republican cadres ceded the path to him for two reasons: they lagged behind him in their mastery of state socialism, and they were slower than he in casting off isolationism. Willkie went much further than official pronouncements of the party, and in part he surmounted reactionary individualism. When he accepted the honor the Republican party accorded him, he declared that "the forces of free enterprise must be regulated" and at the same time accused Roosevelt's supporters of giving private enterprise too little credit for its achievements.[92] More than anyone else among Republican leaders, he was a "yes man" to the New Dealers; and that was his main strength in the campaign of 1940.

The party realignment, important in accommodating and causing socioeconomic and ideological-political changes, in its turn concretely altered the social environment. The realignment of forces in the two-party system helped put in place major reforms of a state-monopolistic character; then it slowed the pace of their implementation. Realignment straightened the leftist list, but retained the bases of the New Deal and prevented a reactionary turn to normal, precrisis times. Thanks to realignment, which turned around the effort of the parties and the entire system to adapt to the consciousness of the masses, the institutionalization of government monopolistic principles pervaded the superstructure. At first pushing the parties apart and then effectively drawing them closer, realignment created a strong double center on the political party spectrum. This center accepted a state-monopolistic platform that strengthened the position of the monopolies.

Although muted by the revival of the consensus-alternative channel, the two-party mechanism during the prewar period still featured anomalies. Major capital believed the Democratic party was not yet free from excess and improvisation in handling socioeconomic problems, from antimonopolistic rhetoric, from Social Democratism, or from an excessively large and undisciplined "column" that harbored leftists who determined the policies of the leadership. Many components of the Republican party had not quite abandoned the dogma of reactionary individualism,

90. Johnson and Porter, *National Party Platforms,* 389–90.
91. A. A. Kreder, "American Monopolistic Bourgeoisie and the New Deal of F. D. Roosevelt (1932–1940)," in *American Annual, 1979* (Moscow, 1979), 148.
92. *Annals of America,* 18 vols. (Chicago, 1968), 16:27–31.

nor accepted state socialism. Some still equated governmentalization with socialism. The realignment of the two-party system during the years of the New Deal was not quite complete. It was during and after World War II that the inner structures of the parties were strengthened and modified and the principles of interparty relationships were stabilized.

James L. Sundquist

Comment on "Realignment in the Two-Party System in the Years of the New Deal," by N. V. Sivachev

Mr. Sivachev issues a provocative challenge to debate when he contrasts the interpretations placed by "bourgeois scholars" and Marxist historians on the political realignment of the New Deal era. The contrast is, indeed, a fascinating one—even though the very choice of terms embodies the first of many semantic difficulties that impede communication between the parties to that debate. In my dictionary, *bourgeois* is defined as *middle class*—to be distinguished, that is, from the proletariat and the upper classes. All American non-Marxist scholars are not necessarily bourgeois, then; some surely were born to the proletariat, and if annual earnings are to be taken as the measure they may never have escaped that status. And some Marxist historians in Western countries are undoubtedly bourgeois, both in origin and in life-style. But the author left this term, like others, undefined; let us assume here that he intended it as an identification by ideology rather than social class, and it simply means non-Marxist.

That problem to the side, we can agree with Mr. Sivachev that Marxists and non-Marxists do have differing approaches to scholarship that are bound to lead to diverging conclusions. "Marxist-Leninist methodology," he writes, "necessitates inquiry into the relationship of party realignment, as political superstructure, to changes in the basis of capitalistic society." Non-Marxist methodology, too, requires inquiry into the relationship of political and economic systems, but at that point the divergence begins. For the Marxist approach necessitates not only that the relation be examined but that the examination lead to conclusions that have been predetermined. Mr. Sivachev's article alone is a convincing demonstration of that (but even more convincing, of course, if read in the context of the larger body of Marxist scholarship on these matters). The author examines American history through a polarized lens that, on crucial questions, admits evidence that supports the conclusion supplied in advance by official dogma and screens out that which does not.

"Bourgeois" scholars are the product of a culture, too, one which in my view does not prescribe any particular interpretation of history. The mores of Western scholarship commit researchers to arrive at conclusions inductively. They may never wholly escape their biases, but they—the best of them, anyway—do try. That leads, in the case of political realignments, to a certain indecisiveness in interpretation, an inability or a reluctance to talk of the "deep roots of change" that Mr. Sivachev regards as a shortcoming of bourgeois scholarship. From the non-Marxist point of view, this is a merit, not a fault. Scholars *should* stop short of translating speculation into fact and asserting conclusions that the empirical evidence does not fully support.

How Mr. Sivachev's preconceptions, by contrast, lead to insupportable conclusions is most clearly demonstrated in the four sentences that begin with the one just quoted. Whether the political alignment is a mere "superstructure" on the economic system—the nature of the former thus being determined by the character of the latter—is not part of the inquiry he conducts but a given, settled matter. Party realignments, he tells us without qualification, result "from successive stages of development in which a capitalist structure characterized by manufacturing undergoes transformation to state-monopolistic capitalism." He applies this generalization to "each" of the "several party realignments" in United States history. His methodology thus compels him to exclude from consideration the possibility that the most profound party realignment in American history—more profound, even, than the New Deal realignment—had precious little to do with capitalism and everything to do with a great moral issue, to wit, slavery. The antislavery movement and the Civil War were not a "class conflict," as Mr. Sivachev contends all our realigning issues had to be, but a moral conflict overlaid with a sectional dimension. Opponents of slavery came from all classes of white society, and so did its defenders. That Western scholars have not interpreted the realignment of the mid-nineteenth century in the language of economic determinism testifies to their open-mindedness, not their lack of insight.[1]

The realignment of the 1930s, in contrast, did arise from what can fairly be called "a crisis of capitalism." But once again, "bourgeois" scholars have quite properly been inclined to emphasize the proximate economic and emotional causes of the political revolution, because its relation to basic changes in a capitalist society remains—in the absence of an ideology that provides a ready-made interpretation—highly conjectural. We can assert beyond doubt that the realignment was precipitated by the collapse of the economy, and by the response of the people and of the Republican and Democratic parties to that event. But we cannot declare with equal authority that the *behavioral* changes in the economy were the inevitable consequence of *structural* changes. That is surely an interesting question, but it is a separate one. For purposes of analyzing the realignment process and the nature and scope

---

1. American scholarship has produced in the past three decades a vast body of literature on the history and processes of political party realignment, of which Mr. Sivachev cites only Seymour Martin Lipset's *Emerging Coalitions in American Politics* (1978), Everett Ladd's *Transformations of the American Party System* (1978), and my own *Dynamics of the Party System* (1st ed., 1973). Realignment as a field of study was first identified, like so many other things, by V. O. Key, Jr., in his "A Theory of Critical Elections" (*Journal of Politics*, February 1955). Among the more important book-length works that build on Key's foundations are Walter Dean Burnham, *Critical Elections and the Mainsprings of American Politics* (New York, 1970); Jerome M. Clubb, William H. Flanagan, and Nancy H. Zingale, *Partisan Realignment: Voters, Parties, and Government in American History* (Beverly Hills, 1980); and John R. Petrocik, *Party Coalitions: Realignments and the Decline of the New Deal Party System* (Chicago, 1981). A noteworthy symposium on realignment theory is Bruce A. Campbell and Richard J. Trilling, eds., *Realignment in American Politics: Toward a Theory* (Austin, 1980). The basic history of party alignments is still William N. Chambers and Walter Dean Burnham, eds., *The American Party System: Stages of Political Development* (New York, 1967). Individual journal articles that make substantial contributions to our understanding of individual realignments and to realignment theory are too numerous to mention.

of the political changes, political scientists and historians do not even have to answer it.

When we try, however, we find that the evidence does not give much support to the economic-determinism doctrine of the Marxists. The temporal connection linking the structural changes to the behavioral results that one would need to discover is missing. The American economy was transformed at a staggering pace during the whole period from the beginning of the Civil War to the crash of October 1929. The structure of modern capitalism, including its giant monopolies (more accurately, oligopolies), was created through what must have been quite a few "successive stages of development." Yet the political alignment produced in the turmoil of the Civil War era remained essentially intact throughout and was never more firmly in place than on the eve of the Great Depression. Had the nation then known enough about economics, would the crash of 1929 have been inevitable—or preventable? Fifty years of post-Depression history suggest the latter answer to that question. Despite all the changes in the economy in the most recent half-century, the second coming of the Great Depression—so confidently predicted by the Marxists—has not occurred.

Moreover, even the Great Depression might not have precipitated realignment on the scale that actually took place had the political leadership of the time responded differently. Suppose that Herbert Hoover had been made of another set of emotional and intellectual ingredients? Any Republican president, of course, would be to greater or lesser extent the prisoner and product of his party's long tradition of nonintervention in the affairs of the private economy—whenever, that is, the intervention met solid opposition from the business and financial community. Yet there had been one Republican president in recent history who made himself anathema to that community—Theodore Roosevelt. He arrived in the White House through a chain of accidental circumstances, but nevertheless he did get there. If TR instead of Hoover had presided over the crash of 1929, it is entirely likely that his response would have been dynamic enough to satisfy the people and he would have been able to drag his party far enough in the direction of activism to avert a major realignment. Liberal activists would hardly have been moved in any great number to abandon a TR-led Republican party to rally behind an opposition that was at that time timorous, budget-obsessed, and floundering in search of both policy and leadership. It was the intransigence of Herbert Hoover, his deafness to the cries of a suffering population, that drove people to the Democratic party for lack of anywhere else to go. It was he who produced the intense and emotional polarization of the citizenry that in turn produced the realignment. And no one, surely, would consider the wisdom and the temperament of particular presidents to be a matter of economic determinism.

The activism of Franklin Roosevelt, his receptivity to ideas that at the time seemed radical, and his bold readiness to experiment with them were essential to the realignment also, but here the ring of inevitability is more audible. Once Herbert Hoover dug in his heels and refused to budge, he was bound to be supplanted by an FDR. Had Roosevelt not possessed the traits that the times demanded, the Democratic party would have found some other leader who did, or the distraught voters would have turned to a third party that promised a forceful response to the Depression. One of the ironies of history is that the New Deal hated with such passion by Herbert Hoover was as much his creation as Roosevelt's. The latter's opportunity to lead was made possible by the former's inability or unwillingness to do so.

In short, while Lenin was right in saying that political realignments occur "in a time of profound crisis, stunning the entire country," he was wrong if he went on to say (and I do *not* read him as saying so in the words quoted by Mr. Sivachev) that such crises must necessarily be rooted in changes in the "capitalist structure." Drastic changes can occur in that structure without precipitating a party realignment on the scale of the 1930s. That was the case during many decades before the Great Depression, and it has been the case also in the decades since. And political realignments can occur from other than economic causes; the Whig party died and the Republican party was born in the 1850s during a political upheaval that was noneconomic in its origins, and even in the current era we are witnessing a minor realignment that is again not rooted in economics, with the movement of religious fundamentalists, not to mention racists, into the Republican party. Finally, the direction and scale of realignments are heavily influenced by the random factors that put particular individuals in positions of leadership at particular times and bear upon the directions in which they lead.

In his treatment of random influences, Mr. Sivachev can perhaps be forgiven a touch of nationalistic and ideological pride in crediting the October Revolution and "the demonstrable success of socialist reconstruction in the USSR" with forcing the United States into its course of governmental activism under Roosevelt. Few American historians would give events in the Soviet Union that much credit. What happened there was, if anything, an impediment to reform of the American economic system, because it enabled opponents of change to condemn each proposed expansion of governmental activity and concern as leading to collectivism, socialism, and Bolshevism (and sometimes fascism in the same breath). Only on the fringes of the New Deal did anything smacking of socialism appear—public housing, notably. Those New Dealers who were attracted by one key element of the Soviet system, its central economic planning, found themselves hobbled by the very fact that planning was associated with the other aspects of "socialist reconstruction" and thus had become un-American. The United States was forced into governmental intervention, surely enough, but by the internal pressures of an aroused electorate, not by external example.

Even the third-party movements that condemned the New Deal as timid and complacent drew little inspiration from abroad. Huey Long, Father Coughlin, Dr. Townsend, and others who challenged Roosevelt from the left used an American vocabulary and offered remedies indigenously designed. Norman Thomas, who had been the voice of old-fashioned European socialism for years, faded. Earl Browder and William Z. Foster, the direct disciples of the October Revolution, could not even begin to compete with America's home-grown radicals.

In many other ways, Marxist concepts—as translated—impede communication between Soviet and American scholars. The phrase *state-monopolistic capitalism*, so often repeated in this chapter, is just not part of the Western—or, if one prefers, bourgeois—vocabulary. In fact, the words *state* and *capitalism* in this context sound antithetical. A monopoly is either state-owned, in which case it is not capitalistic, or private, in which case it is outside the state. How it can be both needs explaining, but the phrase is not even defined, much less explained and justified.

Another baffling phrase is *state socialism*, which likewise appears throughout the chapter. One is accustomed to hearing conservatives accuse liberals of socialistic inclinations but "neo-conservatives" (that is, Dewey and Taft Republicans) would surely have been surprised to learn that they "accepted a state-socialist platform roughly similar to that of the neo-liberals" (that is, New Deal Democrats). Today's Republicans will be astonished to hear that their party, like the Democrats, has "accepted the ideopolitical tenets of state socialism." From the context, however, one can figure out what is meant. If one substitutes the phrase *governmental activism* or *governmental interventionism* wherever *state socialism* appears, the account makes sense. Unfortunately, it is not so simple to find a suitable synonym for *state-monopolistic capitalism*, but simply to delete the hyphenated adjective might do the trick.

One Marxist concept that cannot be dealt with by simple substitution of language, however, is that of America's "ruling class." The very definition of a ruling class, one might assume, is that its members control elections and hence control the government. But in the 1930s America's wealthy, at least, did not. Mr. Sivachev cites statistics that prove this very point: "The fact that Roosevelt won 47 percent of the businessmen to his party illustrated support for the New Deal inside ruling-class circles." And 42 percent of "the people at the top of the social ladder" voted for Roosevelt. Most of the "ruling class," then, was against FDR, while his support among those at the bottom of the ladder was 76 percent and among those receiving unemployment assistance 81 percent. The "ruling class" was soundly defeated, in other words, by the ruled. Those of us who lived through the New Deal era can still hear the thunderous outcries of leading spokesmen for the major institutions of capitalism—bankers, business executives, leaders of the U.S. Chamber of Commerce and the National Association of Manufacturers, and so on—castigating Roosevelt and his New Deal. How can a ruling class still be a ruling class when its hated enemies win the elections and then proceed to staff the White House, the regulatory commissions, and the Department of Justice—even, eventually, the Supreme Court—and write the laws? Perhaps Marxist logic can resolve this conundrum, but Mr. Sivachev does not attempt to do so.

Setting aside that question, however, we can agree with him that those who denounced the New Deal most fiercely were, in the end, among those who benefited most. The "ruling circles and the entire dominating class," as Mr. Sivachev calls them, were forced to accept labor unions and higher levels of corporate and "soak the rich" personal taxation, but the New Deal reforms were mild compared with the punitive and confiscatory measures that would have been, in the mood of the early

1930s, within the range of possibility. Failing industries were propped up and rescued, not nationalized. Wealth was preserved and protected, not shared. When the
economy presently recovered, under the stimulus of defense spending, Roosevelt's
"economic royalists" still wore their purple, his "money changers" were still in the
temple. The rich were still rich and free to become richer. As they proceeded to do
so, they would be the last to recognize that the New Deal had done them the enormous favor of saving their system for them. They would be the last to acknowledge
the truth that Mr. Sivachev discerns: that it was not Herbert Hoover's G.O.P. but
Franklin Roosevelt's Democratic party that proved to be "the most useful tool of
major capital."

V. O. Pechatnov

7 THE DEMOCRATIC PARTY AND ITS ELECTORATE IN THE YEARS OF THE NEW DEAL

The period of the New Deal, unique in its amplitude and significance in the history of the United States, continues to be a center of attention for Soviet and foreign historians. They are discovering in the period new opportunities for productive scientific analysis. Amidst the inadequately explored and unfocused historical data, one sees the deep influence of the social shocks of those years on the primary bourgeois parties of the country. Study of the ways in which the ruling Democratic party adapted to the adverse conditions of the "Red Decade" is of particular interest, especially its interaction with independent political parties and groups, and the strategies and tactics used by the Democrats to attain and preserve their popular base in one of the decisive epochs of American history.

This topic thus far has not been the subject of a great deal of independent research in Soviet historiography, which concentrates on analysis of democratic movements, the social policy of state governments, and the class struggles of those years.[1] So little has been done on this key period of Democratic party history that not one significant specialized work in American historiography has been dedicated to it, although both preceding and following periods in the history of the Democrats are covered by serious works of research.[2] As a result, the party's history during the 1930s appears to be left to political scientists, the labors of whom,[3] despite their significant contributions to the study of the behavior of the electorate, cannot replace valuable historical analysis of all the relevant questions.

The present article is an attempt, even if partial, to fill that gap. It is concerned primarily with displacements among the Democratic electorate and with the tactics of the party leadership in the "struggle for the masses." It is written on the basis of material in the archives of the Democratic National Committee in the Franklin

1. V. L. Malkov, *The New Deal in the United States: Social Movements and Social Politics* (Moscow, 1973); *The History of the Workers' Movement in the Unites States in Recent Times* (Moscow, 1970), vol. 1; N. V. Sivachev, *Political Conflict in the United States in the Mid-1930s* (Moscow, 1966); D. F. Nadzhakov, *The People of the United States—Against War and Fascism, 1933–1939* (Moscow, 1969). This article by V. O. Pechatnov was originally published in *American Annual, 1980* (Moscow, 1981), 61–91. This English translation is by Brenda Kay Weddle.

2. D[avid] Burner, *The Politics of Provincialism: The Democratic Party in Transition, 1918–1932* (New York, 1969); R[obert A.] Garson, *The Democratic Party and the Politics of Sectionalism, 1941–1948* (Baton Rouge, 1974).

3. S[amuel] Lubell, *The Future of American Politics* (New York, 1965); J[ames L.] Sundquist, *The Dynamics of the Party System: Alignment and Realignment of Political Parties in the United States* (Washington, 1973); K[risti] Andersen, *The Creation of a Democratic Majority, 1928–1936* (Chicago and London, 1979).

178

Delano Roosevelt Library at Hyde Park, the private papers of James Farley (chair-man of the Democratic National Committee) that were opened by the Library of Congress in 1975, and a number of other sources.

One of the most interesting pages of party history in the United States concerns the swift transformation of the Democratic party in the 1930s from a party of the minor-ity and of ideological provincialism to a party of reform that received the support of the majority of the country's population. What, in fact, did the party represent on the eve of the 1930s? In the words of Socialist leader N[orman] Thomas, it was "this strange conglomeration of northern wets and southern drys . . . of a handful of hopeful Liberals and the masses of the Tammany and the Hague machines, the party financed by the open shop Raskob, voted for by a probable majority of organized labor."[4]

The "presidential" wing of the party, the National Committee and its finances, were controlled by private capital in the Northeast in the persons of J[ohn J.] Raskob, O[wen D.] Young, B[ernard M.] Baruch, G[erard] Swope, and others, who con-tinued into the very depth of the Great Depression redundant debates over states' rights, decentralization of federal power, reduction of government expenditures, and repeal of prohibition.[5]

Another wing of the party, agrarian in character, had represented the southern states, the party's traditional stronghold, since the end of Reconstruction. This wing was dominant in Congress. Despite their cultural-religious differences, economic conservatism united both wings; and they resolved to debate only antiquated party topics. Urban, predominately Catholic immigrants in the Northeast who were con-trolled by party machines in the big cities also appeared to be a traditional source of popular support for the party. Effective opposition to the politics of Hoover in Con-gress came from a bipartisan block of progressives in which a few Democrats were junior partners to such prominent Republicans as G[eorge W.] Norris, H[iram W.] Johnson, W[illiam E.] Borah, and R[obert M.] La Follette, Jr. Few in the ranks of liberals and progressives linked the Democratic party with their hope of promoting alternatives to the bankrupt Republicans. Any possibility for alternatives would result from the creation of a new party, independent of major capital.[6]

However, both in the genealogy and in the peculiarities of the popular base, as well as in the character of the party's future leadership, there were several predispositions which shaped its reconstruction in the 1930s and made the Democrats, in comparison to the Republicans, more suitable for action under the new circumstances.

The popular base of the Democrats contained in its historically established social, ethnic, and religious diversity not only the weakness, but also the strength of a

4. "Why Not a New Party?" *North American Review,* February 1929, 145. Tammany Hall was the headquarters of the Democratic organization of Manhattan in New York City; F[rank] Hague was the boss of the party machinery of Jersey City, New Jersey, in the 1930s.

5. *Literary Digest,* 12 December 1931.

6. P[aul H.] Douglas, *Why a Political Realignment?* (New York, 1930), 5-6, and *The Coming of a New Party* (New York and London, 1932), 174–75.

"strange conglomerate" of ideological avidity and flexibility, the special art of appealing to the most diverse social groups and strata and protecting them with ideological-political maneuvers. Of particular importance was the long-standing identification of the party with the urban lower classes of immigrant origins who rapidly evolved into the majority of the urban population during the 1910s–1920s.[7] The Great Depression imparted to these bonds a political character and grave consequences.

Finally, in the person of Franklin Roosevelt the Democrats acquired a leader who was acceptable not only to all components of the party, but who also was realistic, who understood that adaptation to the growing popular mood of protest was unavoidable, that the theme of "politics as usual" with its debates about prohibition, high tariffs, and states' rights had passed, and that the suffering of millions of unfortunates dictated an entirely new order of the day. This new way of thinking also reflected itself in the very extensive correspondence of Roosevelt and his aides L[ouis] Howe and J[ames] Farley with the members (115,000 in number) of local party committees during the 1932 election campaign.[8] For example, one Democrat from Illinois who expressed the opinion of many wrote: "This is a new era and conservatism does not fit into it at all. We have a lot of Democrats who are prominent in national affairs and who do not seem to know that T[homas] Jefferson is dead. The Democratic party cannot be a conservative party, and will not be if Governor Roosevelt is elected. What people are demanding is a complete change and I think we are going to get it if the Democrats win."[9]

Roosevelt's rhetoric about the "forgotten man at the bottom of the economic pyramid" and his promises to do something to relieve that man's suffering reflected an understanding of these concerns. And although a heterogeneous and contradictory combination of people throughout the country voted for the Democrats in 1932 in their wrath against the discredited Republicans, basic traits of the group's composition and mind-set were definitely perceptible. An analysis of the vote shows that the main sources of reinforcements for the Democrats were millions of unemployed, the working class, and farmers, who had deserted the Republicans to gain "the defeat of Hoover and all he stands for."[10] This conclusion is confirmed by communications from the grassroots to Roosevelt's headquarters. One party supporter, an oilman, wrote from the Republican bulwark of industrial Pittsburgh that Roosevelt would receive the support of "the million and a quarter men that are out of work, most of

7. Lubell, *The Future of American Politics*, 50–53.

8. *New York Times*, 7 November 1932.

9. H. Rainey to J. Farley, 27 August 1932, James A. Farley Papers, Library of Congress, General Correspondence (hereafter JFP, GC), box 1.

10. From a letter by the known Republican progressive G[eorge N.] Peek (G. Peek to Farley, 19 October 1932, JFP). Concerning shifts in the Democratic electorate by states in 1932, see W[alter D.] Burnham, *Critical Elections and the Mainsprings of American Politics* (New York, 1970), 55–59; Sundquist, *Dynamics of the Party System*, 201–2; M[ichael D.] Rogin and J[ohn L.] Shover, *Political Change in California, 1890–1966* (Westport, Conn., 1970), 119.

whom formerly were voted by the railways and large manufacturers for the Republican ticket." Similar reports came in from other Republican states.[11]

Thus the broad Democratic coalition that would become an important motivating force of the New Deal began to take shape.[12] The political fate of Roosevelt and the Democratic party now depended on how well they succeeded in retaining the support of this coalition of protesters that favored their election.

***

As is well known, the New Deal developed during a time of growing class conflict, during a rapid influx into political life of a wide spectrum of the working class, farmers, and the urban poor. Political activism seriously affected not only the lower levels of the Democratic party, but also political activity beyond the bounds of the two-party system.

So it was that the Roosevelt administration came into conflict with radicalism in its own party as early as 1933–1934 and encountered millions of the unemployed, the working class, and the farmers who had deserted the Republicans. These people believed their well-being depended on the "defeat of Hoover and all that he stands for." This conclusion is confirmed by communications from the grass roots concerning the growing threat from the political left. One possible response to the changing situation was suggested by T[homas R.] Amlie, a prominent progressive in the movement to create a third party: "The real danger that you are in now," he wrote the president in February 1933, "is that of trying to represent the whole Democratic party. In ordinary times this is undoubtedly a proper position to take . . . in the present situation . . . your course cannot be one of compromise or conciliation. You will have to make a tremendous number of enemies within your own party and be subject to no end of criticism. Your course must be bold and daring right from the start."[13]

Following Amlie's course clearly would result in a union of progressives with Democrats and openly alienate conservatives in the ruling party. It was a route that Roosevelt did not rush to take. He believed that in situations where class-political polarization was comparatively undeveloped, the tactics of "compromise and conciliation" offered a useful flexibility. That flexibility might be the advantage needed to maintain "national unity" during the struggle against the economic crisis. Obscuring class-party divisions and accenting the national interest, the president told his cabinet in anticipation of the midterm election of 1934, also would be advantageous in the matter of "gathering votes."[14] Roosevelt's observation provides the key to under-

11. W. Benedum to Farley, 5 July 1932; O. Dern to Farley, 15 August 1932; F. Murphy to Farley, 27 April 1932, JFP, GC, box 1.

12. See *The History of the Workers' Movement in the United States in Recent Times,* 1:243.

13. Amlie to F. Roosevelt, 20 February 1933, Franklin D. Roosevelt Library, Hyde Park, New York (hereafter FDRL), Official File 1600.

14. L[ester G.] Seligman and E[lmer E.] Cornwell, eds., *New Deal Mosaic: Roosevelt Confers with His National Emergency Council, 1933–1936* (Eugene, Oreg., 1965), 230–31.

standing the other side of an "above-the-party" tactic that aimed to keep, besides the traditional components of the Democratic electorate, the new political forces as well—independent voters, progressives, and those Republicans who supported the Democratic party in 1932.

Republicans of the progressive trend whom Roosevelt brought into government positions were especially interested in this. For example, H[enry A.] Wallace wrote to Norris that "it would be a mistake to permit the administration to develop an overwhelmingly partisan character. The President was elected by virtue of the votes of Progressive and independent citizens and we must be very careful to not affront them. I think that this is reasonable in both a clearly political sense and in giving to the politics of the government its due direction."[15] At the same time, many Democrats called the attention of the party leaders to the need for "holding and bringing into the Democratic party the better elements of our electorate, many of whom have for the first time voted the Democratic ticket."[16] During 1933–1934 Roosevelt and his party leaders heeded that advice and strove to retain the widest possible front of political support. They did give special attention to the Left, but they did so with sufficient care so as not to split the party.

The primary issue at hand related, of course, to political reform, but political tactics were of no less significance—questions concerning concrete cooperation with independent political forces and concerning alignments inside the Democratic party itself. Manifestations of this general change were as diverse as were local party political situations.

The states of Minnesota, Wisconsin, and New Mexico and parts of New York presented a particular problem to the administration. In those areas there were liberal party alternatives to the local conservative Democrats. Since 1930 the Farmer-Labor party (FLP), headed by F[loyd B.] Olson, had been in power in Minnesota. The FLP was the most radical of all third parties during the 1930s. Its 1934 platform provided for the nationalization of natural resources, the means of production, transport, and communications within the bounds of a "new, just society."[17] The local conservative Democratic party was not influential, and it was split into two factions. One faction, headed by state party chairman [John F.D.] Meighan, formed an alliance with the Republicans against Olson. Through another, more moderate faction, the Roosevelt administration reached an agreement with the FLP according to which the administration disassociated itself from the Meighan faction in exchange for Olson's support in the presidential election. The Farmer-Labor party received a lion's share of federal patronage and other gestures of support at the instigation of the president himself.[18] Despite the indignation of local party functionaries[19] and Farley's deep

15. 20 October 1933, JFP, GC, box 2.

16. R. Winton to D. Roper, 2 December 1932; see also E. Lorton to Farley, 6 December 1932; D. French to Farley, 5 December 1932, JFP, GC, box 1.

17. A. Naftalin, "A History of the Farmer-Labor Party in Minnesota" (Ph.D. diss., University of Minnesota, 1948), 244; Malkov, *The New Deal in the United States,* 131–32.

18. *New York Times,* 7 October 1934; F. Schiplin to E. Hurja, 25 July 1934, FDRL, Official File

resentment, Roosevelt's agreement with the FLP worked successfully until 1938.

Democratic party leadership in Wisconsin was closely connected to major local capital and was among the most retrograde in the country. The harsh suppression of farmers' strikes and other reactionary measures completely alienated workers and farmers from the local Democrats.[20] Liberals in the state reported to the National Committee that in the Wisconsin organization "there has been no effort to conciliate the disaffected and disgruntled."[21] Under these circumstances, the Progressive party of Wisconsin, created in May 1934 by the La Follette brothers, quickly became the leading political power in the state. Progressives perceived it their duty to support Roosevelt and to defend his policy "from the reactionary elements in the Democratic party."[22] They became greater enemies of the local Democrats than of the Republicans. In the campaign of 1934, the president supported R[obert] La Follette for the Senate. And after the election, when the Progressives became the ruling party of the state, Roosevelt and the La Follette brothers agreed to support each other.[23] As in Minnesota, the agreement was mutually beneficial: the Progressives received the patronage and recognition of the administration, and for the president this arrangement was a way "to keep Wisconsin in the Roosevelt column," even (as one Wisconsin Democrat complained to Farley) "at the expense of the state party."[24]

A complex picture of the party took shape as well in New York City. There the Democratic stronghold, Tammany Hall, lashed out at new political forces: progressive Republicans, trade unions, and liberals who had united by 1933 in the United City party to support the mayoral candidacy of the progressive Republican F[iorello H.] La Guardia. Despite the pressure of the party apparatus, Roosevelt declined to support La Guardia's Democratic rival. Instead he maintained a neutral position.[25]

However, not everywhere was the choice between the Democratic organization and the liberal opposition decided in favor of the liberals. In isolated instances, particularly when liberals appeared weak or vague, Roosevelt formed alliances with the party apparatus. Thus, in New Mexico, where it appeared a small faction of

(hereafter OF) 300 (Democratic National Committee), Minnesota, 1933–1945.

19. "The platform of the Farmer-Labor Party is not Democratic, but Communistic. Playing politics with it, the Democrats in Washington can destroy their own party in Minnesota," complained a local businessman in a letter to Farley, expressing the opinion of the conservative Democrats of the state (O. Thomas to Farley, 17 April 1934, FDRL, OF 300, Minnesota, 1933–1945).

20. L[ouis] Adamic, "La Follette Progressives Face the Future," *Nation,* 20 February 1935.

21. C. Hammersley to Farley, 23 September 1936, FDRL, OF 300, Farley's Correspondence, 1936 Political Trends.

22. *New York Times,* 19 August 1934.

23. C. Backstrom, "The Progressive Party of Wisconsin, 1934–1946" (Ph.D. diss., University of Wisconsin, 1956), 267–68.

24. J. O'Brien to Farley, 15 September 1936, FDRL, OF 300, Farley's Correspondence, 1936 Political Trends.

25. C[harles] Garrett, *The La Guardia Years: Machine and Reform Politics in New York City* (New Brunswick, N.J., 1961), 253–54.

liberal Democrats would unite with the Progressive-Republican coalition behind Senator B[ronson] Cutting, Farley—with the tacit approval of the president[26]—did all he could to the detriment of Cutting's position. In the end, this resulted in domination of the state by conservative Democrats.

States such as these, where the process of revolutionizing the lower levels of society largely occurred outside the Democratic party, were fewer than those where the Democrats prevailed and where the political struggle over New Deal policy took place within the confines of the Democratic party itself. The administration had to choose between different party alignments—often a very difficult task. The natural inclination of the president to support party factions that to one degree or another had split from the main party in disagreement over New Deal policy collided with the conservatism of local leadership, the dominance of corrupt "party machinery" (in the states of Massachusetts, New Jersey, Indiana, and Illinois), and the chaos of factional skirmishes that often were devoid of serious political content (as in Illinois, for example). Party alignments to the left of the New Deal presented the administration no fewer problems. Certainly nothing illustrated so graphically all the difficulties and limits of tolerance for "left deviation" among the ruling Democrats than the dramatic events that unfolded in California during summer and fall 1934.

The swift political revolutionization of the laboring masses, manifested in 1934 by a general strike in San Francisco, met fierce resistance from reactionaries and conservative Republicans headed by governor F[rank F.] Merriam. The discredit of the ruling Republicans accelerated a massive influx into the Democratic party of most of the urban poor.[27] Radical thinking among the lower classes greatly increased. One indication of this change was the appearance of new intraparty organizations— "Democratic Clubs for the New Deal" and "Workers' Committee for the Democrats." The party leadership of the state was embroiled in factional strife between people aligned with Senator [William G.] McAdoo and those aligned with J[ustus] Wardell; it was in no rush to deal with the shift of social opinion to the left. The demand for radical leadership remained unfulfilled. It is not surprising, under the circumstances, that the program "End Poverty in California" (EPIC) found wide support among the state's laborers and petty bourgeoisie, and that its founder, the well-known writer U[pton] Sinclair, quickly became a serious contender for the office of governor.

Registered as a Democrat, Sinclair easily won the primary election and thus became the official party candidate for the governorship. Supporters of the EPIC program, organized into more than two thousand local units in California by fall 1934, became a massive force for the liberalization of the state's Democratic party— the goal toward which Sinclair himself aspired.[28] Yet, Sinclair's obviously utopian

26. J[ames T.] Patterson, *The New Deal and the States: Federalism in Transition* (Princeton, 1969), 173–74; Farley to C. Bowers, 10 November 1934, JFP, box 2.

27. Between 1930 and 1934 the number of registered Democrats doubled. See Rogin and Shover, *Political Change*, 112.

28. *New York Times,* 30 August 1934; Oral History Collection, Columbia University (hereafter OHC), U[pton] Sinclair, 294.

program, with its antimonopoly character, went significantly further than the New Deal.[29] That fact, in the end, determined the stance of the ruling Democrats toward the entire movement.

In September 1934, a convention of California Democrats accepted the EPIC program as the basis for the party platform, and Sinclair's supporters secured a number of responsible posts in the party structure. Conservative bosses, abandoning hope of "taming" Sinclair, deployed an intensive behind-the-scenes campaign to discredit him with the party's national leadership. They depicted the EPIC movement as a "Communist plot" that threatened to spread across the nation, and Sinclair himself as a dangerous opponent of Roosevelt in the upcoming 1936 elections.[30] On his part, Sinclair and his supporters, not unreasonably, solicited the president's support and aligned themselves with the New Deal in defense against reaction.[31]

In his rhetoric, Roosevelt was neutral; but he yielded to the pressure from Farley and influential party supporters in California and sanctioned behind-the-scenes pressure on Sinclair by his own special emissary J[ames F. T.] O'Connor. When Sinclair refused to withdraw his candidacy for governor in favor of the liberal Republican R[aymond L.] Haight, O'Connor and his close friend A[madeo P.] Giannini, head of the Bank of America, concluded a secret deal with Merriam. In exchange for Merriam's nominal assertion of loyalty to the New Deal, they promised to organize Democratic support for him in the fight against Sinclair. And it was done.[32]

The defeat of Sinclair by no means signified the restoration of conservative dominance in the Democratic party of California. Quite the opposite: the elections of 1934 proved to be a turning point in the history of the party in the state. Through EPIC, the party was rejuvenated. The urban poor, an organized working class (around 350,000 Democrats were newly registered between January and June 1934!), formed the solid core of popular support for Democrats in California.[33] At the same time, the leadership became more liberal. In 1934, twenty-seven EPIC party candidates were elected to the state legislature. Their ranks included the future governor, C[ulbert C.] Olson, and Sinclair's partner, S[heridan] Downey, who shortly became a U.S. senator. Conservative factions gradually lost their former influence. "The restoration of the Democratic party of California, begun in 1932 by Roosevelt, was concluded in 1934 by Sinclair."[34]

The congressional and state elections of 1934 were an important milestone for the

---

29. Malkov, *The New Deal in the United States,* 126–28.

30. W. Bryan, Jr., to Farley, 16 October 1934, JFP, box 2; McAdoo to F. Roosevelt, 24 September 1934, FDRL, OF 300, California, 1933–1945.

31. J. Jacobson to F. Roosevelt, 15 October 1934; A. Holst to F. Roosevelt, 27 October 1934, ibid.

32. J. O'Connor to McIntyre, 2 November 1934, FDRL, OF 300, California, 1933–1945; C[harles E.] Larsen, "The EPIC Campaign of 1934," *Pacific Historical Review* 27 (May 1958): 144–45; R. A. Posner, "Giannini and the 1934 Campaign in California," *The Historical Society of Southern California Quarterly* 39 (June 1957): 193–200.

33. Rogin and Shover, *Political Change,* 134–37.

34. C. McWilliams, "Poverty, Pensions, and Panaceas: California in the 30s," *Working Papers for a New Society* (Fall 1974): 40.

party. On the one hand, they revealed the beginning of the consolidation of reactionary power; on the other, they revealed the growth of political activism and the
demands of the laboring class. In violation of the long-standing tradition that the
ruling party is weakened by midterm elections, and in spite of a cautious prognosis
by the National Committee,[35] Democrats increased their majority in Congress and in
the governing organs of the states. Their position was strengthened almost everywhere, the exceptions being minimal losses in Indiana, Nebraska, and Oregon. The
elections confirmed that new voters continued to flood into the party. The number of
voters for Democratic candidates for the House of Representatives, for example,
increased during four years (in comparison with the previous midterm election) by
6.4 million people. At the same time, the increase for Republicans was less than
300,000. More than half the growth came from five industrial states in the Northeast
and Midwest (including Pennsylvania, New York, Ohio, and Illinois), together with
California.[36]

As in California, the mass of new voters in Pennsylvania was particularly active.
This was due largely to the participation of workers in the steel mills and coal industries. Pennsylvania votes for Democratic congressmen increased almost threefold—
from 562,500 to 1,457,000. And the ratio of Democrats to Republicans from the
state in the House of Representatives changed accordingly: 1930—3:35; 1932—
11:25; 1934—23:11.[37] For the first time in forty years, a Democrat, G[eorge H.]
Earle, was elected governor of the state. A converted Republican, Earle became one
of the most liberal governors of the 1930s. From a Republican stronghold, the state
was quickly transformed into an area of substantial Democratic influence. "In Pennsylvania a miracle has been worked," Farley was informed happily by the Catholic
archbishop of Philadelphia, [Denis] Cardinal Dougherty, "in overthrowing the
Republican party, which has had a grip on this state, but particularly on the city of
Philadelphia, for many years."[38] It is not surprising that the "Pennsylvania miracle," reflective of the party's increasing strength in industrial centers, was viewed by
its leaders with particular satisfaction.[39]

But, as Democratic functionaries themselves understood, this was not so much a
success for the Democratic party as a "triumph of the New Deal" that rested on the
shift of public opinion to the left.[40] A letter to Roosevelt from a rank-and-file Democrat in Indiana immediately after the election clearly revealed the new mood and the
demands of workers. The "overwhelming endorsement of the liberal innovations of
the New Deal means emphatically that the people of this country expect further

35. Farley to F. Roosevelt, 3 November 1934, JFP, box 2.
36. Calculated according to E[dward F.] Cox, *State and National Voting in Federal Elections,
1910–1970* (Hamden, 1972), 41, 81, 119, 159, 179, 255.
37. Ibid., 193, 202.
38. 8 November 1934, JFP, box 2.
39. Farley to C. Bowers, 8 November 1934, ibid.
40. From a letter from an aide at the Justice Department, J. Jackson, to Farley, 8 November 1934,
ibid.

progress along the same lines," he wrote. "Old-age pensions, unemployment insurance, socialized medicine, public ownership of waterpower, government banking—these are the things I hear daily on the tongues of people everywhere—the things they believe confidently will come to pass under the New Deal. Let me repeat again: Do not underestimate your personal popularity and the popularity of liberal policies which you have sponsored. Do not 'play politics' and make compromises with the old forces of reaction."[41]

By late 1934 and early 1935, the earlier political course of compromise was in ever greater conflict with the rapidly intensifying polarization of the nation's social classes. The coalition of "National Unity" formed in 1932 sprawled to both the right and the left. Divisions widened within the Democratic party itself. Its former conservative ("Wall Street") leaders openly defied Roosevelt by creating the Liberty League. The threat of a third party—a farmer-laborers' party—emerged on the left. Growing protest movements centered around H[uey P.] Long, C[harles E.] Coughlin, and F[rancis E.] Townsend. The double danger of a "third and fourth party," acknowledged by Roosevelt himself, was the major political problem confronting Democratic leaders by early 1935. Confidential papers from the National Committee to the president regularly reported lost voters on both the right and left flanks.[42] The continued desire of his progressive allies for political independence in 1936 caused Roosevelt particular pain. He wrote E[dward M.] House, expressing his concern about "progressive Republicans like La Follette, Cutting, Nye, etcetera, who are flirting with the idea of a third ticket anyway with the knowledge that such a third ticket would be beaten but that it would defeat us, elect a conservative Republican and cause a complete swing far to the left before 1940."[43]

The president, of course, clearly recognized that the prospects for a third party on the left largely depended on how he conducted himself in the future, a subject about which potential leaders of a third party—the brothers La Follette, Amlie, and others—staunchly warned him.[44] "Unless the new leadership of the Democratic party is able to liberalize that party nationally and locally to a much greater extent than has yet been done," noted the magazine *Nation*, "the progressive movement seems to have a good chance for success on a national scale."[45]

In short, the task of developing a more decisive political orientation stood before the Roosevelt Democrats. In fall 1934 the president received an especially curious letter from K[erwin H.] Fulton, a liberal businessman and Democrat from California. The writer set forth his own plan for eliminating the threat of a third party. "Your line, therefore, is to divide, to circumvent, to squash, to remove the need for this growing third party tendency," he explained. "Failure to do so . . . is sure to ulti-

41. R. Coleman to F. Roosevelt, 15 November 1945, FDRL, OF 299.
42. E[lliot] Roosevelt and J[oseph P.] Lash, eds., *F.D.R.: His Personal Letters*, 2 vols. (New York, 1950), 1:454.
43. Ibid., 452–53.
44. *New York Times*, 9 December 1934.
45. *Nation*, 11 August 1945, 124.

mately defeat the party in power. The best way to circumvent the third party is to go to the left: to make the Democratic party itself 'the third party.' While this will drive out some of our reactionary elements, such a course will positively be good for us. It is time for us again to be able to see some real differences between the two old parties."[46] It is not known whether this offering by the dilettante strategist ever reached the president himself (the answer was a formal note from his secretary). In any case, Fulton very accurately anticipated the policy Roosevelt would soon choose.

Roosevelt chose a new political orientation. He set out deliberately to broaden the popular base of the party as much as possible by using workers as a counterbalance to the growing opposition to the New Deal from the side of reaction. Fully aware that it was not the Democratic party per se that was attracting the masses, but the effective policies of his government, Roosevelt tried to avoid the appearance of a traditional party fight. For a time, he tried to open the party to the general stream of progressive forces. Roosevelt told party officials as they planned for 1936: "It would be a New Deal, not a Democratic party, appeal, with a special effort made to reach the new groups which had a stake in the continuance of the Roosevelt policies—workers, farmers, Negroes, young people, women, independents."[47] Many of Roosevelt's opponents—R[aymond] Moley, A[rthur] Krock, and others—depicted the main social reforms of the New Deal as a crude pursuit of votes from industrial regions.[48]

Of course, conjunctional undertakings played their role. The president and his party aides knew perfectly well that their policies brought a "return" in terms of votes.[49] But Roosevelt was thinking on a higher level, and such considerations became entangled in his strategic calculations. In his view, only restraint by bourgeois leaders toward the powerful wave of democratic movements, which would deaden their class direction, could preserve the foundations of the existing social order. Personal political survival was for him undistinguished from saving the system as a whole. As it turned out, the outcome was decided by new reforms initiated by the government in 1935, but Roosevelt's maneuvers inside the party were of no less significance in retaining the mass support of liberal Democrats. He gave top priority to securing the support of organized labor. The government established direct contact with the unions and supported the work of a special section for worker's organizations in the National Committee. D[aniel J.] Tobin, president of the truck drivers' union, was appointed head of the section. Cooperation between party and union functionaries was carried out secretly, and for the most part effectively, during the election campaign. Both sides were fully informed of the activities and plans of the other. Thus, Farley informed the well-known party functionary C[laude G.] Bowers in fall 1935 that the "Guffey coal bill will help us materially in Missouri, Illinois, Indiana, West Virginia, and Pennsylvania, making it possible for us to carry all of these states.

46. 28 October 1934, FDRL, OF 300, California, 1933–1945.
47. J[oseph P.] Lash, *Eleanor and Franklin* (New York, 1971), 439.
48. Moley, *The First New Deal* (New York, 1966), 379, 525–26; OHC, A. Krock, 65.
49. OHC, F. Perkins, 81–82, 490.

John Lewis, as you know, has always been an outstanding Republican and he supported Hoover. Passage of the coal bill has made him a real Democrat . . . . Lewis is going to help us . . . in Republican quarters where we need the help."[50]

The Non-Partisan League became a very important mechanism for attracting working-class voters to Roosevelt. It was a political coordinating organization of trade unions created in spring 1936 at the initiative of several trade-union leaders who were close to liberal Democrats: S[idney] Hillman, Lewis, D[avid] Dubinsky, and others. Although the NPL insisted that it was independent from bourgeois parties and even viewed itself as the prototype of a future workers' party, it was under Roosevelt's strong influence and limited its activities mostly to mobilizing support for him.[51] Working through a far-flung network of auxiliaries in the states and industrial centers, the NPL proved itself highly competent during the election campaign of 1936, and local party functionaries made the Democratic National Committee aware of the fact.[52]

The strongest branch of the Non-Partisan League was the American Labor party (ALP) in New York State. Its history is particularly instructive in the matter of cooperation between Democrats and organized labor. Organized at the initiative of Hillman and Dubinsky with the active support of E[leanor] Roosevelt, it soon received the blessing of the president himself.[53] Roosevelt saw the opportunity to enlist gradually the ten thousand members of New York trade unions of socialist orientations who were prepared to support his candidacy, but who had long regarded Tammany Hall with hostility.[54] Hillman and Dubinsky set up the arrangement, fully content to be junior partners in a "party which in fact would be ideologically tied to the New Deal and would function as a left wing of the New Deal."[55] "I can never teach them to vote under the Democratic star," Dubinsky explained to F[rances] Perkins. "We have been warning them for years to never vote for Tammany Hall . . . . Now I cannot teach them to vote under that star all of a sudden. I have got to have them vote under something that has got labor in it. They think that is the same thing."[56]

Roosevelt urged New York Democrats and the National Committee to collaborate with the new party, even though they regarded it with open hostility. But even they valued the benefits of a union of convenience during an election year. "The labor movement supported by S[idney] Hillman and others will bring more than 150,000 votes to our ticket," E[leanor] Roosevelt calculated in a letter to Farley. "They are

50. 14 October 1935, JFP, box 3.
51. See *The History of the Workers' Movement in the United States in Recent Times,* 1:396–97.
52. P. Fagan to Farley, 16 September 1936; T. Kennedy to Farley, 10 September 1936, FDRL, OF 300, Farley's Correspondence, 1936 Political Trends.
53. W[arren] Moscow, *Politics in the Empire State* (New York, 1948), 152–53.
54. OHC, E. Flynn, 21–22.
55. OHC, Socialist Movement Project, J. Weinstein, 7:12.
56. OHC, F. Perkins, 511.

going about it all right and we are going to cooperate in any way. Mr. Hillman himself believes that they will be able to get many people to register and vote who have never voted before."[57]

As it turned out the ALP, representing nearly 300 New York trade unions in October 1936, gave Roosevelt 275,000 votes and almost as many to the governor of the state, the liberal Democrat H[erbert H.] Lehman.[58] The hopes of local Democrats that the ALP would disband after the election were not realized. The new organization grew stronger, and friction between the two parties noticeably increased over time. The president himself played the role of arbitrator in this conflict, often siding with the ALP.[59] Recognizing the influence of this party, Roosevelt kept in close contact with its leadership.[60]

The president's evaluation was fully warranted: during 1937–1944, the ALP tipped the voting balance in New York State, insuring victory not only for Roosevelt himself, but also for Senator R[obert] Wagner, Governor Lehman, and other liberal Democratic candidates.[61] At the same time, the cost to the administration of such an alliance was minimal. The ALP limited its activity to one state and was under the direction of trade-union members who were faithful to the president. In reality, the alliance became for Roosevelt a useful form of indirect control over the radical opinions of the trade-union masses of New York, in that it kept them inside the channel of liberal politics.

Progressive Republicans and independent voters were other important groups that became objects of the tactic of "involvement." Roosevelt placed great importance on drawing these groups into his party because their support was as indispensable to Democrats as it was to minority parties in the elections.[62] In 1936, calling on experience gained in the previous campaign, he actively fostered creation of the Progressive National Committee (PNC) to win support among progressive non-Democrats. Committee membership included La Follette, Olson, Norris, La Guardia, and even a few leaders of the CIO. Acting independently of Democratic party machinery and through local organizations and farmer-laborers' parties, the PNC made a substantial contribution to Roosevelt's victory in 1936.[63]

The Good Neighbor League was another well-camouflaged force for the Demo-

57. Farley to E. Roosevelt, 26 July 1936, JFP, box 4.

58. R. Carter, "Pressure from the Left: The American Labor Party, 1936–1954" (Ph.D. diss., Syracuse University, 1967), 20, 24.

59. Farley, *Jim Farley's Story: The Roosevelt Years* (New York, 1948), 11–113; Garrett, *La Guardia Years,* 259.

60. L. Antononi and A. Rose to F. Roosevelt, 29 August 1936; F. Roosevelt to L. Antononi and A. Rose, 16 September 1936, FDRL, President's Personal File (hereafter PPF), 3892.

61. Thus, in the presidential election of 1940, when Roosevelt led across the state by 224,400 votes, the ALP gave him 417,500; in 1944, when he led by 316,900, ALP gave him 405,000 votes (Carter, "Pressure from the Left," 138, 212–13; *New York Times,* 9 November 1944).

62. J[ames M.] Burns, *Roosevelt: The Lion and the Fox* (New York, 1956), 286.

63. D[onald R.] McCoy, "The Progressive National Committee of 1936," *Western Political Quarterly* 9 (June 1956): 455–68.

crats. It was created in April 1936 by the National Committee at the suggestion of Roosevelt's advisors. The league occupied itself with mobilizing pro-Roosevelt elements among liberally minded businessmen, intelligentsia, blacks, and religious figures in the middle classes.[64] Collaborating with the NPL and PNC, it proved generally effective. By the end of the 1936 campaign, it had branches in twenty-eight states and counted nearly one million members. But the main function of the league was to serve as a "halfway house for those political independents and liberal Republicans who were making their way to the ranks of the Democratic party."[65] The National Committee, in confidential instructions to its functionaries, gave special attention to the task of winning the support of independents and Republicans.[66]

The creation of such a "driving belt" to encourage new political groups to support the Democrats was Roosevelt's favorite method. H[enry] Wallace remembered this as a "technique that Roosevelt's friends were expert at."[67]

Another method for this purpose was use of the left flank of the Democratic party itself. One of the best examples can be seen in the little-known relationship between Roosevelt and C[ulbert L.] Olson, a Sinclair ally who led the liberal-progressive faction of California Democrats while serving as chairman of the state party committee. The president found Olson especially helpful because he would use his considerable influence among former supporters who were newly converted or potential Democrats. Besides, Olson was more easily controlled than Sinclair. Local functionaries had advised the leadership that Sinclair's political demise offered new opportunities to consolidate his former allies behind the Democrats. They emphasized that leftist groups were responsible for the huge increase in registered Democrats in the state. Now the task was "to hold these left-wing voters for Roosevelt."[68]

Since 1935 Roosevelt had maintained confidential contacts with Olson for the purpose of combining energies against any rising third party in California.[69] By the election of 1936 Olson and his partners had diverted the energy of the radicals into the liberal channel of the local Democratic organization, and they supported Roosevelt's candidacy.[70] "Loyal Democrats" did everything possible to snare votes from the Left, including penetration of their organizations. Not without prompting from the president, they came to view as their main task, so Olson wrote to Farley, "the necessity of holding the extreme leftist voters in line, as well as those misguided by

64. See Malkov, *The New Deal in the United States*, 229.

65. D[onald R.] McCoy, "The Good Neighbor League and the Presidential Campaign of 1936," *Western Political Quarterly* 13 (December 1960): 1019–20.

66. M. Dewson, "Request to All Speakers"; F. Wichlem, "To Every Young Democratic Leader," 2 October 1936, JFP, Letters to J. Farley as Democratic National Chairman, box 26.

67. OHC, H. Wallace, 744.

68. J. Pachard to Farley, 5 September 1936; T. Crawford to Farley, 7 September 1936; T. Ford to Farley, 26 August 1936; FDRL, OF 300, Farley's Correspondence, 1936 Political Trends.

69. Secretary of War W. Dern to F. Roosevelt, 6 September 1935, FDRL, OF 300, California, 1933–1945.

70. Manifesto of Liberals and Progressives of the Democratic Party of the State of California, 20 January 1946, FDRL, OF 300, California, 1933–1945.

crack-pot spokesmen of the Townsend-Lemke-Coughlin element." For his part, Olson expected support from the party leadership.[71]

The election of 1936 revealed impressively the effectiveness of Roosevelt's political tactics and how much the popular bases of the party had changed. In summer 1936, the National Committee sent a questionnaire to local party functionaries in order to better understand the political situation on the eve of the election. Now preserved in the Franklin Roosevelt Library, the responses make it possible to sense the nature of the change. The election brought about a displacement of social-political forces unprecedented in the history of the country; and this displacement was reflected in the realignment of voters between the two bourgeois parties.

The term *class schism*, which was unusual in routine intraparty communications, frequently appeared in dispatches from many states, including such agricultural areas as Kansas, Nebraska, and Arizona.[72] New Deal programs had alienated conservative-minded elements among the upper and middle bourgeoisie from the Democrats. According to correspondence received by the National Committee, this alienation of conservative Democrats, so visible among the party elite (A[lfred E.] Smith, Raskob, J[ouett] Shouse, and J[ohn W.] Davis),[73] was duplicated at the local level.[74] Working with incomplete data from public-opinion polls, the well-known American political scientist V. O. Key concluded that the most well-to-do classes predominated among the deserters.[75]

However, in 1936 this phenomenon was not far advanced. Attempts by "Jeffersonian Democrats" at conferences in Detroit and Macon, Georgia, to organize a mass exodus of "true believer" Democrats from the "party of Roosevelt" failed. According to a Gallup Poll, 98 percent of those who considered themselves Democrats voted for Roosevelt.[76]

The withdrawal of conservatives had a more adverse effect on the party treasury. Contributions to the National Committee from traditional Democratic donors among the bankers and brokers of Wall Street decreased by six times in comparison with 1932—from a former share of 24 percent to 4 percent.[77] A similar picture could be seen across the country: "Leading contributors to our past campaign," lamented the party treasurer of Nebraska, "are now 'Liberty Leaguers' and . . . are putting their

71. 28 July 1936, FDRL, OF 300, Farley's Correspondence, 1936 Political Trends.

72. W. Barnum to Farley, 11 August 1936; A. Engield to Farley, 1 September 1936; W. Coy to Farley, 1 October 1936, FDRL, OF 300, Farley's Correspondence, 1936 Political Trends.

73. On displacement in the leadership of the Democratic party, see Sivachev, *Political Conflict in the United States in the Mid-1930s,* 196–97.

74. L. Lewis to Farley, 26 August 1936; J. Quigley to Farley, 21 July 1936; T. Parkinson to Farley, 14 September 1936, FDRL, OF 300, Farley's Correspondence, 1936 Political Trends.

75. V[ladimir] O. Key, Jr., *The Responsible Electorate: Rationality in Presidential Voting, 1936–1960* (Cambridge, 1964), 35–37.

76. E[verett C.] Ladd, Jr., and C[harles D.] Hadley, *Transformations of the American Party System* (New York, 1975), 83–84.

77. L[ouise] Overacker, "Labor's Political Contributions," *Political Science Quarterly* 54 (March 1939): 60.

money in Landon's pot for president."[78] Additions from other social sectors compensated the Democrats with interest for their losses on the right. Of the increased number of participants in presidential elections from 1932 to 1936 (six million people), almost five million supported Roosevelt, and more than 60 percent of this increase came from California and the aforementioned industrial states of Pennsylvania, New York, Michigan, Ohio, and Illinois.[79] From what elements did these millions of new votes come? Answering an analogous question about his own state, one Missouri correspondent wrote the National Committee, "Democrats who before were apathetic have come back to life, and first voters as a general rule feel that Roosevelt has done something for them. The Negro vote which we took from the local Republican organization four years ago has not been led back to the Republican party by the ghost of Abraham Lincoln . . . . The labor vote locally has abandoned the party line and is strongly pro-Roosevelt."[80] This assessment can reasonably be applied to the country as a whole.

The trend toward unanimous support of Roosevelt by the working class was reported in summaries from practically every state. The following are examples: "Soft-coal miners, of whom we have a great many, are with us almost to a man" (Pennsylvania). "Never in the history of the nation has the labor movement in Colorado been so solidified as far as a presidential candidate is concerned" (Colorado). "United Mine Workers are 100 percent for Roosevelt" (West Virginia).[81] It was especially noteworthy that Anglo-Saxons and Protestants among the working class (who had previously supported Republicans) shifted to the Democrats.[82] So sharp a break with long-standing tradition was possible only because spontaneous class consciousness had grown so much among workers and because class understanding of "economic interest" had led people to "vote as his or her pocketbook and conscience dictates." "By far the greater majority of those earning $50 or less per week vote for Roosevelt," one of Farley's New York correspondents reported.[83] Economic interest became a decisive factor in political behavior and pushed back ethnic, religious, and other factors.

No less an abrupt reorientation in party loyalty occurred in the black community. There, the concrete benefits of New Deal programs outweighed allegiance to the

78. G. Proudfit to Farley, 7 September 1936, FDRL, OF 300, Farley's Correspondence, 1936 Political Trends.

79. Cox, *State and National Voting*, 40, 80, 118, 178, 192.

80. E. Kane to Farley, 15 October 1936, FDRL, OF 300, Special Correspondence, 1936 Political Trends.

81. A. Braden to Farley, 22 September 1936; J. Brownlow to G. Collins, 12 August 1936; J. Hague to Farley, 11 September 1936, FDRL, OF 300, Farley's Correspondence, 1936 Political Trends.

82. Ladd and Hadley, *Transformations of the American Party System*, 56–57, 70–71.

83. B. Easton to Farley, 9 September 1936, FDRL, OF 300, Farley's Correspondence, 1936 Political Trends. "The overwhelming majority of persons with incomes of $50 or less a week will vote for Roosevelt," reported another New York Democrat (J. English to Farley, 30 September 1936, ibid.).

long tradition of supporting the "party of Lincoln."[84] Also, Democratic leaders skillfully involved black functionaries in the northern states. With the sanction of the president and Farley, "Negro political leaders were accepted in the inner councils of the party," and their participation was visible at the 1936 party convention. All this "convinced voters that the Democratic party was playing square with the race."[85] The National Committee actively encouraged work among the colored population. The goal was to direct the rising political awareness among blacks toward party registration and voting.[86] On the eve of the election, functionaries from Michigan, Illinois, New York, California, Indiana, and Pennsylvania reported the influx of a majority of "colored voters."[87] As a result, four years after they had supported Hoover, nearly two-thirds of black voters cast their votes for Roosevelt. Although this contribution was not great, taking into account the number of blacks who voted, it is nevertheless difficult to overestimate the significance of this early rapprochement for the future of the party.

The primary source of renewal for the party, as is corroborated by recent political analyses,[88] was not former Republicans, but "the new voters"—youth and those whose former participation in elections had been shunned. The number of new voters rose sharply during the 1930s because there was strength in their combined votes and because of the unanimity of their political sympathies. The majority, particularly the lowest paid, chose the Democrats.[89] According to a Gallup poll, 67 percent of the people who achieved voting age in 1933 became Democrats.[90] Similar percentage statistics do not exist for those who formerly were apathetic, but it is clear that participation in the elections of those years increased markedly in the industrial states and that the new voters favored Roosevelt.[91]

In 1936, 75 percent of the independents voted for a Democratic candidate; only 14 percent of registered Republicans did so.[92] This was indeed an unprecedented addition of new social forces to Roosevelt's party, and it violated all party traditions. "It must be realized," wrote Olson to Farley, "that the majority now registered with our party in this state are not traditional Democrats. The trends and accomplishments of

84. The common factors of this shift can be seen in Malkov, *The New Deal in the United States,* 224–27.

85. E[arl] Brown, "How the Negro Voted in the Presidential Election," *Opportunity,* December 1936, 360.

86. J[ames A.] Harrell, "Negro Leadership in the Election Year 1936," *Journal of Southern History* 34 (November 1968): 555–56; Democratic National Committee, Colored Division Releases, 1936, FDRL, OF 300, Patronage and Campaign Correspondence.

87. S. Boumann to Farley, 3 September 1986; E. Heine to Farley, 10 September 1936; W. Coy to Farley, 1 October 1936, FDRL, OF 300, Special Correspondence, 1936 Political Trends.

88. Andersen, *Creation of a Democratic Majority,* 63, 105.

89. Key, *Responsible Electorate,* 39.

90. Ladd, Hadley, and L[auristron] King, "A New Political Realignment," *Public Interest,* Spring 1971, 49.

91. For example, between 1928 and 1940, the level of participation in elections rose by 52 percent in Michigan and 43 percent in New York (Patterson, *The New Deal and the States,* 162).

92. Ladd and Hadley, *Transformations of the American Party System,* 83, 84.

New Deal policies, the President's forceful stand against opposition and predatory interests, and the political enemies he has made in reactionary circles, have brought a majority of voters of California behind President Roosevelt."[93]

A large proportion of the new Democrats lived in the major cities of the northern states. The New Deal strengthened the party in cities that contained a high percentage of Catholics, a feat first achieved by Smith in 1928. It also brought the party to dominance in the remaining industrial centers of importance. Voting in the cities acquired a uniformity as never before.[94] Recent statistical studies of the voting population of states that were developing industrially have confirmed that during this time the Democrats gained greatest strength in urban regions essentially populated by the working class and national, religious, and racial minorities.[95] These conclusions are fully consistent with what local party functionaries reported to the National Committee.

The formation of support for the Union party in the election campaign of 1936 was significant. The leadership of the Democratic party and Roosevelt himself, as is well known, followed the movement of Long and his followers with great anxiety and with a clear understanding that Long was capable of seriously weakening petty-bourgeois support for the party. From local responses to a special inquiry that Farley circulated in summer 1936, it emerged that the Union party and the followers of Townsend were perceived as a threat to be taken seriously in the agricultural regions of North Dakota, Illinois, Ohio, Michigan, and Nebraska, among elderly voters in California, and even to an extent in the Catholic circles of Massachusetts, Michigan, and Ohio where the Union party absorbed Catholic Democrats from the ranks of Coughlin's followers. The politicians of Massachusetts and Ohio even credited W[illiam] Lemke with the power to tip the political balance in their states.[96]

But as the election approached, the popular base of these movements eroded and flowed toward the Democrats. Evidently part of this development was accounted for by the traditional reluctance of American voters to "throw their votes to the wind." More important reasons, confirmed by letters from across the country, were the growing popularity of Roosevelt's policies (especially the programs of social insurance) and the negative reaction of the voters to violent attacks on Roosevelt by Lemke himself.[97]

As a result, the *New York Times* noted, "the efforts of the Union party to establish itself as a 'common front' of the discontented . . . were checkmated by FDR's strat-

93. 28 July 1936, FDRL, OF 300, Farley's Correspondence, 1936 Political Trends.

94. Lubell, *The Future of American Politics,* 62–63.

95. J[ohn H.] Fenton, *Midwest Politics* (New York, 1966), 215–16, 221; Burnham, *Critical Elections,* 57–59; Sundquist, *Dynamics of the Party System,* 205–10.

96. S. Loftin to Farley, 6 August 1936; C. White to Farley, 10 September 1936; J. Curley to Farley, 10 September 1936, FDRL, OF 300, Special Correspondence, 1936 Political Trends.

97. C. Foraber to Farley, 10 September 1936; Farley to F. Roosevelt, 13 August 1936, FDRL, OF 300, Special Correspondence, 1936 Political Trends; W. Barnum to Farley, 11 August 1936; H. Briggs to Farley, 27 July 1936, FDRL, OF 300, Farley's Correspondence, 1936 Political Trends.

egy. By taking WPA groups under his economic tutelage and lining up radical agrarian and industrial elements of farmer-labor parties in several Western states as campaign allies, the President has left several millions less acutely discontented voters for Mr. Lemke and his organizers to 'front' with."[98]

In 1936 most farmers supported Roosevelt for the first time, although local correspondents reported they already had reservations about "extravagant" government spending, taxes, and the like. The first signals that the party was losing strength in the agricultural sections of a number of states were soon forthcoming. From Illinois, for example, one writer reported, "The farm vote is drifting away from us [i.e., from the party], rapidly influenced by the Republican propaganda about the enormous cost of farm aid and its burden for the future."[99] A Pennsylvania writer volunteered that thus far "the New Deal is more popular in cities than among farmers."[100] The election results confirmed that the peak of Democratic influence in agricultural communities of the North had passed.[101]

Of course, the Democratic party as such remained in character the party of the ruling class. Its leadership in 1936 by no means personified Roosevelt supporters or the broad New Deal coalition. That coalition, over which liberal Democrats retained leadership with difficulty, included a number of other democratic forces that previously had not been connected closely with the old party. The newspaper of American Communists emphasized after the elections that "it has been admitted on all sides that Roosevelt's landslide was not the result, primarily, of a well-functioning Democratic party machine, but rather of new forces and organizations that rallied behind Roosevelt, and in the first place the labor-nonpartisan league."[102]

Whether or not the main groups that constituted the party would remain committed to it depended on many things: the course of class conflict, the solidarity of the democratic movement, the politics of the leadership, and, finally, the result of future conflicts within the Democratic party itself. The fact that conflict in the Democratic party currently extended to the level of local organizations was confirmed in several states. From Utah, for example, came word of antagonism between the conservative party faithful "paying lip service to the New Deal and F.D.R." and the alignment of independents who united the "farm bureau, labor unions, railroad brotherhoods, miners' union, and Democrats of progressive tendencies." Marylanders reported that many of the local party leaders, headed by Governor A[lbert C.] Richie, were "strongly anti-Roosevelt." Some said the president had "drifted too far to the left to suit conservative elements in the Democratic party." Reports from New York and

---

98. 18 October 1936.
99. W. Gleeson to Farley, 7 August 1936; V. Dallman to Farley, 9 September 1936, FDRL, OF 300, Special Correspondence, 1936 Political Trends.
100. W. Van Dyke to Farley, 8 September 1936, ibid.
101. Sundquist, *Dynamics of the Party System,* 201.
102. *Daily Worker,* 13 November 1936. See also Sivachev, *Political Conflict in the United States in the Mid-1930s,* 239.

Michigan, California and Nebraska, West Virginia and Iowa described schisms in the local organizations.[103]

The vast expansion of the popular base chiefly through additions from the urban lower classes quickly changed both the social-political and the regional arrangement of power inside the party. The proportional influence of the formerly strong southern agricultural wing seriously declined, and the role of the northern industrial states significantly increased. While in 1928 southerners constituted 63.2 percent and 66.7 percent, respectively, of Democrats elected to the House of Representatives and the Senate, by 1936 southern percentages were reduced to 35 percent and 34.2 percent.[104] In 1936, as in the previous election, Roosevelt could have won without the support of the South. And from that time forward, twelve densely populated northern states became the unavoidable and decisive factors in the elections for the Democratic party.[105]

The transformation of the Democratic party from a chiefly regional party into a national party was accompanied by the South's loss of its special standing. From "the faction of the majority in the party of the minority, the South became the faction of the minority in the party of the majority." The hundred-year-old rule that required no less than two-thirds of all convention delegates' votes in order to nominate a candidate for the presidency was repealed by the party convention in 1936. The old two-thirds rule, in fact, had given the South the right of veto in the selection of future presidents.[106] Now its repeal brought the southern bloc closer together and laid the groundwork for the future division of the party. That division was postponed only so long as both sides broadly conformed in their thinking about the New Deal. Later, in connection with reviving southern conservatism, southern politicians more than once remembered 1936 as "a black year" that was marked by the loss of "the best weapon the South had to stay the hands of radical Northern forces raised against it [i.e., the two-thirds rule], by the Negro vote coming to the Democratic Party in the North, and by the rise of left-wing organized labor as an important influence in the Democratic Party."[107]

The very size of Roosevelt's victory in 1936 obscured the approaching complications. At its peak, the New Deal coalition seemed too wide and heterogeneous to

103. O. Michelson to Farley, 12 September 1936; G. Dailey to Farley, 10 September 1936; W. Curran to Farley, 4 September 1936, FDRL, OF 300, Special Correspondence, 1936 Political Trends.

104. R[alph M.] Goldman, *Search for Consensus: The Story of the Democratic Party* (Philadelphia, 1979), 173.

105. S[amuel J.] Eldersveld, "The Influence of Metropolitan Party Pluralities in Presidential Elections Since 1920: A Study of Twelve Key States," *American Political Science Review* 43 (December 1949): 1202–5.

106. R[ichard L.] Rubin, *Party Dynamics: The Democratic Coalition and the Politics of Change* (New York, 1976), 115–17.

107. C[harles W.] Collins, *Whither Solid South? A Study in Politics and Race Relations* (New Orleans, 1947), 251–52.

remain stable during a period of rapid change. Previously hidden centrifugal tendencies and contradictions among its component parts gradually gathered strength.

The exodus from the New Deal of a substantial number of farmers and of the middle class occurred quickly and visibly. Worried about stabilizing their own economic situation, middling and large farmers of the North and Midwest quickly lost interest in continuing the course of reform. These developments brought traditional petty-bourgeois attitudes to the surface anew: an aversion to regulation of production and bureaucracy that often enhanced the New Deal; financial conservatism and dissatisfaction with the growth of government spending on the needs of the urban population; and fear that radicalism in the workers' movement would undermine the sanctity of private property and bourgeois law and order.[108]

Correspondents of the National Committee who analyzed the results of the 1938 congressional elections provide most of the documented proof that these attitudes resurfaced. The chairman of the Democratic party committee in Indiana volunteered that there were "excessive labor gains and legislation"; local functionaries in Iowa and Idaho wrote to explain that "farmers were jealous of relief to cities" and referred directly to the "fear of radicalism."[109] Writers from practically all the agricultural states and areas noted growing dissatisfaction with the administration's handling of social work, sit-down strikes, labor legislation, the Communist party, and government spending.[110] Even so, less than uniform opinions among farmers illustrated the great differences among them. A report on conditions in the agricultural areas of Illinois, Indiana, and Ohio, to cite one example, stated that "antagonism toward Roosevelt . . . seemed to be concentrated in the farm belt and appeared to come from farmers who owned from 360 acres up. Farmers who owned less land were more pro-Roosevelt and Roosevelt policies."[111]

The election of 1938 settled a strongly developing trend—the serious loss of farmers' votes by the Democratic party. The loss was especially pronounced in the agricultural states of the Northwest with traditional Republican ties. In those states, farmers "went back home to the Republican Party."[112] Riding the crest of the New Deal, the Democratic party had been enlivened during the first half of the 1930s in

---

108. On reasons for the waning of agricultural radicalism during this period, see V. P. Zolotukhin, *Farmers and Washington* (Moscow, 1968), 140–44; Malkov, *The New Deal in the United States,* 110–11, 222–23.

109. W. Gutziller to Farley, 3 December 1938; R. Ingram to Farley, 12 December 1938; A. Wilson to Farley, 17 December 1938, FDRL, OF 300, Election Forecasts and Analysis of Election Results, 1938.

110. U. Paul to Farley, 23 December 1938; D. McClugage to Farley, 19 December 1938; T. Diamond to Farley, 23 December 1938, ibid.

111. C. Vanderbilt, Jr., to Farley, July 1938, FDRL, OF 300, Patronage and Campaign Correspondence.

112. W. Mercer to Farley, 14 December 1938, FDRL, OF 300, Election Forecasts and Analysis of Election Results, 1938; J. Nolen to Farley, 16 December 1938; C. Manion to Farley, 14 December 1938, FDRL, OF 300, Political Scene after Election 1938.

such old pro-Republican states as Nebraska, Wyoming, Iowa, and Kansas. After the 1938 election, party efforts practically came to naught.[113]

The same process occurred in Minnesota and Wisconsin with several other consequences for the Democrats. For the most part farmers abandoned the Farmer-Labor and Progressive parties that had affiliated with the New Deal. In Wisconsin conservative Democrats even united with the Republicans against their common enemy (the party of La Follette) and were openly malicious about its defeat.[114] The progressive decay of third parties in Minnesota and Wisconsin graphically illustrated the general breakdown of connections between workers' movements and farmers—the "gap between farmers and laborers," as a report from Minnesota put it.[115] These developments struck a serious blow to the Roosevelt coalition.

Another breach in the coalition occurred in the South. Before 1937 the South was the region most loyal to the party, both in popular support for the government's policies and in the behavior of its southern congressional delegation, particularly its representatives in the lower house.[116] From 1933 to 1936 this poorest area of the country accepted federal aid and the economic programs of the New Deal enthusiastically. But from 1937 the level of party loyalty among southerners in Congress began to diverge markedly from that of northern Democrats.[117]

The decision of Democratic southerners to turn away from the New Deal involved complex economic, political, and ideological reasoning that was conditioned by the emergence of the South from the worst of the economic crisis. The 1938 Fair Labor Standards Act struck at the pockets of southern employers, who had become rich on the difference in labor costs between North and South. The battle around the anti-lynching bill that flared in Congress in 1937 encroached on the hitherto inviolable principle of southern autonomy in racial questions. Both these measures promoted the greatest divisions between northern and southern Democratic congressmen during the 1930s, and their resolution headed the South's list of claims to party leadership.[118] Add to this the threat to establish trade unions in the South and the increased assertiveness of blacks, and it becomes clear why the ruling class of the South began to perceive the continuation of the New Deal as a direct challenge to its

113. J[ames F.] Pedersen and K[enneth D.] Wald, *Shall the People Rule? A History of the Democratic Party in Nebraska Politics, 1854–1972* (Lincoln, Nebr., 1972), 298–99; T[homas C.] Donnelly, ed., *Rocky Mountain Politics* (Albuquerque, 1940), 139, 185–86.

114. W. Lautz to Farley, 14 December 1938, FDRL, OF 300, Political Scene after Election 1938. This opinion of the Wisconsin Democrats was fully shared by Farley. See Farley to F. Roosevelt, 7 November 1938, FDRL, OF 300, Patronage and Campaign Correspondence.

115. FDRL, OF 300, Election Forecasts and Analysis of Election Results, 1938.

116. Ladd and Hadley, *Transformations of the American Party System*, 131–32; J[ulius] Turner, *Party and Constituency: Pressures on Congress* (Baltimore, 1970), 173.

117. Turner, *Party and Constituency*, 173; 4 January 1938, FDRL, PPF 2405; J. Bailey to Farley, 10 October 1938, JFP, box 7.

118. L. Juggits to F. Roosevelt, 4 January 1938, FDRL, PPF 2405; J. Bailey to Farley, 10 October 1938, JFP, box 7.

monopoly of power.[119] By 1937–1938, southern politicians not only had cooperated openly with conservative Republicans in Congress, but also had begun to play with the idea of a two-party bloc in the elections.[120]

It should be noted that during this period conservative opposition in the South, more than in other regions, had a controlling, elite character. Southern politicians were more isolated from the pressures of the lower classes. Discrimination in voting practices was undergirded thoroughly by a social system that isolated the overwhelming part of the black and poor white population from participation in political life.[121] For this reason, and also by virtue of the general political backwardness of the South, attempts to liberalize the party leadership in large measure passed without effect.

In 1937 and 1938 the party split widened in the industrial regions of the northern states. The struggle for party control intensified between conservatives and the new forces that had sided with the Democrats in previous years—the unions and progressive and liberal elements. This struggle occurred in the context of the stronger class conflict brought on by the monopolies' frontal attack on the organized labor movement and by labor's powerful wave of strikes.[122] The sit-down strikes of 1937 were unacceptable to the "middle class, business, and farmers" (as Michigan Democrats informed the National Committee),[123] and at the same time they demonstrated the increased strength of militant unions. It was not an accident that this year saw the unions actively fighting for influence in local Democratic organizations.

In Akron, Ohio—the center of the rubber industry—the newly recognized trade union of rubber workers joined the local branch of the Nonpartisan Workers' League to nominate its own candidates in the municipal election on the Democratic ticket. They did so to frustrate the reactionary gubernatorial Democrat M[artin L.] Davey and his "party machine." Nevertheless, Ohio labor, so the magazine *Nation* reported, "made it clear that it was under no illusions about the Democratic Party as such."[124]

Michigan also became an arena of struggle between liberal Democrats who actively supported labor unions and the local conservative faction. Governor F[rank] Murphy, who led the liberal group, opposed forced suppression of sit-down strikes in Detroit. He became one of the primary targets for defamation by reactionaries throughout the country. Tagging him a "dangerous radical" who tolerated "the Communist elements of the CIO," conservatives successfully undermined Murphy's position with nonproletarian voters in the state, and they took revenge in the election.

119. R. Fossett, "The Impact of the New Deal on Georgia Politics, 1933–1941" (Ph.D. diss., University of Florida, 1960), 278–79.

120. Patterson, "The Failure of Party Realignment in the South (1937–1939)," *Journal of Politics* 27 (August 1965).

121. V[ladimir] O. Key, Jr., *Southern Politics in State and Nation* (New York, 1949), 491–503.

122. *History of the Workers' Movement in the United States in Recent Times*, 1:418–30.

123. J. Luecke to Farley, 29 December 1938, FDRL, OF 300, Election Forecasts and Analysis of Election Results, 1938.

124. D[onald M.] Pond, "Ohio Labor Tries the Ballot," *Nation*, 28 August 1937, 220.

The governor, claimed one of Farley's Michigan correspondents, clearly paid insufficient attention to farmers and local businessmen, forgetting that "the Democratic
Party can never win with the votes of labor alone." The liberal faction also was
weakened by the economic crisis of 1937–1938. As Murphy himself explained in a
letter to Farley, the recession "put the party on the defensive."[125] Regardless of this
temporary retreat, it was during Murphy's tenure that the foundation of the future
coalition of Michigan Democrats with the autoworkers union was laid. From the end
of the 1940s, the unionized autoworkers became the leading political force of industrial Michigan.[126]

In Oregon, the Federation for Universal Good, created in 1937 by liberals of both
parties and the local labor unions, contested an ardent opponent of the New Deal,
Democratic governor C[harles H.] Martin.[127] The federation supported the
nationalization of energy resources and, having the support of several representatives
of the administration, assumed the task of liberalizing the local Democratic party.
There was no end to the protests and insinuations from Oregon conservatives. The
patronage of H[arold L.] Ickes, B[enjamin V.] Cohen, and T[homas G.] Corcoran,
Martin complained to Farley, "resulted in infiltration and capture of the party by
radicals, demagogues and self-seekers." Others saw in the bloc of the CIO and
liberals the beginning of a "Communist trend in the Democratic Party."[128] In the
election of 1938 the federation candidate did not win the governorship. An important
federal employee in the state confirmed that "Republicans played upon conservative
prejudices against labor and liberal legislation."[129] But a moderate Republican
replaced Martin, and the liberalization of the party in Oregon continued into the
1940s and to the beginning of the 1950s.[130]

Events in the neighboring state of Washington developed in a similar manner.
There the local branch of the Federation for Universal Good battled conservative
Democrats headed by Governor C[larence D.] Martin for control of the Democratic
party.[131] And the growing political activity of trade unions in New Jersey, New York,
and Pennsylvania provided considerable worries for party bosses in those states.

On the national level these intraparty divisions and the upsurge of conservative
resistance were reflected in strained relations between the "presidential" (Roosevelt)

125. F. Murphy to Farley, 7 December 1938, FDRL, OF 300, Election Forecasts and Analysis of
Election Results, 1938. See also P. O'Brien to Farley, 3 December 1938, ibid., Political Scene after
Election, 1938.

126. Fenton, *Midwest Politics*, 11.

127. R[obert E.] Burton, *Democrats of Oregon: The Pattern of Minority Politics, 1900–1956*
(Eugene, Oreg., 1970), 84.

128. C. Martin to Farley, 13 October 1938, JFP, box 7; L. Irwing to Farley, 13 December 1938,
FDRL, OF 300, Political Scene after Election, 1938.

129. E. Griffith to Farley, 16 November 1938, FDRL, OF 300, Election Forecasts and Analysis
of Election Results, 1938.

130. Burton, *Democrats of Oregon*, 103–24.

131. "Progressives in Seattle," *New Republic*, 20 October 1937, 285; Patterson, *The New Deal
and the States*, 155–56.

wing of the party and the swelling conservative opposition in Congress.[132] Roosevelt's supporters wanted to "smoke these traitors and hypocrites out of their rabbit warrens and scourge the Tories from the Democratic party."[133] "The Kings, Copelands, Glasses, Georges and Byrds are no more liberal than the Hoovers and Knoxes," the Democratic mayor from Ohio reminded Roosevelt. "It is foolish to imagine that the Democratic party will remain liberal without a struggle."[134] The behavior of reactionary Democrats thoroughly angered the president. In the words of J[osephus] Daniels, they "hang on the coat tails of Roosevelt before elections, and then try to strangle his policies."[135] This, and preoccupation with the party's loss of its liberal reputation, inclined the president to initiate more decisive forms of intraparty battle.

The midterm election of 1938 provided a suitable opportunity to try to rid the New Deal of several of its enemies in Congress. Roosevelt's unprecedented and open interference in the primary elections yielded, however, very modest results. Of the victims marked, only one, New York congressman J[ohn J.] O'Conner, suffered defeat. This unsuccessful "purge" showed how well the local party apparatus had preserved its position and how the opportunity for rebuilding the party "from the top" was so limited. Besides this, the "purge" complicated Roosevelt's relations with the party hierarchy[136] and increased confidence among his conservative opponents.

In general, the election of 1938 confirmed a constriction of the party coalition. It was caused by the withdrawal of farmers and the middle class, as well as by the intensification of the intraparty struggle. It was no accident that, outside of agricultural areas, the most significant losses for Democrats were in the states where this struggle was most serious: Michigan, Ohio, Pennsylvania, and New Jersey. These factors, the conservative resurgence, and the unsuccessful "purge" made a more compromising course increasingly attractive to the party leadership. Intraparty differences might now be smoothed over in the name of completing the period of reform.

Such a course, more popular now in the president's circles,[137] acquired additional support as foreign policy required more attention. Party functionaries in the South, for example, contacted the president confidentially to point out the necessity of an amicable agreement with past enemies of the New Deal—Senators [Harry F.] Byrd, [Carter] Glass, [Walter F.] George, [Millard E.] Tydings, and others—in order to

132. The formation and essence of the conservative opposition have been examined in detail in both Soviet and American historiography. See Malkov, *The New Deal in the United States,* 331–40; Patterson, *Congressional Conservatism and the New Deal* (Lexington, Ky., 1967).

133. From a letter from Congressman J. Coffee to Roosevelt (14 August 1937, FDRL, PPF 607).

134. G. Abbot to F. Roosevelt, 16 March 1937, FDRL, OF 41.

135. J. Daniels to Farley, 3 August 1938, JFP, box 6.

136. Farley, *Jim Farley's Story: The Roosevelt Years,* 146; Farley to F. Roosevelt, 30 December 1938, FDRL, OF 300, Political Scene after Election, 1938.

137. M. McIntyre to Farley, 11 April 1939, JFP, box 7; S. Reed to F. Frankfurter, 14 April 1938, Library of Congress, Felix Frankfurter Papers, General Correspondence, box 92; OHC, H. Wallace, 559.

assure southern support for the government's foreign policy. The president's foreign policy offered "a common ground from which to begin the healing of past wounds." Roosevelt welcomed such probes and in response stated, "I am, like you, desirous of having the factions of our party come together under a common banner."[138] Thereafter, consolidation of the party guided his declared and actual policies. Even though "union under a common banner" implied different things to different people, it remained unattainable.

For Roosevelt Democrats it was quite clear that restoration of the precrisis status quo was impossible. Roosevelt himself repeatedly warned in public and in private that a return to conservatism would be suicide for Democrats, in terms of "preserving of the system" and in terms of retaining the voters won during the 1930s.[139] A letter from a liberal Wisconsin publisher to the president and Farley expressed the same belief well: "If the Democratic party is to continue in power in the nation, it must remain a liberal party. The Democratic party will return to the position of minority party if it fails to hold the support of the millions of progressives and liberals who voted for Roosevelt in 1932 and 1936. If the Democratic party becomes once more a reactionary party, then a new political alignment will surely emerge."[140] Precisely so, added Daniels, who speculated that if the Democrats nominated a conservative for president in the next election, "a new party, organized by Phil La Follette and others, would ultimately be as strong as the Republican party was in 1856."[141]

These ideas about consolidation did not settle the conservatives. They had not abandoned hope of "turning back the New Deal tide"[142] and of restoring their former position in the party. Therefore, after a short-lived respite, intraparty conflict broke out again on the eve of the 1940 election campaign. This time it took the form of whether Roosevelt should be nominated for a third term; and the divisions in the conflict were quite clear. Conservative Democrats from all regions, led by those from the South, and with the support of a significant part of the party apparatus, opposed the labor unions and liberal-minded elements.[143] To conservative Democrats, blocking Roosevelt's nomination appeared to be the last decisive chance for "saving the party from radicalism."[144] They found a valuable ally in the person of Farley, who was popular with the party hierarchy and whose own presidential ambitions

138. L. Jiggits to F. Roosevelt, 15 December 1939; F. Roosevelt to Jiggits, 20 November 1939, FDRL, PPF 2504.

139. *The Public Papers and Addresses of Franklin D. Roosevelt* (New York, 1969), 7:517; F. Roosevelt to R. Manner, 8 August 1939, FDRL, PPF 236; F. Roosevelt to S. Nettles, 29 January 1940, FDRL, PPF 6460.

140. W. Evjue to Farley (1938–1939), FDRL, OF 300, Wisconsin 1933–1945.

141. J. Daniels to Farley, 29 June 1938, Library of Congress, J. Daniels Papers, Special Correspondence, box 76.

142. W. Williams to Farley, 17 October 1940, Library of Congress, JFP, box 11.

143. J. F[rederick] Essary, "The Split in the Democratic Party," *Atlantic Monthly,* December 1937, 751.

144. J. Bailey to Farley, 6 July 1939, JFP, box 8.

prompted a certain hostility to the New Deal. Texas—the ancestral land of Vice-President J[ohn Nance] Garner, who also was thinking about the White House—was another hotbed of opposition to a third term. With great difficulty, S[am] Rayburn and L[yndon B.] Johnson, loyal to Roosevelt, succeeded in warding off an open mutiny by the Texas state delegation at the convention of 1940.[145] Still, the candidacies of Garner and Farley brought together conservatives of every suit who united in hostility toward Roosevelt and the New Deal.

Faced with boycott by significant numbers of his own party even more than in 1936, Roosevelt found it necessary to rely on the support of unions and liberal and independent organizations. He limited himself to a minimum of promises about "preservation of the achieved." But in light of a weakening labor movement and of the threat of counterreform, this was sufficient to maintain working-class loyalty. Neither the ballyhoo of propaganda about a third term nor the open mutiny of J[ohn L.] Lewis shook the president's position.[146] Johnson wrote from Michigan that farmers were "less exposed to such counteracting influences as union membership and public meetings."[147] The defection of farmers, begun in 1938, now accelerated. In the 1940 election Democrats lost the agricultural states of Kansas, Iowa, Nebraska, both Dakotas, Indiana, and Colorado. But "it was in industrial centers that Republican hopes were blocked out in factory smoke," S[amuel] Lubell wrote.[148] Precisely here, in the major cities of the country, the election was decided. Thanks to votes from the urban lower classes, Democrats compensated for losses in agricultural areas. They also strengthened their position in comparison to 1938 in Pennsylvania, Michigan, Minnesota, and the states of New England.[149] Abandonment by farmers and the middle classes imparted to the Democratic electorate an even more distinct social-economic coloring than it had possessed in 1936. Specifically, 1936 Gallup polls showed that 63 percent of workers (both unskilled and slightly skilled) supported the Democrats, as did 47 percent of the remaining population. In 1940 the percent of the voters in these categories was 65 and 40.[150]

The result of the election and, even more, of the party convention clearly confirmed the changing relationship of liberal and conservative forces in the party's leadership. It was specifically in the actions of the convention that the overwhelming

145. S. Rayburn and L. Johnson to A. Wirtz, 1940, Lyndon B. Johnson Library, Austin (hereafter LBJL), House of Representatives, 1940 Convention; E. Germany to Farley, 5 August 1940, JFP, box 9.

146. R. Tenerowicz to L. Johnson, 26 October 1940; J. Dingell to L. Johnson, 26 October 1940; W. Larrabee to L. Johnson, 27 October 1940, LBJL, House of Representatives, 1937–1949, 1940 Convention.

147. W. Jund to L. Johnson, 28 November 1940, ibid. (The future president, Congressman Lyndon Johnson, worked in the party committee on congressional elections.)

148. "Post-mortem: Who Elected Roosevelt?" *Saturday Evening Post,* 25 January 1941, 9.

149. P[aul T.] David, *Party Strength in the United States 1872–1970* (Charlottesville, 1972), 112, 116, 166, 170, 174, 198, 238, 242.

150. R[obert R.] Alford, *Party and Society* (Chicago, 1963), 352, 227–28; Lubell, "Post-mortem," 10, 92–96.

majority of Farley's conservative correspondents concluded that "the old regime had completely broken up." The conservatives lamented "the betrayal of the finest things . . . the party and the organization has stood for" and the party's degeneration into a "New Deal radical party."[151] After the convention Roosevelt himself wrote with satisfaction to G[eorge] Norris about frustrating the "revenge of the conservatives," who, "encouraged by the results of the 1938 elections, tried to return the Democratic party to the status of the years of 1920–1928."[152]

Nonetheless, intraparty shifts continued. The start of the war slowed, but did not stop, them. In the North agricultural support for the party diminished even further. At the same time, unions and liberal and black organizations became even more influential. Conservatives among northern Democrats in Congress, strong in the recent past, also lost influence.[153]

Other tendencies became apparent in the southern wing. Southern aspirants to the party's national leadership now added new grievances. The activity of the Committee on Fair Labor Standards; the campaign of the CIO to unionize the South; the renewed efforts of liberals in Congress to abolish the South's pervasive poll-tax; the stronger movement in the South to prohibit segregation in public places, lynching, and discriminatory voters' practices—all these things southern Democrats attributed to the intrigue of northern Democrats who pursued northern black votes.[154] By 1943 dissatisfied southern politicians had found new forms "of movement toward independence" from the national party. Possible variants of a "schism" began to be discussed openly.[155]

The election campaign of 1944 was a clear revelation of displacement inside the party. The Political Action Committee of the CIO—the most important instrument of liberal Democrats for mobilizing support among the working class—fought hard against southern reactionaries. Although Texas conservatives did break away, Roosevelt succeeded in averting the formation of a third party in the South (which he had feared greatly since 1943),[156] thanks to the specific circumstances of wartime and to keen political maneuvering. But this was the last time the weakened party coalition of the New Deal era could present a united front.

151. J. Wolfe to Farley, 7 August 1940; R. Smith to C. Glass, 8 August 1940; J. Hansen to Farley, 29 July 1940, JFP, box 9, 28.

152. *F.D.R.: His Personal Letters*, 2:1047.

153. Sundquist, *Dynamics of the Party System*, 212–13.

154. Garson, *Democratic Party*, 14–26, 28.

155. S. Jones, "Will Dixie Bolt the New Deal?" *Saturday Evening Post*, 6 March 1943; *New York Times*, 12 December 1942.

156. OHC, H. Wallace, 2896, 2918.

John M. Allswang

Comment on "The Democratic Party and Its Electorate in the Years of the New Deal," by V. O. Pechatnov

For those of us who are acquainted with writing on American history only in English and western European languages, the translation of current Soviet historiography is valuable and illuminating. Moreover, if Professor Pechatnov's essay is in any way typical, we can conclude that Soviets interested in American history are being well served by their academic historians.

Professor Pechatnov provides an informed and impressive synthesis of his topic, well-researched in both primary and secondary materials, and integrated in a sophisticated fashion. He has used a variety of materials, mined them carefully, and reached conclusions that contribute to our understanding of the period. In large part, his conclusions correspond to those of American scholars; where he verges away from them, his points are interesting and worthy of consideration.

Professor Pechatnov is primarily concerned with analyzing the political development of the Democratic party and its mass base during the New Deal years. He wants to see how what he calls the "social shocks" of the Depression decade affected the party, how it responded to the challenges of individual and group demands from the political system, and how it changed as it responded to those stimuli. He does this looking in both directions—at the forces impinging upon the Democratic party, and at the activities of the party and its leaders in trying to shape the flow of events. This is an entirely reasonable approach, and Professor Pechatnov, within the framework of his own sense of history, summarizes the forces involved.

Professor Pechatnov is also concerned with what seems to me a combination of methodology and ideology. He is looking for what he calls the "opportunities for productive scientific analysis" that the New Deal period offers. That is a complex can of worms, as most American historians will realize, since the definition of *scientific* is an open, always controversial matter. To some, it implies the application of concepts, such as modeling, and methods, such as content analysis and the use of quantitative techniques, from the other social sciences. To others, it is more general, implying primarily an effort to escape from previously normative orientations. And to still others, it implies an ill-advised effort to jettison a traditional humanistic focus.[1]

Professor Pechatnov's own approach, while consciously aware of much of this literature, is itself quite traditional and not what an American historian would call

1. One introduction to the topic is David S. Landes and Charles Tilly, eds., *History as Social Science* (Englewood Cliffs, N.J., 1971). Its application to popular voting behavior, which is a key element of Professor Pechatnov's essay, has been treated by a number of scholars, including Walter Dean Burnham, "The Changing Shape of the American Political Universe," *American Political Science Review* 59 (March 1965).

scientific. That is not meant to be taken as a dismissive criticism, since I hold to the common belief of the "many mansions" of history, with no one approach necessarily better suited than another to discovering the hows and whys of human behavior. But the raising of the idea of *scientific* history immediately calls for clarification, since it can mean so many different things. The reader needs a precise working definition, consistently applied in the body of a work. Professor Pechatnov does not provide such a precise statement of methodology and leaves the reader unclear about just what he means by the term *scientific analysis.*

Professor Pechatnov also appears to underestimate the amount of work that American historians have done on the politics of the New Deal years. He says that analyses of the Democratic party's response to the challenges of the decade have been done primarily by political scientists, and that "not one significant specialized work in American historiography has been dedicated to it." This is questionable in two ways. First, the line he draws between political scientists and historians is not nearly that solid. American scholars tend to move freely back and forth across the formal definitions of the two disciplines. And, second, while there is indeed room for more work, historians have by no means avoided the subject.[2] His own essay, I am happy to note, deserves ranking with those of American scholars as a part of that literature.

Professor Pechatnov has a good sense of the division in the Democratic party on the eve of the New Deal, particularly that between its southern/rural and northern/urban elements. The issues between them, however, were not really "redundant," as he suggests, at least from the voters' perspective. Prohibition especially, which he cites as one of the "redundant" issues, was in fact an issue of extreme importance, both practically and as a symbol of cultural conflict between these two elements in the party. This was true as early as 1924, and would continue to be the case through the election of 1932, where it was, arguably, more influential with various ethnic voters than even the Depression.[3]

Professor Pechatnov is quite correct in recognizing the germ of the new Democratic party in this "popular base," particularly the urban working-class element, which did indeed provide the crux of the New Deal coalition. It was sociocultural factors, as much as economic ones, however, which brought this to pass.[4]

---

2. For example, James MacGregor Burns, while admittedly a political scientist by profession, was certainly functioning as a historian in *Roosevelt: The Lion and the Fox* (New York, 1956), which deals in large part with the kind of analysis here called for. *The Politics of Upheaval,* vol. 2 of Arthur M. Schlesinger's *The Age of Roosevelt* (Boston, 1960), is only the first of a number of lengthy considerations of the topic by historians. A couple of more recent examples are John M. Allswang, *The New Deal and American Politics: A Study in Political Change* (New York, 1978), and James C. Cobb and Michael V. Namorato, eds., *The New Deal and the South* (Jackson, Miss., 1984).

3. See, for example, David Burner, *The Politics of Provincialism: The Democratic Party in Transition, 1918–1932* (New York, 1968), 98–101, and John M. Allswang, *A House for All Peoples: Ethnic Politics in Chicago, 1890–1936* (Lexington, Ky., 1971), 97–98, 118–28, 136–37.

4. Allswang, *House for All Peoples,* chap. 5; *New Deal and American Politics,* chap. 3; Richard Kirkendall, "The New Deal and American Politics," in *Fifty Years Later: The New Deal Evaluated,* ed. Harvard Sitkoff (Philadelphia, 1985), 18–19.

These factors also played a role in the New Deal's relationship with established political organizations, whether at the city or state levels. Professor Pechatnov concludes that "in isolated instances . . . Roosevelt formed alliances with the party apparatus" rather than with liberals like La Guardia or the Non-Partisan League. The opposite, I think, is closer to reality. Political considerations generally triumphed over ideological ones in the New Deal for both practical purposes and as a function of FDR's own nonideological orientation (see below). Roosevelt's effort to purge the party of some conservatives in the 1938 Democratic primaries was very much the exception, not the rule. Moreover, it was directly related to policy implementation, not ideology in any absolute sense. It is not surprising that it came late in the New Deal years, when things were going badly, and ideological factors resultantly increased; while things were going well, Roosevelt was quite content to work with established political organizations of all kinds.[5]

This tendency for political considerations to have a higher priority than ideological ones was even more pronounced in urban politics than it was among the states. It was also more important at this level, since the New Deal years saw a steady enhancement of urban political power at the expense of that of the states in which major cities were located.[6] Roosevelt and his political advisers saw the urban machines, with very few exceptions, as an important source of strength that should be supported, rather than as a threat that should be opposed. Thus patronage continued to flow to them, they were strengthened by the welfare and other programs that they had a role in administering, and their interests were deferred to in political decisionmaking.[7]

This was done not simply because the machines were powerful, which they often were. It was also very much a reciprocal and mutually beneficial relationship. The machines needed the New Deal and the Roosevelt-dominated national Democratic organization quite as much as it needed them, perhaps even more so. The fact was not, as Professor Pechatnov suggests, that the machines controlled the urban lower class; this had never really been the case. Machine control existed only so far as it responded to urban groups' perceived needs.[8] And their perceived needs in the 1930s were very much influenced by what was going on in Washington, which they came to support with steadily increasing enthusiasm.

Thus the New Deal supported established political organizations at the city and state levels both because those organizations had something to offer and also because

5. On the New Deal's political relations with state Democratic organizations, see James T. Patterson, *The New Deal and the States: Federalism in Transition* (Princeton, N.J., 1969), and Allswang, *The New Deal and American Politics,* chap. 5, and 121–26.

6. Allswang, *The New Deal and American Politics,* 110–11.

7. This supportive position of the New Deal vis-à-vis the urban political machines has been documented consistently over time. See, for example, Bruce M. Stave, *The New Deal and the Last Hurrah: Pittsburgh Machine Politics* (Pittsburgh, 1970), Lyle Dorsett, *FDR and the City Bosses* (Port Washington, N.Y., 1977), and Roger Biles, *Big City Boss in Depression and War: Mayor Edward J. Kelly of Chicago* (DeKalb, Ill., 1984).

8. See John M. Allswang, *Bosses, Machines, and Urban Voters,* rev. ed. (Baltimore, 1986), especially chap. 1.

they, by necessity, were strong supporters of the president and his administration. Ideology was minimized because FDR, most of the time, was not very ideological, and because it was simply politically inexpedient, even disruptive.

As Professor Pechatnov notes, the New Deal emerged at a time of growing class conflict and radicalism, and had to deal with these challenges in order to maintain its voter majority and its control of the Democratic party. Indeed, the role of challenges from both the left and the right in shaping the development of the New Deal, particularly in the second hundred days, is well known.[9] But most historians tend to agree, also, that even at the end of Roosevelt's first term the New Deal continued a politics of moderation. Not all New Dealers agreed with their president that they were part of a nonideological broker-state approach to public issues; some of them saw that approach as too limiting and conservative. Nonetheless, most of them did agree with the New Deal's pragmatic seeking of a humanitarian middle ground.[10] Politically, as economically, the New Deal under FDR's control never really varied from a basic approach of moderation, whose "radical" extreme, perhaps, was the Wagner Act (something the president approached with reluctance), and whose mainstream focus is well exemplified by the conservative Social Security Act and an on-again, off-again approach to welfare.

This bourgeois approach to reform was not simply a function of Roosevelt's own ideas and personality, however. Rather, it reflected the views of the vast majority of Americans, whether in factories, farms, or offices. Richard Kirkendall is correct, I think, in saying that FDR "seems to have understood the American people better and known how to communicate with them more effectively than any actual or potential leader of the Left."[11] And this is the case because almost all Americans shared his bourgeois liberalism.

Roosevelt's major critics, that is the ones with relatively large followings, were radical only in a relative sense. Huey Long and Father Coughlin, for example, were populist inflationists, of a sort, and Dr. Francis Townsend had a very limited sense of social reform. Even the labor leaders, including the relatively leftist ones like Walter Reuther, were in the final analysis reformers within the tradition of free enterprise.[12] Radical *tactics* had always been common among the American working class, and a sense of class division certainly increased with the Depression; but this hardly meant a real *political* radicalization of the American worker.

No better testimony to the essentially moderate nature of the American working class exists than that of those who would have moved that class further to the left.

9. This theme was developed by Burns and Schlesinger, as cited above, and has been generally accepted by all historians of the New Deal. A convenient summary can be found in William E. Leuchtenburg, *Franklin D. Roosevelt and the New Deal, 1932–1940* (New York, 1963).

10. Harvard Sitkoff, Introduction to his *Fifty Years Later,* 5. See also Kirkendall, "The New Deal and American Politics," 11.

11. Kirkendall, "The New Deal and American Politics," 16.

12. John Barnard, *Walter Reuther and the Rise of the Auto Workers* (Boston, 1983), 59–60 and passim.

Most Socialist and Communist leaders, certainly, were never attracted to the New Deal; it was to them, as Harvard Sitkoff has put it, "a flawed attempt to prolong the life of an archaic and defunct economic system."[13] But they realized that they were piping a tune that few were willing to dance to. Norman Thomas got only twenty thousand votes in 1936, and Socialist party membership dropped by 50 percent, to less than seven thousand by 1937.[14] Norman Thomas himself acknowledged that FDR, "a good Machiavellian," had implemented enough of what the Socialist party had been advocating to undercut its support. He felt that the New Deal commitment to alleviate poverty, and the labor legislation particularly, hurt the Socialists.[15]

Earl Browder, head of the American Communist party, agreed that the New Deal "cut the ground from under both the Socialist and Communist parties." The Communists' only real gains in the decade, he concluded, were in "reformist" activities: "As a revolutionary party it had not advanced an inch." Even among blacks, where the Communists were in the vanguard of defense against persecution and exploitation, the number of converts to the party was minuscule.[16] It was just not possible to move an essentially bourgeois working class beyond a level of activism keyed to improving their status in the social system to which they were committed. This particular characteristic of the American working class is crucial to an understanding of modern American history, not least that of the 1930s.

Equally problematic is the interrelationship between the New Deal, on the one hand, and blacks and the South, on the other. Professor Pechatnov is concerned in his essay with this problem and its effects on the New Deal and its politics. It is quite true, as he notes, that there was some diminution of the South's power in the Democratic party, due to numerous factors: the ending of the two-thirds rule for nominations, the large-scale increase of Democrats in Congress from other regions, particularly the urban north, and so on. But one should beware of a too facile write-off of southern influence. Southerners continued to hold numerous committee chairmanships and other positions of influence. And by the second administration they had begun to develop the "conservative coalition" with Republicans that would plague presidents from FDR to Carter.[17] Southern politics and politicians, overall, were little changed in the short run by the New Deal.[18]

Consequently, Roosevelt and the New Dealers had to constantly consider ramifica-

13. Sitkoff, *Fifty Years Later*, 6. See also Max Schachtman, "Radicalism in the Thirties: The Trotskyite View," in *As We Saw the Thirties: Essays on Social and Political Movements of a Decade*, ed. Rita James Simon (Urbana, Ill., 1967), 25.

14. Kirkendall, "The New Deal and American Politics," 31.

15. Norman Thomas, "The Thirties in America as a Socialist Recalls Them," in Simon, *As We Saw the Thirties*, 111–12.

16. Earl Browder, "The American Communist Party in the Thirties," in Simon, *As We Saw the Thirties*, 226–27, 233–34. See also Nancy J. Weiss, *Farewell to the Party of Lincoln: Black Politics in the Age of FDR* (Princeton, 1983), 297.

17. An excellent introduction is in James T. Patterson, *Congressional Conservatism and the New Deal: The Growth of the Conservative Coalition in Congress, 1933–1939* (Lexington, Ky., 1967).

18. Alan Brinkley, "The New Deal and Southern Politics," in Cobb and Namorato, *The New Deal and the South*, 112–15.

tions on southern support when formulating policy relative to blacks. It remained the issue that southern politicians were most adamant about, even to the extreme of virulently opposing antilynching legislation.[19] Thus there was no meaningful New Deal effort to undercut Jim Crow systems of segregation. And many New Deal programs had little or no impact on the predominantly rural blacks in the South: National Recovery Administration programs did not apply to agricultural or domestic workers, for example, nor did the Agricultural Adjustment Administration ultimately affect the power of blacks vis-à-vis whites.[20]

That had to be balanced against two other factors, however. First, there was real concern among some New Dealers for the lot of blacks in the United States, both as members of the poor generally and as members of an especially depressed minority group. Leading figures like Eleanor Roosevelt, Harold Ickes, and Aubrey Williams served as the administration's conscience in this regard. Second, and ultimately more important, southern political power was not necessarily more important, in the long run, than black political power, particularly in the northern cities where the New Deal's primary support was found. Thus there were very practical reasons for responding to black ambitions, particularly outside the South.[21]

Blacks did profit, especially outside the South, from New Deal relief and welfare programs. Rising black politicians were supported by receiving their share of patronage and appointments. Indeed, almost every New Deal agency ultimately had a black adviser by 1937, and Mary MacLeod Bethune had convened the "Black Cabinet" as early as 1935. The last was not an official government agency, but functioned almost as if it were; it had direct access to Eleanor Roosevelt, and its suggestions were at least heard in the administration.[22]

One can readily overstate the effects of the New Deal on blacks. FDR was no more directly devoted to blacks as a group than he was to industrial workers or any others. Rather, he sought to bring them into his coalition in order to strengthen it, and in the process hoped that they, too, would reap the general benefits of a more humane society. This was not civil rights, by any means; it was, rather, part of the broader politics of the New Deal.

As Alan Brinkley has noted, the New Deal was less concerned with changing politics than it was with controlling politics and using it to its own ends, whether that applied to southern whites or northern blacks.[23] Each group got a part of what it wanted; none got it all.

These are some of the important issues Professor Pechatnov raises relative to the

19. A good overview of the politics of the antilynching issue can be found in Weiss, *Farewell to the Party of Lincoln,* chap. 5.

20. Harvard Sitkoff, "The Impact of the New Deal on Black Southerners," in Cobb and Namorato, *The New Deal and the South,* 120–22.

21. Weiss, *Farewell to the Party of Lincoln,* is quite good on this, especially chap. 4 on the new black politicians.

22. Sitkoff, "The Impact of the New Deal on Black Southerners," 123–25; Robert C. Weaver reminiscences in Katie Louchheim, ed., *The Making of the New Deal: The Insiders Speak* (Cambridge, Mass., 1983), 260–64; Weiss, *Farewell to the Party of Lincoln,* chap. 7.

23. Brinkley, "The New Deal and Southern Politics," 97–115.

politics of the New Deal, the Democratic party, and American voters in the 1930s. He raises them suggestively and well, providing interesting ideas for Soviet readers. If I have focused primarily on aspects of the problem which I think require some rethinking, that is not to suggest that I am not often in agreement with Professor Pechatnov's generalizations. He has provided a creative synthesis and interpretation of subject matter New Deal historians still need to work on and reevaluate, even if most of them will see the problem in somewhat different terms.

American historians of the United States live in and study a society with a tradition of pragmatism that has been steadily reinforced from colonial times to the present. The nature of our environment, the development of our institutions, and our demography have all supported this pragmatism. Moreover, our long-term economic development and our democratic polity have offered possibilities of peaceful change beyond those of most other organized societies. Most American historians are impressed by this pragmatic tradition, particularly as it affects American politics. As such they are unconvinced that any rigid historical definitions do a good job of explaining our national development.

Certainly, ideological definitions of history, be they theistic, mechanistic, or Marxist, see American development in quite different terms. They may or may not apply to other places (basically, I doubt that they do), but have some real problems in explaining the American experience. Even so simple an example as our two-party system, inevitably nonideological and moderate, defies such categorizations.

The New Deal and the 1930s are a good place to see these differences. Few American historians find ideological or class considerations decisive in the behavior of American voters, on the one hand, or in the operation of the New Deal, on the other. Rather, they are impressed by the interplay of long-term forces (urban growth, wealth distribution, population change, cultural conflict) with the immediate ones of the Depression. And they are impressed by sociocultural forces (Prohibition is the classic example, nativism another) in American politics, wherein groups of Americans make political decisions quite irrespective of, or even contrary to, the class or ideological position one might expect them to take.[24]

This is a key area, then, where Soviet and American historians are likely to diverge in their understanding of the development of American history. It is quite a basic difference. Additionally, just as most of us see the American experience as pragmatically derived, we see it also as heterogeneous and impossible of reduction to one or even a small number of causative variables. We are also impressed, I think, by the role of chance. Soviet historians, as I understand them, are less impressed by the vagaries and the varieties, and more impressed by the certitudes that condition history. In this, we clearly disagree. Hopefully, in endeavors like the current one, we can learn some things from one another.

24. See, for example, Allswang, *A House for All Peoples*, 118–38.

Response by V. O. Pechatnov

I was very pleased to find Professor Allswang's response to my article to be overall quite favorable and his critical suggestions so very civil and thoughtful. Still, there are several specific points in his review to which I would like to respond, not so much for the sake of argument as for clarification.

I did not attach any deep methodological meaning to the term *scientific analysis*, which in our academic discourse has quite a different connotation and in this particular case should have been more accurately translated as *scholarly analysis*. Nor did I claim to be very innovative methodologically, although I tried to reach a deeper synthesis of history and political-science methods applied to this particular period—a synthesis that has not been quite achieved yet in my view, although the gap has been considerably narrowed in recent years (mostly, we must admit, due to the efforts of historians).

I am very much aware of and respectful of the work that American historians have done on the politics of the New Deal; unfortunately, I could not incorporate the most recent writings (including Professor Allswang's excellent *The New Deal and American Politics*) since my work on this article was completed in 1979 and I did not have a chance to update it since then. So by mentioning a lack of research, I simply meant a much narrower field of Democratic party history during the 1930s and the absence of a single specialized volume of synthesis comparable, for example, to David Burner's *The Politics of Provincialism*.

As for the rest of Professor Allswang's comments, most concern natural differences of emphasis and interpretation. While he tends to emphasize the moderation and continuity of New Deal politics, I accentuated the differences that those years brought for the Democrats, whether in terms of relations between the party's established organizations and its new allies or in the level and the role of the class consciousness of its electorate.

In this article I did not question the moderate character of the New Deal reforms (although it is so evident only in retrospect), but to what extent that moderation was merely a reflection of the popular mood or a function of political leadership is still a debatable point. We historians can endlessly argue about how really radical (or moderate) the masses were, but it is an undisputable fact based upon much historical evidence that for FDR and his circle the *threat* of further radicalization on the left was a very important factor affecting their political strategy and tactics. I also happen to think that the latter was rather important in channeling the political energy of the "red decade" into the bourgeois reformist mold on the policy level and into a considerably reconstructed Democratic party on the electoral one.

E. V. Kurochkina

8 THE SOUTHERN WING OF THE DEMOCRATIC PARTY OF THE UNITED STATES FROM 1933 TO 1935 AND THE NEW DEAL OF F. ROOSEVELT

The 1930s, known in United States history as the era of F[ranklin] Roosevelt's New Deal, were important years in the evolution of the Democratic party. The economic crisis of 1929–1933 and the Depression that followed resulted in greatly intensified class opposition. The desire to preserve their supremacy forced the ruling circles of the United States to find a way of dealing with the new reality. Internal restructuring of the two main political parties and realignments in the two-party mechanism occurred as a consequence of major socioeconomic and ideopolitical changes.

The most important role in transforming the mechanism of the Democratic party was played by reform-minded circles within its leadership. Once in office, Roosevelt, as party leader, proposed a program of socioeconomic measures that signaled forced development in the direction of state monopoly. He rallied around his program a coalition of class forces in which the ideopolitical leadership was assumed by a liberal wing of the bourgeoisie. The processes of party reorientation proceeded against a background of battle between adherents to the old-but-still-influential philosophy of individualism and supporters of bourgeois reform. Southern Democrats, the traditional mainstay of the party electorate, were to be an important component of Roosevelt's coalition and one of the party factions that greatly affected the formation of government policies.

The part played by southern Democrats in Roosevelt's policies is still disputed in American bourgeois historiography. The conclusions that the southern states were conservative in their very foundation and that they constituted the most conservative region of the country have received the most widespread dissemination.[1] Several modern historians (G[eorge B.] Tindall, W[illiam C.] Havard, E[verett C.] Ladd, C[harles D.] Hadley, and G[eorge E.] Mowry) have rejected these assessments. They believe the opposite—that the South in the 1930s was a reliable supporter of liberalism.[2] The present article attempts to analyze the relationship of the southern states

---

1. W[ilbur J.] Cash, *The Mind of the South* (New York, 1941); F[rank] Freidel, *F.D.R. and the South* (Baton Rouge, 1965); C[linton L.] Rossiter, *Parties and Politics in America* (New York, 1960). This essay by E. V. Kurochkina first appeared in *Social Structure and Social Movements in the Countries of Europe and America,* ed. Eugene Yazkov (Moscow, 1984), 70–88. This English translation is by Brenda Kay Weddle.

2. Tindall, *The Emergence of the New South, 1913–1945* (Baton Rouge, 1967); Ladd and Hadley, *The Transformation of the American Party System* (New York, 1975); Mowry, *Another Look at the Twentieth Century South* (Baton Rouge, 1979); Havard, *The Changing Politics of the South* (Baton Rouge, 1972).

to Roosevelt's program during the most active period of bourgeois reform (1933 to 1935) and to define the ideopolitical character of the southern Democrats.

The southern region enveloped thirteen states[3] that were united by a common history and common political and ethnic-cultural traditions. W[ilbur J.] Cash, a well-known journalist of the 1930s and author of the classic book *The Mind of the South*, compared these states to "a tree with many age rings, with its limbs and trunk bent and twisted by all the winds of the years, but with its tap root in the Old South."[4] The long domination in the South of a system of plantation slavery and its survival in the form of the semifeudal sharecropping system doomed it to economic stagnation and gave birth to a severe problem of poverty. The "peculiar institution" of slavery and the prevalence in the southern population of disfranchised and exploited blacks turned the region into a preserve of racism and laid the base for the flourishing of the doctrine of states' rights and of regional sovereignty.

The Civil War of 1861 to 1865 brought an end to slavery and cleared the way for extensive capitalist development. Nonetheless, the strong agricultural base on which the plantation owners had built their economic and political power was preserved. Even until the 1930s two-thirds of the South's population was engaged in agriculture. At the same time, the industrial development of the South was managed by its own bourgeoisie, who operated on the periphery of major monopolistic amalgamations in the Northeast. Those individuals specialized in initial processing of raw materials and frequently harbored anti–Wall Street opinions. During the 1930s the region contained only one-sixth of the country's industrial enterprises and only one-fifth of the capitalists who had million-dollar fortunes.[5]

As it developed in the aftermath of slavery, capitalism in the South was characterized by an almost complete absence of financial oligarchies, major machine industries, trade unions, and a large industrial proletariat among the working class. These characteristics left their mark on class relations and the structure of political institutions. The weakness of class conflict and the political passivity of the masses, reinforced by limited voters' rights, enabled the bourgeoisie and plantation owners to achieve political supremacy with the help of one bourgeois party. A one-party system gradually established itself in the region and foreshadowed the wide influence of southern Democrats in Congress and the national party conventions. Generally speaking, the southern wing of Congressional Democrats was a group of aged professional politicians who professed archaic views and considered themselves "the preservers of the sacred traditions of the United States." For a long time they held the highest ranks in the hierarchy of power—and they used the Democratic party as a weapon to defend their regional interests.

The South's particular race problem, the political inertia of the masses, the tendency to expect lower levels of government to fulfill social functions, and the related belief in the doctrine of states' rights created an identifiable microregion. The rela-

3. The eleven states of the former Confederacy, plus Kentucky and Oklahoma.
4. *The Mind of the South*, xi.
5. C[alvin B.] Hoover and B[enjamin U.] Ratchford, *The Economic Resources and Politics of the South* (New York, 1951), 34, 116; J[ohn S.] Ezell, *The South Since 1865* (New York, 1963), 153.

tionship of southerners to New Deal reforms depended primarily on the degree to which Roosevelt took into consideration the traditions of the region's political culture.

When Roosevelt first took office, the southern states were experiencing the worst of economic crises. A decrease of industrial production, mass unemployment, a slump in prices for agricultural products, and the growth of farm mortgage debts struck painfully at the southern states and sharply intensified the problem of poverty. The origin in 1931 of a Communist-led sharecroppers' union in Alabama and the mass action of textile workers[6] testified to the intensification of social conflict. Despairing and frightened by the approaching social storm, the majority of the propertied class in the South saw in Roosevelt a prospective leader. Typical of influential Americans, North Carolina governor O. Max Gardner remarked, "If I were Roosevelt . . . I would march with the crowd, because I tell you the masses are marching and if we are to save this nation it has to be saved by liberal interpretations of sentiments now ruling in the hearts of men."[7]

By the time the National Democratic Convention opened in July 1932, Roosevelt had won decisive primary victories in Georgia, Alabama, and Florida and had received pledges from all other southern delegations except Texas, Virginia, and Oklahoma. Those three nominated favorite sons—J[ohn N.] Garner, H[arry F.] Byrd, and W[illiam H.] Murray.[8]

Taking the reins of leadership, Roosevelt's government swiftly carried out reforms during the so-called "one hundred days." The tactic of performing "in the name of all the people" during the one hundred days was directed at retaining the broad coalition of sociopolitical forces that had supported the Democratic party in 1932.[9] The composition of Roosevelt's government reflected regional alignments.

Specifically, three Democrats from the South—C[ordell] Hull (Tennessee), C[laude A.] Swanson (Virginia), and D[aniel C.] Roper (South Carolina)—occupied the responsible posts of secretary of state, secretary of the navy, and secretary of commerce, respectively;[10] and Senator J[ames F.] Byrnes from South Carolina became an influential member of the "brain trust."[11] The desire to cement the Democratic coalition explained both Roosevelt's decision to run for election with Garner (Texas) and one of his innovations—that of inviting the vice-president to top-level meetings.[12]

The political weight of southerners in the mechanism of national power was even

6. Tindall, *Emergence of the New South,* 375–86; *The New Republic,* 1 January 1933, 226.

7. J[oseph L.] Morrison, *Governor O. Max Gardner: A Power in North Carolina and New Deal Washington* (Chapel Hill, 1977), 112.

8. R[oy V.] Peel and T[homas C.] Donnelly, *The 1932 Campaign: An Analysis* (New York, 1932).

9. V. O. Pechatnov, *The Democratic Party of the United States: Voters and Politics* (Moscow, 1980), 12.

10. R[aymond] Moley, *27 Masters of Politics in Personal Perspective* (New York, 1949), 252–53.

11. Byrnes, *All in One Lifetime* (New York, 1958).

12. F[rances] Perkins, *The Roosevelt I Knew* (New York, 1946), 133–35.

more clear in Congress. Southerners occupied 26 of 60 Democratic seats in the Senate and 130 of 310 in the House of Representatives. In accordance with the seniority system, southern Democrats headed 9 of 14 of the most important committees in the Senate and 12 of 17 in the House of Representatives. Moreover, southerners made up most of the Committee on Agricultural Affairs, the Ways and Means Committee, and the Rules Committee in the House of Representatives. At the same time, southerners secured for themselves the strategically important posts of majority leader in the Senate (J[oseph T.] Robinson from Arkansas) and speaker of the House of Representatives (J[oseph W.] Byrns from Tennessee, who was replaced in turn by W[illiam B.] Bankhead from Alabama and then S[amuel] Rayburn from Texas). The most important roles in the leadership of congressional Democrats were played by Byrnes (South Carolina), Robinson (Arkansas), and the "Patriarch of the Senate," P[at] Harrison (Mississippi).[13]

There seemed every reason to conclude, according to the *Washington Evening Star*, that "Dixie is in the saddle on Capitol Hill all right." However, this optimism was a little premature. As a result of the growth of the urban population and the disappointment of the masses with the politics of Republican presidents, a wave comprised of urban lower classes swept into the Democratic party. This phenomenon changed both the sociopolitical and the regional arrangements of power within the party. The reorientation of the party toward the industrial centers of the Northeast weakened its southern enclave. By the election of 1932, Roosevelt already could win without the support of the southern states; they possessed only 26.3 percent of the vote of the electorate.[14]

The waning of the South's political greatness could be seen in Roosevelt's Cabinet, where southerners were only minimally represented. The change is especially clear if one recalls that five members of Wilson's cabinet and two of his advisors were southerners.[15] During the years of prosperity, southerners had held 56 percent to 82 percent of the Democratic seats in the Senate and 55 percent to 70 percent of those in the House of Representatives. Then, in 1930, they began to lose their position in both houses (53.2 percent and 55.3 percent). The election of 1932 severely weakened their influence (37.4 percent and 37.3 percent of the Democratic seats).[16] The southern wing, which had formerly constituted the majority in the party of the minority, now had become the minority in the party of the majority.[17] Under these circumstances the control of congressional committees, where their position remained strong, took on new importance for southerners. Roosevelt's advisor R[exford G.] Tugwell con-

13. *Historical Statistics of the United States* (Washington, 1975), pt. 2, 1083; D[avid M.] Potter, *The South and the Concurrent Majority* (Baton Rouge, 1972), 48–50.

14. A[lexander A.] Heard, *A Two-Party South?* (Chapel Hill, 1952), 18; cited in M[artin H.] Swain, *Pat Harrison: The New Deal Years* (Jackson, Miss., 1978), 253.

15. Mowry, *Another Look*, 37.

16. R[alph M.] Goldman, *Search for Consensus: The Story of the Democratic Party* (Philadelphia, 1979), 173.

17. Potter, *The South and the Concurrent Majority*, 68.

sidered those in the southern wing to be hard-line conservatives. By the beginning of the New Deal he could see potential conflict in the depths of the altered coalition.[18] Taking into account the ability of southerners to turn the "minimum of their representation into the maximum of power"[19] through manipulation of their committees, Roosevelt built his own relations with the southern wing of the party on the basis of political bargaining.[20]

The New Deal hastened the transition to state-monopolistic methods of conducting the economy. The transition occurred with great speed under crisis circumstances. The new policies meant a substantial revision in the federal-state relationship, the ascendancy of centralized government over local political groups, and a clear advance in political consciousness among the bourgeoisie. Byrnes, expressing the opinion of the majority of southerners, later admitted that his strong convictions about the character of relations between central and local authorities should have been sacrificed temporarily to the necessity of some experimentation.[21]

At first, relations between Roosevelt and the southern wing of the party were conditioned by the principle of "friendly neutrality"[22] and by the region's interest in subsidies from the federal treasury and patronage from the White House. As early as 1931, Senator Bankhead (Alabama) counseled his colleagues "to burn some old bridges . . . and . . . the old prejudice against direct relief . . . might be one of the first bridges to be burned."[23] Burdened with regional problems, southerners, in fact, did not argue, but helped Roosevelt conduct a number of reforms through Congress. Thus, H[ugo] Black from Alabama authored a bill for a thirty-hour work week, Bankhead played an important role in passing a bill that regulated the agricultural economy, and the conservative W[alter F.] George (Georgia) persistently advocated federal expenditures to help the states.[24] The liberal press exposed the inconsistency of Robinson and Harrison, saying, "It was difficult to repress a smile when such Southern Democrats as good old Joe Robinson and good old Pat Harrison battled manfully for inauguration of a policy against which they had battled just as manfully in the past. But, in heaven, the repentant sinner is thrice welcome and Robinson in these days might easily be taken for a Progressive."[25] During the one hundred days, southerners acted as a regional bloc for the first time in the debates on the bill to regulate agriculture. They were united by the demand for fast and effective government aid. This bill did stipulate a substantial cut in production and did seem a rather radical anticrisis measure. Some southern Democrats—believers in conservative tra-

18. Tugwell, *In Search of Roosevelt* (Cambridge, Mass., 1972), 240.

19. J[ames] M. Burns, *The Deadlock of Democracy: Four Party Politics in America* (Englewood Cliffs, N.J., 1963), 311.

20. Tugwell, *In Search of Roosevelt,* 240.

21. *All in One Lifetime,* 69–70.

22. Freidel, *F.D.R. and the South,* 57.

23. W[alter J.] Heacock, "William Bankhead and the New Deal," *Journal of Southern History* 21 (1955): 350.

24. *Congressional Record* (hereafter *CR*), vol. 77, pt. 2, 1177, 1648.

25. *Nation,* 12 April 1933, 395.

ditions—first reacted with disbelief. The chairman of the Senate Agricultural Committee, E[llison D.] Smith (South Carolina), sharply condemned the proposal and tried to delay the beginning of debate. His colleague in the House of Representatives, M[arvin] Jones (Texas), considered the bill unconstitutional and even refused to bring it up for discussion. However, it was Jones's committee that eventually pushed through the bill: individual convictions temporarily yielded to political pragmatism.[26] When the bill came to the vote, the southern wing of the party joined with senators from Western agricultural states to present a united front.[27]

Roosevelt's reforms, with their accent on the regulatory function of government, were seriously at odds with the traditions of southern political culture. Therefore, from the beginning, Roosevelt found among southerners both unstable supporters and ardent opponents. It is noteworthy that the first Democrats in Congress to confront Roosevelt openly were the influential "irreconcilable" southerners—leaders of the "invulnerable" party machine of Virginia, C[arter] Glass and Byrd, and T[homas P.] Gore (Oklahoma)—and also J[osiah W.] Bailey (North Carolina). However, comparing Tugwell's assessment of southerners as hard-line conservatives with summaries of their votes in Congress, the researcher comes to the conclusion that the majority consistently supported Roosevelt. They considered themselves, in the expression of Congressman E[dward E.] Cox, good soldiers and followed their party leader. Not one southerner risked opposing all six important bills introduced during the one hundred days of reform: Glass and Byrd rejected two bills; Bailey, three; and Gore, four.[28] Even so, these Democrats united with a conservative nucleus of Republicans to form the earliest congressional opposition to the New Deal.

Several American political scientists explain the "digression" of southerners from their traditional conservatism as a simple matter of party loyalty. Undoubtedly, loyalty was a factor in their behavior, but it was not, in the view of the present writer, a determining factor. Their acceptance of liberal measures was primarily due to the extreme depth of the crisis, which in fact made the South a parasite on the federal treasury. Southerners considered the reforms of the one hundred days pragmatic measures and supported them because, in their opinion, only unqualified support of the country's popular president and his program could bring an end to the crisis and the return of social stability. Even Bailey, who accused Roosevelt of "superfluous liberalism" from the beginning, said, "I still think the element of faith in the president is the most valuable asset in the country and we ought to pursue a course tending to maintain this faith."[29]

However, the posture of most southerners toward the New Deal soon changed from positive or deferential to critical. A measure of improvement in the economic

26. *CR,* vol. 77, pt. 1, 539–40; M[arvin I.] May, *Marvin Jones: Agrarian Advocate* (Baton Rouge, 1979), 102.

27. *CR,* vol. 77, pt. 2, 1351. The bill passed by a vote of 53 to 28.

28. *CR,* vol. 77, pt. 1, 735, 1042, 1350; pt. 3, 2562; pt. 6, 5424–25.

29. Cited in J[ames T.] Patterson, *Congressional Conservatism and the New Deal* (Lexington, Ky., 1967), 12.

situation and rising social protest in the region served as an impetus to opposition. Implementation of the law to regulate agriculture drove massive numbers of share-croppers, tenants, and small farmers from the land. This displacement incited the Share Croppers Union of Alabama to action; and in 1934 the socialist-led Southern Tenant Farmers' Union took form. The quickening of agricultural protest coincided with major strikes of textile workers in Alabama and Georgia. These strikes, which were called when employers violated Section 7A of the National Industrial Recovery Act (NIRA), signaled the appearance of the first unions in the South.[30] In addition, Roosevelt's policies toward blacks caused intense hostility in the South. To a certain extent the president had taken the financial interests of black Americans into account and even granted them a number of posts in the government. Thus, in the "Black Cabinet," created in 1933, there were fifty-five representatives of the black community.[31]

Despite the fact that the president's policies toward blacks rested on discriminatory beginnings, in the midterm election of 1934 in Pennsylvania and Kentucky, blacks actively supported liberal Democrats.[32] Perceiving in the New Deal the source of free thinking by the lower classes, the ruling classes of the South nonetheless eagerly availed themselves "of all opportunities to seize benefits from the government on their account"—this while "they were heartily cursing Mr. Roosevelt for all that they found wrong."[33] Another, no less important, reason for new opposition among southern Democrats was the continued decline of their congressional influence. After the 1934 election, southern representatives filled only 36.7 percent of Democratic seats in the House and 37.7 percent of those in the Senate.[34]

The government's greater concern for social programs occasioned shifts within the factions of the Democratic party in Congress and complicated relations between the South's professional politicians and the coalition of liberals. Although they continued to support Roosevelt's economic reforms, southerners vehemently objected to the government's social programs. In 1935 new social legislation fundamentally changed the political orientation of the United States and became the basis of ongoing disputes within the party. Under the threat of class conflict, the New Deal was transformed. As its leaders single-mindedly took up the politics of bourgeois reform, the New Deal continued to bear the stamp of excess. By early 1935 southern Democrats no longer showed their previous reverence toward the government. The *New Republic* speculated that one reason for the moderate tone of the New Deal was insufficient liberalism among the southern Democrats who led the Senate. Outwardly they seemed loyal and zealous, but they were not convinced of the necessity of further experimentation.[35] In his own assessment of southerners in Congress,

30. Tindall, *Emergence of the New South,* 507–10, 420.
31. M[onroe N.] Work, ed., *Negro Year Book* (Tuskegee, Ala., 1937–1938), 112–14.
32. "New Congressmen," *The Crisis* 41 (1934): 359.
33. Cash, *Mind of the South,* 394.
34. Goldman, *Search for Consensus,* 173.
35. *New Republic,* 24 April 1935, 311.

Roosevelt was forced to admit that Robinson and Harrison had nothing more to give in support of his politics and had become preoccupied with "where the man in the White House is taking the old Democratic party."[36] Roosevelt's close advisors F[elix] Frankfurter and H[enry A.] Wallace considered Robinson and Harrison to be obstructionists of new reform and advised the president to undercut their influence as soon as possible.[37] As it turned out, leading southern Democrats preferred not to make a true show of their views on the threshold of the 1936 presidential election and in view of so much new social protest. They remained loyal and continued to support the New Deal; and at the same time they used all their influence to make the New Deal more moderate.[38] Their politics of friendly neutrality changed to a diplomacy of cautious silence.

Southern attitudes emerged during discussion of a $4.88 billion appropriation bill for social welfare. Various proposals to set the amount of aid to the unemployed met resistance from conservative southerners and Republicans, who considered reforms of this sort a tribute to socialist propaganda and an erosion of "the great principles of the philosophy of individualism." The economic concept of extreme individualism was linked inseparably with references to the defense of personal freedom and particularly to the doctrine of "states' rights." Demanding that federal agencies withdraw from the business of dispensing aid and transfer the responsibility to local authorities, Glass declared: "Every state and every civilized community in every state is competent to take care of its own indigent." Byrd echoed the thought, charging, "Government cannot compete with private business in the employment of people. It is not a wise thing for government to undertake to give jobs to those unemployed."[39] Those opinions were reflected in the voting on Byrd's amendment to reduce the appropriation for social welfare to $1.88 billion (21 voted for it, and 66 against) and in Glass's effort to limit federal aid to direct grants that states could use according to their own discretion.[40] A coalition of "old guard" Republicans and southerners supported Byrd's amendment. Simultaneously, southerners (not renouncing subsidy policies) voted down an amendment offered by leftist Republican R[obert A.] La Follette to increase the appropriation to $9.88 billion.[41] The bill passed in the Senate (68 for, 16 against) despite the steadfast opposition of Republicans and the conservative southerners Glass, Byrd, and Gore. However, in the opinion of the *Baltimore Sun*, congressmen who passed the bill only gave it lip service; their real interest was accessing

36. *Roosevelt and Frankfurter: Their Correspondence 1928–1945,* ed. M[ax] Freedman (Boston, 1967), 282.

37. H[arold L.] Ickes, *The Secret Diary,* 3 vols. (New York, 1953–1954), 1:363.

38. During the entire period of the New Deal, Harrison opposed it in 12 percent of the roll-call votes, and Byrnes in 14 percent, mostly during Roosevelt's second term (Patterson, *Congressional Conservatism,* 349).

39. *CR,* vol. 79, pt. 3, 2394; pt. 4, 3938.

40. Ibid., 3962, 2966–3967; *Editorial Research Reports* (Washington, 1935).

41. Among Southern Democrats, only T[heodore] Bilbo (from Mississippi) supported it (*CR,* vol. 79, pt. 4, 4160).

the national treasury.[42] The South reacted similarly during discussions of the Wagner Act, the law that guaranteed the right of the workers to organize into unions and make collective agreements. Southern industrialists, convinced that unionization of the workers would collapse the regional economy, rose in opposition to the original proposal. Congressman E[dward E.] Cox (Georgia) asserted that the bill was unconstitutional and that its provisions encroached on the rights of the states. H[oward W.] Smith (Virginia) appealed to Congress "not to further strip the states of their police power in purely local matters by means of legislation of this character forced through under the whip and spur of a real or fancied emergency." The chairman of the Southern States Industrial Council, J[ohn E.] Edgerton, called on congressmen to use all their influence to protect southern interests from the planning in Washington.[43]

Robinson and Harrison feared discussion of the bill would lead to a schism in the Democratic camp and asked Roosevelt's approval to postpone the debate. These senators, as other southerners, supported the bill out of considerations for party unity and with the hope of a subsequent change through judicial interpretation.[44] The concerns of the South's special interest groups took the form of an amendment by Congressman R[obert] Ramspeck (Georgia) directed against the creation of unions.[45]

Discussion of the bill to provide social insurance was more strained. The introduction of this bill was prompted by visibly heightened class conflict and the necessity of neutralizing a petty-bourgeois right-extremist movement headed by H[uey P.] Long, C[harles E.] Coughlin, and F[rancis E.] Townsend. The bill provided a measure of material security in old age and insurance against unemployment. While financing and immediate implementation of the pension program were to be carried out by federal agencies, unemployment insurance was to be administered through a combined federal-state system.[46] Ten of the twenty members of the Ways and Means Committee of the House of Representatives and the Senate Finance Committee considered themselves conservative; and they used their positions to oppose what they perceived as the growth of governmental interference.[47] While the bill was under discussion in the Finance Committee, Byrd introduced a series of amendments that substantively changed the definition of financial security and expanded the right of the states to establish the requirements for receiving grants. Committee chairman Harrison philosophically disagreed with the basic premise of the bill, but out of loyalty to the president he reported it to the Senate for consideration.

Debate on the bill took the form of arguments over the constitutionality of giving

---

42. Ibid., 4366; *Baltimore Sun*, 26 March 1935; *CR*, vol. 79, pt. 4, 4497.

43. *CR*, vol. 79, pt. 9, 9679, 9692–93; pt. 6, 6635–37.

44. Swain, *Pat Harrison*, 97–98; *New Republic*, 5 June 1935, 99.

45. *CR*, vol. 79, pt. 9, 9727–28; pt. 7, 7681. The amendment was not considered.

46. N. V. Sivachev, *The United States: Government and the Working Class* (Moscow, 1982), 213–18.

47. The committee consisted of twelve Democrats (of whom seven were southerners), two Progressives, and six Republicans (*CR*, vol. 77, pt. 1, 13; E[dwin E.] Witte, *The Development of the Social Security Act* [Madison, Wis., 1962], 95).

the executive "excessive strength," over states' rights, and over "unfounded taxation." In the course of the Senate debate, southerners made their position clear on the expansion of states' rights. Two amendments introduced by the Republican W[illiam E.] Borah (Idaho) and the Democrat [Bennett C.] Clark (Missouri) related directly to their concern. The first would fix the basic old-age payment at thirty dollars a month. Expressing the displeasure of his fellow southerners, Harrison protested that "The federal government cooperates with states, each giving one-half. The amendment would necessitate a change so that decisions would be made by a bureau here in Washington . . . . I prefer to leave jurisdiction in the states." Only four southerners joined liberal Democrats and progressives in support of the amendment.[48] What is more, southerners induced R[ichard B.] Russell (Georgia) to introduce an amendment that would protect the South's special interests from federal planning.[49]

The Clark amendment proposed to exclude workers who were covered by private insurance. This amendment divided southerners. A[lben W.] Barkley (Kentucky) became the propositions' implacable opponent. He asked his colleagues to support the existing government scheme. "One of the wisest things the Nation has done," he said, "has been to recognize the duty of the government towards indigents." To pass the amendment, the senator insisted, would be to flaw the federal system of insurance and to compromise the grant policy. Despite Barkley's agitation, eleven southerners supported the amendment, and it became part of the bill.[50] In this context, it is important to stress that southerners—with the exception of Smith (South Carolina), George (Georgia), and Gore (Oklahoma)—voted against an amendment offered by Republican W[alter] Hastings, who wanted to eliminate the section on social security in old age.[51]

Thus, the southern position in questions on social insurance took shape. Southerners would accept federal legislation only on condition that local leaders implement it and that the South's regional problems be approached conservatively. But an interest in subsidies demanded southern loyalty and forced them to approve the bill.[52]

Southerners were even more active during debate on the antiracist Wagner–Van Nuys–Gavagan bill. This bill declared lynching a criminal offense and gave jurisdiction to the federal courts. The bill extended the government's right of regulation into the field of race relations. Roosevelt's strategy for strengthening the Democratic coalition preordained his own position on the question of civil rights for blacks. The American historian [Frank] Freidel has characterized it as "benevolent neutrality." Although he was quite independent of southerners in Congress, Roosevelt in 1934 made an important declaration: "If I come out for the anti-lynching bill now, they will block every bill I ask Congress to pass to keep America from collapsing. I just

48. *CR*, vol. 79, pt. 9, 9632, 9634. The amendment was rejected by a vote of 60 to 18.
49. The amendment was not discussed and was accepted without vote (ibid., 9640–41).
50. Ibid., 9626, 9631. The amendment was accepted by a vote of 51 to 35.
51. Ibid., 9648. Glass and Byrd did not participate in the voting. The amendment was rejected by a vote of 63 to 15.
52. Ibid., 9634. Of the southern Democrats only the "irreconcilable trio" renounced the bill.

can't take that risk."[53] The position of the president could have been different if a minority of southern Democrats had been the only racists. However, even politicians of liberal and moderately conservative orientation—H[ugo] Black (Alabama), T[om] Connally (Texas), T[heodore G.] Bilbo (Mississippi)—and the leaders of the party and the Senate actively supported the racist elements.[54] The bill was brought up in the Senate in 1934 and then a second time the next year. The obstruction of the southerners was so unruly that even the press in the South called their conduct a parody of parliamentary debate. Robinson, to whom Roosevelt had assigned responsibility for shepherding the bill, preferred not to participate in the debate; Bailey, ever faithful to racist principles, christened the bill violent; and Smith declared he would consider himself free to choose his own allies if the bill became part of party doctrine.[55] In these debates the southern wing of the Democratic party showed its regional cohesion. It acted so decisively in the early stages of the New Deal that Roosevelt conceded autonomy in the question of jurisdiction over equal rights for blacks. This was one reason the southern wing continued to support the president's policies. However, fear of obstruction by southern Democrats does not explain the president's passive position. Roosevelt tolerated the existence of southern segregation and the disfranchisement of blacks within the framework of the Democratic party basically because political pressure from the black electorate was insufficient to force the party's national leadership to challenge the racist order.[56] It was under these circumstances, at the end of April 1935, that the Senate postponed debate on the bill with the unanimous consent of its opponents.[57]

The influence of conservative southerners on Roosevelt's policies can be seen as well in agricultural reforms. Under pressure from large farmers, the administration dismissed a group of advisors from the Department of Agriculture. It was known widely that this measure upheld the interests of petty farmers and agricultural workers. Harrison, Smith, and Robinson warned Roosevelt that the future activity of this group could be a serious obstacle to congressional support of new legislative proposals.[58] This conservatism, however, should not be exaggerated. Although southerners did hinder bourgeois agricultural reform, they also initiated agricultural reform in Congress. For example, Senator Bankhead was known as the author of a bill (which became law in 1934) to force a decrease in cotton sales. He also introduced a bill in 1935 that gave financial credits to tenant farmers for the purchase of farms and created an agency for migrants. After prolonged discussion the bill passed

53. Freidel, *F.D.R. and the South*, 97; W[alter] White, *A Man Called White: The Biography of Walter White* (New York, 1948), 169–70.

54. *CR,* vol. 79, pt. 6, 6353–72.

55. Ibid., 6774, 6615, 6616; J[oseph] Huthmacher, *Senator Robert F. Wagner and the Rise of Urban Liberalism* (New York, 1968), 238–39.

56. Pechatnov, "The Democratic Party and Black Voters during the Upsurge of the Civil Rights Movement," in *Political Parties of the United States in Contemporary Times,* ed. N. V. Sivachev (Moscow, 1982), 175.

57. *CR,* vol. 79, pt. 6, 6632. The bill was rejected by a vote of 48 to 32.

58. *Newsweek,* 16 February 1935, 7.

the Senate by 45 to 32.[59] The fate of this bill should have been decided in the Committee on Agricultural Affairs, where an alignment of conservative southerners deliberately delayed hearings and postponed its consideration. Roosevelt himself responded to the will of the landed bourgeoisie and declined to include this bill on his list of high-priority measures.[60]

Despite this moderation of his program, Roosevelt became the object of dissatisfaction among leaders of the financial oligarchy and the majority of politicians in his own party. This dissatisfaction became clear in 1935 during the discussion of bills on holding companies and taxes on large fortunes. By this time Roosevelt not only had to contend with the opposition of Republicans and "irreconcilable" southerners, he also had a falling out with the party leadership in Congress and with the idol of the southerners, Vice-President Garner. Trouble with Garner stemmed from disagreement over tax policy.[61] R[aymond] Moley, one of Roosevelt's advisors, believed the schism in the Democratic party began while Congress worked through the aforementioned bills. The vote on an amendment to the bill on holding companies made the differences clear. The amendment, offered by [Oscar] DePriest (Illinois), would prevent federal authorities from liquidating a number of companies for a specified period of time. Liberals scored victory in the tense battle by only one vote, with the southern wing of the Democratic party almost equally split between supporters and opponents of reform. The conclusion drawn by Moley, however, was exaggerated somewhat.[62] Southerners—in the persons of Harrison, Byrnes, Robinson, and Rayburn—chose as their tactical objective the preservation and consolidation of party unity; and as much as possible they attempted to limit debate.[63] Debate on the bill concerned with taxes on large fortunes centered on two amendments sponsored by La Follette (Wisconsin). These were propositions for additional taxes on yearly income. Southerners stuck to a position of silence, and with the exception of Black (Alabama), Russell (Georgia), and Thomas (Oklahoma), voted against these amendments. The bill passed the Senate over the objections of ten Democrats (among whom were the southerners Glass and Byrd) and of "old guard" Republicans.[64]

The concept of the "solid South" has long been a part of the lexicon of American politicians and historians. Their use of the term connotes the devotion of the region to the Democratic party. The present writer believes this concept more likely reflects the geographic unity and common historical background of the southern states than a unified political outlook and unity of action on the part of southern representatives.

59. *CR*, vol. 79, pt. 9, 9960. The "irreconcilable trio," the southerners E[llison] Smith, W[alter F.] George, and H[uey P.] Long, several Democrats from other states, and Republicans voted against the bill.

60. S[idney] Baldwin, *Poverty and Politics: The Rise and Decline of the Farm Security Administration* (Chapel Hill, 1968), 153.

61. Perkins, *The Roosevelt I Knew*, 171.

62. Moley, *After Seven Years* (New York and London, 1939), 312.

63. Swain, *Pat Harrison*, 113; *CR*, vol. 79, pt. 9, 9053.

64. *CR*, vol. 79, pt. 12, 13213, 13215, 13254.

An analysis of voting shows a lack of unity as early as 1933, when the "irreconcilable trio" and Bailey took their stand against a number of reforms during the one hundred days. In 1935, Senators George (Georgia) and Smith (South Carolina) joined them. As economic conditions improved, George and Smith more openly reflected the opinions of the propertied classes, who thought in terms of stability rather than experimentation.[65] The union of this alignment with the Republicans became the primary weapon of major capital as the battle of bourgeois reformation unfolded.

The bulk of southerners in the Senate (sixteen Democrats) continued to view Roosevelt as their leader and supported—to be sure for differing reasons—his policies. Robinson, Harrison, and Byrnes supported the New Deal primarily out of loyalty to the president and were potential allies of the forming two-party coalition. Southerners Black, Bilbo, and Thomas proved their liberality. In a number of cases, they favored the more leftist course, and they supported progressive Republicans. The ideas of bourgeois liberalism, however, were not disseminated widely and for the most part only enjoyed popularity among university scholars.[66] Finally, somewhat apart in the group of southerners stood Long, a man who alternately supported the liberals and progressives, then the conservatives.

There are grounds to maintain that the ideopolitical character of southerners in the 1930s was determined neither by the dyed-in-the-wool conservatives Glass and Byrd nor by solitary liberals like Black, but rather by figures of a moderately conservative orientation—Rayburn, Bankhead, Harrison—who combined in their outlooks elements of old theories and new liberal doctrines. Voting almost unanimously for expansion of the federal bureaucracy and for government regulation of the economy, these individuals, with their own hands, destroyed the individualism they professed. At the same time, they directed the development of the New Deal into the channel of moderate reformism.

In other words, the "solidarity" and "durability" of the South were relative in the party's political battles. Southerners were members of the same closed clan, and at times membership seemed more important than political ideas and beliefs.[67] Militant racism was inherent to the clan. It was the distinguishing feature of the southerners' idealistic creed and to a certain extent limited their liberalism.

Thus, from 1933 to 1935, the southern wing of the Democratic party was an influential component in Roosevelt's coalition. Pressured by class conflict, it generally supported the course of the New Deal. Still, the southern wing thwarted the evolution of the Democratic party in the direction of liberalism and served to counterbalance the growing strength of trade unions and liberal factions. It remained for the party leadership to keep southerners inside the Democratic ranks.

65. Patterson, *Congressional Conservatism*, 75.

66. M[onroe L.] Billington, *The Political South in the Twentieth Century* (New York, 1975), 67.

67. W[illiam S.] White, *Citadel: The History of the U.S. Senate* (New York, 1956), 74.

A. S. Manykin

9 THE REPUBLICAN PARTY OF THE UNITED STATES IN SEARCH OF AN ALTERNATIVE TO THE NEW DEAL

The economic crisis of 1929 shook the system of private property in the United States to its very foundation and showed that monopoly alone was incapable of effectively resolving the problems that confronted American society. The necessity of socioeconomic regulation became absolutely clear. However, neither the Republicans nor the Democrats could take action of the sort that the extraordinary conditions of those years demanded. Their political philosophy, based on Social Darwinism and ideas about individualism, prohibited government regulation of socioeconomic processes. This meant that the two-party system had lost the ability to fulfill effectively its most important task—preserving the supremacy of the monopolistic bourgeoisie.

The situation urgently required an immediate restructuring of the two-party system and its adaptation to new conditions, for only by means of government regulation could preservation of the existing order be guaranteed in the United States. Democrats and Republicans did accommodate themselves to the demands of the times, but in different ways—ways that were determined primarily by the positions each party held in the two-party system.

Defeat in the 1932 election forced the Republicans to assume the unfamiliar role of the opposition party. Yet, the opposition party had an important place in the makeup of the two-party system. It had several historically determined functions, and the stability of the entire two-party system depended largely on how well it played its role.

Because the ruling Democratic party in the 1930s as a whole adhered to neo-liberal views, Republicans had to come up with a constructive conservative alternative to the New Deal. In time, neo-conservatism became the alternative to the New Deal and to neo-liberal ideology. The essence of neo-conservatism was a combination of traditional conservative ideological postulates with state-socialist principles that reflected the reality of state monopoly.[1]

For a number of reasons the transition of the Republican party took a relatively long time (from the mid-1930s to the 1940s). The present article is an effort to explain the extent to which Republicans changed in the second half of the 1930s when they took the first steps. This subject actually involves investigation of three related topics: the change in Republican attitudes toward government intervention in socioeconomic problems; the gradual repudiation of isolationist dogma in foreign

1. For more on the essence of neo-conservatism, see N. V. Sivachev, "State-Monopolistic Capitalism in the United States," *Questions of History,* 1977, no. 7. This article by A. S. Manykin was first published in *Herald of Moscow State University,* History series, 1978, no. 5, 44–59. This English translation is by Brenda Kay Weddle.

policy; and the crisis and ideopolitical regeneration among Republicans. The present article, however, deals with only one of these: precisely how the Republican party gradually changed its internal position on government's role in resolving socioeconomic problems.

During the 1936 election campaign, Republicans made their first timid efforts to replace traditional, conservative ideopolitical principles in light of the changing role of government. Candidates in the Republican camp espoused a number of political outlooks. Candidates [William E.] Borah, [Frank] Knox, [Arthur H.] Vandenberg, [Alfred] Landon, and [Herbert] Hoover each enjoyed the favor of a faction of the party. Hoover, the former president, was considered the strongest candidate. After 1932 Hoover had remained the nominal head of the "Grand Old Party," and several influential members among the various factions still supported him. One was [Henry P.] Fletcher, head of the party's National Committee. In the greatly depleted Republican faction in the Senate, J[ames J.] David (Pennsylvania), D[aniel O.] Hastings (Delaware), and J[ames N.] Metcalf (Rhode Island) came out in active support of Hoover, as did House veteran F[rederick] Hale (Maine).

Delegates to the party's convention responded enthusiastically when the "Great Engineer" appeared. But Hoover, for all his support, could not win the nomination. His speech to the convention, "The New Deal and European Collectivism," has gone down as a classic in the ideology of individualism. Given the conditions that existed in 1936, the speech seemed a little strange, to say the least. It left the impression that the country would not survive the awful economic crisis, nor the sweeping upward spiral of the labor and democratic movements, nor the numerous New Deal reforms. Hoover acted as if this was the election campaign of 1928, not 1936.

The New Deal was the central issue among the delegates to the convention. Passing judgment on Roosevelt's policies, Hoover declared, "The evidence [is] that the New Deal is a definite attempt to replace the American system of freedom with some sort of European planned existence."[2] Of course, Hoover understood that a simple condemnation of the New Deal was not enough; it was necessary to offer a constructive political alternative. To that end he insisted, "The Republican party must achieve true social betterment, but we must produce measures that will not work confusion and disappointment. We must propose a real approach to social evils, not the prescription for them, by quacks, of poison in the place of remedy."[3] However, he failed to specify just how social well-being should be achieved, and that was one of the reasons his party rejected him.

Another reason for Hoover's defeat was that a significant group of leftist Republicans, primarily from the Western states (Senators [William] Borah, [Smith] Brookhart, [Lynn J.] Frazier, [Gerald P.] Nye), sharply opposed his nomination. Nye openly announced, "Unless the Republicans nominate a real liberal, I imagine

2. *Annals of America* (Chicago, 1968), 15:385.
3. Ibid., 386.

I'll support Roosevelt in 1936, provided he remains liberal. Otherwise I'll support a third party candidate, always with the proviso that it isn't a demagogue."[4]

The Republicans selected as their presidential candidate Governor A[lfred] Landon of Kansas. He was little known nationally, but the Hearst newspapers christened him "the new Lincoln." His candidacy pleased all constituent parts of the party (with the exception of the most radical Republicans like [Robert] La Follette, [George W.] Norris, and Nye). Landon's political views reflected all the contradictions of that complicated period when the Republican party, still holding to a position of rugged individualism, made its first efforts to find a more acceptable conservative alternative to the New Deal.

In his book published not long before the election, *America at the Crossroads*, Landon wrote, "The choice ahead of the American people is not whether to keep on with the mistakes of the so-called New Deal or return to the mistakes of the old order. The old order belongs to the past but sound American principles persist."[5] Positing the issue this way somewhat distinguished Landon from Hoover—for whom the "old order" seemed ideal. At the same time, Landon agreed with the old guard of his party that the New Deal as a whole was unacceptable. "This argument," he maintained, "instead of being progressive, is 40 years behind the times."[6] Landon identified with the individualists of the Hoover school in their apology for the system of private enterprise. America owed all its successes, he believed, to that system.

At the same time, there were some important differences between Landon and the former president. The state of Kansas, where Landon had built his political career, had long been famous for its antimonopoly sentiments, and these could not help but have some influence on the moderate Republican candidate. "My experience has convinced me," he wrote, "that monopoly is bad for everyone, including business itself."[7] And further, "one of the chief causes of our economic difficulties is the tendency of monopoly to fix prices and retain special privilege."[8] Of course, the antimonopolistic opinions of the governor should not be exaggerated. They were, in larger part, a tribute to the winnowing of time and the political traditions of the Western states.

Millions of voters waited for Landon to answer the question of how he would lead his party. The Republican position on government's role in resolving society's socioeconomic problems was of highest significance. But precisely here was the most vulnerable part of Landon's position; he simply did not have a firm opinion on the matter.

On the one hand, the reactionary individualism espoused by Hoover had strongly influenced the entire party, and Landon was no exception. Hoover-like rhetoric rang

4. W[ayne] Cole, *Senator Gerald P. Nye and American Foreign Relations* (Minneapolis, 1962), 136.
5. Landon, *America at the Crossroads* (New York, 1936), 13.
6. Ibid., 14.
7. Ibid., 83.
8. Ibid., 82.

out from every page of Landon's book. "I believe," he declared, "the greatest need of the American people today is a revival of confidence in themselves and in their ability to work out their own problems."[9] The lexicon of the Kansas governor contained many such expressions.

On the other hand, Landon could not help but sense that complete restoration of the Republican party along the old lines was impossible. It was becoming clearer that Republicans could compete with Democrats only if they shared common ground, or some small part of it, in recognizing government's positive role in social and economic life. Landon broached this strong feeling in American society very timidly. "There should be regulation of industry," he wrote, "wherever regulation keeps opportunity open and protects, not hampers, the people in the exercise of their rights."[10] Understanding that this statement was too vague and diffused for such an important issue, Landon tried to define more precisely—although without much success—the kind of functions government should take upon itself.[11] Measured against traditional conservatism, Landon said nothing new. His most valuable contribution was the very attempt to raise the question.

In subsequent efforts to compose a constructive conservative alternative, Landon took the position that the federal government should intervene in this or that matter only when it became clear that state and local powers could not resolve it effectively. So long as it was possible to act on the state and local level, it was necessary to do so, he maintained.[12] A similar thought about the use of federal and state power in social life later became one of the basic tenets of neo-conservatism.

Although it is true that this primarily was a hypothetical position and remained undeveloped, Landon defended this position on minimal federal intervention throughout the 1936 campaign. As a whole the 1936 Republican platform was in complete accord with the tradition and dogma of old-fashioned Republicanism. In true Hoover style its creators declared in the preamble: "America is in peril. The welfare of American men and women and the future of our youth are at stake . . . . The rights and liberties of American citizens have been violated. Regulated monopoly has displaced free enterprise."[13] And the Republicans further vowed to battle for the preservation of the principles of the American Constitution and the inviolability of the system of free enterprise.[14]

The Democrats proclaimed in their platform that "government in a modern civilization has certain inescapable obligations to its citizens"[15] and enumerated a number of specific measures to expand the system of social insurance, to guarantee

9. Ibid., 34.
10. Ibid., 82.
11. Ibid., 71.
12. Ibid., 27.
13. D[onald B.] Johnson and K[irk H.] Porter, comp., *National Party Platforms 1840–1972*, 5th ed. (Urbana, Ill., 1974), 365.
14. Ibid., 366.
15. Ibid., 360.

the rights of unions, to improve the farmers' situation, and so forth.[16] The Republicans proposed to eliminate all forms of federal government control over free enterprise and tried to persuade the voters that by so doing they would be taking the true road to prosperity.[17]

Republicans were least successful in electing their candidates to the Senate. They lost eight seats, and the number of Republican senators dropped to seventeen, the lowest level in the history of the party. Under these circumstances, Republicans lost the capacity to function independently in the important role of the opposition—to put political pressure on the administration with the goal of effectively defending, as American political scientists say, the "interests of the minority." In other words, the opposition party lost an important means of consolidating its social base.

A general assessment of the Republican party in the 1936 campaign must conclude that the organization continued to base its activities on ideas about individualism. And even the overwhelming defeat did not convince loiterers in the old guard that the old political prescriptions were wrong. Thus O[gden L.] Mills commented on the election not long before his death: "We are on perfectly sound ground in pointing out the inevitable results of the New Deal policies. But no one has yet actually felt their consequences, and people have to feel things before they are actually influenced."[18]

For all that, several ideas that crept into Landon's speeches made it possible to argue that Republicans, at precisely this time, were taking the first tentative steps on the difficult path toward a new ideopolitical orientation—neo-conservatism. Although individualism remained central to Republican party ideology, Landon's interpretation of it was not completely compatible with Hoover's outlook. When Landon spoke of individualism during times of deep socioeconomic stress, he did not seem so uncompromising and aggressive as had Hoover when times were prosperous.

Landon's defeat, after a campaign that was fully consistent with Republican traditions, changed relationships inside the party. The defeat was a serious blow to Hoover's claims to party leadership. Landon, considered the nominal head of the party after the convention, gravitated toward Republican organizations in the Midwest, where the tone was set by Vandenberg, [Robert A.] Taft, and Knox, i.e., people who were ambitious to occupy the command posts in the party's hierarchy. J[ohn D.] Hamilton replaced Fletcher as chairman of the National Committee in 1936 and openly advocated Hoover's retirement from active political life.

Hamilton, undeniably a conservative, nonetheless understood the need to give the party a new ideopolitical framework. When asked by the *Baltimore Sun* in February 1937 how he viewed the party's future, he said, "The Republican party will be an opposition, yes, but, I hope, a party of constructive proposals."[19] Following Hamilton, Governor H[arold G.] Hoffman of New Jersey offered a stinging critique of

16. Ibid., 360–62.

17. Ibid., 366.

18. J[oseph] Boskin, "Politics of an Opposition Party: The Republican Party in the New Deal Period, 1936–1940" (Ph.D. diss., University of Minnesota, 1959), 82.

19. *Baltimore Sun*, 7 February 1937.

Hoover: "The Republican party is hampered by leaders who are still living among cobwebs and mothballs," he declared.[20] Almost simultaneously, a very influential Republican senator, Arthur Vandenberg, took a stand against Hoover. In an interview with the *Saturday Evening Post* he condemned Hoover's leadership, albeit with characteristic caution. In explaining the party's current misfortunes he declared, "We were entirely too self-satisfied, too smug in the lush and easy days. It would be silly to deny these realities."[21]

Discussion of the reasons for this major Republican defeat was not restricted to the high echelons of party leadership. Newspapers and magazines sympathetic to the party carried lively commentary about the party's future prospects. The primary characteristic of all this discussion, of course, was embarrassment. "In 1920, 1924, 1928, and 1932 *The Literary Digest* polls were right," stated an editorial in the magazine. This year "we were far from correct. Why? We ask that question in all sincerity, because we want to know."[22] It is impossible to say whether Republican newspapers understood the real causes of the party's defeat. All the same, the idea crept in on several occasions that the basis of the defeat was to be found in the discrepancy between the ideological position of Republican leaders and the mood of the voters—the reality of life in the country. The *Kansas City Star*, a leading midwestern newspaper long famous for its Republican sympathies, contended the election simply showed that voters approved of Roosevelt's actions.[23] The *Milwaukee Journal* in its analysis noted that farmers had deserted the Republicans and maintained they had done so because of New Deal agricultural legislation, for the Democratic administration had regulated agriculture.[24] The *Portland Press Herald* argued that blind adherence to traditional Republican dogma had led the party to the verge of disaster.[25] Of course, the influence of such views on the party leadership should not be exaggerated. Nonetheless, they did have a certain impact on the Republican party's internal struggles.

The years 1937 and 1938 saw a new phase in the Republican party's adaptation to state-monopolistic capitalism and its creation of a constructive, conservative alternative to the New Deal. These two years were also landmark years in the reconstruction of the two-party system. After the first stormy and troubled years of the New Deal, the Republican party began to reestablish a more normal situation characterized by flexibility and equilibrium. Two developments made this possible. First, the outline of a coalition of conservative Democrats and Republicans took shape during these years. This coalition began to function as a counterbalance to the exceptionally strong liberal wing of the Democratic party. The formation of the coalition also allowed Republicans to shift from passive criticism to more creative activities.

20. *New York Times*, 7 February 1937.
21. *Saturday Evening Post*, 27 February 1937.
22. *Literary Digest*, 14 November 1937, 7.
23. Ibid., 12.
24. Ibid.
25. Ibid.

Second, conservative Republicans during these years began to switch from unsubstantiated rejection of all Roosevelt's measures to a more flexible position, one directed at limiting (and not eliminating) government regulation. Thus, to a certain extent they had come to recognize a limited role for government in the resolution of economic and social affairs, and they had found a point of agreement with a number of Democrats. The prerequisite interparty consensus that is necessary for the two-party system had been created. At the same time, the majority of Democrats and Republicans remained widely divided over approaches to most important political problems. These developments occurred simultaneously, quite often intertwining and clashing with each other.

As these events evolved, conflict over reforming the Supreme Court, which had become the main bastion of reaction in America, played an important role. Roosevelt came more and more into conflict with the Court over expansion of New Deal reforms. Using its right to interpret the Constitution, the Court declared many laws unconstitutional that Congress had passed from 1934 to 1936. The White House gradually lost patience. The 1936 Democratic election platform contained an unambiguous threat to the Supreme Court: "If these problems can't be effectively solved by legislation within the Constitution, we shall seek such clarifying amendments as will assure . . . the power to enact those laws which the state and federal legislatures, within their respective spheres, shall find necessary."[26]

However, limiting the power of the Supreme Court by winning acceptance of constitutional amendments would be an extremely lengthy process, and therefore Roosevelt took another course. He addressed Congress on 5 February 1937 to propose that the members consider reforming the judicial system of the United States, and particularly the Supreme Court. The president did not hide his concern. He pointed out that "the judiciary, by postponing the effective date of the acts of Congress, is assuming an additional function and is coming more and more to constitute a scattered, loosely organized and slowly operating third house of the national legislature."[27] However, if the current state of affairs did not suit Roosevelt, it was precisely what American conservatives wanted. In 1935 Knox declared, "Hoover feels as I do that the New Deal program has collapsed and if the Supreme Court decision on the oil code is followed by others . . . the Roosevelt program is thrown into inextricable confusion."[28] In 1936 Mills wrote to Professor G[lenn] Frank, a well-known conservative American ideologist: "Roosevelt's policies did not cause recovery, quite the contrary, if government did help recovery, the only branch of government entitled to credit is the Supreme Court."[29]

It is easy to understand why Roosevelt's proposal to reform the judicial system received such a hostile reception. Hoover soon charged, "He wants one [a Supreme

26. *National Party Platforms,* 362.
27. *The Public Papers and Addresses of F.D.R.* (New York, 1941), 37:58.
28. Boskin, "Politics of an Opposition Party," 70.
29. Ibid., 247.

Court] that will revise the Constitution so it will mean what he wishes it to mean."[30] Taft echoed him: "The President now desires to secure personal control of the entire government."[31] Hamilton had noted that Madison viewed the Supreme Court as a bastion against encroachment on human rights by the legislative and executive branches.[32]

Leaders among Senate Republicans were more cautious. They fully understood that they were a clear minority and that the fate of the court reform bill was in the hands of the Democrats. Therefore, when three of the most influential Republican senators—Vandenberg, Borah, and [Charles L.] McNary—met in mid-February to consider their faction's response, they reached a unanimous decision: they would wait. Vandenberg explained their position: "Only a coalition could succeed—a preponderantly Democratic coalition . . . . Republicans voluntarily subordinated themselves and withdrew to the reserve line."[33]

Vandenberg was by no means building on sand. Grounds for creating a coalition had been established in the middle 1930s as a result of the dissatisfaction of many Democrats with several of Roosevelt's policies. For example, as early as 1933 the influential Democratic senators C[arter] Glass and H[arry F.] Byrd (both of Virginia) and J[osiah W.] Bailey (North Carolina) periodically challenged the New Deal. After 1935 they were joined by E[dward R.] Burke (Nebraska), P[eter G.] Gerry (Rhode Island), W[alter F.] George (Georgia), and E[llison D.] Smith (South Carolina). Famished for power and fearful of the magnitude of the crisis, these individuals first had accepted the president's political leadership. But as the New Deal expanded, their patience and willingness to submit to White House leadership gradually diminished. However, there were not sufficient grounds for them to bring their dissatisfaction completely into the open.

Roosevelt's proposal for judicial reform provided such grounds. The proposed legislation "violates all precedents in the history of our government and would in itself be a dangerous precedent for the future." "The theory of the bill is in direct violation of the spirit of the American Constitution"; "this bill is an invasion of judicial power such as has never before been attempted in this country." These words come not from the mouths of Hoover, Landon, or [James W.] Wadsworth, but from the report of the Senate Judiciary Committee after its hearings on the proposal.[34] Of the eighteen members of this committee, thirteen were Democrats, and their signatures appeared beneath the document's conclusion. Senators B[ennett] Clark (Missouri), T[om] Connally (Texas), Byrd and Glass (Virginia), Smith (South Carolina), and Bailey (North Carolina) worked on the substance of the document and took a full share of responsibility during the hearings. Behind

30. Hoover, *Addresses upon the American Road, 1933–1938* (New York, 1938), 233.

31. *Literary Digest,* 13 February 1937, 5.

32. *Baltimore Sun,* 7 February 1937.

33. J[ames T.] Patterson, "A Conservative Coalition Forms in Congress," in *The Growth of American Politics,* ed. Frank O. Gatell et al. (New York, 1972), 2:362.

34. *Annals of America,* 15:438–45.

the many accusations of these southerners that Roosevelt had defamed the Constitution, they hid their fear that liberalizing the Supreme Court would remove the barriers to federal intervention in the "peculiar" institution of the southern states, i.e., race relations.

Not surprisingly, others joined the conservative forces in opposing Roosevelt's proposal. The well-known Democratic official J[osephus] Daniels wrote in March 1937: "What troubles me most about the Court matter, is to see men like Wheeler and Nye and other men who have been on the liberal line failing to appreciate the significance of the issue. Unless Roosevelt wins, most of the important New Deal policies will fail."[35]

Until Roosevelt's inauguration, and even during the first years of the New Deal, a majority of radical Republicans had taken places in the front ranks of those who believed in expanding the functions of government.[36] R[obert] La Follette had stressed in 1931 that the "philosophy of laissez-faire had ended in disaster . . . . the ideas of an agricultural society have been outmoded, and a new set-up of society is necessary in order to establish society on a prosperous basis."[37] And in 1934 he went even further, declaring, "The right to life, liberty, and the pursuit of happiness cannot survive in the modern world without the right to work. It is the duty of government to guarantee to every home, economic security and the enjoyment of the fruits of labor."[38]

This occurred ten years before Roosevelt announced his radical "Economic Bill of Rights." In 1934 La Follette had introduced a proposal in Congress to appropriate $5.5 billion for social work, again anticipating Roosevelt's recommendations. For many years he had fought persistently for passage of Senator Norris's bill to authorize government construction of hydroelectric plants. H[enry A.] Wallace, who switched to the Democrats' camp in the 1930s, also tried to convince others of the necessity of expanding government functions. In an article which became very well known in radical circles, "Old and New Frontiers," he wrote, "The keynote of the new frontier is cooperation [between individuals and the government], just as that of the old frontier was individualistic competition."[39]

Even so, most radical Republicans never supported a state-monopolistic structure. In the eyes of these people, monopoly was the primary enemy of American society. Senator Borah once wrote, "Monopoly is at war with democratic institutions, and the

---

35. E. [David] Cronon, "A Southern Progressive Looks at the New Deal," *The Journal of Southern History* (May 1958): 170.

36. Pittman, for example, wrote Roosevelt in February 1935: "Progressive Republican membership [is] determined upon going further to the left, than you will go" (cited in Boskin, "Politics of an Opposition Party," 72). Daniels also indicated to Roosevelt in 1934 that "La Follette went down the line with us in essentials. He has now left the Republican Party" (cited in Cronon, "A Southern Progressive," 174).

37. *Current History,* August 1935, 479.

38. Ibid., 479–80.

39. *Annals of America,* 15:277.

conflict is as irrepressible as was the conflict between freedom and slavery."[40]

The system of government regulation and the political linkages then forming in America responded primarily to the interests of monopoly. Senator B[urton K.] Wheeler, who was close to radical Republicans, claimed that several people who supported the New Deal were related closely to monopolists. "It is sickening to me to see some of these people who call themselves liberals," declared the senator from Montana.[41] Disappointment in the ability of government regulation to curb the ever-increasing power of monopolies flowed from the neo-liberals.

The opposition of so many well-known radical Republicans to Roosevelt's court proposal had important consequences inside the Republican party as well. Change had created opportunity for leaders of the party's conservative wing. For the first time since the beginning of the twentieth century, prospects brightened for an internal consolidation of the party and for strengthening the right-center of the spectrum in the two-party system.

During the stormy debates over judicial reform, conservative Republicans generally held to the old tactic of denying the efficacy of Roosevelt's policies. This course undeniably strengthened the hand of Hoover's supporters. It was fully consistent with their assessment of political reality. Hoover had no doubt that Roosevelt's days and those of the New Deal were numbered and that the 1940 election would bring a Republican victory, particularly since Roosevelt, according to tradition, could not be a presidential candidate a third time.

F. Waltman, head of the propaganda department of the Republican National Committee, stressed in a letter to the *Washington Post:* "Outside of the solid South a majority of the voters in the country are registered Republicans. It is the Democratic party, not the Republican party, that must attract the voters from the other side of the fence."[42] Under the circumstances, said conservative analysts, the strongest threat to Republicans came not from Democrats but from forces within the party that tried to divert it from true Americanism. In numerous speeches, Hoover tried to explain that "our national mission is to keep alight the lamp of true liberalism."[43]

In an effort to keep the ideology of his party from being compromised, Hoover proposed to hold a midterm convention, an "intellectual session of the party" to write a political platform for the 1940 election. Landon, Mills, and [Harrison E.] Spangler (a member of the National Committee from Iowa) supported him. To be sure, Hoover categorically denied that he would use this convention to further his personal political plans. However, given the realities of the two-party system—that is, the lack of party charters and by-laws, no precise responsibility of leaders to their constituencies, and restricted power of the national committees—a midterm conven-

40. *Bedrock* (Washington, 1936), 11.

41. U.S. Congress, Senate, Committee on the Judiciary, *Reorganization of the Federal Judiciary* (Washington, 1937), 499.

42. Boskin, "Politics of an Opposition Party," 220.

43. Hoover, *Addresses upon the American Road*, 322.

tion and composition of a prospective platform would indeed strengthen the internal hierarchy of whatever group dominated that convention.

Hoover's opponents were well aware of this. Knox wrote, "The party is in danger of becoming Hooverized."[44] J. Hamilton, chairman of the party's National Committee, understood the disaster Hoover's course could mean for the Republican party and worked hard to squelch the proposal. Skillfully playing on interparty opposition and on the reluctance of congressional factions (and particularly of senatorial grandees Vandenberg, McNary, and Borah to be connected with the venture), Hamilton succeeded in burying the proposition at a meeting of the National Committee on 5 November 1937. A substitute resolution created a special commission headed by former University of Wisconsin professor G[lenn] Frank that would draw up recommendations (by no means binding instructions in the form of a party platform) for the party's consideration. Frank himself considered it the commission's task to "rethink, restate, and reinterpret to the nation the political and economic philosophy with which the Republican party faces the new circumstances of this new age."[45] The social composition of this commission was curious. Among its members were fifty-two lawyers, twenty-seven businessmen, twenty-five farmers, twenty-three home-makers, fifteen newspaper editors, ten university chancellors, seven bankers, six heads of insurance companies, four union functionaries, two doctors, and two clergymen. The rest of the members indicated in the "occupation" column that they were "public figures."

In 1940 the commission published its report, "A Program for a Dynamic America." It may be considered the first neo-conservative political document. In accordance with party tradition, commission members ascribed the most flattering characteristics to the system of private enterprise that Republicans loved so fervently. "It is," they wrote, "the only kind of economic system under which a people has a decent chance to realize a sustained high standard of living."[46] The New Deal was "defeatist in its philosophy and reactionary in its policies."[47] But at the same time, the members of the commission agreed with a number of Roosevelt's specific actions. They endorsed aid to the unemployed, although they believed it should be rendered by the states and not by the federal government. They favored paying a subsidy to farmers, although they would repeal provisions that regulated the size of the harvest. They approved the idea of collective bargaining, although they insisted the National Labor Relations Board had too much power in resolving labor conflicts. It was a curious picture. Commission members criticized the New Deal and at the same time approved a great many of the reforms of the period—stipulating that states should play a larger role in their implementation. The *Nation* accurately charac-

44. Boskin, "Politics of an Opposition Party," 228.
45. D[onald B.] Johnson, *The Republican Party and Wendell Willkie* (Urbana, Ill., 1960), 23.
46. *A Program for a Dynamic America: Report of the Republican Program Committee* (Washington, 1940), 25.
47. Ibid., 11.

terized the document. "The report shows," the magazine noted, "the extent to which the Republican party has been forced to accept the leadership, not of Mr. Hoover or of Mr. Landon, but of Mr. Roosevelt."[48]

Many ideas contained in the document were based on proposals advanced by Republicans in Congress. One notes that after the debates on judicial reform, and despite the blockade they formed with conservative Democrats, they somewhat changed their position toward the administration.

Changes in the Supreme Court had an effect on restructuring the Republican party. After spring 1937, the Court quite quickly began to change its position on New Deal legislation. Republicans traditionally showed the Court strong respect and accepted its judgments unconditionally. Therefore, when the Supreme Court proclaimed the constitutionality of the Wagner Act and the social security law, many Republicans began to change their minds about the government's social functions.

Well-publicized changes in attitude by big business also fostered change in the Republican party. As they came to accept that unions were not guilty of "superfluous" connivance, the "captains of industry" began to accept the regulatory role of government somewhat more calmly. Many of them began to see that the principle of regulation was not particularly un-American. Characteristic of this new attitude was a verbose article written in 1937 by head of the U.S. Chamber of Commerce, G[eorge H.] Davis, titled "Organization: Compulsory or Voluntary?" This was one of the clearest statements of early neo-conservatism, and it came from the pen of a man in the highest echelon of American's monopolistic bourgeoisie. Davis stressed that the complexities of social relationships inevitably gave rise to the necessity of regulating them. It was natural that government should assume that function. However, in fulfilling its task, government should proceed not with the idea of regulating, but of cooperating with, business.[49]

About the same time, certain changes were apparent in the position of the leading amalgamation of monopolistic capital, the National Association of Manufacturers (NAM). Its annual convention in 1939 approved the *Declaration of Principles Relating to the Conduct of American Industry*, which demanded a revision of labor laws that would give government greater regulatory power over unions.[50] It is important to stress that in the upper circles of American business the conviction was gradually forming that under certain conditions government regulation might be a plus. It made sense that when business adapted to the reality of state monopoly, the party, representing itself as the political stronghold of business, would be changed. Also, the midterm election of 1938 was approaching, and Republicans had to say something realistic to the voters in order to hold their seats in Congress.

Two developments strengthened their hand. First, a new economic crisis occurred at the end of the summer in 1937. Republicans immediately blamed Roosevelt. "This

48. *Nation*, 9 March 1940, 325.
49. *Nation's Business*, September 1937, 87.
50. NAM, *Declaration of Principles Relating to the Conduct of American Industry* (Washington, 1939), 3–4.

is solidly our own depression," Hoover declared. "Its causes must be searched for right here, at home . . . . This depression is the direct result of governmental action."[51] He was echoed by the Republican leader of the House of Representatives, B[ertrand H.] Snell: "These things have been caused by the blighting hand of the reckless New Deal experimenter."[52]

Second, so-called average Americans were deeply frightened by the sharply heightened class conflict they saw in the radicalization of the labor movement. These people saw the "Grand Old Party" as a bastion against the instability that was sweeping the world. Republicans had to prove, on the one hand, that theirs was a conservative party, but, on the other hand, that it was not the party that had led the country into the great economic crisis. K[enneth F.] Simpson (New York), a member of the Republican National Committee, characterized the situation that had developed by 1938: "The people have left the President, but they will turn to the Republican party only if they are sure that it is not under the domination of Mr. Hoover, the Liberty League, and some of the reactionary influences of the past."[53] Governor G[eorge D.] Aiken of Vermont identified with Simpson. He said Republicans had to orient themselves to people who "want experimentation to stop for awhile, to sift the results . . . to keep the percentage of that which has been found good and to discard the great bulk that has proven extravagant, inefficient, and un-American."[54]

The Republican congressional faction gradually modernized itself during the debates on key bills of the period: the Black-Connery bill (the Fair Labor Standards Act), the Wagner-Steagall Act (on financing housing construction), the Wagner bill (on the transfer of cases that involved lynching to federal courts), and the bill to reorganize the executive branch. On the whole, Roosevelt failed in these reform efforts: the latter two were rejected, the Wagner-Steagall bill became law in a very truncated form, and the administration succeeded only in discussions on the Black-Connery bill.

Although they opposed these legislative proposals, Republicans did not reject them from the outset. The regulatory role of government did not strike in them such holy terror as it had a few years before. Allegedly they were striving only for the "constructive improvement" of these bills. They even proffered an explanation of why they made "constructive improvements" to Democratic propositions. Congressman B[ruce] Barton (New York) pointed out that the Democrats "have proved, perhaps, that they have more ideas than we have . . . they have ideas but they do not seem to be able to make the ideas work."[55] By means of the party he assumed the role of transforming the idealistic proposals of the Democrats into effective, workable laws.

When Republican leaders spoke, their themes were more frequently new, espe-

51. Hoover, *Addresses upon the American Road,* 348–49.
52. Boskin, "Politics of an Opposition Party," 201.
53. *Time,* 12 December 1938, 16.
54. Boskin, "Politics of an Opposition Party," 152.
55. *Time,* 11 July 1938, 14.

cially when compared to those of the earlier period when individualism and Social Darwinism dominated Republican ideology. Vandenberg's statement that "We must put human rights ahead of property rights" was frankly a seditious thought for Republicans.[56] It is true, however, that he immediately retreated to the standard position that "property rights are among the most precious and the most significant of human rights."[57] R[obert] Taft, a rising star in the Republican party after his election as senator in 1938, also gradually moved away from Hooverian views about the proper role of government. Although Taft zealously hurled the traditional charges against the New Deal and sang the praises of private enterprise (which, he said, brought wealth and prosperity to America),[58] he reconciled himself to a number of Roosevelt's innovations. Specifically, Taft held that "government competition with private industry should be confined to its present limits, and assurance given that it will not be expanded into other fields."[59] For Hoover, Mills, [Simeon D.] Fess, and people like them, the whole proposition was unacceptable. They did not wish to reconcile with any innovation. Congressman B[ruce] Barton (New York) expressed it more forcefully: "The time has come to review the mass of New Deal legislation, preserve the good, and modify or repeal the rest."[60]

Considering that the Republican party was beginning to restructure itself, and considering a serious schism in Democratic ranks, the 1938 midterm election was bound to be important. It was a clear indicator of how well each party had adapted to the changing situation.

The election brought no special laurels to the liberals. Roosevelt's attempt to intervene in the primaries had little effect. He could only state that on most public questions he and the conservative Democrats did not speak the same language.[61] Therefore, conservatives became more attentive.

Republicans relished the election results. They won a number of victories in what would be key states in the upcoming presidential election: Ohio, New Jersey, New Hampshire, and Connecticut. They also ran successfully in several gubernatorial contests: they won in such important states as Ohio, Massachusetts, and Minnesota. In the course of the election several new political personalities entered the national arena. Taft, [Thomas E.] Dewey, [John W.] Bricker, [Harold] Stassen, [Leverett] Saltonstall, and [Joseph C.] Baldwin quickly came to occupy significant posts in the Republican party hierarchy. The election reinforced the position of H[enry] C[abot] Lodge, Jr., H[arrison E.] Spangler, and [H. Styles] Bridges, who had won in 1936. These were very different people in their political views, and even the most conser-

56. *Vital Speeches of the Day*, 15 March 1940, 336.
57. Ibid.
58. *Annals of America*, 15:572.
59. Ibid.
60. *Collier's Weekly*, 21 January 1939, 12.
61. B[asil] Rauch, ed., *F.D.R.: Selected Speeches, Messages, Press Conferences, and Letters* (New York, 1960), 202.

vative among them thought differently than had Republicans during the time of "prosperity."

One can see in this rank of Republican leaders the desire to convince voters that the party had changed fundamentally during the stormy years of the New Deal. Thus, young Dewey maintained that Republicans were by no means a conservative, reactionary force. Quite the opposite: they were a bulwark of genuine liberalism in the fight against the radicalism that was alien to America, the radicalism in the Democratic party.[62]

The desire to portray himself to the voters as a modern liberal was characteristic also of W[endell L.] Willkie, who was beginning his political career. Willkie tried to combine traditional Republican distrust of a strong federal government with recognition of the need for the reforms that had occurred during the years of the New Deal. Defining his creed, he declared in May 1938, "The liberal will, of course, be sympathetic with the principles of much of the social legislation of recent years, but the liberal will also be on his guard lest this trend go too far and suppress the individualism and initiative which are the basic factors in the continuing advance of any civilization."[63]

Even in that traditional stronghold of American conservatism, the states of the Midwest, Republicans on a number of occasions during the 1938 election campaign departed from the usual course of ignoring the social legislation of recent years. The chairman of the Republican National Committee, J[ohn D.] Hamilton, announced at an election meeting in Toledo, Ohio, that "instead of weakening Social Security, Republicans will strengthen it."[64] To be sure, he quickly made clear that this system should be administered by the states.

It can be said that the election significantly reinforced the position of people inside the party who supported the concept of limited federal participation in resolving the socioeconomic problems of American society—in other words, the position of future neo-conservatives. Summing up the events of 1938, Republican senator Bridges (New Hampshire) proclaimed with satisfaction: "This is our year. This is a young Republican year. The New Deal forces are on the run everywhere."[65] But the *Christian Science Monitor* contended, "In state after state, the combination of conservative city groups with the farmers appeared to nullify that balance of power which labor exercised two years ago."[66]

The first steps toward forming a new conservative ideology based on recognition of state-socialist principles were taken during the two years following Roosevelt's second election. This beginning was extraordinarily important for both the ruling

62. *Time*, 5 September 1938, 12.
63. *This Is Wendell Willkie: A Collection of Speeches and Writings on Present Day Issues* (New York, 1940), 165–66.
64. *Time*, 31 October 1938, 12.
65. *New York Times*, 10 April 1938.
66. 12 November 1938.

circles of the United States and the two-party system. It represented a realistic alternative to neo-liberalism. At the same time and in a number of cases it made possible a consensus between adherents of the two ideologies. This process illustrated one of the most important features of the two-party system: the interaction and interdependency of the parties and their components. Truly, both Democrats and Republicans to some degree participated in the formation of the new conservative ideology.

The bipartisan conservative bloc played a vital role in the process just described during 1937–1938 and in many ways helped return the two-party system to its state of elastic equilibrium. True, complete stabilization demanded the restoration of an important element of the system—the two-party center, which had been destroyed during the years of the crisis and the New Deal. But few of the first ideas of neo-conservatism were put into practice by the Republicans. The entire party would have to assimilate the ideopolitical principles of "Modern Republicanism" (i.e., to turn from the ideas of rugged individualism and imperialistic isolationism and to remove radical Republicans from their ranks).

The process of restructuring the Republican party was completed only in the 1950s by [Dwight D.] Eisenhower. However, the intense factional strife inside the organization during 1937 and 1938 partially prepared the way for passing key leadership positions in the party into the hands of a new generation of politicians. Their world view generally included the acceptance of state-monopolistic realities. Willkie's nomination in 1940, and later Dewey's, would have been impossible without the changes that occurred in the Republican party during the second half of the 1930s. This restructuring, admittedly timid, increased Republican chances in their struggle against the Democrats and restored the principle of balance of power. This was extremely important (from a bourgeois point of view) in restoring the optimum functioning of the two-party system. The restored two-party system was increasingly effective in protecting the supremacy of the monopolistic bourgeoisie. And critical analysis of the events of the second half of the 1930s helps one better understand the tactics of modern American conservatives.

James T. Patterson

Comment on "The Southern Wing of the Democratic Party of the United States from 1933 to 1935 and the New Deal of F. Roosevelt," by E. V. Kurochkina, and "The Republican Party of the United States in Search of an Alternative to the New Deal," by A. S. Manykin

The essays by Ekateryna V. Kurochkina and Alexander S. Manykin demonstrate that Soviet scholarship on the political history of the 1930s is alive and well. Both essays are solidly grounded in contemporary magazine and newspaper sources, as well as in some of the relevant secondary literature.[1] They show an informed awareness of American political institutions and constitutional forms. The authors understand that American political parties are far from ideologically pure—or even consistent. Regional, ideological, and economic divisions within the parties—as much as divisions between them—characterized American politics in the 1930s.

It is reassuring to note the relative absence of Marxist-Leninist jargon in the two essays.[2] Though there are occasional references to ill-defined phrases such as *bourgeois liberalism*, *neo-liberalism*, and *state-monopoly capitalism*, they do not impede the flow of the narrative or obscure the thrust of the arguments. More striking, perhaps, the authors eschew overtly theoretical frameworks. In sticking close to their sources, they succeed in offering empirically careful and convincing analyses of their chosen subjects.

Kurochkina tells a fair-minded and familiar story of the South as a micro-region united by geography and historical memory yet never wholly "solid" in its political ideology. Some southern congressmen quickly opposed Roosevelt and all that he stood for, and all of them united to defend racial mores in the region. But most southern politicians backed the early New Deal, some out of party loyalty, others out of fear of social unrest, others because they wished to tap the federal treasury. Moderates like Sam Rayburn and Pat Harrison indeed represented dominant forces

---

1. The authors fail to cite some recent sources. Some of these include the essays in Harvard Sitkoff, ed., *Fifty Years Later: The New Deal Evaluated* (New York, 1985), especially Alan Lawson, "The Cultural Legacy of the New Deal," 155–66, and Richard Kirkendall, "The New Deal and American Politics," 11–36. Other relevant sources focusing on political developments include John Braeman et al., *The New Deal* (Columbus, Ohio, 1975); John M. Allswang, *The New Deal and American Politics: A Study in Political Change* (New York, 1978); David Porter, *Congress and the Waning of the New Deal* (Port Washington, N.Y., 1980); and Larry Gerber, *The Limits of Liberalism* (New York, 1983). Pertinent scholarly articles include John Shover, "The Emergence of a Two-Party System in Republican Philadelphia, 1924–1936," *Journal of American History* 6 (March 1974): 985–1002; and Allan J. Lichtman, "Critical Election Theory and the Reality of American Presidential Politics, 1910–1940," *American Historical Review* (April 1976): 317–51.

2. By contrast, for instance, to N. V. Sivachev, *Russia and the United States* (Chicago, 1979).

and attitudes in southern politics at the time. As Kurochkina reminds us, they also did much to facilitate important New Deal legislation.

By 1935, however, relations between Roosevelt and southern congressmen began to deteriorate. Though well-represented in Congress, the South gradually lost influence within the Democratic party as a result of the political revolution worked by the Depression and the rise of the New Deal. These dramatic changes, which Kurochkina mentions mainly in passing, deserve greater attention. They transformed the United States into a country in which masses of relatively poor and working-class voters, including immigrants and (more slowly) blacks, secured enhanced political power within the Democratic party—and consequently in policy formation.[3] By the mid-1930s they were sufficiently vocal to frighten many of the more conservative Democratic politicians who had until then enjoyed great influence within the party. For this reason, and because of controversial legislation such as the public utility holding company and Wagner acts, many southerners grew restive in 1935. Kurochkina indicates this restiveness by sketching varied reactions to key legislative amendments. By 1936 southerners were doubtful about the New Deal. "Their politics of friendly neutrality changed to a diplomacy of cautious silence."

I have no serious quarrel with these conclusions, and wish only that Kurochkina had the space to develop some of them more fully. For instance, she suggests that the decline of southern influence within the Democratic party contributed to a growing sense of impotence among southern congressmen. As early as 1935? How important were such fears in altering attitudes toward the New Deal? Kurochkina also notes that many southerners backed the New Deal in 1933 out of a concern for "social stability." It is not entirely clear what this means, or how important a matter it was for the majority of southern congressmen. Is the author offering here a "social control" thesis to explain the support of moderate-to-conservative southern politicians for the New Deal?

Manykin, too, tells a balanced story. He shows clearly that national leaders of the Republican party rejected Herbert Hoover's anti–New Deal excesses and became more moderate by 1940. His assessment of Alf Landon—an unhappy transitional figure—is perceptive. He gives due attention to the role of Roosevelt's court-packing scheme in bringing a conservative coalition out in the open against the president. Though Manykin may exaggerate slightly the rise of "neo-conservatism" within the G.O.P. in these years, there is no doubting his main point: that the domestic proposals of men such as Wendell Willkie and Thomas Dewey were more liberal than those of Herbert Hoover. Much changed in the late 1930s.

A special strength of Manykin's essay is its recognition of shifting but nonetheless

---

3. See Everett Ladd with Charles Hadley, *Transformations of the Party System* (New York, 1978). Soviet readers especially need to be aware of the important role of federalism (and of localism) in American politics. See John Jeffries, *Testing the Roosevelt Coalition: Connecticut Society and Politics in the Era of World War II* (Knoxville, Tenn., 1979); and Jo Ann Argersinger, *Toward a New Deal in Baltimore* (Chapel Hill, N.C., 1988). Also Richard Lowitt, *The New Deal and the West* (Bloomington, Ind., 1984); and my *The New Deal and the States: Federalism in Transition* (Princeton, N.J., 1969).

significant divisions within the Republican party. Like Kurochkina, he understands the pluralism of the American political universe and the ideological compromises that underlie our two-party system. I wish, therefore, that he had said more about sectional aspects of these divisions. It was during these years that the G.O.P. (like the Democratic party) became more liberal in the urban areas of the Northeast (and California) while becoming if anything more conservative in many parts of the West and Midwest. Progressive Republicanism in some of the midwestern and Plains states, a notable presence in American politics from 1900 to 1936, virtually disappeared thereafter.[4] Rooted in part in economic change, these enduring sectional shifts are significant political legacies of the 1930s.

Having offered these small suggestions, let me focus on wider matters. What is striking about both these essays is not what they say, but what they omit. Their strengths—a carefully grounded empiricism focusing on the rhetoric of party leaders— lead to a narrowness of focus and to neglect of other, deeper aspects of the politics of the era. Three such aspects seem especially worthy of further consideration.

1. Constitutional and structural aspects. As Theda Skocpol and others have observed, the American State grew considerably in the 1930s.[5] The executive branch, in particular, assumed new roles and stature.[6] Manykin, to be sure, does not ignore reactions to these changes; he recounts Hoover's alarm at the expansion of the federal government. But neither author pays much attention to these developments, which many conservatives loudly deplored at the time. To what extent were these complaints based on constitutional principles? How much, especially among Republicans, did they represent partisan rhetoric? It would be useful to have a thorough look at conservative reactions to the growth of the state and of the presidency during the 1930s.

In the same context, the authors say little about the growing hostility that developed between the executive and legislative branches, especially after 1935. Indeed, while such conflict is guaranteed by the constitutional separation of powers, it has seemed particularly sharp since 1937—so much so that James MacGregor Burns has written insightfully about "Four Party Politics" (two in the executive, two in the legislative branch) in modern America.[7] Because Kurochkina stops in 1935, and

4. See Ronald Feinman, *Twilight of Progressivism: The Western Republican Senators and the New Deal* (Baltimore, 1981); John E. Miller, *Governor Philip F. La Follette, the Wisconsin Progressives, and the New Deal* (Columbia, Mo., 1982); Patrick Maney, *"Young Bob" La Follette: A Biography of Robert La Follette, Jr., 1895–1953* (Columbia, Mo., 1979).

5. Skocpol and John Ikenberry, "The Political Formation of the American Welfare State in Historical and Comparative Perspective," *Comparative Social Research* 6 (1983): 87–148. Another comparative study is James Patterson, "Comparative Welfare History: Britain and the United States, 1930–1945," in *The Roosevelt New Deal: A Program Assessment Fifty Years After,* ed. Wilbur Cohen (Austin, 1986). This collection of essays, like the one by Sitkoff cited above, looks at a variety of political and cultural developments during the Roosevelt era.

6. Theodore Lowi, *The Personal President: Power Invested, Promise Unfulfilled* (Ithaca, N.Y., 1985).

7. Burns, *The Deadlock of Democracy: Four Party Politics in America* (Englewood Cliffs, N.J., 1963).

Manykin focuses on the national Republican party, neither author deals much with this important legacy of the 1930s. How much was the sharpening of such conflict related to the contemporaneous growth of the executive branch under FDR? To what extent did congressmen worry that executive agencies would disrupt channels of political patronage and power?

2. Cultural, symbolic, and psychological aspects. Largely missing from both of these accounts is the passion, indeed the rage and hatred, characteristic of politics in the 1930s. Much of this passion surrounded the person of FDR, perhaps the most widely loved and hated politician in American history.[8] Some of it helped to elevate minor differences into angry symbolic controversies.[9] More importantly, the authors underplay the lasting influence of the Depression and the New Deal, which in myriad ways promoted a cultural as well as a political revolution.[10] Many conservatives literally trembled when they thought about Roosevelt and the New Deal, imagining that FDR stood for everything that was new, radical, and loathsome in American life. They were alarmed not only by public policies, but also by what they perceived—not altogether inaccurately—as the New Deal's subversion of the cultural hegemony of the mostly white and Protestant business classes in American politics and society. In slighting these cultural and psychological matters the authors unintentionally minimize the angry partisan warfare of the 1930s. They also offer a model of politics that is more narrow and dry than it might be.

3. Socioeconomic aspects. Perhaps because I expected to find overtly Marxist presentations here, I was most surprised at the neglect in these essays of the social and economic roots of political behavior. Apart from scattered references to "bourgeois" reactions and to "monopoly," there is little here to link conservatism (or liberalism) with social background or economic interest.[11] Were conservatives defending small-town, rural patterns of life, or were they representing large business interests? Which interests? What was the influence on the G.O.P. of organizations such as the Chamber of Commerce and the National Association of Manufacturers? Or on the Democrats of the newly invigorated labor-union movement of the era? Where did campaign financing come from?[12] What economic interests were being

8. For FDR's legacy see William Leuchtenburg, *In the Shadow of FDR: From Harry Truman to Ronald Reagan* (Ithaca, N.Y., 1983).

9. Mark Leff, *The Limits of Symbolic Reform: The New Deal and Taxation, 1933–1939* (Cambridge, Eng., 1984).

10. See Lawson, who draws heavily on T. V. Smith, "The New Deal as a Cultural Phenomenon," in *Ideological Differences and the World Order*, ed. F. S. C. Northrup (New Haven, Conn., 1949). Also Warren Susman, "The Culture of the Thirties," in his *Culture as History* (New York, 1984), 150–83.

11. Examples of such analyses are Lowi, *The End of Liberalism: Ideology, Policy, and the Crisis of Public Authority* (New York, 1969); and Grant McConnell, *Private Power and American Democracy* (New York, 1966).

12. See Robert Caro, *The Years of Lyndon Johnson: The Path to Power* (New York, 1982), for very revealing information on the financing of Democratic congressional campaigns in these years. Johnson did much to systematize fund-raising, especially from southwestern oil interests.

protected by opponents of the social security or wealth-tax bills? The essays by Manykin and Kurochkina, while informative in dealing with political rhetoric and ideological developments, would have profited considerably from greater emphasis on the socioeconomic roots of political behavior.

In the same vein, the essays might have probed more deeply into the rhetoric of the national party leaders. How ideologically consistent, really, were opponents of New Deal domestic policies? "Conservatives," for instance, often supported costly farm subsidies. Many New England Republicans, confronting the rise of the southern textile industry, backed minimum-wage legislation in the ultimately fruitless quest to undercut competition from the southern textile industry (which employed cheap labor). Historians who take the rhetoric of politicians at face value run the risk of slighting important regional and constituent pressures that sometimes make a mockery of ideological consistency.

What can be said, finally, about changing ethnic and racial patterns in the politics of the era? This is a very important area of research that American scholars have explored in order to discover the base (as opposed to the rhetorical superstructure) of American political behavior. Some of this work employs quantitative methods (though mostly of a fairly simple order), and much of it—again—turns to state and local developments in order to try to explain the social aspects of politics.[13] This kind of research, of course, generally requires access to local election statistics, demographic records, and newspapers: it is much harder for an overseas scholar to do than are studies of political rhetoric. Still, political history without it loses much of its richness and complexity.

In making these observations, I recognize that I am asking the authors to undertake more than they set out to do. One senses, indeed, that they have deliberately focused on empirically manageable research questions, and that they have purposefully steered clear of broader speculations. The result is mostly admirable analysis of a number of legislative and party developments. At the same time, the essays concentrate on political rhetoric and legislative maneuver and therefore represent somewhat narrow and old-fashioned political history. Both essays will be richer when and if they are expanded to place this maneuvering in the broader context of cultural change and interest-group behavior.

---

13. See Allswang, *A House for All Peoples: Ethnic Politics in Chicago, 1890–1936* (Lexington, Ky., 1971); Harvard Sitkoff, *A New Deal for Blacks: The Emergence of Civil Rights as a National Issue: The Depression Decade* (New York, 1978); Nancy Weiss, *Farewell to the Party of Lincoln: Black Politics in the Age of FDR* (Princeton, N.J., 1983); and Charles Trout, *Boston, The Great Depression, and the New Deal* (New York, 1977).

Response by E. V. Kurochkina and A. S. Manykin

Allow us to express our gratitude for the detailed analysis of our articles. It was with great interest that we learned Professor Patterson's opinion of the ideas they contain. In our view, his observations are constructive in character and undoubtedly deserve the most careful consideration. We believe they are quite justified. And this is not merely a compliment or an expression of politeness. The articles reviewed were published in 1978 and 1982—that is, between six and ten years ago. We have continued to examine the same range of problems, and much of what is rightly described in the commentary as shortcomings has to this or that degree been taken by us into account in subsequent studies. In particular, there recently appeared a collective monograph entitled *The U.S. Constitution: History and the Present*, in which the changes that took place in the 1930s in the area of the formulation of constitutional norms are analyzed. Recently a monographic study was completed (it will be published in approximately a year and a half) in which, in particular, the role of these developments in the evolution of the party system in the U.S. in the 1930s is examined.

Professor Patterson expresses a certain puzzlement in connection with the fact that these articles paid considerably less attention than he expected to socioeconomic questions such as have traditionally occupied Marxist historians. But it is precisely because Soviet historiography already boasts a whole number of very thorough studies of the socioeconomic development of the United States during the period of the New Deal that we thought it possible to devote most of our attention to topics relating to the political parties. When analyzing the processes that took place within the structures of the Republican and Democratic parties, we naturally relied on the achievements of our predecessors.

Finally, you draw attention to a certain underestimation on our part of sociopsychological issues. In principle this reproach is justified. We should only like to point out that it is difficult enough to take into account within a single article all the factors that affected the development of the two-party system. Undoubtedly, in our future research we shall have to pay the closest attention to the points you have made. We believe that the exchange of views begun in this edition will stimulate a more profound examination of the fundamental problems of American history and will increase our understanding both of the historical process itself and of the interpretation it has been given by our scholars.

I. B. Tverdokhleb

10 THE MOVEMENT FOR CREATION OF A PROGRESSIVE THIRD PARTY IN THE UNITED STATES DURING THE MID-1930s

The "two-party system" is the most important political institution in the United States that ensures the supremacy of the monopolistic bourgeoisie.[1] The causes of its long life are a continuing concern in Marxist historiography. Within this context, there has been a special interest in analyzing the place of third parties in the two-party system and in clarifying the factors that contributed to their weaknesses and short lives. In modern Soviet historiography, interest has increased noticeably in the methodological problems of studying the two-party system and the political parties themselves. This interest extends to theoretical problems related to third parties. I. P. Dementiev, V. L. Malkov, A. S. Manykin, N. V. Sivachev, V. V. Sogrin, E. F. Yazkov, and others[2] have developed a multifaceted approach to analyzing the role and place of third parties in the political structure of the United States. In a number of studies of efforts to create third parties, these authors point out the need for further historical investigation of the role of those parties during transitional periods of American history. The role of mass movements in political change requires special attention because, in the final analysis, the movements always lacked the multiple features required to sustain a third national party.

Bourgeois American authors who study the complexities of political party history generally contend that mass movements are not a component in the analysis of third parties.[3] Although they correctly observe that new parties have appeared during "periods of reconstruction," of "heightened tension" or "great political friction," of "economic crises" during which the aroused masses became increasingly disappointed with the main bourgeois parties, American scholars consider third parties no

1. V. I. Lenin, *Complete Collected Works,* 22:193. This essay by I. B. Tverdokhleb was first published in *American Annual, 1985* (Moscow, 1985), 210–28. This English translation is by Brenda Kay Weddle.
2. V. I. Borisiuk and N. V. Sivachev, "Problems in the History and Methodology of Study of the Two-Party System of the United States," in *The Role of Bourgeois Political Parties in the Social Life of the United States* (Moscow, 1981); I. V. Galkin, "The Political Party History of the United States in the 1920s and 1930s in General American Bourgeois Historiography," *Modern and Contemporary History,* 1983, no. 5; I. P. Dementiev et al., "On the Question of Periodization of the History of the Two-Party System of the United States," *Questions of Methodology and History of Historical Science,* 2d ed. (Moscow, 1978); A. S. Manykin and N. V. Sivachev, "The Two-Party System in the United States: History and Contemporaneousness (Several Methodological Problems in Research)," *Modern and Contemporary History,* 1978, no. 3; A. S. Manykin and E. F. Yazkov, "The Role of Third Parties in the Political Party System of the United States," *Questions of History,* 1981, no. 2.
3. The work of D[aniel A.] Mazmanian on the problems of third parties serves as an example. See his *Third Parties in Presidential Elections* (Washington, 1974).

more than "indicators of the health" of the two-party system. In so doing, they ignore the socio-class aspect of the problem.[4]

The definition of third parties as merely "means of agitation and enlightenment,"[5] as "suppliers of new ideas," became firmly established in bourgeois American historiography. The accent has been on their short lives, a characteristic explained by the alleged ability of the two-party system to "absorb dissatisfaction."[6] In the end, third parties have been denied a notable role in the political life of the country, as have been mass movements for political change. The result has been to obscure the process by which the policies of the two major parties have in many ways been liberalized by mass movements. Third parties have formed during periods of heightened social conflict, have set definite limits on turns toward conservatism, and have contributed to the comparatively peaceful development of capitalism.

The history of the effort to establish a progressive third party during one of the key periods in United States history—the New Deal of [Franklin D.] Roosevelt—is conspicuous.[7]

The effort to create a third national party in the United States during the middle 1930s was an important stage in the development of a national democratic movement. Building on antimonopolistic traditions that had developed during preceding popular movements (those of the Grangers, Green Backers, Farmers' Alliance, Populists, the Progressive Era, and the early 1920s), the movement for independent political action

4. S[amuel J.] Eldersveld, *Political Parties in American Society* (New York, 1982): F[rederick E.] Haynes, *Third Party Movements Since the Civil War* (New York, 1966); W[ilber R.] Hesseltine, *The Rise and Fall of Third Parties* (Washington, 1948); *The History of U.S. Political Parties, 1789–1972,* ed. Arthur Schlesinger, Jr., 4 vols. (New York, 1973); R[ichard] Hofstadter, *The Age of Reform from Bryan to FDR* (New York, 1956); Christopher Lasch, *The New Radicalism in America (1889–1963)* (New York, 1965); H. Lovin, "The Fall of Farmer-Labor Parties, 1936–1938," *Pacific Northwest Quarterly,* January 1971; H[oward P.] Nash, *Third Parties in American Politics* (Washington, 1959).

5. Haynes, *Third Party Movements,* 1.

6. Eldersveld, *Political Parties,* 40.

7. For the history of Roosevelt's New Deal and also various aspects of the battle for a third party during this period, see V. L. Malkov, *The New Deal in the United States: Social Movements and Social Policy* (Moscow, 1973); Malkov and D. G. Nadzhofov, *America at the Crossroads: Essays on the Socio-Political History of the New Deal in the United States* (Moscow, 1967); Sivachev, "The Movement for Creation of a Third Party in the United States in the Middle 1930s," *Herald of Moscow State University,* History series, 1961, no. 3; Sivachev, *Political Conflict in the United States in the Middle 1930s* (Moscow, 1966); Sivachev, "The New Deal in the United States," *Questions of History,* 1981, no. 9; N. N. Yakovlev, *Franklin Roosevelt—Man and Politician* (Moscow, 1965); J[oseph] Alsop, *The Life and Times of Franklin Roosevelt* (London, 1982); P[aul] Dennis, "On Independent Political Action," *Political Affairs,* December 1971; T[homas] Ferguson, "From Normalcy to New Deal: Industrial Structure, Party Competition, and American Public Policy in the Great Depression," *International Organization* 38 (1984); A. Koeniger, "The Politics of Independence," *South Atlantic Quarterly,* Winter 1981; William Leuchtenburg, *Franklin D. Roosevelt and the New Deal, 1932–1940* (New York, 1963); D[onald R.] McCoy, *Angry Voices: Left-of-Center Politics in the New Deal Era* (Lawrence, Kans., 1958); A[rthur M.] Schlesinger, Jr., *The Age of Roosevelt* (Boston, vols. 1–3, 1957–1960).

during the 1930s took on an anticapitalistic coloring from the very beginning. Compared to traditional progressivism, it was a significant shift to the left.

Although it did not become a formal party, this movement demonstrated the possibility that certain social groups, at that time, could separate themselves from the influence of the two-party system and play a prominent role in the nation's political life. Among other things, it imparted a more liberal-progressive character to the policies of the Roosevelt administration.

The third-party movement of the 1930s developed slowly. Its beginnings can be traced to the 1928 election campaign,[8] during which the liberal press appealed for the creation of a new party, and to the world economic crisis of 1929–1933, which dispelled forthwith prevailing ideas about the exceptional nature of American capitalism. Deteriorating material conditions, growing disappointment in the major bourgeois parties, and deepening doubts about capitalism resulted in new strength for radical politics. The political awakening of America's masses was apparent in their turn to independent political action as a means of satisfying their demands. That action, in turn, stimulated the movement to create a third party.

The primary landmarks during the early history of this movement to create a third party (1928–1933) were the creation in 1928 of the Non-Partisan League (NPL) by radical intellectuals and the formation in September 1933 of the Farmer-Labor Political Federation.

These organizations represented petty-bourgeois radicalism in the third-party movement.[9] The ideological tenets of petty-bourgeois radicalism were an eclectic blend of T[horstein] Veblen's technocratic ideas and E[dward] Bellamy's utopian socialism, which criticized "private capitalism" and advocated nationalization and petty-bourgeois cooperativism as the means of achieving a new "ideal society." Petty-bourgeois radicalism also incorporated the most popular liberal-reformist ideas about the necessity of planning and government regulation of the nation's socioeconomic development. As a result, the three most immediate demands in the programs of the NPL and the Farmer-Labor Political Federation—establishment of public-works projects, a system of social insurance, and direct aid to the farmers and others—anticipated future programs of the New Deal.[10] At the same time, the demands of these two organizations for the nationalization of banks, utilities, and basic industries went beyond the bourgeois liberalism that bounded the Roosevelt administration. Moreover, the left wing among bourgeois democrats gravitated toward political radicalism, and their ideology affected the trend toward anticapitalism in the third-party movement—from sharp criticism of the existing system

8. On the decline of the movement for independent political action during the middle of the 1920s, see E. F. Yazkov, *The Farm Movement in the United States (1918–1929)* (Moscow, 1974), 248–55.

9. On the problem of petty-bourgeois radicalism in the 1930s, see Malkov, *New Deal in the United States*, 97–153.

10. For the text of the program, see *Nation*, 17 February 1932, sec. 11; *Common Sense*, September 1938, 27, and October 1938, 13–19.

of government to a call for a new cooperative society characterized by a planned economy and production for consumption instead of production for profit.[11]

Despite obvious theoretical weaknesses and a failure to comprehend American reality, the petty-bourgeois leaders of the third-party movement projected anti-capitalist themes in their proposals and propaganda that made it possible to radicalize participants in the movement for independent political action. Conditions were right for resolving the most important task—the union of antimonopolistic, anticapitalistic ideology with the popular movement.

People who favored the creation of a third national party considered the Farmer-Labor party of Minnesota (FLP) its potential core. The FLP was the largest third party in the country, and its head, F[loyd B.] Olson, became governor of Minnesota in 1930. The strength and sweep of popular uprisings, the activities of the Farmer-Labor administration of the state in behalf of the masses, the intensity of conflict between leading liberal-progressives and conservatives, all served the interests of Minnesotans because of who identified with the Farmer-Labor party. And the number of party rank-and-file members increased. All this created a certain receptivity among the masses for radical ideas; and the platform of the Farmer-Labor party gave expression to such ideas in 1934. The platform demanded a basic transformation of the economic system, and specifically the creation of a cooperative society based on nationalization of basic production and natural resources. It was the most radical document of its time among political parties in Minnesota.[12]

Wisconsin was second to Minnesota as a center of independent political action. Widespread dissatisfaction with the state's Democratic and Republican organizations prompted formation in 1934 of the Progressive party of Wisconsin. It was headed by Robert and Philip La Follette—brothers and leftist Republicans.[13] The Progressive party embraced the platform provisions of the Farmer-Labor Federation and older third parties, particularly the FLP of Minnesota. Despite the domination of the Progressive party by moderate radicals headed by R[obert] La Follette, the very fact that it joined forces in Wisconsin with the growing popular movement for independent political action was an event of great importance.

A distinguishing trait of mass protest in the first half of the 1930s was broad

11. Historical experience has repeatedly proved the truth of the Marxist contention that there are limited possibilities in the cooperative movement. Karl Marx noted, "However excellent in principle and useful in practice cooperative labor might be, it can never check the growth of monopolies, which occurs in a geometric progression, nor liberate the masses, nor even noticeably ease the burden of their poverty." Marx and Engels, *Collected Works,* 2d ed., 16:10.

12. On the Farmer-Labor party of Minnesota, see Malkov, *New Deal in the United States,* 131–34; Sivachev, *Political Conflict,* 96–98; A. Naftalin, "History of the Farmer-Labor Party in Minnesota" (Ph.D. diss., University of Minnesota, 1948).

13. On the Progressive party of Wisconsin, see Malkov, *New Deal in the United States,* 136–38; Sivachev, *Political Conflict,* 98–100; I. B. Tverdokhleb, "The Formation of the Progressive Party of Wisconsin (Middle 1930s)," in *Problems of Modern and Contemporary History of the Countries of Europe and America* (Moscow, 1972); E[dward N.] Doan, *The La Follettes and the Wisconsin Idea* (New York, 1947); R[oger] Johnson, *Robert M. La Follette, Jr., and the Decline of the Progressive Party in Wisconsin* (Madison, Wis., 1964).

participation by the most destitute and backward classes. Semiskilled workers, small farmers, immigrants, the unemployed, urban petty bourgeoisie, and the aged comprised the great army in pursuit of "panaceas." This was the least-organized part of the democratic movement. Most of those who sought panaceas inclined toward the utopian movement: U[pton] Sinclair's "End Poverty in California" (EPIC); [Francis E.] Townsend's old-age pension scheme; the demagogic "Share Our Wealth" plan proposed by Louisiana's dictatorial senator, Huey Long; and the National Union for Social Justice, organized by the fascist demagogue Father C[harles] Coughlin.[14]

Support of utopian and demagogic social schemes by the masses illustrated their extremely low level of political awareness. In fact, supporters of "panaceas" ran the risk of becoming tools of the reaction. At the same time, the poverty of millions of Americans, which was the cause of the uprising and the development of a movement that was antimonopolistic in its orientation, in the final analysis actually drew together the seekers of "panaceas" with the discontented working class and all progressive forces in the country who would strengthen and expand the programs of the New Deal. This created conditions that liberated supporters of panaceas from the influence of their leaders and made independent political action more attractive. That is, they reoriented themselves more decisively to the critical situation—toward creation of a progressive third party in the United States.

A notable change in the movement for independent political action occurred in 1934, when it became clear that the New Deal had not resolved the most important problems that affected the broad masses. Growing disillusionment with Roosevelt's policies led to stronger disappointment in the Democratic party. This, together with the recent failure of Republicans to lead the country out of the crisis, made possible gradually increased interest in the idea of independent political action among workers, farmers, and the intelligentsia.

Subsequent development of the movement for independent political action occurred in a setting in which "disappointment with the achievements of the New Deal is growing just as rapidly on the left as is opposition to its declared aims and measures on the right."[15] Roosevelt's reverence for big business during the 1934 election campaign and the first months of 1935 did not go unnoticed by radical groups, including the leaders of the Farmer-Labor Political Federation. As T[homas R.] Amlie, a leader of the Farmer-Labor Political Federation, acknowledged, the good intentions with which the path of the New Deal was strewn were allowed to become law only when they coincided with the wishes of business.[16]

Passage by Congress in July-August 1935 of a number of progressive laws that

14. On the "panacea" movement, see V. I. Lan, *The United States: From the First to the Second World War* (Moscow, 1976), 411–23; Malkov, "A Comparative Historical Study of the Radical Social Movements in the United States," *Historical Science and Several Problems of Contemporaneousness* (Moscow, 1969); Sivachev, *Political Conflict,* 86–88, 92–95; A[braham] Holtzman, *The Townsend Movement: A Political Study* (New York, 1963); A[lan] Brinkley, *Voices of Protest: Huey Long, Father Coughlin, and the Great Depression* (New York, 1982).

15. *New Republic,* 22 May 1935, 33.

16. *The Progressive,* 17 August 1935, 2.

constituted the establishment of a second stage of the New Deal only strengthened the belief among progressive forces that it was necessary to create a third party. Undoubtedly, the Roosevelt administration's shift to the left was an attempt to co-opt the political initiative of the masses and to channel their support in behalf of liberal reform.[17] The desire on one side to prevent the creation of a third party that might rouse and radicalize the working class and all other democratic forces was no less important than the desire to thwart the growing popularity of reactionary demagogues, especially Long, on the other. In changing the direction of his policies, Roosevelt, in his words, took into consideration "progressive Republicans like La Follette, Cutting, Nye, who are flirting with the idea of a third ticket." There was, in his opinion, a "dangerous situation" that demanded attention and "corresponding reaction."[18]

Those who favored the creation of a third party were aware of their influence on liberalizing the government's policies. One liberal reformer who supported the effort, the well-known economist Paul Douglas, wrote in his memoirs that "Roosevelt's change of policy was perhaps partially affected by our movement."[19] Radical-progressives also remained in the third-party movement after Roosevelt implemented the second stage of the New Deal. What was at hand was both a growing opposition of conservative-reactionary circles to government policy and the fear that the president would shift to the right under this pressure.

The president's declaration in September of a "respite" for business was taken by progressive-radical circles as a dangerous indicator that this could occur. According to Amlie, this declaration signaled the end of the "liberalism of the New Deal."[20] Petty-bourgeois progressives, differing in their degree of radicalism, asserted various responses: the "new rise of the movement for independent political action" (A[lfred] Bingham, journalist and leader of the Farmer-Labor Political Federation); "a united-front labor party, including all labor, farm, cooperative and professional organizations" (E[rnest] Lundeen, a congressman from the Farmer-Labor state of Minnesota); "a third party should be created now to be used as a progressive agency with an eye to the future" (G[erald] Nye, progressive Republican senator). In other words, advocacy for creating a third party was based primarily on thwarting the conservative influence on Roosevelt, on safeguarding the liberal-progressive trend, and on making that trend stronger and more radical.[21]

A direct result of independent political action during 1935 was a significant increase in the number of people who supported the creation of a third national party. The origins of this national movement were rooted in the activities of the rank and file at the state level. The Farmer-Labor party and progressive federations that emerged

17. Pechatnov, *The Democratic Party of the United States: Voters and Politicians* (Moscow, 1980), 14.
18. *F.D.R.: His Personal Letters, 1928–1945*, ed. E[lliott] Roosevelt (New York, 1950), 1:452.
19. *In the Fullness of Time* (New York, 1970), 74.
20. McCoy, *Angry Voices*, 94.
21. *Common Sense*, 2 April 1936, 2; *The Progressive*, 3 August 1935, 1.

in 1934 intensified their efforts to form a third national party by the election of 1936.[22]

At the same time, new organizations for independent political action arose, even in such remote territories as Hawaii and Alaska.[23] The center of the movement was in the western states—the traditional region of petty-bourgeois radicalism. In addition to the farmers (especially members of the Farmers Union), whose interest and activity was most intense, many petty bourgeoisie and intelligentsia—teachers, doctors, lawyers, and clergymen—were attracted to the movement.[24]

Actual achievements of farm-labor and progressive organizations and parties at the grassroots,[25] together with growing public skepticism about the Democratic administration in Washington, stimulated opinion in favor of a third national party. Some testimony to this effect can be found in letters written to the party press and to organizations for independent political action.[26]

Because the greatest interest in independent political action came from below, the position of trade-union and farmers' organizations and of leaders of third parties at the community and regional levels (not only of the FLP in Minnesota and the Progressive party in Wisconsin, but also of the fascistic "Share Our Wealth" program and the "National Union for Social Justice") became decisive. The chances of creating a third national party that was progressive depended on taking a positive first step. Just at that time, Long and Coughlin launched more severe charges against the New Deal and thereby threatened to lead the movement for independent political action into the camp of reaction.

The popularity of Long and Coughlin among the masses continued to grow, largely due to the fact that "continuation of the six-year depression allows them to amass political capital on the dissatisfaction of seventy percent of the population still in a poverty condition."[27] With the air so full of talk about a third party, there was the possibility that any leader with popular support who criticized the New Deal might join the third-party movement. Coughlin, however, despite his growing differences with Roosevelt, for the time being continued to deny insistently that either he person-

22. *The Progressive,* 8 March 1935, 1; 25 May 1935, 3.

23. Ibid., 16 March 1935, 1.

24. Ibid., 18 January 1936, 4, 18; 22 February 1936, 6–7; 7 March 1935, 3.

25. Particularly telling was the example of the activity of the Farmer-Labor party of Minnesota, which came out in support of the program, many points of which were directly related to easing the conditions of the broad masses. Thus, the state legislature was forced to pass the bill introduced by the FLP that appropriated $10 million for a "program of aid." The law establishing qualifications for an old-age pension became considerably more liberal, as did other laws. See *New York Times,* 17 March 1935, 133; *Common Sense,* February 1936, 21; Naftalin, "History of the Farmer-Labor Party," 278–88. Similar achievements were made by the Progressive party of Wisconsin. See *Congressional Record,* vol. 79, pt. 12, pp. 13586–87.

26. See, for example, the section of correspondence in the newspaper of the Progressive party of Wisconsin for February, March, and May 1935: *The Progressive,* 23 February 1935, 2; 23 March 1935, 2; 18 May 1935, 2. The comment of W. Bradley of California was typical: "What we need is united action and not half a dozen minor parties" (ibid., 18 May 1935, 2).

27. *Literary Digest,* 9 February 1935, 13.

ally or the National Union for Social Justice would participate in any political move-ment, particularly one to establish a third party. He declared, "We are above politics and politicians."[28]

After Long openly announced his intent to become president,[29] he assessed the prospects of a third party. With characteristic inconsistency, he said he was 100 percent certain that a third party would arise before the 1936 election and that "we will sweep the entire country."[30] Then, he said he had not decided whether to head the third-party movement—that would depend on whether or not he could win over the Republican or Democratic party.[31]

The attitude of any particular category of the population toward independent polit-ical action was not simple. Among farmers the attitude reflected the complexities and contradictions that divided them.[32] From the very beginning of the third-party move-ment in the 1930s, a number of farmers' organizations—the Farmers Union and particularly the Farmers' Holiday Association (the most radical)—and their leaders looked upon the idea of independent political action with keen interest. They joined the camp of third-party supporters primarily because, as representatives of middling and small farmers, they understood the hostility of their clients toward New Deal agricultural policies. When the Farmer-Labor Political Federation was created in September 1933, Farmers' Holiday Association leader Milo Reno was among those who signed the call for a special convention.[33] However, deep ideological differences precluded close contact between the farm-labor political federations and the Farmers' Holiday Association. Reno, a true populist, steadfastly defended the right to private property, and his aspirations were for no more than inflation and the establishment of guaranteed prices. He could not accept the radical program of the Farmer-Labor Political Federation and publicly disavowed Amlie's proposal for a constitutional amendment that would guarantee principles upon which a cooperative society could be built.[34]

Although he did not completely break with the Farmer-Labor Political Federation, Reno tried to organize an independent movement. He placed great hope in Towns-end, Coughlin, and Long. Their programs, which promised quick solutions to nearly

28. *New York Times,* 6 May 1935.

29. *The Progressive,* 18 May 1935, 3.

30. Schlesinger, *Age of Roosevelt,* 3:66–67.

31. *The Progressive,* 18 May 1935, 3.

32. On the farm movement during the New Deal, see V. P. Zolotukhin, *Farmers and Washington* (Moscow, 1968); Malkov, *New Deal in the United States,* 103–17; Yazkov, "The Agricultural Pol-icy of the Roosevelt Administration and the Farm Movement in the United States in 1933–1935," *Modern and Contemporary History,* 1957, no. 3; Yazkov, *The Strike Movement of the Agricultural Proletariat in the United States in 1929–1935* (Moscow, 1962); Theodore Saloutos and John D. Hicks, *Agricultural Discontent in the Middle West, 1900–1935* (Madison, Wis., 1951); J[ohn] Shover, Jr., *Cornbelt Rebellion: The Farmers' Holiday Association* (Urbana, Ill., 1965).

33. R[oland] White, *Milo Reno: Farmers Union Pioneer* (Ames, Iowa, 1951), 138; Shover, *Corn-belt Rebellion,* 188; *The Progressive,* 13 January 1934, 2.

34. Shover, *Cornbelt Rebellion,* 189.

every problem, were more attractive to Reno than plans to gradually develop society through a government for universal good. In spring 1935, he took steps to unite the disparate groups and parties. Not understanding the vast differences between the radical movement that sustained the Farmer-Labor party of Minnesota, the Utopian movement of Townsend, the EPIC movement, and the reactionary demagogic agitation of Coughlin and Long, Reno invited [Floyd B.] Olson, [Upton] Sinclair, Townsend, Coughlin, and Long to the third annual convention of the Farmers' Holiday Association. Reno "saw in the Louisiana senator, the Detroit priest, and the author of the revolving pension plan, three men who might cause history to repeat itself," that is, return it to the "Golden Rule and Declaration of Independence principles."[35] Thus, by constantly looking to the past and refusing to acknowledge the vast changes in American society, by steadfastly defending private property, by opposing fundamental social reforms, Reno actually led the organization into the camp of reaction—into the hands of fascist demagogues.

Only Long accepted Reno's invitation to appear at the third annual convention of the Farmers' Holiday Association. On 27 April 1935, the first day of the convention, the delegates enthusiastically adopted Long's "Share Our Wealth" plan to the accompaniment of Long's anthem, "Every Man a King."[36] Some members of the Farmers' Holiday Association rejected Reno's scheme for affiliation with the forces of Huey Long and Coughlin. A substantial left wing emerged in support of the radical ideas of the Farmer-Labor Political Federation. This group rejected the views of more staid farmers about the causes of poverty and the ways and means of overcoming it, and also rejected their illusions about the beginning of inflation. These ideas developed fully in the Farmers' Holiday Association of Minnesota, headed by J. Bosch. Besides the basic progressive demands of farmers, documents generated by this very radical branch of the national organization[37] included assertions that "Farmers do not propose to limit their demands to what they can get under a system dominated by international bankers. They will demand justice, and then, if necessary, endeavor to change the system so that justice will be attainable."[38] As for the ultimate goals of the Farmer-Labor Political Federation, vague provisions (somewhat naive and simple expressions of anticapitalism) also evolved into more concrete demands to create a cooperative society based on production for consumption.[39]

Radical ideas of the Farmers' Holiday Association of Minnesota found broad support among the members of the national organization, as the results of the national convention in April 1935 attested. Once the strong emotions unleashed by Long's appearance had subsided and the delegates proceeded to draw up resolutions, they ignored the spirit of the "Share Our Wealth" plan. Moreover, at this convention, at

35. *Farm Holiday News,* 25 April 1935, 2.
36. *New York Times,* 28 April 1935, 1.
37. For the text of the platform of the Farm Holiday Association, and the Declaration of Independence of 1934, see *Farm Holiday News,* 23 June 1933, 1; 2 April 1934, 2.
38. Ibid., 23 June 1933, 1.
39. Ibid., 10 May 1935, 4.

the very podium from which Huey Long's speech resounded, a platform was read that included for the first time in the history of the Farmers' Holiday Association the demand for "production for consumption."[40] There was also a resolution in support of creating a third "national political party, expressing the interests of the workers and the farmers."[41] Acceptance of these radical documents by the national convention of the Farmers' Holiday Association testified to the growth of political awareness among the traditionally moderate farmers.

At the same time, the fact that Long was received so enthusiastically by the delegates to the convention—that is, by representatives of organized, more or less politically knowledgeable farmers—showed how great was the threat that the growing movement might be influenced by the Louisiana dictator.

In this situation, the growing insistence of trade unions that reactionary demagogues be thwarted and conservative forces denied was particularly timely. Interest in the idea of independent political action became significantly stronger among the working class in 1935; and participation of workers in the third-party movement increased at the local level. In many state labor federations and branches of trade unions, there were numerous discussions about a new party, during which it became quite clear that workers wanted to make the issue a national one. They tried to do so at the stormy fifty-fifth convention of the AFL, held 7–19 October 1935 in Atlantic City, New Jersey. The delegates, representing five hundred thousand trade-union members, introduced thirteen resolutions, as opposed to two at their previous convention. The resolutions reflected the need for the AFL to create a workers' or farmer-labor party. The resolutions differed little from one another in their main point and focused attention on the fact that the "nonpartisan" position of the AFL leadership created the opportunity for the major political parties, which did not represent workers' interests, to recapture their votes. The most important argument in favor of a new party was the existence of labor-party movements in several states—in Connecticut, Michigan, New Jersey, and Illinois, where special conferences were held on the subject.[42]

However, the conservative leadership again persuaded the committee on resolutions to accept the point of view of the organization's executive committee, and it came out in favor of continuing the nonpartisan stance.[43]

A subsequent event, which was of decisive significance in determining the position of the working class toward a third party, was the creation in April 1936 of the Non-Partisan League. The major trade unions of the AFL joined it.[44] It proclaimed its primary task to be "assistance in the affairs of liberalism in the United States,"

40. *New Republic*, 15 May 1935, 12.

41. *Farm Holiday News*, 10 May 1935, 4.

42. R[obert R.] Brooks, *When Labor Organizes* (New Haven, Conn., 1937), 301; *AFL Proceedings* (1935), 177, 181–82, 199–200, 202, 239–40, 250–54, 275, 290, 293.

43. *AFL Proceedings* (1935), 759.

44. McCoy, "The Good Neighbor League and the Presidential Campaign of 1936," *Western Political Quarterly* 13 (1960): note 4.

defense of workers' rights, struggle for preservation of all democratic freedoms, cessation of the threat of fascism, etc.[45] The reelection of Roosevelt was considered a guarantee that the vital tasks of the day would be dealt with quickly. By supporting the cause of liberal government in its struggle against reaction, the labor movement responded to the needs of the nation; its position was a positive factor.[46] However, by supporting Roosevelt's candidacy, the Non-Partisan League automatically removed the question of its participation in the movement for a third national party in 1936. In the final analysis, and in many ways, this action brought the movement for a third national party to an end. With the creation of the league, the Socialist party also ceased to participate in the third-party movement. Although the party's leaders recognized that a third party could be a force strong enough to avert the threat of fascism,[47] most of them took up a temporizing position. After the decision of the Non-Partisan League to support Roosevelt, the creation of a Farmer-Labor party in 1936, in the opinion of the Socialists, was useless.[48] This conclusion was fixed officially in the documents of the national convention of the Socialist party in Cleveland in May 1936.[49]

As a result, only two major forces provided leadership to expand the movement for a third national party in the mid-1930s—the Communist Party of the United States and the petty-bourgeois radicals in the Farmer-Labor Political Federation. By this time the American Communists had accepted the criticism and recommendations contained in the report presented by G. Dimitrov at the VII Congress of the Comintern[50] and were on the road to overcoming the sectarianism and dogmatism that previously had characterized the party on the issues of a mass democratic movement and the creation of a third party. The plenum of the Central Committee of the U.S. Communist party in November 1935 accepted the resolution "The Farmer-Labor Party and the Struggle Against Reaction." The platform of the future party drawn up by the Communists contained the most important demands of the country's laboring masses, around which workers, farmers, the unemployed, veterans, the middle classes, the intelligentsia, and blacks could unite.[51]

The November 1935 plenum of the Central Committee outlined Communist party activity from discussion to the actual creation of a new party. There were efforts to establish close contacts with groups led by the bourgeois radicals, and work intensified within the existing third parties at the local level.[52]

45. *Daily Worker,* 12 May 1936, 1.

46. Sivachev, *Political Conflict,* 211.

47. *The Progressive,* 4 January 1936, 1.

48. Ibid., 25 April 1936, 7.

49. *New York Times,* 24 May 1936, 1. For more on the policies of the Socialist party in the 1930s, see Malkov, "Communists, Socialists, and the New Deal of Roosevelt: From a History of Conflict to Unity of the Anti-Monopolistic Forces in the United States," *Modern and Contemporary History,* 1977, no. 5.

50. Dimitrov, *Selected Works* (Moscow, 1957), 1:403–5.

51. *The Communist,* December 1935, 1191–92.

52. *Daily Worker,* 12, 28 December 1935; 21 February 1936; 7, 19, 20 April 1936; 23 May 1936.

Simultaneously with the Communists, petty-bourgeois radicals also adopted new methods for expanding and strengthening ties with the masses. The Farmer-Labor Political Federation, which after July 1935 became known as the American Commonwealth Political Federation, served as the ideological center. The decision to change the organization's name resulted from a proposal by Amlie and his supporters. They explained that "farmer-labor" did not correspond with the organization's leading thesis and that "the title would place middle-class emphasis on the movement."[53] Already there was distrust, typical of petty-bourgeois radicals, of the proletariat as an active political force.[54]

The active participation of the Communist party, the American Commonwealth Political Federation, progressive leaders of the workers, and farmers' organizations strengthened the movement for independent political action. As a result, by the beginning of the election campaign of 1936, third parties existed or were being created in thirty-seven states.[55]

Seven international and national unions of the AFL, five independent trade unions, federations of labor in four states, the central workers' councils of twenty-seven counties and cities, hundreds of local unions, the Workers' Alliance of America, the Farmers' Holiday Association—and also progressive democratic organizations such as the American League Against War and Fascism, the American Student Union, the Negro Congress, the Civil Liberties Union, and others—came out in support of a national Farmer-Labor party.[56]

This evolution of the movement toward independent political action made it possible to take concrete steps toward organizing a third national party. However, not paradoxically, it was the functionaries of the American Commonwealth Political Federation who split the movement at the crucial moment. The reason is to be found in the anti-Communist position of its main leaders, T[homas] Amlie and A[lfred] Bingham. When it came to expanding the participation of the Communist party in the movement and strengthening its authority among the rank and file, these leaders sharply objected. Citing the party's past mistakes, they were unwilling to join forces with the Communists in the struggle for common goals.[57]

When the Farmer-Labor Association of Minnesota issued the call for a national conference in Chicago of third-party supporters and did not exclude Communist participation, Amlie and Bingham refused to attend.[58] The national executive committee of the Socialist party also used reluctance to collaborate with the Communists as a pretext for not attending.[59] In 1936 the leaders of the Non-Partisan League, J[ohn L.] Lewis, D[avid] Dubinsky, and S[idney] Hillman, in whom conference organizers placed great hope up to the last minute, finally clarified their position on a

53. *New York Times*, 7 July 1935, 21.
54. Malkov, *New Deal in the United States*, 119.
55. *Congressional Record*, vol. 79, pt. 9, 9715.
56. *Daily Worker*, 23 May 1936, 2.
57. *The Progressive*, 23 May 1936, 1; *New York Times*, 6 March 1936, 9.
58. *The Progressive*, 23 May 1936, 1.
59. *New York Times*, 28 May 1936, 24.

third party. They limited their participation to letters of welcome to conference delegates; and the letters repeated their admonition to support Roosevelt's candidacy in the election.[60] Leading functionaries in the movement for independent political action at the local level, such as Olson and La Follette, also failed to attend the conference. Although they generally supported the idea of a third national party, they concentrated all their attention on affairs in the states. Needing the administration's material support in order to implement reforms in their communities, Olson and La Follette did not want to irritate the leadership of the New Deal, which, in its turn, did everything possible to keep the independent parties at the state level under its control.[61]

The conference in Chicago opened on 30 May 1936. Eighty-five delegates from twenty-eight states of all regions of the country attended. They represented farmer-labor groups, associations, state parties, and farmers' and workers' organizations. The progressive ideas that permeated the conference were fixed in the "Declaration of Principles of the Farmer-Labor Movement." This document contained the most important socioeconomic demands of the masses, which gave it a clearly expressed antimonopolistic character. It turned out to be a radical alternative to the New Deal and had every requisite around which the liberal-progressive, democratic forces of the country could begin to unite.[62]

The main item on the conference agenda—the creation of a national farmer-labor party—was, in many ways, resolved before the conference began. The reason was that the conference organizers had announced that the nomination of a candidate for president would not be discussed.[63] During the conference, the idea of creating a national farmer-labor party based on the trade unions and led by them, or on organizations of the unemployed, farmers, and cooperative groups "united for independent political action, was recognized only in principle."[64] The practical resolution of the matter was put off until September 1936.[65]

In the end, timing determined the fate of a national farmer-labor party during that period. Conditions changed as the election approached, especially in the camp of petty-bourgeois supporters. However, the movement did not disappear; it continued to expand. New farmer-labor parties appeared in New Hampshire, Connecticut, and Montana, where the principle organizers were Communists and Socialists.[66] An important event was the creation in July 1936 of the American Labor party in New York by the state's trade unions.[67] One of the party's documents noted that it came into existence at a time when there undoubtedly was growing working-class recogni-

---

60. *The Progressive*, 6 June 1936, 1.

61. Pechatnov, *Democratic Party of the United States*, 23–24, 32–33.

62. Malkov and Nadzhafov, *America at the Crossroads*, 135; Sivachev, *Political Conflict*, 212–13.

63. *New York Times*, 25 May 1936, 2.

64. *The Progressive*, 6 June 1936, 1.

65. *New York Times*, 31 May 1936, 26; 1 June 1936, 2.

66. *Daily Worker*, 1, 13, 16 July 1936.

67. *The Progressive*, 26 September 1936, 5.

tion of "the need to build a genuine and permanent labor party for independent political action."[68] Like the Non-Partisan League, the new party endorsed Roosevelt's candidacy for president because that course seemed the best means of thwarting the offensive of the conservative camp.

The creation of the reactionary Union party on the initiative of Coughlin in June 1936[69] showed how real the danger was and how necessary it was to support Roosevelt. The party nominated as its presidential candidate William Lemke, a well-known politician in farm states and a member of the House of Representatives from North Dakota. The appearance of the Union party showed the validity of fears that demagogic leaders would use ideas popular among the broad spectrum of third-party supporters in their program. Considering the situation, this development actually lent support to the Republican candidate [Alfred] Landon, who personified the forces of reaction.

Without a mass, progressive third national party, the most effective way to rebuff the challenge of the reactionary conservative camp, to defend the liberal course taken by the Democratic administration, was to support President Roosevelt. It was no accident that the Communist Party of the United States conducted a policy of "objective, although not official, support of Roosevelt" during this period.[70]

Radical-progressive forces, including those in the movement for a third party, became an important component in the broad democratic coalition[71] that brought victory to the New Deal in the election of 1936. In August 1936, the Farmer-Labor party of Minnesota and the Progressive party of Wisconsin accepted resolutions that denied support to Lemke or any other anti-Roosevelt candidate.[72]

On the initiative of leading progressive functionaries, headed by Senator R[obert] La Follette, a conference of two hundred liberal-progressive leaders was convened in Chicago in September 1936. A resolution was passed to create a progressive national committee that would conduct "as vigorous a campaign as possible to unite the progressive and liberal forces into an effective organization to aid in the reelection of President Roosevelt."[73]

Commenting on the creation of the national committee, *The Progressive* quite precisely defined the position of liberal-radical forces in the 1936 election campaign: "The men who met at Chicago realistically faced the situation that exists in 1936 and

68. Ibid.

69. On the Union party, see D[avid H.] Bennett, *Demagogues in the Depression: American Radicals and the Union Party, 1932–1936* (New Brunswick, N.J., 1969).

70. W[illiam Z.] Foster, *History of the Communist Party of the United States* (New York, 1952), 333.

71. On the formation of a new social base of the Democratic party in the 1930s, see Pechatnov, *Democratic Party of the United States,* 7–41; Sivachev, "Realignment in the Two-Party System in the Years of the New Deal," in *Political Parties of the United States in Contemporary Times* (Moscow, 1982).

72. *The Progressive,* 22 August 1936, 1.

73. Ibid., 19 September 1936, 8. Similarly, see R. Feinman, *Twilight of Progressivism: The Western Republican Senators and the New Deal* (Baltimore, 1981).

saw clearly that the choice of honest liberals in the present campaign is Roosevelt against Landon . . . . The delegates agreed that the liberalism of President Roosevelt has done a great deal to further the cause of liberalism in America . . . . Nor did they [the conference delegates] seek to convey the impression that the Roosevelt administration was anything like perfect from the viewpoint of the liberal movement in the record it has made."[74]

In truth, the support of Roosevelt did not mean satisfaction with the moderately liberal character of the Democratic administration's socioeconomic program, nor did it signify a turning away from the idea of creating a third party. The position of the Communist party was quite clear on the matter.

Consequently, it advocated strengthening the political organization of the working class, the farmers, and the urban petty bourgeoisie as the only hopeful defense against reaction and fascism. The way to achieve the goal, stressed in the decision of the IX plenum of the Central Committee of the Communist Party of the United States (June 1936), lay in creation of a farmer-labor party as a special kind of national front.[75] At the height of the 1936 election campaign, petty-bourgeois radicals discussed creating a third national party in time for the elections of 1938 and 1940.[76]

The undying interest in radical ideas among different layers of the American population was reflected in the results of the 1936 election. The most important victory came when local third parties and organizations fighting to create farm-labor parties achieved the election to Congress of four senators and twelve members of the House of Representatives. In three states—Minnesota, Wisconsin, and North Dakota—their candidates became governors. Many members of state legislatures were elected on third-party slates with the support of independent political-action groups. This important achievement of progressive-democratic forces was a substantial contribution to the ascendance of the liberal-progressive trend. The movement to create a progressive third party was an antimonopolistic struggle, and it influenced the shift to the left in Roosevelt's New Deal policies.

From the founding of the Non-Partisan League in 1928 until the election of 1936, the movement for independent political action had trod a difficult path. As it steadily expanded, it encountered numerous problems which, in the final analysis, preordained the failure of efforts to create a progressive third national party. Equally as important as external factors (legal rights, psychological factors, government policies of social maneuvering, etc.), the character of the movement itself determined the fate of the party.

Despite the basic strength and appeal of independent political action among the working class, the participation of the working class in the third-party movement was weak. It remained under the political and ideological influence of the bourgeoisie. Also, the link of the Communist Party of the United States to the broad masses was

---

74. 19 September 1936, 8.
75. *Daily Worker,* 23 June 1936, 1; *The Communist,* July 1936, 385.
76. *The Progressive,* 25 July 1936, 3; 22 August 1936, 1.

not strong enough. In many ways this fact predetermined that the leadership of the movement would represent petty-bourgeois radicalism.

Petty-bourgeois radical functionaries played an important part in critiquing capitalism's defects, in composing progressive-radical solutions to socioeconomic problems, and in mobilizing the masses to battle for social reforms against conservatism and reaction. At the same time, the limit of their aspirations and the diverse nature of their ideological-theoretical views (which rejected proletariat socialism) led to a notorious political inconsistency that left its mark on every development of the third-party movement. There was no unity among leaders as to methods, and the degree of radicalism varied. The moderate wing, represented by leaders of third parties in the Midwest, concentrated vital strength on combating the conservative-reactionary forces that pervaded the ranks of the state Democratic and Republican parties. It relied more on supporting the Roosevelt administration than a new national party in this battle. The left wing of the third-party movement—functionaries of the Farmer-Labor Political Federation—more consistently advocated creation of a new party on a national scale. It saw this development as the best means of carrying out necessary and major transformations in society. But it did not have the same popularity and influence among the broad masses as leaders of local third parties in their communities.

A specific factor that thwarted the third-party movement was the necessity of consolidating the liberal-progressive camp in order to counteract the consolidation of reactionary circles. In the end, this factor influenced the most ardent advocates of a third party to support the moderately liberal wing of the Democratic party headed by President Roosevelt. This wing was viewed as an active, powerful force. With the help of all participants in the movement for democracy and progress, it was capable of preventing a turn to a reactionary course in domestic policies.

The 1936 election was a definite landmark in the development of the third-party movement. But while it somewhat weakened the movement, it did not eliminate the popularity and influence among the masses of ideas about independent political action as such. The inclination toward breaking with the two-party system was preserved and is being preserved; it has reappeared in certain periods to a greater or lesser degree. In modern times the democratic movement has strengthened the voices of protest in broad layers of the population against the social contradictions of capitalist society. It has created, in the opinion of American Communists, certain opportunities to agitate for the formation of an "independent anti-monopolistic political party, headed by the working class, that would take on itself the task of implementing a program of radical reform."[77] The movement for a third party during the 1930s illustrates that democratic forces did have an active, positive influence on the political course of the country.

77. "New Program of the Communist Party of the United States," *USA: Economics, Politics, Ideology,* 1983, no. 3, 126.

Mark Naison

Comment on "The Movement for Creation of a Progressive Third Party in the United States during the Mid–1930s," by I. B. Tverdokhleb

Irene B. Tverdokhleb's essay on third-party movements in the 1930s provides an interesting basis for dialogue between Soviet and American scholars. Ms. Tverdokhleb's portrait of Depression Era political insurgency is often astute. She understands both the breadth of grass-roots discontent and the limits of its influence. She realizes that the United States, despite unprecedented economic problems, never approached a revolutionary crisis. She offers convincing evidence of the conservatism of the labor movement, the weakness of the Left, the strength of capital, and the ability of the two-party system to absorb discontent, even amidst powerful movements for economic security and recognition of worker rights within the industrial system.

Unfortunately, Ms. Tverdokhleb couches her arguments in language that will satisfy few American scholars working in the field. Terms like *monopolistic bourgeoisie*, *petty-bourgeois radicalism*, and *bourgeois American historiography* seem more like broad caricatures than descriptive categories, relics of a Stalinist epoch when Marxism became frozen into a catechism rather than reaching its potential as a tool for understanding social change. Moreover, Ms. Tverdokhleb assumes a unanimity of interpretation among American scholars that simply does not exist. Readers of his article (both text and footnotes) would never know that much of the important new work on third-party movements and the history of American Communism has been done by young scholars influenced by the Marxist tradition. If Ms. Tverdokhleb wishes to give her Soviet readers an accurate picture of the complexity of American society and the diversity of its intellectual life, she would do well to rethink the categories she uses to describe economic divisions, political ideologies, and historiographical perspectives in the United States.

To begin with, Ms. Tverdokhleb should immerse herself in some of the recent historical writing on third-party and radical movements in the Great Depression. Some of the seminal works she makes no reference to are Richard Cloward and Frances Piven, *Poor People's Movements*, John Haynes, *Dubious Alliance: The Making of the Minnesota DFL Party*, Harvey Klehr, *The Heyday of American Communism*, James Weinstein, *Ambiguous Legacy: The Left in American Politics*, Maurice Isserman, *Which Side Were You On?*, Mark Naison, *Communists in Harlem During the Depression*, and Lowell Dyson, *Red Harvest: The Communist Party and American Farmers*. In addition, *Radical America*, *Socialist Review*, and the *Radical History Review*, three journals that arose from the New Left movement of the 1960s, have conducted a vigorous debate on the strength of labor-party sentiment among the American working class.[1] James Weinstein and Staughton Lynd initiated this controversy by arguing that

---

1. Staughton Lynd, "The United Front in America: A Note," *Radical America* 5 (July-August

the Depression offered an opportunity to create a mainstream political party far to the left of the New Deal, something that would have reestablished a permanent socialist presence in American politics. They blamed leaders of the Congress of Industrial Organizations and the Communist party for undermining this possibility by throwing their support to Roosevelt in the 1936 presidential election. Critics of this position, notably Max Gordon and Kenneth Waltzer, have argued that grass-roots sentiment for Roosevelt was so strong among American workers that labor leaders would have jeopardized their movement by supporting a third party. Communists, too, made a reasonable decision; pressing for a third party would have assured their isolation.

Another significant but related debate has occurred over the nature of American Communism. Until the late 1960s, most scholars of American Communism argued that the CPUSA was a captive of Soviet interests, unable and unwilling to undertake significant initiatives in response to American conditions. New Left scholars have challenged this interpretation, arguing that the party served as an outlet for indigenous streams of working-class and black protest even while obeying Comintern discipline. Ms. Tverdokhleb seems unaware of these controversies, and in particular unaware of the influence that Marxist scholars have had on the mainstream of American historiography (a phenomenon bemoaned by Theodore Draper in recent issues of the *New York Review of Books*).[2] She needs to discard the term *bourgeois American historians*, or at least employ it in a far less sweeping manner.

Secondly, Ms. Tverdokhleb should reevaluate the category *petty-bourgeois radicalism*, especially reconsidering the pejorative connotations she attaches to it. She applies this term to movements that call for the redistribution of wealth, inflationary monetary policies, or restrictions on monopoly, but that do not challenge private ownership of capital or legal protections for property rights in civil society. Such movements, she argues correctly, have been unusually strong in the United States, often stronger than working-class radicalism. But Ms. Tverdokhleb's implication that such movements are a sign of political backwardness, that they retard the natural and inevitable movement toward "proletariat socialism," fails to take into account peculiarities of American history and social structure that prevent it from falling neatly into an orthodox Marxist pattern of political "progress."

Many Europeans, examining nineteenth- and twentieth-century U.S. labor history, have been perplexed by the strength of movements calling for inflationary monetary policy, easy access to credit, land distribution, and other programs that

---

1974); "The Possibility of Radicalism in the Early 1930s: The Case of Steel," *Radical America* 6 (November-December 1972); Max Gordon, "The Communist Party of the 1930s and the New Left," *Socialist Revolution* 6 (January-March 1976); Peggy Dennis, "On Learning from History," *Socialist Revolution* 6 (July-September 1976); Kenneth Waltzer, "The Party and the Polling Place: American Communism and an American Labor Party in the 1930s," *Radical History Review* 23 (December 1980).

2. Draper, "American Communism Revisited," 9 May 1985, and "The Popular Front Revisited," 30 May 1985. Also see "Revisiting American Communism: An Exchange," 15 August 1985.

seemed designed to protect opportunities for petty proprietorship instead of the social ownership of industrial monopolies. Given the relentless tendency toward concentration of capital, so brilliantly described by Marx in the *Communist Manifesto*, such "populist" movements seem hopelessly atavistic. But throughout much of American history, widespread ownership of land and productive property, along with universal male suffrage, helped give American political culture a uniquely democratic substance. Many farmers and workers wished to retain opportunities for economic independence, even as the march of modern capitalism seemed steadily to restrict its scope. They found it difficult to welcome the prospect of homogenization into an industrial proletariat or to assume the mantle of human liberation that Marx assigned to it.

In addition, by the 1920s many American workers in basic industry had become enmeshed in the accumulation of consumer commodities. A survey of 100 workers for the Ford Motor Company taken in that epoch discovered that 32 owned their own homes, 47 owned cars, 45 phonographs, 36 radios, and 49 washing machines.[3] A combination of relatively high wages and the development of installment buying allowed many American workers to accumulate personal property.

Because of such circumstances, proletarian collectivism, the elimination of private property, and the vision of a classless society had little appeal to the American working class. Many workers and farmers associated property with self-fulfillment, personal dignity, and social advancement. When the Depression took away their jobs, destroyed their savings, and led to foreclosure on their homes and farms, they protested fiercely, both through the techniques of mass action (strikes, boycotts, marches) and through support for insurgent candidates. But on an ideological level, they showed a marked preference for movements that did not challenge the concept of private property, but focused on the power of wealthy monopolists (real or imagined) who were keeping the common people in thrall. Hence programs such as those of Huey Long (who called for confiscatory tax policies, but not nationalization) and Father Coughlin (who called for an inflationary monetary policy) attracted a tremendous following. To refer to them as "fascist" is more confusing than illuminating. They fit squarely within a populist tradition aimed at restoring the grandeur of the small property owner and petty entrepreneur; they did not put forth the program of a corporate state.

Side by side with these populist movements, the American labor movement experienced an extraordinary revival, sparked by a small but vigorous political Left. American workers displayed great militancy both in industrial disputes and in protests to force the government to provide aid to the unemployed. But when the Depression began, few independent working-class institutions existed to give focus to this activity. The Communist party had less than ten thousand members, many of whom spoke no English. The Socialist party stood at a fraction of its World War I strength.

---

3. David Brody, *Workers in Industrial America: Essays on the 20th Century Struggle* (New York, 1980), 63–64.

Labor unions had slightly more than three million members. The weakness of socialist political culture meant that radicals had to mobilize on the basis of immediate needs rather than a widely accepted core of common values. Millions of workers joined marches for unemployment benefits, movements against foreclosures and evictions, and union-organizing drives led by Socialists and Communists. But many of the same workers who followed Communist leadership in sit-down strikes listened to Father Coughlin on the radio! No coherent, oppositional ideology emerged to unite the diverse streams of Depression Era protest. However, their cumulative result was to create a climate of political instability that elected officials could not afford to ignore.

As Ms. Tverdokhleb observes, the Democratic party, under the leadership of Franklin Roosevelt, moved to coopt this discontent and became its major beneficiary. During 1935, in the midst of great labor unrest and growing grass-roots support for Long and Coughlin, the New Deal administration passed three pieces of legislation that spoke directly to working-class grievances: the Social Security Act, providing for old-age pensions and unemployment insurance; the Wagner Labor Relations Act, offering federal protection for the right of collective bargaining; and the Works Progress Administration, a huge and diversified government-employment program for those who could not find work in the private sector. These actions undermined popular enthusiasm for third-party activity, especially among industrial workers. By 1936, the most influential leaders of the American labor movement, especially in the newly founded CIO, had come to believe that the success of their organizing efforts depended upon a sympathetic president and congress. Hence they reluctantly withdrew support from movements for a national farmer-labor party and mobilized to reelect Roosevelt and key Democratic legislators.

The CPUSA, with some reluctance, supported this political strategy. Party leaders had returned from the Seventh World Congress of the Communist International (in 1935) with hopes of participating in the creation of a national farmer-labor party. But party work within the CIO, where it played an important role in a third of the constituent unions, convinced the leadership that working-class sentiment for Roosevelt was too strong to challenge without risking isolation. Hence party activists chose to support labor parties locally where they had sizable trade-union support, while working for Roosevelt's reelection nationally. Through this strategy, Communists were able to maintain their alliance with liberal industrial-union leaders and play a role in a vast expansion of working-class influence in state and local politics that helped secure labor's gains.

The alliance between the labor movement and the Democratic party, undertaken with the support of the political Left, helped pave the way for an extraordinary rise in labor's organizational strength and political influence. Union membership rose fivefold from 1933 to 1946, from three million to over fifteen million. Without direct intervention in labor disputes from the National Labor Relations Board, and later the War Labor Board, without the refusal of local governments to intervene on the side of management, such gains would have been impossible.

But this left the issue of third-party movements on the back burner. Most labor leaders believed their unions thrived best with the support of the federal government, something best achieved when elected officials felt obligated to the labor vote. Diluting labor's influence through third-party activity had little appeal. When John L. Lewis sought to lead a third-party challenge to Roosevelt in 1940, he found himself removed from the leadership of the CIO. When Communist trade unionists supported Henry Wallace's candidacy in 1948, it helped pave the way for their expulsion from the labor movement. By 1936, ties between the labor movement and the national Democratic party had become so powerful that labor leaders, whether radical or mainstream, could not challenge them without jeopardizing their careers. Communists could survive in the labor movement so long as they accepted this consensus; once they challenged it (as the Cold War escalated) they rapidly became "persona non grata."

The lessons of the labor-party movement of the 1930s are therefore not particularly encouraging to exponents of third-party politics. Ms. Tverdokhleb ends her essay with a quote from a CPUSA spokesperson describing *contemporary* opportunities for "an independent anti-monopolistic political party . . . implementing a program of radical reform." A sober evaluation of the Depression Era, a time when U.S. capitalism faced its most severe crisis, suggests that prospects for a modern third-party movement are rather dim. Radical reform may indeed occur, as an outcome of popular unrest and electoral insurgency. But it is highly improbable that such insurgency could develop without a concerted effort to absorb it into the Democratic party, both nationally and locally. Hence activists would face a conflict between the desire for practical results (that is, reform) and prospects for the creation of a new party. Given the experience of protesters in the 1930s (and the 1960s), it is likely that the new party would be sacrificed in the quest for legislative influence.

It is terribly important that Soviet scholars not possess illusions about prospects for major realignments in American politics, especially those which conform to an orthodox Marxist paradigm. The U.S. constitutional structure makes it extremely difficult for third-party movements to have more than a temporary local impact. The widespread distribution of personal property has associated property rights with personal fulfillment. Socialist ideas have little popularity with rank-and-file American workers. The abuses and injustices of capitalism have provoked and will continue to provoke fierce resistance. The forms this will take in the future are difficult to predict, but if history is any guide, they will probably be expressed through mainstream electoral insurgency and populist rhetoric rather than a third-party movement for socialism.

Response by I. B. Tverdokhleb

M. Naison's comments on the article "The Movement for Creation of a Progressive Third Party in the United States in the Mid–1930s" show that Soviet scholars and American historians of the radical tendency share much in common with regard to the interpretation of the main theoretical aspects of the problem of a third party in the United States. Thus, a large part of M. Naison's review is devoted to an explanation of the "nuances of American history," which in his opinion determined the lack of receptiveness among the American working class toward the idea of a third party and socialist ideology. That problem—the problem of the distinctive character of the historical development of the United States, which brought about the prolonged domination of the two-party system and explains the political weakness and fragility of third parties—was comprehensively studied in the works of Soviet historians like I. P. Dementev, V. L. Malkov, A. S. Manykin, N. V. Sivachev, V. V. Sogrin, E. F. Yazkov, and others, references to which are made in the article under review. In their explanation of the stability of political institutions and the homogeneity of the politico-ideological and value beliefs of American society, including the American working class, Soviet scholars have singled out, among the many causes of this phenomenon, the prevalence of private-ownership ideals in the mass consciousness, attention to which is also drawn by M. Naison.

At the same time we believe that it is precisely these features of the socioeconomic system in the United States that explain the importance of studying the experience of those movements for independent political action that operated within the confines of the national system of values. This is necessary not so much for predicting the likelihood of a viable third party being established in the United States as for ascertaining the possibility of the emergence of public sentiment in favor of independent political action, and the degree of influence and effect on the two-party system and current government policy such sentiment might have. In the article under review, an attempt was made to analyze these questions on the basis of the history of the development and role in the political life of the United States in the early 1930s of the movement for the creation of a third party, which, within the framework of capitalist society, championed a program of broad democratic reforms which in their radicalism surpassed the liberal reforms of Roosevelt's New Deal. Representatives of the radical intelligentsia and the political federation of farmers and workers they created initiated and led this movement in the early 1930s. The social composition of the movement was quite heterogeneous, with an active part being played by the middle class.

M. Naison, on the other hand, suggests that attention should be focused on the activities of the Communist Party of America (CPA) and the position of the labor movement concerning the idea of a third party, which was in fact done in the studies by American historians published in the 1970s and 1980s that are listed in the commentary. This topic undoubtedly deserves special attention,[1] but it lies outside the

---

1. A contribution to its study was made by V. L. Malkov in his article "Communists, Socialists, and Roosevelt's New Deal," in *Modern and Recent History,* 1974, no. 5.

scope of the article under review, since the main effort by the CPA to create a farmers' and workers' party and the struggle in the labor movement, particularly within the Congress of Industrial Organizations, around this issue took place in the late 1930s. What was of interest to the author of this article was the issue of cooperation between the CPA and the Farmer-Labor Political Federation in the matter of creating a national third party. In this connection it must be made clear that the position of implacable hostility adopted by the leaders of the Farmer-Labor Political Federation toward the Communists did not act as a brake on the "natural and inevitable movement toward 'proletariat socialism,' " as the reviewer ironically says, misinterpreting the article's conclusion, but rather became an obstacle to the unification of the different currents within the movement for a progressive third party, which was another reason why that movement was weakened. It must be stated once again that, despite the eventual failure of the attempts to create a progressive third party for the 1936 election, the movement for independent political action during that period was an important part of the struggle of the broad masses of the American people for social reforms, in many ways making possible and stimulating the development of the liberal policy of the Roosevelt administration. It is this that makes the significance and topicality of studying the historical experience of such movements obvious and enables us to offer a less pessimistic evaluation of their role in the political life of the United States than does M. Naison.

T. V. Galkova

11 THE EVOLUTION OF THE SOCIOECONOMIC PROGRAM OF FDR's ADMINISTRATION IN THE CLOSING YEARS OF THE NEW DEAL (1937–EARLY 1938)

The election campaign of 1936, which took place during a period of popular resistance to conservative forces, was an important event in the history of the New Deal.[1] The election brought triumphant victory to Franklin Roosevelt (who received 60.79 percent of the votes of the electorate) and his party. The election also demonstrated unequivocally the support of a broad range of workers, farmers, and petty and middle-class bourgeoisie for the reforms of the New Deal and their desire for stronger and more extensive social legislation. However, the results by no means signified a total defeat for the conservative forces. They did not lay down their arms; rather, they considered Franklin Roosevelt's victory a call to action. With the beginning of 1937 a new phase began in the history of the New Deal. The present author has attempted to examine the evolution of the leadership's program during these changing times.

The situation in the United States at the beginning of 1937 was very complicated. Against the background of an improving economic situation there was a significant upsurge in the workers' movement, which was accompanied by a sharp polarization of the nation's political forces. The workers' struggle, noted John L. Lewis, head of the Congress of Industrial Organizations (CIO), basically took two directions: toward attracting millions of unorganized workers into unions, and toward congressional enactment of truly democratic laws. Lewis said, "Labor demands legislation . . . making realistic the principles of industrial democracy."[2] Pursuing the struggle for the right to create unions was prompted, first and foremost, by the fact that many entrepreneurs simply ignored the Wagner Act, which had proclaimed that right. As a result, labor conditions in many enterprises were very oppressive. An effective struggle to improve conditions first required the proletariat to organize. And a significant

1. This article by T. V. Galkova was originally published in *Social Movements and Political Conflict in the Countries of Europe and America in Contemporary Times* (Moscow, 1985), 51–67. This English translation is by Brenda Kay Weddle. On the history of the New Deal, see N. V. Sivachev, *The Political Conflict in the United States in the Mid-1930s* (Moscow, 1966); Sivachev and E. F. Yazkov, *Recent History of the United States* (Moscow, 1980), chap. 4; Sivachev, *The United States: The Government and the Working Class* (Moscow, 1982), chaps. 8, 9, 10; V. L. Malkov and D. G. Hadzhafov, *America at the Crossroads: Essay on the Social-Political History of the New Deal in the United States* (Moscow, 1967); Malkov, *The New Deal in the United States: Social Movements and Social Politics* (Moscow, 1973); M. Z. Shkundin, *The History of the Governmental-Monopolistic Social Politics of the United States* (Moscow, 1980).

2. *Daily Worker,* 2 January 1937, 6.

number of the proletarian uprisings in 1936 and 1937 took place under the slogan that the Wagner Act be enforced.[3] The workers, besides the proven means of battle, employed new and radical methods such as "sit-down strikes," during which they did not leave their job sites and thereby precluded any opportunity for strike-breaking.

The workers' movement for social legislation took the form of support for the Black-Connery bill (labeled the Fair Labor Standards Act), a bill designed to establish a federal minimum wage and a maximum work day. Workers' organizations also supported expanded legislation on social security.

The improvement of the economic situation had an impact on the general arrangement of power in the country. The volume of industrial production approached the level of 1929, and several "new" branches of industry, according to the *Wall Street Journal*, surpassed the 1929 level by 50 to 100 percent.[4] The prognoses of economists about the development of the economy were reassuringly bright.[5]

At the same time, employers began to intensify their opposition to the administration's activities. The reason lay in the fact that as the economic situation improved, business again found confidence in its own strengths. In that setting, employers tried to limit the regulating role of the government as much as possible in these areas where, they believed, they could get along without it. Influential publications claimed that Roosevelt wanted jurisdiction over the economy of the country and other spheres of public life.[6] Business circles sharply criticized the president for his policies toward workers. They saw in them the primary cause for the popular uprising of the proletariat. In January the *Wall Street Journal* asked, "Today is there anyone who believes seriously that the government is not strongly sympathetic to labor's cause? Not only is it the federal government that is sympathetic, but also state and municipal government."[7] In a situation in which the holy of holies of capitalist society, private property, was exposed to danger, the business world united to battle against encroachment on their rights by workers; and they demanded that the administration restrict the workers' movement through its policies.

The government faced the complicated task of fashioning a political position in this uneasy situation. On 6 January 1937, Roosevelt presented his annual address to Congress. Although he noted some progress toward economic recovery, he pointed out that the desired standard was yet to be achieved, and he singled out entirely different problems that were, in his opinion, more important. These were housing conditions among urban dwellers, the condition of the farm economy, and a future system of social security and aid to the unemployed.[8] Roosevelt considered the Supreme Court the primary obstacle to fulfillment of his plans. As is well known,

3. *Historical Statistics of the United States: Colonial Times to 1957* (Washington, 1960), 99.
4. 3 January 1937, 336.
5. *Business Week*, 3 January 1937, 22–23; *Wall Street Journal*, 2 January 1937, 336–37.
6. *Business Week*, 23 January 1937, 55; *Wall Street Journal*, 16 January 1937, 412.
7. 2 January 1937, 361.
8. *Congressional Record*, vol. 81, pt. 1, 85.

during the course of his first term the Supreme Court had declared a number of New Deal laws unconstitutional, including the National Industrial Recovery Act (NIRA) and the Agricultural Adjustment Act (AAA). These actions brought a storm of indignation from workers and made the social-protest movement more radical. Therefore, at the beginning of 1937, the reform of the Supreme Court became the president's main political concern. His aim was to obtain recognition of the basic measures of the New Deal and to safeguard the achievements of the previous four years. Eleanor Roosevelt wrote in her memoirs that Roosevelt believed "if it was going to be possible to pass progressive legislation, only to have it declared unconstitutional by the Supreme Court, no progress could be made."[9] American laborers also supported the idea of reform. Labor "demands that Congress exercise its constitutional powers and brush aside the autocratic rule as presented by the Supreme Court," John Lewis said in his New Year's address.[10] Sensing strong support, the president made reform of the Supreme Court his first priority and decided against introducing any new socioeconomic changes.

Recognizing the need to respond somehow to millions of ordinary Americans, the president took up the question of the nation's well-being in his inaugural address of 20 January: "But here is the challenge to our democracy: In this nation I see tens of millions of its citizens . . . who at this very moment are denied the greater part of what the very lowest standards of today call the necessities of life . . . . I see one-third of a nation ill-housed, ill-clad, and ill-nourished."[11] Roosevelt especially wanted to enhance the role of the government in resolving socioeconomic problems. "Instinctively we recognized a deeper need—the need to find through government the instrument of our united purpose to solve for the individual the ever-rising problems of a complex civilization," he said. "Repeated attempts at their solution without the aid of government had left us baffled and bewildered . . . . To do this we knew that we must find practical controls over blind economic forces and blindly selfish men."[12]

But Roosevelt proposed no concrete socioeconomic program in this speech, asserting, "We are determined to make every American citizen the subject of this country's interest and concern."[13] The American historian William Leuchtenburg has written that in place of new social legislation for improving the condition of "one-third of the nation," as the country expected, to everyone's amazement Roosevelt proposed reform of the Supreme Court.[14] In a special address to Congress on 5 February, the president laid out his plan for reorganization. He proposed that when a member of the Supreme Court reached age seventy, but did not retire, the president

9. *This I Remember* (New York, 1949), 166.

10. *Daily Worker,* 2 January 1937, 6.

11. *The Public Papers and Addresses of Franklin D. Roosevelt* (hereafter *FDR Public Papers*), 1937 vol. (New York, 1938), 4–5.

12. Ibid., 1.

13. Ibid., 5.

14. *Franklin D. Roosevelt and the New Deal, 1932–1940* (New York, 1963), 231.

could name (with the consent of the Senate) an additional member, provided that the total number of judges did not exceed fifteen. This would have provided Roosevelt the opportunity, at the beginning of 1937, to appoint six new members. In the words of Roosevelt himself, the goal of Supreme Court reform was to infuse it with "new and younger blood."[15] At this time of increasing resistance by conservatives to new legislation, the president decided to strike at the heart of the opposition. By so doing he could strengthen what had been achieved and open the way for future reform.

Reaction to the president's proposal varied. The working classs reacted sympathetically. The Communist Party of the United States and black organizations offered support.[16] The CIO, however, contended that it was only a first step. "The long range program against the court still stands," said J[ohn L.] Lewis.[17] Various other unions supported the president. His plan was backed by the Labor Nonpartisan League as well as by public organizations, students, and intellectuals.[18] Even the Executive Committee of the AFL and its chairman, W[illiam] Green, accepted the idea of reform.[19] However, the rank and file, who were not fully satisfied with the imprecise contours of the administration's program, insisted on more detail. Charging that Roosevelt "turned his back on the auto strikers,"[20] unions demanded administration support for their strike policies. "What you promised so definitely during the campaign," Lewis reminded the president, "the workers now expect you to perform."[21]

Even before Roosevelt's official announcement about Supreme Court reform, cautious business circles had announced their disapproval.[22] However, the campaign against the reform took on greatest strength after 5 February. The author of an article published in *Business Week* wrote that of all Roosevelt's measures, even the very worst "has not been so dangerous to our constitutional structure, our social institutions . . . , the future happiness of our country as his demand for authority to pack the Supreme Court."[23] The main danger was that with the aid of judges obedient to him, Roosevelt could have all his bills declared constitutional, including the NIRA and the AAA, and primarily "the Wagner Labor Relations Act," which the author believed was written "by the American Federation of Labor in order to compel every employee in the land to join a union."[24] Strengthening the unions particularly angered employers. Accusing Roosevelt of supporting the AFL and CIO, *Business Week* emphasized, "He could procure the enactment of any bill that John L. Lewis

15. *FDR Public Papers* (1937), 127–28.
16. *Daily Worker,* 9 February 1937, 6; 10 February 1937, 6; 19 March 1937, 3.
17. Ibid., 18 February 1937, 6.
18. Ibid., 18 February 1937, 6; 5 March 1937, 2, 6; 13 March 1937, 3; 15 March 1937, 5; 26 March 1937, 5.
19. *American Federationist,* April 1937, 353.
20. *Daily Worker,* 14 January 1937, 6; 23 January 1937, 7.
21. Ibid., 23 January 1937, 6.
22. *Business Week,* 23 January 1937, 55.
23. Ibid., 13 February 1937, 56.
24. Ibid.

may suggest as a means of unionizing the automobile, rubber, and steel industries. The President's entire legislative program would go through Congress, undeterred by fears that the Supreme Court would invalidate it. For a Supreme Court packed by the President would invalidate nothing the President wanted."[25]

Wall Street Journal columnist C. Benedict, in his analysis of the proposed reform, noted that it would violate the constitutional system of balances between the executive, legislative, and judicial branches and lead to the concentration of all power in the hands of the former. He especially stressed the role of the Supreme Court as the branch "which corrects the activities of the administration." Applauding the measures designed to help business, Benedict wrote, "Thus far, in spite of the splendid work he has done, many glaring errors have been made, of which the NIRA and AAA represent the least successful of his major policies. It was the Supreme Court that made it possible to correct these mistakes; while, on the other hand, it was also the Supreme Court which upheld and backed up the most important social and financial measures advocated by the President. What reason, therefore, have we to believe that the Supreme Court blocks the effectiveness of the New Deal's progress?"[26] From these statements, which echoed the opinions of business circles, it is clear how strongly employers opposed new legislation as well as enforcement of reform legislation already passed.[27] The same division among political forces continued during discussion of the new budget. The budget deficit was cause for constant attacks on the president by big business. At the beginning of 1937 a campaign intensified to force Roosevelt to reduce spending on assistance to the unemployed. This campaign greatly affected the administration's stance toward the new budget, and balancing the budget was the main point in Roosevelt's budget address on 8 January. To achieve it, he asked that several programs be cut—particularly unemployment relief. In 1937, $2.166 billion had been appropriated for unemployment relief; in 1938 the figure should be cut to $1.5 billion.[28] This way, under pressure from conservatives, the government not only refrained from proposing new reforms but also decreased allocations for social needs.

Laborers met this decision with a storm of indignation. Communists and workers in various cities sharply criticized the budget message.[29] Leftist forces in Congress, headed by Robert La Follette, also opposed decreased spending on social needs.[30] However, the overwhelming majority in business circles came out in support of such a decrease. Some businessmen, in fact, believed that aid to the unemployed should be reduced to nothing. Thus, the journal of the U.S. Chamber of Commerce, *Nation's Business*, reported, "Under our present scheme, relief, which everyone was led to

25. Ibid.

26. *Wall Street Journal*, 13 March 1937, 667.

27. *Commercial and Financial Chronicle*, 9 January 1937, 143–44; *Wall Street Journal*, 2 January 1937, 340–341; *Business Week*, 16 January 1937, 17–18.

28. *Congressional Record*, vol. 81, pt. 1, 116–17.

29. *Daily Worker*, 13 January 1937, 6; 1 March 1937, 6.

30. *Literary Digest*, 17 April 1937, 5.

picture as a temporary phase, is to continue until the last taxpayer has died."[31] Other businessmen believed the government should go further and cut costs of government operations.[32]

The president's recommendations, which he asked Congress to approve in April 1937, increased controversy over the budget. Roosevelt proposed still larger cuts in social programs than he had in January.[33] Leftist liberal groups were critical. They pointed out in May 1937, when the first indications of an economic decline took shape, that balancing the budget was possible only if economic conditions improved. They proposed increased government spending, with possible decreases only in military appropriations.[34] In the fall of 1937 (by which time no one doubted that the country would survive the economic crisis), the *Nation* bluntly called the politics of cutting federal spending for "social services" a mistake.[35] Secretary of Agriculture H[enry A.] Wallace opposed making less money available for the needy in the agricultural economy, and the president of the American Farm Bureau, E[dward A.] O'Neal, said, "We are for economy, but we are not for an economy that will paralyze agriculture."[36] However, many politicians, mostly conservative ones, supported the budget cuts and even proposed a reduction in the category of unemployment relief to $500 million. Among these politicians, the most visible were southerners, such as J[ames F.] Byrnes, who, as *Newsweek* wrote, was "never friendly to huge relief expenditures for blacks."[37]

In 1937 the labor movement, particularly the CIO, greatly influenced political life in the United States. "Sit-down strikes" strongly affected the president's relations both with unions and with business. Roosevelt found himself between a rock and a hard place, with workers demanding stronger social reforms and employers an end to his flirtation with unions.

The president decided to wait. He could not yield to the zealous opponents of the unions who wanted him to use force to end strikes. In Roosevelt's opinion, repressing the struggle of working-class America during the highly explosive strikes of 1933–1937 was tantamount to suicide for the two-party system.[38] The president wisely urged unions and business to cooperate and "criticized the tendency of business to lengthen working hours and thereby carry an increased volume of business without an increase in personnel."[39] Although he strongly opposed "sit-down strikes," Roosevelt feared to condemn them openly. The class struggle had reached such a fevered pitch that the workers' anger might easily be directed against the

31. April 1937, 21.
32. *Wall Street Journal,* 13 March 1937, 667.
33. *FDR Public Papers* (1937), 165–67.
34. *New Republic,* 5 May 1937, 372–73.
35. 30 October 1937, 461.
36. *Newsweek,* 1 May 1937, 8.
37. Ibid.
38. See Malkov, *The New Deal in the United States,* 285.
39. *New Republic,* 20 January 1937, 339.

president. Therefore, he considered it necessary to denounce both the police who shot at participants during a sit-down strike in Chicago on 30 May 1937 (at the instigation of Republic Steel Corporation officials) and the excessive activities of the unions.[40]

So careful an approach by the president prompted a barrage of sharp criticism from business representatives who blamed him for "superfluous gentleness" and at times even of "the betrayal of America's interests." In June 1937, *Business Week* published a series of articles that violently attacked the president and the "subservient Congress." The indignant author of one wanted to know how long the administration would abet the unions and permit workers to take control of industries.[41] Another article, referring to Roosevelt's new approach to unions that allegedly "violated property rights," concluded with the words, "That is really a new deal!"[42] Other organs of prominent bourgeoisie advanced similar arguments against the president's position.[43]

The position of the administration was complicated by the fact that serious opposition to its basic programs existed in Congress. The opponents objected primarily to reform of the Supreme Court, but also opposed a large number of legislative proposals, including the Black-Connery bill. Employers viewed Black-Connery as a government scheme to limit their freedom of action, as "a program directed against business," and as still another concession to the unions.[44] The industrialists most opposed to the bill were from the South, "where even the lowest federal standards of labor wages would demand an increase of the minimum wage."[45] There was no unity on the Black-Connery bill even among the leaders of the unions. While the leadership and rank and file of the CIO spoke out in support of this legislation, leaders of the AFL, pointing out the low minimum wage, tried to convince members that they would achieve more through collective bargaining. As Secretary of Labor F[rances] Perkins put it, the internecine struggle between the AFL and the CIO, the absence of a united policy among unions, perniciously bespoke the fate of the bill.[46] In many respects all these factors influenced the administration's position, which in spring 1937 was fully supportive of the legislation;[47] but in direct proportion to increased opposition the government insisted less on enactment. Perkins wrote that at the end of the spring, "on the advice of Attorney General Cummings, the President embarked upon the ill-fated court plan" and decided that "the wage-hour legislation

40. *F.D.R.: His Personal Letters, 1928–1945,* ed. Elliott Roosevelt, 2 vols. (New York, 1950), 1:693.

41. 12 June 1937, 68.

42. 26 June 1937, 62.

43. *Wall Street Journal,* 19 June 1937, 252; *Commercial and Financial Chronicle,* 29 May 1937, 3553.

44. *Business Week,* 21 August 1937, 13; *Commercial and Financial Chronicle,* 24 April 1937, 2726; *Wall Street Journal,* 19 June 1937, 292.

45. Sivachev, *The United States,* 226.

46. Perkins, *The Roosevelt I Knew* (New York, 1946), 258.

47. *FDR Public Papers* (1937), 209–14.

would have to wait."[48] Although the Senate passed the bill on 31 July 1937, the failure of the administration to change its position caused discussion to drag on in the House of Representatives.

A similar fate befell other bills. At the end of the regular session of Congress, out of five important bills the administration had championed (the bill to reform the Supreme Court, the bill to construct inexpensive housing, the Black-Connery bill, the bill to control agricultural production, and the bill to reorganize the federal administrative structure), only the bill on housing construction had received the support of both houses of Congress—and that bill had been significantly changed.[49] The press that voiced business concerns talked about Roosevelt's defeat and the "revolt" of Congress against the "dictatorship" of the president. These writers considered the attempted reform of the Supreme Court, which "undermined confidence in the President,"[50] the primary cause. However, the causes lay primarily in the reluctance of ruling circles to continue the politics of reform. During the entire session the press wrote constantly of the "danger" to business of the president's plans and insisted that Congress "fight for its independence" and not pass the new laws.[51] The president himself, aware of the strong opposition to the new measures, pursued them with less energy and in several matters, such as the new budget, was inclined to make concessions to conservatives.

By fall 1937 the situation in the country had changed significantly. The economic crisis, which by that time had become serious, magnified all the contradictions, contributed to a strong upsurge in the workers' movement, and modified the position of business circles. A decline in production began in spring 1937 and continued until spring 1938; at its lowest point in May 1938 the level of production was 30 percent lower than the level of 1929.[52] The number of unemployed rose from 7.7 million in 1937 to 10.39 million in 1938.[53] The deterioration in the condition of workers brought on by the crisis incited the proletariat to more decisive action. Laborers now fought harder for enactment of the Black-Connery bill and for the bills on construction of inexpensive housing and on regulation of agricultural production. Having taken no concrete steps in the sphere of socioeconomic legislation, the government brought on itself the greater dissatisfaction of the working class; the threat of a schism between the New Deal and the workers' movement became all the more real.

As the situation deteriorated, Roosevelt decided to travel across the country. Presi-

48. *The Roosevelt I Knew*, 256.

49. *Commercial and Financial Chronicle*, 28 August 1937, 1315.

50. Ibid.; *Wall Street Journal*, 17 July 1937, 402–3, 440.

51. *Commercial and Financial Chronicle*, 24 April 1937, 2726; 29 May 1937, 3553; 12 June 1937, 3896–97; 7 August 1937, 823–24; 14 August 1937, 1002; 28 August 1927, 1315–16; *Wall Street Journal*, 16 January 1937, 412; 13 March 1937, 667; 5 June 1937, 212; 19 June 1937, 292, 330; 17 July 1937, 402–3, 440; 14 August 1937, 514–15, 566–67.

52. The gross national product in 1938 was $84.7 billion, compared to $103.1 billion in 1929. *Historical Statistics of the United States: Colonial Times to 1970* (vols. 1–2, Washington, 1975), 1:224.

53. Ibid., 1:135.

dential aide S[amuel I.] Rosenman wrote that the aim of the president was to "talk about the things he was trying to do in Washington. He knew how much his voice and smile and presence could do with the people."[54] In the course of his trip the president became convinced that workers strongly supported the Black-Connery bill. He pointedly devoted his speech in St. Paul, Minnesota, to this subject.[55] On his return, Roosevelt decided to call a special session of Congress in November-December 1937. As he explained in a speech on 12 October, "I shall ask this special session to consider immediately certain important legislation which my recent trip through the nation convinced me the American people immediately need."[56] As he established the agenda for the session, the president calculated that during the time before it began, since he had demonstrated to the voters his desire for action, they would exert pressure on the members of Congress who had gone home to their districts.[57] Included in the business of the special session were all the basic legislative proposals that had been before the regular session. The working class supported the president. The Black-Connery bill now was included in the program of the CIO. The union accepted it at its conference in October 1937, where Lewis made a special point of the proletariat's desire for shorter hours and higher wages.[58] However, the appeals of business to boycott the proposed legislation[59] had a decisive influence on Congress, and not one of the bills was passed. The conservatives celebrated their victory and proposed that Congress shift from the politics of boycott to the composition of an alternative program to the New Deal.[60]

Press comments reflected certain changes in the position of business. As business saw it, Roosevelt had supported them loyally, but then had turned to social reform, "forgetting about the employers."[61] These social policies, in the opinion of one group of commentators, had caused the new economic recession, and they demanded that the president actively aid business.[62] These press comments were a clear consequence of the economic crisis of 1937–1938. They also came at a time when government regulation of socioeconomic processes was becoming an inalienable function of society. A way out of the existing crisis was to increase the regulatory activity of the government in the future. A few business people immediately recognized this; however, it took the economic crisis to force this understanding on most employers.

On 3 January 1938, Roosevelt delivered his annual message to Congress. The

54. *Working with Roosevelt* (New York, 1952), 170.

55. *FDR Public Papers* (1937), 403–5.

56. Ibid., 429.

57. Rosenman, *Working with Roosevelt,* 170.

58. *Daily Worker,* 14 October 1937, 4; 16 October 1937, 3.

59. *Business Week,* 16 October 1937, 13; *Commercial and Financial Chronicle,* 23 October 1937, 2590; 30 October 1937, 2748–49; 6 November 1937, 2911; 13 November 1937, 3106–7; 20 November 1937, 3249; *Wall Street Journal,* 20 November 1937, 138.

60. *Commercial and Financial Chronicle,* 25 December 1937, 4024–25.

61. *Wall Street Journal,* 6 November 1937, 76.

62. *Literary Digest,* 25 December 1937, 20–22; *Wall Street Journal,* 18 December 1937, 272–74, 322–23.

message included a detailed analysis of the economy and the condition of various classes of society. He placed passage of the Fair Labor Standards Act high on the agenda. In doing so, on the one hand, he publicized it as a means of improving the condition of labor. On the other hand, the president tried to calm businessmen with the contention that passing the bill would improve the national economy and that "more desirable wages are and should continue to be the product of collective bargaining."[63]

The economic crisis and pressure from labor forced the administration once again to increase spending for social programs. Roosevelt announced that the budget deficit would be less, but the budget could not be balanced during the next year. While the president condemned advocates of a balanced budget and their idea of reducing appropriations for the unemployed,[64] at the same time he sought an opportunity to win business support. His annual address stressed cooperation among different social groups as a means of overcoming the crisis. He also put monopolization and concentration of the means of production on the national agenda. These problems also were to be central in the political life of the country at the beginning of 1938.

In the last days of 1937 liberals in the president's circle launched an antimonopoly campaign. It began on 26 December 1937, with a radio talk by a Department of Justice aide, R[obert H.] Jackson. Jackson placed the blame for the economic recession on monopolistic capital, and three days later he declared that the government now was concerned with "the general strike of capital against reform." He rejected business contentions that workers who demanded higher wages were to blame, and concluded by saying, "The only just criticism that can be made of the economic operations of the New Deal is that it set out a breakfast for the canary and let the cat steal it."[65]

On 30 December H[arold L.] Ickes, secretary of the interior and administrative head of public works, delivered a similar speech. He also assailed monopoly, asserting that America was threatened by "big business fascism."[66] The speeches of Jackson and Ickes genuinely alarmed business circles, who wanted to know whether the speeches had been sanctioned by the president. The point was that Roosevelt's statements were much more moderate. In a speech on 8 January, the president did criticize the activity of monopolies, but in contrast to Jackson and Ickes he expressed the hope that "evils and abuses and unfortunate actions will in greater part be eliminated by the cooperative action of that overwhelming majority. The White House door is open . . . to all citizens who come offering to help eradicate the evils that flow from that undue concentration of economic power or unfair business practices."[67] In this manner Roosevelt proposed that business leaders contact him directly. The subsequent

63. *FDR Public Papers* (1938), 6.
64. Ibid., 8–9.
65. *Newsweek*, 10 January 1938, 9.
66. *The Secret Diary of Harold L. Ickes*, 3 vols. (New York, 1954), 2:282–83; *Nation*, 29 January 1938, 119–20; Leuchtenburg, *Franklin D. Roosevelt and the New Deal*, 249.
67. *FDR Public Papers* (1938), 43–45.

activity of the president revealed the true goals of his antimonopoly campaign. He conducted a series of "round table" discussions, mostly for representatives of major businesses. Following up on his idea of "collaboration" among different social classes, he also invited union leaders, particularly Lewis. Still, establishing contacts with the heads of major corporations, such as General Motors and U.S. Steel, was the first priority. The number of participants in these meetings was large. "During the first three weeks of 1937 when boom was in the air, President Roosevelt saw about a half-dozen businessmen. Since the turn of this year, he has talked with more than 100,"[68] *Time* reported in January 1938. The administration's position surprised commentators at first, but by February the majority agreed that it was a well-thought-out policy designed to frighten business through a loud antimonopolistic campaign and force it to be more amenable and to seek out contact with the president. Ickes wrote that at a cabinet meeting in January 1938 Roosevelt, who had just returned from a conference with businesses, remarked, "Do you know that this conference would not have been possible if it had not been for the speeches of Bob Jackson and Harold Ickes? Prior to the speeches these businessmen refused even to come in to talk to me. After the speeches, they were only too glad to come in."[69]

Newsweek reported that the main reasons New Dealers brought up the antitrust issue were, first, the desire to place blame for the economic recession on the shoulders of business, and, second, in order to frighten business and prepare the public to accept "any reforms that may later be decided on."[70] The theory of the propagandistic character of the campaign was corroborated, in the opinion of the magazine, by the symbolic increase of expenditures in the new budget for antitrust activity.[71]

Roosevelt also tried to use these meetings to make his legislative program a reality. The outcome of one meeting with forty-nine members of the Chamber of Commerce testified to the fact that he had chosen the right way. The Chamber drew up a plan of action that included all the basic proposals the president had advocated: the Black-Connery bill, the bill to construct inexpensive housing, the bill to regulate agricultural production, and the demand to revise the antitrust laws.[72]

Roosevelt's first success was congressional passage of the law to regulate agricultural production (the second AAA). Signing this law on 16 February 1938, the president said its enactment "represents the winning of one more battle for an underlying farm policy that will endure."[73]

The decline in production, having now reached its lowest point, demanded drastic measures. However, in mid-January 1938 Roosevelt initiated no radical measures because he expected production to rise. By his calculation that should have occurred in April.[74] Time passed, and the decline continued. Then, the head of the administra-

68. 31 January 1938, 7.
69. *Secret Diary,* 2:295.
70. 17 January 1938, 10–11.
71. Ibid., 11.
72. Ibid., 31 January 1938, 12–13.
73. *FDR Public Papers* (1938), 86–87.
74. *Newsweek,* 17 January 1938, 11.

tion offered a series of new proposals for overcoming the crisis. On 23 March he devoted a speech to the economic problem in Gainesville, Georgia, a small town that had been victim to a tornado in 1936. Noting that the "rebirth" of the town had occurred with the help of federal dollars, the president optimistically declared that the entire country would soon "revive" and rise above its economic problems with the help of the government. The most important means of overcoming the crisis, he said, was increasing the purchasing power of the people.[75] On 14 April the president turned to Congress with a similar recommendation for battling the crisis. On the same day he gave his regular "fireside chat." "The purpose of the chat," Rosenman wrote, "was to tell the people in very simple terms what was wrong, what he was doing about it, what he had recommended that the Congress do."[76]

Roosevelt explained the importance of his legislative proposals to Congress and contended that several were urgent. These included additional appropriations to aid the unemployed and needy, creation of additional bank credits, and various propositions directed at increasing the purchasing power of the people. The battle for the latter, he stressed, would require large government expenditures.[77]

The economic crisis, ongoing pressure from labor, and skillful politics led to passage of much of the president's legislative program in mid–1938. This included the Black-Connery bill and the law to regulate agricultural production, as well as a new commission to investigate the activity of monopolies. The enactment of these laws was the result of a lengthy struggle by the administration; but more fundamentally it was the result of a complicated and contradictory process of evolution of the government's socioeconomic program. At the beginning of 1937 conservative opposition to the new legislation sharply increased. As economic prospects improved, the desire to weaken the role of government intensified in the minds of the American bourgeoisie (both large and petty). Given these better conditions, so the employers thought, government aid was no longer necessary; and opposition to new socioeconomic reforms grew amongst entrepreneurs. Undoubtedly the democratic movement during the election campaign of 1936 and the wave of "sit-down strikes" that enveloped the country at the end of 1936–1937 led to a sharp polarization of political forces. Frightened by the sweep of the workers' movement and the growth and strength of unions, entrepreneurs tried to stop the outpouring of new legislative proposals that workers supported. Business protested that government already had given too much to labor. The position of business had a strong impact on the arrangement of power in the leading political parties and on the situation in Congress. There was a clear shift to the right in the ranks of the Democrats.[78] In many respects the mood of business could be seen as well in the activity of the administration, which in early 1937 fought primarily to reform the Supreme Court and concentrated on reinforcing legislation that had already passed. New socioeconomic measures were not

75. *FDR Public Papers* (1938), 164–68.
76. *Working with Roosevelt*, 174.
77. *FDR Public Papers* (1938), 240–42, 244–45.
78. See further Sivachev, "Realignment in the Two-Party System in the Years of the New Deal," in *Political Parties in the United States in Contemporary Times* (Moscow, 1982).

introduced at first. In early 1937 the government made concessions to entrepreneurs and tried to balance the budget. This reduced spending on social needs.

However, during the second half of 1937, clear changes took place in administrative policy. The economic crisis that aggravated all contradictions, the wave of protest from laborers who favored expanding and deepening social legislation, the changed views among employers who began to recognize that without government help they would not survive the economic recession—all these factors could be seen in the position of the government. And the government found it necessary to introduce plans for reform and to begin to implement them. The result of the administration's activity was a new—and, as time told, the last—wave of legislation during the New Deal.

Otis L. Graham, Jr.

Comment on "The Evolution of the Socioeconomic Program of FDR's Administration in the Closing Years of the New Deal (1937–Early 1938)," by T. V. Galkova

The topic of T. V. Galkova's essay, the New Deal in the 1937–1938 period, is well chosen, for this was indeed a critical period in American political development. Galkova's interest is in the conjuncture of economic and political pressures upon the course of the New Deal. The essay begins convincingly, setting out the essential elements of the background—a triumphantly reelected president who had run a campaign infused with more antibusiness and generally "radical" rhetoric than any in American history, an improving economy completing (as 1937 arrives) four years of expansion, continuing labor unrest. Well before FDR made his 20 January 1937 State of the Union address, with the language about "one-third of a nation ill-housed, ill-clad, ill-nourished," labor militancy had altered the American political and social terrain. John L. Lewis had aimed an organizing offensive against the steel industry in the early summer of 1936, and days before the end of the year there broke out the "sit-down" tactics of an aroused labor movement in the auto industry. While FDR wrote his annual message, a great drama was being played out, and on 11 February 1937, General Motors Corporation surrendered and accepted collective bargaining. U.S. Steel would capitulate a month later. The heartland of American industry was breached by unionism in 1937—steel, autos, rubber, farm equipment, consumer electronics. This was an epochal shift of power, felt more strongly by contemporaries than by those of us with the advantage of distance. There was some violence and much high emotion, and a tide of anxiety surged among corporation executives and the millions of middle-class citizens who shared their doubts about unionism. The future was uncertain enough, when a sharp economic recession in autumn 1937 made this one of those critical occasions so attractive to Marxist historians.

Labor-management conflict is, as Galkova assumes, a productive starting point for analyzing governmental politics and policy in the years 1936–1938. This was a historical moment especially inviting to an analysis of American society, such as Galkova's, which locates causal forces and consequences in class alignments. She argues that the crisis so aroused American workers that the Roosevelt administration was pushed toward an ambitious second-term program with essentially six elements—in the order of their importance to her analysis, the Fair Labor Standards Act, the Court reform, relief spending, and of much less importance, public housing, a new agricultural bill, and executive-branch reorganization. Business and rightist congressional forces resisted fiercely, but the crisis deepened, the administration adroitly manipulated the threat of antimonopoly action to convert at least the U.S. Chamber of Commerce to support of its measures, and in 1938 a burst of legislation completed the New Deal.

I have disagreements with significant parts of this argument, but one might begin with the negotiable ones. To recognize that class conflict appeared sharper in the middle years of the 1930s than at any time in (at least) the twentieth century should provide no occasion to simplify political alignments of major economic groups merely for economy of statement. Galkova sees more class unity than is found in the historical record, to my mind. Statements such as "the working class supported the president" while "business protested" this or that are too loosely drawn to advance our understanding. Such language may in a general way depict main trends in political loyalties, but we should be most interested in the detailed accounting of which parts of the working class and of business, whatever these may be defined to mean, played what roles in politics and policy.

Galkova, indeed, is fully aware that "business" was not always a monolithic thing, though she does not extend this awareness to "the working class." She observes that southern industrialists were vociferously opposed to the FLSA, and she might have noted more strongly that northern industrialists with rival plants sited in the South were among the act's supporters. I would urge that Soviet historians question the usefulness of such broad generalizations as "the working class" or "business" in describing and explaining events and take a keener interest in intra-capitalist political divisions especially. American historians are more than passingly interested in such divisions inside the business/capitalist community. To what degree was there a "corporate liberalism" in the form of a conception of the active State guided by a corporation-politician-labor elite? This is a vital question to students of modern American political economy.

Another feature of Galkova's essay deserves notice. One might have expected her to describe this tense period at the close of the New Deal as a time in which working-class pressures forced important concessions within the liberal, welfare-state-capitalist framework, and in so doing to depict Franklin Roosevelt as merely a mediator between class forces. An interesting aspect of Galkova's account is, however, her decision to place him near the center and implicitly to impute to him a large degree of individual agency.

Amid these currents of intensified class conflict moves Franklin D. Roosevelt, the real focus of her essay. I am struck by the sympathy which Professor Galkova brings to this account of FDR's struggles to find a way ahead. How does he appear to Soviet historians? In this essay, we do not get to know him very well as a person, but this child of the Hudson River Valley propertied class seems in the Soviet view to be, most of the time, on the right side. His annual message of January 1937 Galkova describes, correctly, as both socially progressive and indeterminate. FDR spoke as no other American president had of the plight of the bottom one-third and asserted in strong terms that government must be a permanent part of the remedy for those unequal results. Thus FDR uttered fighting words as his second term opened, suggesting that he would at once pursue the fulfillment of a New Deal which had been arrested. But on this occasion he was also evasive, proposing "no concrete socioeconomic program."

Then came his stunning decision to proceed first with Supreme Court reform. It is interesting to find a Soviet historian appearing to sympathize with FDR on this complex issue, and finding—and sympathizing because of finding?—that journals of business opinion opposed the Court reform. The administration is the target of a business-led attack against not only the unfortunately presented Court-reform plan, but the entire range of "its basic programs" of that period.

But what are the New Deal's "basic programs" in this second term? Galkova's reconstruction of them recognizes a cluster of legislative proposals—FLSA, Court reform, relief spending, public housing, a replacement AAA, the reorganization of executive-branch structure. These were supplemented with a mildly (but unprecedented) prolabor stance during the intense labor-management conflicts of 1936–1938, and the threat of some sort of antimonopoly drive. Perhaps I read too much into tone, and between the lines, but it is my impression that the author of the essay finds this also the program of progressive forces, the working class—and of right-thinking historians, whether American or Soviet. Certainly no contrasting substitute program of superior virtues is proposed. There is the implication that, on the whole, it must have been a progressive and correct program because business and conservative forces opposed it with such animus.

And what was the outcome of it all? Galkova tells the story of political pressures, of shifting positions within the administration, the business community, and once or twice, even, within the "working class" (organized labor). The progressive forces know what they want, the business forces want to defeat this. Roosevelt, of course, is not always tactically on the right side. He is conservative on the budget in 1937, liberals put pressure upon him and attempt to rouse public opinion for spending, and in the spring of 1938 he is convinced. To my mind, Galkova underplays FDR's vacillation on the matter of the volume of relief spending and the adoption of a massive Keynesian stimulus. For her, "during the second half of 1937, clear changes took place in administrative policy," after which "the government found it necessary to introduce plans for reform and to begin to implement them." Roosevelt "found it necessary" to present a well-defined and class-recognized program before 1937 was out. Such was the power of an aroused labor force. But if in her account the government's program was decided more in the sweeping contest for political power that raged in the great industrial cities than in Roosevelt's head and heart, his role remains important. Once he read the political currents, the president began to convince the business community that he was right and they were wrong (see Galkova's discussion of Roosevelt's meeting with the Chamber of Commerce in January 1938). On the basis of an article in *Newsweek*, it is said that "forty-nine members of the Chamber of Commerce testified that he [FDR] had chosen the right way," and "the Chamber drew up a plan of action that included all the basic proposals the president had advocated." Roosevelt had apparently persuaded an important segment of the business elite to submit to his program. Within not too many months, "a new and . . . last wave of legislation" completed the New Deal. It is not clear whether this is an account of the autonomous State that forces the capitalists to accept these last left-centrist additions to public policy, or the corporate-liberal State in which the liberals in the White House convince their rational allies in the business community to make sensible concessions at the eleventh hour, or the State as a relatively passive mediator arbitrating the struggling titans of labor and business.

***

Few historians of the New Deal, whatever their nationality or persuasion, would deny that this essay grapples with the major policy and political issues as contemporaries saw them. Galkova's array of topics and events is accurately drawn from the media, organizational, and personal records of that time. It is interesting to notice what does not enter this version of the 1937–1938 part of the New Deal. A central part of the administration's 1937–1938 program is missed entirely when the agenda is thought to be what the newspapers thought it to be—laws which FDR wanted Congress to pass in the winter and spring of 1937–1938, as Galkova and others array them.

But there was another reform arena, a Roosevelt-designed thrust of the second-term New Deal program that has until recently been either missed or misunderstood by historians. This was the reform of electoral, judicial, and executive components of the State-political structure, in pursuit of Roosevelt's vision of what has recently and with reason been called the Third New Deal.

This reform agenda was often unappreciated, in its entirety, by some who saw clearly one or more of its parts. Barry D. Karl, of the University of Chicago, was the author of *Executive Reorganization and Reform in the New Deal* (1963), a study of the struggle over FDR's proposal to reorganize the executive branch. In that exemplary book, Karl had not fully seen the larger importance of the reorganization proposal within the politics of the second term, but his *The Uneasy State* (1983) made some connections he had missed earlier and described the existence in 1937–1938 of a Third New Deal. The first reorganization plan, developed for FDR by the (Louis) Brownlow Committee (President's Committee on Administrative Management, launched quietly in early 1936), boldly combined ideas and proposals that had roots in the progressive era. The plan would reorganize all federal agencies into twelve departments, abolish all independent regulatory commissions and subsume them within the Cabinet departments, strengthen the presidency further with the assistance of a formal Executive Office of the President containing a Budget Bureau for central legislative clearance, and add a national planning board.[1]

With the enactment of such reforms, there could at last be Planning. This was

1. See Barry D. Karl, *The Uneasy State: The United States from 1915 to 1945* (Chicago, 1983), especially Chap. 8, "Thermidor and the Third New Deal," and Karl, "In Search of National Planning: The Case for a Third New Deal," paper delivered at the annual meeting of the Organization of American Historians, 7 April 1983. Another useful study of the 1937–1938 reorganization plan is Richard Polenberg, *Reorganizing Roosevelt's Government: 1936–1939* (Cambridge, 1966).

Roosevelt's consistent objective, and one in which Soviet historians should have a special interest. Roosevelt had concluded that there was no coherent administration program in 1933, or in 1937, since the compromises forced upon a president by the checkmated system inherited from the past made a coherent program impossible. Overwhelmingly reelected and with a mandate for further change, the reforms Roosevelt sought in 1937 would be sweeping and procedural. Karl understands this Third New Deal to include the reorganization plan, the Court reform, and the realignment of the party system attempted so late and hesitantly in the so-called "Purge" of 1938. I would add to this the radical change in the government's engagement with local land-use practices being pushed forward in the Department of Agriculture's formulation of a national land-use planning system, and FDR's proposal for "seven little TVAs" to complete the network of regional governments that the TVA had begun.[2]

"Roosevelt had tried to bring off a genuine revolution and had failed to do so," Karl concludes, and with no exaggeration, either as to intent or result.[3] The president was beaten in virtually every element of the Third New Deal. The reorganization bill was seized upon by conservatives as, like the Court plan, a godsend, allowing them to rouse part of the public to kill the Court reform (though Roosevelt did alter the makeup and outlook of the Court) and emasculate the reorganization; party realignment was a failure, Roosevelt abandoning the effort after the 1938 primaries and pondering glumly the need for a new progressive party some day in the future; seven new TVAs and national land-use planning were both rebuffed entirely; the TNEC study of the economy, wherever that might have fit into the rethinking of New Deal economic policy, was entangled in confusion and its report swallowed up in the coming of war.

These reforms in governmental machinery were the core of Roosevelt's 1937–1938 program. The news media of the day and the forces on Capitol Hill skewed the agenda toward the issues treated in Galkova's essay. American historians have only recently discovered the importance of the 1937–1938 proposals aiming at a

---

2. My own view of the Third New Deal is briefly sketched in "The New Deal," in *FDR, His Life and Times: An Encyclopedic View,* ed. Graham and Meghan R. Wander (Boston, 1985), and in "Franklin D. Roosevelt and the Intended New Deal," in *Essays in Honor of James MacGregor Burns,* ed. Michael Beschloss and Thomas Cronin (Englewood Cliffs, N.J., 1988). Late New Deal plans for expansion of regional governments may be followed in William E. Leuchtenburg, "Roosevelt, Norris, and the 'Seven Little TVAs,' " *Journal of Politics* 14 (August 1952); late New Deal steps toward a national land-use planning system to be operated out of the Department of Agriculture may be glimpsed in Richard Kirkendall, *Social Scientists and Farm Politics in the Age of Roosevelt* (Columbia, Mo., 1966).

3. The most recent monograph on the last months of the New Deal is David L. Porter, *Congress and the Waning of the New Deal* (Port Washington, N.Y., 1980), a useful study of selected congressional battles over legislation suggested by the president, but hardly a book which explores the issues discussed above.

radical restructuring of the government apparatus itself—electoral, judicial, executive at the federal level, and reaching also local government and the intergovernmental relations of federalism itself—and one would expect Soviet scholars to share their keen interest. For the Third New Deal might be called Franklin Roosevelt's *perestroika* for American governance.

Response by T. V. Galkova

First, I should like to express my deep appreciation to Professor O. Graham for his sympathetic approach to my article and the very interesting thoughts about it that he expressed. It is with great pleasure that I can say that in the course of working on my topic I, too, came across many of the questions Professor Graham raises in his comments and tried to answer them.

The interest shown by Soviet Americanists in this stage of the New Deal is not solely due to the intensity of the class struggle and the actions taken by the working class. These years are of interest not only from the point of view of a whole series of anticrisis measures and the social legislation adopted at the time, but also because of the simultaneous process whereby the role and place of the State within the framework of the socioeconomic structures of society underwent a transformation and the functions of the executive, legislative, and judicial branches of authority were to a certain extent redefined. All these developments took place in the complicated situation of the late 1930s and were affected to a significant degree by both internal factors (for example, the economic crisis of 1937–1938) and the worsening of the international situation.

I should like to say a few words about the peculiarities of the antitrust movement during those years. Antitrust traditions, whose roots may be traced to the period of the 1900s, were widespread among the New Dealers and were characteristic of such prominent members of the administration as R[obert H.] Jackson and H[arold] Ickes, who inaugurated the antitrust campaign of 1938. At the same time, the liberal press noted the serious change that had taken place in antitrust attitudes. The *New Republic* wrote that if the aim of antitrust campaigns had previously been largely to defend small business from big business and if particular emphasis had been placed on "fair competition . . . in the 1930s, it was high prices and their effect on production that were at the center of attention." It must be said that Roosevelt himself was hardly an active supporter of these attitudes. Most frequently his actions reflected a desire to use the antitrust campaigns in his own interests.

There is no doubt that by the end of 1937 the disagreements within the administration on matters of socioeconomic policy had not been resolved. The struggle within the administration during the economic crisis of 1937–1938 grew much more intense and in many ways became dramatic in character, a development examined in great detail by D[ean L.] May in his study of the conflict between the groups of Morgenthau and Eccles. Of particular interest in this connection is the position adopted by the president himself, who authorized anticrisis appropriations only under the impact of a whole number of factors: the continuing fall in production, the deterioration in the international situation in connection with the Austrian Anschluss of 12 March 1938, the approaching elections, and his fear of losing the prerogative of presidential initiative in the formulation of economic policy.

The attitude of Congress during this period was complex and ambivalent. In the conditions of crisis it sanctioned the government's anticrisis measures, but in the course of the debates on the proposed socioeconomic measures some Democrats displayed a desire to limit those articles of the draft laws that were long-term in character, and in particular the powers of those federal agencies that were entrusted with putting the laws into effect. This reflected the complex and contradictory nature of the positions of many of the members of the ruling party, who understood the necessity of state intervention during the crisis but at the same time did not want government regulation to turn into a permanently operating factor. For these Democrats the most important aspect of the legislation adopted in 1938 was the anticrisis one, yet the objective content of these measures entailed a further extension of government regulation. In this way the crisis forced a whole number of Democrats to sanction the expansion of the regulatory functions of the state, even though they themselves were far from recognizing the necessity of promoting this process.

The attitude adopted not only by the Republicans but also by a large number of Democrats toward what Professor O. Graham calls "the third New Deal" was the logical extension of that approach. I completely agree with Professor Graham that these measures, namely the reform of the Supreme Court, the reform of the federal administrative organs, the "party purge" of 1938, and others are of particular importance and require comprehensive and attentive study. Their special character was determined above all by the fact that they were the most long-term in their implications and affected not just individual developments, but the entire complex of government, party, and political problems.

The fate of these measures, the tenacity with which the Republicans as well as a significant number of Democrats opposed them, and the countermeasures adopted by Congress to prevent the realization of the plans of Roosevelt also testify to the magnitude of the tasks the president had undertaken. These problems should undoubtedly be subjected to thorough analysis.

CONTRIBUTORS

SOVIET CONTRIBUTORS

Victor I. Borisiuk is Chairman of a sector at the Institute of U.S. and Canadian Studies of the Academy of Sciences of the U.S.S.R.

Tatiana V. Galkova is a Research Associate at the Institute of U.S. and Canadian Studies of the Academy of Sciences of the U.S.S.R.

Ekateryna V. Kurochkina is a postgraduate student at Moscow State University.

Victor L. Malkov is Professor of History and Chairman of a sector of the Institute of General History of the Academy of Sciences of the U.S.S.R.

Alexander S. Manykin is a Senior Research Associate in the Department of Modern and Contemporary History at Moscow State University.

Vladimir O. Pechatnov is Chairman of a sector at the Institute of U.S. and Canadian Studies of the Academy of Sciences of the U.S.S.R.

Alexey A. Popov is Chairman of a sector at the Institute of U.S. and Canadian Studies of the Academy of Sciences of the U.S.S.R.

Nikolai V. Sivachev was Director of the Department of Modern and Contemporary History in the School of History at Moscow State University from 1977 until his death in 1983.

Irene B. Tverdokhleb teaches at the Moscow State Institute of History and Archives.

AMERICAN CONTRIBUTORS

John M. Allswang is Professor of History at California State University, Los Angeles.

David Brody is Professor of History at the University of California, Davis.

Otis L. Graham, Jr., is Distinguished University Professor of History at the University of North Carolina, Chapel Hill.

William E. Leuchtenburg is William Rand Kenan Professor of History at the University of North Carolina, Chapel Hill.

Nelson Lichtenstein is Associate Professor of History at the Catholic University of America.

Mark Naison is Professor of Afro-American Studies and History at Fordham University.

James T. Patterson is Professor of History at Brown University.

Theda Skocpol is Professor of Sociology at Harvard University.

James L. Sundquist is a Senior Fellow at the Brookings Institution.

INDEX